QUICK & DELICIOUS

READER'S DIGEST

QUICK & DELICIOUS

READER'S DIGEST

Reader's Digest

The Reader's Digest Association, Inc.
Pleasantville, New York • Montreal

QUICK & DELICIOUS was created and produced by
Carroll & Brown Limited

Project Editor	*Jennifer Rylaarsdam*
Art Editors	*Sara Kidd, Lisa Tai*
Assistant Editor	*Madeline Weston*
Recipe Developer	*Lucy Wing*
Recipe Testers	*Sarah Bush, Marthajean White*
Photographer	*David Murray*
Photographer's Assistants	*Ian Boddy, Jules Selmes*
Food for Photography	*Eric Treuillé, Mandy Wagstaff*
Prop Stylist	*Elaine Charlesworth*
Production Consultant	*Lorraine Baird*

READER'S DIGEST STAFF

Project Editor	*Fred DuBose*
Senior Art Editor	*Henrietta Stern*

Printed in the United States of America

Library of Congress Cataloging in Publication Data
Quick & delicious : how to fix great meals in minutes / the Reader's Digest Association, Inc.
   p. cm.
   Includes index.
   ISBN 0-89577-491-7
   1. Quick and easy cookery. I. Reader's Digest Association.
   II. Title: Quick and delicious.
   TX833.5.Q53   1993
   641.5'55—dc20   92-34604

COVER PHOTO Penne with Shrimp and Peppers, page 232
PREVIOUS PAGE (clockwise from top right) Spinach, Bacon, and Egg Salad, page 320; Spicy Cream of
Carrot Soup, page 78; Fresh Strawberry Pie, page 381; Rotelle with Cheese and Walnuts, page 219;
Paprika Chicken, page 139; Gingered Beef Kebabs, page 174

FOREWORD

Everyone agrees that the best meals are homemade ones, lovingly prepared by someone who cares about good cooking. Yet our busy time schedules keep getting in the way: While we're determined to serve great-tasting food, we also want to make it quickly and with a minimum of fuss.

Quick & Delicious takes care of both of these needs beautifully in each of more than 480 recipes. The idea behind this book is that cooking with fresh ingredients need not mean long and complicated preparation—and that fresh foods can sometimes be combined with pre-packaged ones in order to streamline the cooking process. The result is a wholesome and delicious dish served by one relaxed cook.

The recipes in *Quick & Delicious* include filling main dishes made with meat, poultry, fish, eggs, cheese, pasta, and vegetables. There are also main-dish soups and salads, plus snacks that are hearty enough to be served as a casual meal. Inventive side dishes include party appetizers, easy breads, lighter salads, and vegetables. And, so that you can bring your meals to a triumphant close, we include desserts you can whip up in a jiffy—fruit desserts, fresh pies, ice cream sundaes, and even cakes.

HOW QUICK IS QUICK?
With the exception of a few make-ahead recipes in the first chapter, every recipe in this book can be made in 45 minutes or less. This includes preparation and cooking time, from the point that the ingredients are taken from the pantry or shopping bag to the point that the dish is ready to be eaten. Each recipe has been fully tested in home kitchens, where the preparation and cooking were timed realistically, with the average home cook in mind.

The book's first chapter shows you how a little advance planning, including organizing your kitchen, can save time later. But even if you are a spontaneous cook who decides what to prepare only at the last minute, you'll find that most of the recipes are surprisingly simple to make. Your family and friends are sure to applaud the impressive results.

Whether you want to serve an elegant dinner for guests or make a casual weeknight supper for the family, *Quick & Delicious* will provide you with all the inspiration you need to set a table that pleases you and those you love.

—The Editors

CONTENTS

FROM THE TOP:
CHUNKY SALSA, PAGE 48
CHICKEN SOUP, PAGE 81
CHICKEN BREAST WITH HONEY MUSTARD SAUCE, PAGE 157

FROM THE TOP:
PASTA WITH BROCCOLI PESTO SAUCE, PAGE 223
GREEN SALAD WITH CURRIED YOGURT DRESSING, PAGE 305
TUTTI-FRUTTI SUNDAE, PAGE 365

ABOUT THIS BOOK

Quick & Delicious has been designed to provide a complete range of recipes that require little cooking time yet produce irresistible and satisfying dishes for your family and friends.

THE QUICK COOK

In order to make full use of this book, begin by looking at the ideas set out in *The Quick Cook* chapter. In it you will find suggestions for equipment from big items like food processors and microwave ovens (which can provide substantial time-saving in the kitchen but are very rarely necessary for the recipes in this book), to little items like citrus juicers and pastry blenders. There are also some preliminary recipes for stocks, pie crusts, and other basics that you can make ahead and store for later, as well as abundant entertaining tips and creative menu suggestions that allow you to spend less time cooking and more time having fun with your guests. Perhaps the most important feature in *The Quick Cook* is a list of staples to keep on hand that frequently appear in the recipes in this book.

SHELF MAGIC

Certain super-quick recipes throughout the book take full advantage of the staples and convenience foods you probably have in your pantry or freezer. Look for the *Shelf Magic* headings to find main-dish and side-dish recipes that are ready to serve in 15 minutes or less.

TIME SAVERS

Another feature you'll find throughout the book is called *Time Savers*. These are tips and information for dozens of ways to speed up preparation time. Their beauty is in their simplicity—once done they won't be forgotten, because they make such practical sense.

SPECIAL VARIATIONS

In every chapter of *Quick & Delicious* you'll find one or two special two-page features with creative ideas for dressing up simple dishes. One type of spread, called *Start With ...*, shows how to take ready-made foods such as soup stock, cooked chicken, or pizza crust and, with just a few easy additions, turn them into delectable dishes in minutes. The second type of spread is *Variations on the Basic ...*, in which we explain how to make a quick and basic recipe such as an omelet, a hamburger, or a baked potato, then suggest a number of creative variations that will turn the dish into something really special. You'll find the range of recipe variations so wide that you'll probably be inspired to come up with some of your own culinary innovations.

RECIPE NOTES

At the top of many of the recipes are introductory notes, such as *Cook's Tip, Serving Suggestion, Diet Note*, or *Food Note*. In these introductions we offer some new ideas for cutting yet more preparation time, suggest simple side dishes that can be made in minutes or bought ready-made, provide information about a particularly healthful aspect of the recipe, or mention an interesting point about the history of the dish.

SYMBOLS

Important information is given for each regular recipe by means of the following symbols:

indicates the number of servings (or in some cases, pieces) that the recipe will make.

is the time it takes to prepare the ingredients before or after cooking, including any additional cooling or resting time.

is the total amount of the recipe's cooking time, not including the preparation of the ingredients.

At the top of each recipe you will also find the complete nutritional breakdown for each serving, including calories and mineral values.

Once you start cooking, you'll see that *Quick & Delicious* has been planned first and foremost with you, the busy cook, in mind.

THE QUICK COOK

THE QUICK COOK'S PANTRY

A well-stocked kitchen is essential to the Quick Cook's peace of mind. If you keep a supply of staples in your pantry, refrigerator, and freezer, you'll never be at a loss when putting together a last-minute recipe—all you will have to shop for are a few fresh ingredients, and the rest will be there for you.

The recipes in this book rely on fresh ingredients first and foremost. But any cook will tell you that on some occasions you simply can't do "fresh" and "quick" at the same time. This is why we suggest putting to prudent use a selection of canned goods, frozen foods, or other ready-made products, combining them with fresh ingredients in such a way so as not to compromise taste. (In the special Shelf Magic features, you'll find that the recipes rely almost entirely on packaged products—but the advantage is that each of these recipes is ready in only 15 minutes or less.)

The list of pantry items that follows does not mention the traditional staples—flours, sugars, and oils—that you already have. Instead, it consists of ingredients especially geared to the Quick Cook.

In addition, the boxes on page 13 list other dry ingredients, canned goods, and refrigerated and frozen items that you may want to keep on hand. Keep in mind that when you prepare one of the recipes in this book, you may want to save still more preparation time by using ready-made products, even when fresh ingredients are called for; it's up to you to decide. Stock up your pantry, refrigerator, and freezer, and find how you can make your kitchen work for you.

RECIPE SHORTCUTS

These ready-made staples help you cut out time-consuming preparation steps.

Canned chopped tomatoes This invaluable ingredient is listed in many recipes throughout the book. The tomatoes are already peeled, seeded, and chopped, and they usually have better flavor in cooked dishes than the pretty but tasteless fresh tomatoes sold in the supermarket.

Chopped garlic Packed in oil and sold in jars, chopped garlic can often be found in the deli or vegetables sections at the supermarket. One-half teaspoon of pre-chopped garlic equals one clove of freshly chopped garlic, which means, for example, using 1 teaspoon in Veal Parmigiana (page 188); you can adjust accordingly for other dishes.

Grated cheeses Cheddar, Monterey Jack, and mozzarella, the three most-used cheeses in our recipes, are sold already grated in various package sizes. You'll shave off lots of preparation time in making dishes such as Huevos Rancheros (page 254) and Mozzarella Ramekins (page 265), or in filling a simple omelet.

Packaged bread crumbs Keep a carton of plain bread crumbs in the pantry for toppings on baked dishes such as Stuffed Zucchini (page 283) and crumb coatings on dishes like Savory Pan-Fried Chicken Breasts (page 136) and Fish and Potato Pie (page 107). They'll save the step of grinding fresh bread crumbs in the blender, and, sealed tightly, they'll store for a few months.

Prepared salad dressings The selection of bottled salad dressings available in the supermarket is getting more extensive all the time. Any of the salads

that call for dressing in this book can be tossed with the prepared dressing of your choice. If you prefer to make your own, there are many dressing recipes throughout the Salads chapter, including those in the special spread on page 305. If you're in a hurry,

though, a favorite brand of bottled dressing will fill in very well.

Cornstarch This flavorless powder makes it possible to thicken sauces quickly, without having to make a roux of butter and flour. Most liquids can be thickened within two minutes after cornstarch has been added. It is usually dissolved in a small amount of the cooking liquid or cold water before being

added, in order to prevent lumps. Many of the poultry, meat, and stir-fry dishes in this book make use of cornstarch to thicken sauces quickly.

Buttermilk baking mix Known to cooks as Bisquick, this pre-mixed powder of flour, shortening, baking powder, salt, and buttermilk can do a lot more than make pancakes. Keep it on hand to use in dishes such as Crustless Garden Quiche (page 258) and Raisin Granola Muffins (page 333). If you want to keep a simple pancake mix on hand, prepare the Basic Pancake Mix on page 29. However, the basic mix does not replace Bisquick in the recipes that specifically call for it in this book.

Quick-cooking oats Oatmeal makes a quick and warming meal on its own as a breakfast cereal, but you may also want to keep an extra box of it on the shelf for recipes like Oatmeal Date Muffins (page 332) and Oatmeal-Raisin Drop Cookies (page 348).

Chopped nuts Packaged chopped nuts make dishes like Caramel Bananas (page 353) a snap to prepare. Store a supply of a variety of nuts in your freezer to keep them fresh much longer than they would on the shelf. There's no need to thaw the nuts before adding them to a recipe.

Refrigerated and frozen pie crusts Many of the recipes in this book call for prepared pie crusts. Unless the list of ingredients specifically calls for refrigerated pie crust, you may use either those from the freezer section of the supermarket (packaged in aluminum pie dishes) or those from the refrigerator section (packaged as folded dough). The refrigerated crusts work best when the dough must be handled in some way, as with Crusty Dogs (page 70) and Nectarine Cheese Tart (page 378).

Frozen whipped topping This non-dairy whipped-cream substitute has been around for a long time, and it remains a real time saver when you compare it to whipping real cream (and cleaning up afterward). It's mentioned as an optional ingredient in many of the dessert recipes in this book.

Nonstick vegetable spray This staple not only saves time by omitting the necessity of spreading butter or shortening into pans, but it also saves on calories since you use less of the spray than you would with butter or oil.

EASY BASICS

These are staples of a different kind: They are a few key items that form the base of dozens of dishes laid out in the special spreads throughout this book. Some you may want to make on your own and store for later, and some you will want to purchase; all of them are the building blocks for a variety of easy-to-make recipes.

Pizza crust For a basic pizza dough that you can make ahead and freeze, see the recipe on page 26. There are also some delicious packaged crusts available in the supermarket that you can freeze. You'll find a complete selection of pizzas to make on the special spread on page 62.

Canned beef stock and low-sodium chicken stock Throughout the Soups chapter, including the special spread on page 80, you will find canned broth on the list of ingredients. Since many people prefer to make their own, we've provided the recipes for homemade stocks on pages 22 to 24. But if you prefer the simpler route, keep a few cans of stock in the cupboard as an indispensable ingredient in the majority of soups as well as many meat and poultry dishes.

Packaged smoked ham Smoked ham is one of the easiest meats to work with because it's ready-cooked when you buy it. For ideas on how to use it as the base for lunch and dinner recipes, see the special spread on page 198.

Pasta Spaghetti, penne, fusilli, and linguine are just a few of the many shapes of pastas you'll find in the market. Keep a selection of your favorite shapes and sizes in the pantry. For a mouth-watering selection of sauces to go with your pasta, refer to the special spread on page 222.

Pound cake See the special spread on page 338 for ideas on how to turn this endlessly adaptable cake into homey or fancy desserts. If you want make

your own from scratch, see the recipe on page 28. Otherwise, purchase one ready made and keep it in the freezer.

Ice cream and frozen yogurt The special spread on page 364 offers ideas on how to turn a pint of ice cream or frozen yogurt into a special dessert.

Crumb crusts These pie crusts can be purchased at the supermarket, or made at home and stored as explained in the recipe on page 28. Chocolate, vanilla, and graham cracker crusts are the base for the variety of pies in the special spread on page 384. Keep one or two on hand for a quick dessert.

PANTRY: DRY INGREDIENTS

- Soup stock cubes
- Croutons
- Ramen noodles
- Crackers and chips
- Instant and flavored rices
- Raisins
- Packaged pudding mixes
- Chocolate chips
- Chocolate syrup

PANTRY: CANNED GOODS

- Chick-peas
- Kidney beans
- Tomato paste
- Tomato sauce
- Tuna fish
- Chopped clams
- Crabmeat
- Chicken
- Black olives
- Peaches
- Pineapples
- Pears

REFRIGERATOR

- Marinated artichoke hearts
- Prepared barbecue sauce
- Prepared spaghetti sauce
- Prepared tomato salsa
- Cream cheese
- Grated Parmesan cheese
- Fruit preserves
- Pimientos
- Lemon juice
- Unsweetened applesauce
- Refrigerated biscuit dough

FREEZER

- Orange juice concentrate
- Mixed vegetables
- Green beans
- Spinach
- Corn
- Blueberries
- Strawberries
- Raspberries

WHEN YOU'RE FRESH OUT OF ...

Regardless of the number of trips to the supermarket, there always seems to be one ingredient in the recipe missing from your pantry or refrigerator. Rather than having to go out yet again, look to this list of convenient alternatives and you may find a substitute that you can use with almost the same results.

INGREDIENT SUBSTITUTIONS

If the recipe calls for:	Replace it with:
baking powder, 1 teaspoon	= 1/4 teaspoon baking soda & 1/2 teaspoon cream of tartar
bread crumbs, 1 cup	= 3/4 cup cracker crumbs
butter or margarine, 1 cup	= 1 cup vegetable shortening & 1/2 teaspoon salt
buttermilk, 1 cup	= 1 cup yogurt = 1 cup whole milk & 1 tablespoon vinegar
chocolate:	
semisweet, 1 2/3 ounces	= 1 ounce unsweetened chocolate & 4 teaspoons sugar
unsweetened, 1 ounce	= 3 tablespoons cocoa powder & 1 tablespoon shortening
bittersweet	= semisweet

If the recipe calls for:	Replace it with:
cottage cheese	= ricotta
cornstarch, 1 tablespoon	= 5 teaspoons flour & 2 teaspoons arrowroot = 2 teaspoons potato starch = 2 egg yolks
cream cheese	= Neufchâtel
cream, heavy, 1 cup	= 7/8 cup buttermilk or yogurt & 3 tablespoons butter = 3/4 cup whole milk & 1/3 cup melted butter
eggs (for thickening or baking), 1 whole	= 2 egg yolks
fish stock	= diluted bottled clam juice, or chicken stock
flour:	
all-purpose (for thickening sauces), 1 tablespoon	= 1 1/2 teaspoons cornstarch = 1 1/2 tablespoons arrowroot = 1 tablespoon quick-cooking tapioca
cake, 1 cup sifted	= 1 cup less 2 tablespoons all-purpose flour

If the recipe calls for:	Replace it with:
fresh herbs, 1 tablespoon	= 1/3 to 1/2 teaspoon dried herbs
honey, 1/4 cup	= 5 tablespoons sugar & 1 tablespoon liquid
hot red pepper sauce, 2 to 3 drops	= 1/8 teaspoon cayenne pepper
lemon juice, 1 teaspoon	= 1 teaspoon lime juice or white wine, or 1/2 teaspoon vinegar
milk, whole, 1 cup	= 1/2 cup evaporated milk & 1/2 cup water = 1 cup skim milk & 2 tablespoons melted butter or cream
mushrooms, fresh, 4 cups sliced	= one 10-ounce jar mushrooms, drained
olive oil	= vegetable oil
onion, chopped, 1 cup	= 1 tablespoon dried minced onion, reconstituted
raisins	= finely chopped soft prunes or dates

If the recipe calls for:	Replace it with:
sour cream, 1 cup	= 3/4 cup milk & 2 1/2 teaspoons lemon juice & 1/3 cup melted butter: allow to stand 10 minutes
stock, canned	= 1 bouillon cube dissolved in 1 cup hot water
sugar:	
granulated, 1 tablespoon 1 cup	= 1 tablespoon maple sugar =1 3/4 cups confectioners sugar =1 cup molasses & 1/2 teaspoon baking soda
confectioners, 1 cup	= 7/8 cup granulated & 1 tablespoon cornstarch processed in the blender
dark brown	= light brown sugar
tomato sauce, 2 cups	= 3/4 cup tomato paste & 1 cup water
vinegar:	
balsamic	= slightly less red-wine vinegar
wine	= cider vinegar & a dash red wine = white distilled vinegar & a dash white wine
yogurt	= light sour cream

TIME-SAVING EQUIPMENT

Considering all the time-saving gadgets just waiting to clutter up your kitchen, there are only a few key items that truly reduce your time in the kitchen. To add to the standard pots, pans, bowls, and spoons you already have on hand, here are a few pieces of equipment and valuable tools that will speed up the cooking process considerably. You won't need all of them, but you can decide which ones would be most helpful to you.

Kitchen shears for quickly cutting up meat, herbs, and some vegetables; often faster than a knife

Hand-held blender
This new gadget is one step easier than a conventional blender. It quickly liquifies food directly in the dish or saucepan you are using. The machine also makes milkshakes in an instant, directly in the glasses. You'll save preparation and cleanup time by not having to transfer the mixture to the blender container.

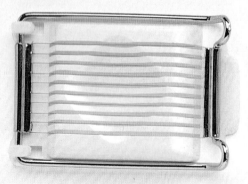

Egg slicer for evenly slicing a hard-boiled egg in one motion

Four-sided grater for shredding cheeses, chocolate, and some vegetables

Garlic press for quickly crushing garlic

Sharp 8-inch chef's knife for speeding up slicing and dicing; always keep knives well sharpened

Sharp paring knife for cutting small items

Pastry blender for easily cutting butter or shortening into flour

Compact food processor
The compact version of a full-size food processor is designed to handle smaller-scale jobs of chopping and grating. The mini-processor is more economical in price and countertop space. If you tend to cook for only a few people at a time, this piece of equipment may be your best kitchen helper.

Long-handled slotted spoon for easily removing foods from their cooking liquids; prevents having to lift the pan to drain

Citrus juicer for squeezing lemons, limes, and oranges; neat and simple using either design

Salad spinner for drying salad leaves and fresh herbs with a few turns of the handle

Melon-ball cutter for easily scooping melon into neat balls

Apple corer for coring fruit and vegetables in one motion

Tongs for easily grasping hot pieces of food while cooking

Flexible rubber spatula for scraping out mixing bowls

OTHER EQUIPMENT

Food processor

This is the best invention for reducing a cook's preparation time on big jobs, and it's become an essential tool in many modern kitchens. It will easily slice, chop, shred, and purée nearly any food in a fraction of the time it would take to do the same task by hand. With some careful reading of the instruction manual, you will be able to master all of the machine's many functions and labor-saving tricks. With a couple of additional attachments you can quickly whisk cream or egg whites, or knead bread dough.

Blender

The blender is an old standby that is still valuable to the Quick Cook. It can be used instead of the food processor for puréeing soups, making bread- and cookie crumbs, as well as its most-used function, blending drinks.

Microwave oven

Without a doubt, this is the greatest modern advance for cutting cooking time. The best machines have a turntable so you do not have to keep stopping the machine to turn the dish around. Though microwaves are used most often for cooking frozen food and reheating leftovers, they can also be invaluable in assisting with preparing ingredients to go into a larger recipe, such as melting butter and chocolate, or toasting nuts.

Toaster oven

This has long been a standby on many kitchen counters, but it is frequently used only for small jobs like toasting breads and warming muffins. Due to its small size it takes very little time to preheat, thereby cutting down on the baking and broiling time for many other small dishes like chicken breasts and fish fillets.

MICROWAVE BASICS

Although very few recipes in this book require a microwave oven, we offer microwave variations on a number of conventionally cooked recipes so you may choose which method you prefer. By and large the best way to make use of your microwave in the conventional recipes throughout the book is to assist you with various stages of food preparation, such as melting butter and chocolate or defrosting frozen ingredients. Some simple precautions, at right, are important to keep in mind. The list on the opposite page will help you get the most out of your machine by explaining the 10 most useful ways you can make it work for you.

TIPS AND SAFETY FACTS

• You cannot use metal, most aluminum foil, or dishes with metal trim in the microwave. In some of the newer ovens, lightweight aluminum foil can be used to shield the parts of the food that cook fastest, such as the bony parts of chicken.

• Uniformly sized pieces of food are best for even cooking in the microwave.

• Stirring or rearranging food during cooking helps ensure even results. Rotating the dish in the oven does the same thing. Using the turn-table built into the microwave oven or one sold as a microwave accessory is a good way to make sure the food cooks evenly.

• Paper towels prevent the food from splattering, and they absorb grease and moisture. When using paper towels, it is best to use plain white towels without any dye in them.

• Plastic wrap is often used in microwave cooking since it holds in moisture and heat so well. To prevent chemicals from leaching from the plastic wrap into the food, don't allow the plastic to touch the food. Be sure to turn back the corner of the plastic to allow steam to vent. Wax paper or parchment makes a good, loose covering when you simply want to hold in some heat. For long-cooking foods that should be covered, glass lids are preferred to plastic wrap. Always be careful of the steam when you lift the lid.

• Because even microwave ovens with the same wattage will perform differently from each other, you cannot depend on the cooking time alone as a guide for doneness. Be sure to follow the recipes' instructions for stopping to check the progress of cooking, stirring the food if required.

POWER SETTINGS

The recipes in this book were tested in microwave ovens with a power level of 650 to 700 watts. If your oven's maximum is 600 watts or less, adjust the cooking time accordingly—add a minute or so, and rely on tests for doneness.

High	100%
Medium-high	70%
Medium	50%
Medium-low	30%
Low (defrost)	10%

TOP 10 TIME SAVERS

Put your microwave to work in cutting preparation time, even when you're making a recipe by conventional methods. Here are the most useful ways that it can help you.

1 To get the most juice from an orange, lemon, or lime, heat it in the microwave oven on high power (100%) just until warm, about 30 seconds. Cut it in half and squeeze to get fresh juice.

2 To cook bacon, place a double sheet of paper towels on a microwave-safe plate or paper plate. Lay the bacon in a single layer on the paper towels and cover it with another paper towel. Cook on high power (100%) for 1 1/2 to 2 minutes, then allow it to stand for 5 minutes. Thinly sliced bacon cooks more rapidly than thick slices, and a few pieces cook faster than a dozen or so.

3 Frozen vegetables packaged in plastic bags can be cooked right in their bags in the microwave. Pierce the package several times for venting and cook the vegetables for 5 to 8 minutes on high power (100%).

4 Fresh vegetables wrapped in damp paper towels steam very well in the microwave. Use vegetables of similar size or density, such as broccoli and cauliflower florets, or cut them into pieces of uniform size. Cook on high power (100%) until crisp-tender, 4 to 5 minutes for 8 ounces of vegetables.

5 When heating muffins or bread, put it in a microwave-safe container with a tight fitting lid and heat it for 20 to 30 seconds on medium-low power (30%). This will keep the bread from turning hard.

6 Butter can be softened on a microwave-safe plate; remove the wrapper if it's made of foil. Heat the butter on medium-low power (30%) for 30 to 40 seconds per 4 ounces until spreadable. Cream cheese may be softened the same way. To melt 4 ounces of butter, heat it on medium power (50%) for 30 seconds at a time until completely melted.

7 Toast nuts in a shallow microwave-safe dish. Heat 2 1/2 ounces of shelled nuts on high power (100%) until they are lightly browned, 2 1/2 to 4 minutes, stirring occasionally.

8 To heat pancake syrup, remove the lid from a glass syrup bottle or transfer the syrup to a microwave-safe pitcher. Heat it on high power (100%) for 1 1/2 to 2 minutes for each 1 to 2 cups of syrup.

9 When ice cream is too hard to scoop, soften it slightly by placing an unopened 16-ounce carton of ice cream in the microwave. Heat it on medium-low power (30%) until the ice cream just begins to soften, 10 to 20 seconds.

10 Melting chocolate in the microwave is a quick and convenient way to avoid using a double-boiler. Place 1 ounce of chocolate in a small microwave-safe bowl. Heat it on high power (100%) just until it is shiny, 1 to 2 minutes, stopping once to stir it. (The chocolate will still hold its shape.) Stir the chocolate until it is completely melted and smooth.

Make-ahead Recipes

Often the shortest way to a quick meal is by advance preparation. For those who prefer to start from scratch, here are 10 recipes and variations that you can freeze or keep in your refrigerator for weeks. Most of these make-ahead recipes refer to one of the special features you'll find throughout the book. For some great ideas on how to turn the basic into something special, turn to the page mentioned at the beginning of the recipe.

Vegetable Stock

MAKES 3 TO 4 CUPS

SEE PAGE 81, *Start with a Stock*

2 **large carrots, coarsely chopped**
1 **large yellow onion, coarsely chopped**
2 **stalks celery, coarsely chopped**
1 **large tomato, cut into 1-inch chunks**
1 **medium-size turnip, coarsely chopped**
1 **small parsnip, coarsely chopped**
1 **cup shredded lettuce**
6 **sprigs parsley**
1 **clove garlic**
1 **bay leaf**
³/₄ **teaspoon dried thyme leaves**
6 **cups water**

1 In a large stockpot, place carrots, onion, celery, tomato, turnip, parsnip, lettuce, parsley, garlic, bay leaf, and thyme. Add water and bring the mixture to a boil over moderate heat. Skim the surface if necessary.

2 Reduce the heat to low and simmer the stock, partially covered, for 2 hours. Line a strainer with two layers of dampened cheesecloth. Strain the stock, and allow it to cool. Discard the vegetables and herbs.

3 Pour the stock into 1-pint freezer containers, leaving ¹/₂ inch of space at the top. Seal the containers, label with date and contents, and freeze for up to 6 months.

BEEF STOCK

SEE PAGE 81, *Start with a Stock*

4 **to 5 pounds meaty beef bones, cut into pieces by the butcher**

2 **large yellow onions, cut into chunks**

2 **stalks celery with leaves, coarsely chopped**

2 **large carrots, cut into chunks**

1 **large tomato, cut into chunks**

1 **teaspoon black peppercorns**

1 **bay leaf**

6 **sprigs parsley**

3 **to 4 quarts water**

1 In a large stockpot, combine all of the ingredients, adding enough water to cover them. Bring the water to a boil over moderate heat, skimming off the foam as it accumulates.

2 Reduce the heat to low and simmer the stock, uncovered, for 4 to 5 hours, skimming occasionally. Do not stir or allow the stock to boil vigorously as this will cloud the liquid.

3 Using a slotted spoon, lift the meat bones from the stock; set them aside. Line a strainer with two layers of dampened cheesecloth. Strain the stock and allow it to cool. Discard the vegetables and herbs. Chill the stock until the fat solidifies and can be removed with a spoon, 2 to 8 hours. (Save meat for another use, if desired.)

4 Pour the stock into 1-pint freezer containers, leaving $\frac{1}{2}$ inch of space at the top. Seal the containers, label with date and contents, and freeze for up to 6 months.

CHICKEN STOCK

SEE PAGE 81, *Start with a Stock*

4 **pounds chicken backs, necks, wings, or bones, and giblets without the liver (or a whole chicken, cut into pieces)**

2 **large yellow onions, cut into chunks**

2 **stalks celery with leaves, coarsely chopped**

2 **large carrots, cut into chunks**

1 **large tomato, cut into chunks**

1 **teaspoon black peppercorns**

1 **bay leaf**

6 **sprigs parsley**

3 **to 4 quarts water**

1 In a large stockpot, combine chicken, vegetables, and herbs. Add enough water to cover the ingredients. Slowly bring the water to a boil over moderate heat, skimming off the foam as it accumulates.

2 Reduce the heat to low and simmer the stock, uncovered, for 2 to 3 hours, skimming occasionally. Do not stir or allow the stock to boil vigorously as this will cloud the stock.

3 Using a slotted spoon, lift the chicken meat and bones from the stock and set it aside. Line a strainer with two layers of dampened cheesecloth. Strain the stock and allow it to cool. Discard the vegetables and herbs. Chill the stock until the fat solidifies and can easily be removed with a spoon, 2 to 8 hours. (Save the meat for another use, if desired.)

4 Pour the stock into 1-pint freezer containers, leaving 1/2 inch of space at the top. Seal the container, label it with date and contents, and freeze for up to 6 months.

Basic Roast Chicken

SEE PAGE 142, *Start with a Roast Chicken*

1 **roasting chicken (3½ to 4 pounds)**
  Salt and ground black pepper
1 **small yellow onion, quartered**
1 **stalk celery, halved**

1 Preheat the oven to 350°F. Remove giblets and neck from chicken; rinse the chicken in cold water and pat it dry with paper towels. (If desired, rinse neck and giblets; wrap and freeze for later use in chicken stock.)

2 Sprinkle salt and pepper in the chicken's body cavity; stuff it with cut onion and celery. Truss the chicken, if desired. (It is not necessary to truss, or tie the legs together, if the bird is being cut up to use for cooked meat. An untrussed chicken roasts faster.) Place the chicken on the rack of a large roasting pan. Tuck the neck skin and wings under the bird to secure.

3 Roast the chicken for 1½ to 2 hours, basting it with its pan juices every 20 minutes. Check for doneness by piercing the leg with a knife; the chicken is done when the juices run clear.

4 Let the chicken cool until it is easy to handle; slice the meat or cut it into cubes. Wrap the chicken in freezer storage bags, or place it in plastic storage containers. Seal the containers, label them with the date and contents, and freeze for up to 3 months.

PREBAKED PIZZA CRUSTS

SEE PAGE 62, *Start with a Pizza Crust*

  2 **envelopes active dry yeast**
  1 **tablespoon sugar**
1¾ **cups lukewarm water**
  ¼ **cup olive oil**
5½ **to 6 cups unsifted all-purpose flour, divided**
  2 **teaspoons salt**
     Olive oil
     Cornmeal (optional)

1 In a large bowl, dissolve yeast and sugar in the water. Let the yeast mixture stand until foamy, about 10 minutes.

2 Add olive oil, 2 cups flour, and salt to the yeast mixture; stir until well mixed. Add 2 to 3 cups of the remaining flour kneading until the dough comes away from the bowl and holds together.

3 On a floured surface, knead dough, adding flour, if necessary, until smooth and elastic, about 5 minutes. Coat the inside of a large bowl with olive oil. Place the dough in the bowl, turning it so the top of the dough is lightly oiled. Cover the bowl with a towel; let the dough rise in a warm place until doubled in size, 1 hour.

4 Punch the dough down and divide it equally into three pieces for large pizzas or six pieces for smaller pizzas. Shape each into a ball and set aside for 15 minutes.

5 Preheat the oven to 475°F. Grease three 12-inch pizza pans or large baking sheets. If desired, dust each pan with cornmeal. For large crusts, roll out each ball into a 13-inch round. For small crusts, roll each into an 8-inch round. Place the crusts on the baking sheets and brush them with olive oil.

6 Bake the unfilled pizza crusts, preferably on the lowest shelf of the oven, until lightly browned, 10 to 12 minutes. If baking two crusts at once, switch the pans' position halfway through the baking time. If the dough puffs up while baking, puncture it with a fork. Let cool on wire racks. Wrap the crusts in freezer paper or plastic wrap and freeze for up to 3 months.

To make pizzas: Preheat the oven to 450°F. Place the frozen pizza crusts on lightly greased pizza pans or baking sheets. Add the topping of your choice. Bake until the crust is browned and the topping is bubbly, 10 to 15 minutes.

VARIATION

Whole-wheat pizza crust: Substitute 2 cups whole-wheat flour for 2 cups all-purpose flour.

BASIC BISCUIT MIX

MAKES 10 CUPS

- 9 cups unsifted all-purpose flour
- 1/3 cup baking powder
- 1 tablespoon salt
- 1 1/3 cups vegetable shortening

1 In a large bowl, combine flour, baking powder, and salt. Using a pastry blender or two knives scissor-fashion, cut in shortening until the mixture resembles fine crumbs.

2 Measure 2-cup portions, place each portion in a plastic food-storage bag, and seal tightly. Refrigerate the mix for up to 6 months.

To make biscuits: Preheat the oven to 450°F. In a bowl, place 2 cups Basic Biscuit Mix; stir in 3/4 cup milk just until the mixture forms a soft dough. Turn the dough out onto a lightly floured surface; knead 6 to 8 strokes and roll it out to a 1/2-inch thickness. Using a 2 1/2-inch biscuit cutter, cut out biscuits. Place them on an ungreased baking sheet. Press the dough scraps together, roll out, and cut out more biscuits. Bake 12 to 15 minutes. (Makes 6 to 8 biscuits.)

BASIC CRÊPES

MAKES 12

SEE PAGE 328, *Start with a Crêpe*

- 1 1/2 cups milk
- 3 large eggs
- 2/3 cup unsifted all-purpose flour
- 2 tablespoons butter or margarine, melted
- 1/8 teaspoon salt
- Melted butter or nonstick vegetable spray

1 In a medium-size bowl, using a wire whisk, combine milk, eggs, flour, 2 tablespoons melted butter, and salt until smooth. (Alternatively, blend the ingredients in a blender until smooth.) Cover and refrigerate for at least 30 minutes.

2 Coat a nonstick 7- or 8-inch omelet pan or small skillet with butter or nonstick vegetable spray. Heat over moderate heat until a drop of water spatters in the pan. Pour in 1/4 cup batter.

3 Swirl the pan to spread the batter to make a 6-inch crêpe. Cook until the underside is golden, about 1 minute. Turn the crêpe over and cook until set, a few seconds. Slide it onto a plate; cover it with wax paper. Repeat until all batter is used, placing wax paper between each crêpe.

4 Let the crêpes cool. Place them in a freezer storage bag, and freeze for up to one month.

Pound Cake

MAKES 2 LOAVES

SEE PAGE 339, *Start with a Pound Cake*

2 **cups (4 sticks) butter, softened**
2 **cups sugar**
9 **large eggs**
4 **cups sifted cake flour**
1 **tablespoon baking powder**
½ **teaspoon salt**
1 **cup milk**
2 **teaspoons vanilla extract**

1 Preheat the oven to 350°F. Lightly butter two 9- by 5-inch loaf pans and set them aside.

2 In a large bowl, using an electric mixer at medium speed, beat butter with sugar until light and fluffy. Add eggs, one at a time, beating well after each addition.

3 In a small bowl, combine cake flour, baking powder, and salt. Add the flour mixture alternately with milk into the butter mixture, beginning and ending with the flour mixture. Beat the batter until smooth. Add vanilla and mix well. Pour an equal amount of batter into the prepared pans. Bake for 55 to 60 minutes or until a cake tester or toothpick inserted in the center of the cake comes out clean.

4 Cool the cakes in the pans on wire racks for 10 minutes. Invert the cakes onto the racks and remove the pans. Let the cakes cool completely. Place the cakes in freezer storage bags. (Alternatively, slice the cake, then reassemble it with pieces of wax paper between each slice. Remove single slices and defrost for quick desserts.) Freeze the cakes for up to 4 months.

Graham Cracker Crumb Crust

MAKES 1 CRUST

SEE PAGE 384, *Start with a Crumb Crust*

18 **to 20 graham crackers**
¼ **cup sugar**
⅓ **cup melted butter or margarine**

1 Preheat the oven to 375°F. Using a blender or food processor, process crackers until crumbled, making 1½ cups crumbs. In a medium-size bowl, mix the crumbs, sugar, and butter.

2 With the back of a spoon, press the mixture to the bottom and side of a 9-inch pie plate, forming a rim. Press a second pie plate into the crust to spread it evenly, then remove the second pie plate. Bake the crust for 8 minutes. Place the crumb crust on a wire rack to cool.

3 Wrap the cooled crust with plastic wrap and store in the refrigerator for up to 2 weeks.

To prepare pie: Fill the crumb crust according to recipe directions. Refrigerate if necessary until ready to serve.

Variations

Vanilla- or chocolate-wafer crumb crust: Substitute about 35 vanilla or 18 chocolate wafers (1½ cups crumbs) for the graham crackers; omit the sugar. Mix with ⅓ cup melted butter; bake, cool, and refrigerate as in Steps 2 and 3 above.

BASIC PANCAKE AND WAFFLE MIX

9⅓ cups unsifted all-purpose flour

1⅔ cups nonfat dry milk

⅔ cup sugar

⅓ cup baking powder

2 teaspoons salt

1 cup vegetable shortening

1 In a large bowl, combine flour, dry milk, sugar, baking powder, and salt. Using a pastry blender or two knives scissor-fashion, cut in shortening until the mixture resembles fine crumbs.

2 Measure 2½-cup portions, place each portion in a plastic food-storage bag, and seal tightly. Refrigerate the mix for up to 6 months.

To make pancakes: In a large bowl, combine 1 large egg with 1 cup water. Stir in 2½ cups of the Basic Pancake and Waffle Mix just until moistened. If the batter is very thick, add more water, 1 tablespoon at a time. For each pancake, pour about ¼ cup batter onto a greased hot skillet or griddle, forming a 5-inch pancake. (Makes about 12 pancakes.)

To make waffles: In a large bowl, combine 2 large eggs with ¾ cup water and 2 tablespoons vegetable oil. Stir in 2½ cups Basic Pancake and Waffle Mix just until moistened. Pour enough of the batter into the center of a hot waffle iron to reach within 1 inch of the edge. (Makes about three 9-inch square waffles.)

MIX VARIATIONS

Whole-wheat mix: Substitute 3 cups whole-wheat flour for 3 cups of the all-purpose flour. Follow Steps 1 and 2 above.

Buttermilk mix: Substitute 1⅔ cups dry buttermilk powder for the nonfat dry milk. Reduce the baking powder to ¼ cup and add 1 tablespoon plus 1 teaspoon baking soda. Follow Steps 1 and 2 above.

BATTER VARIATIONS

Banana: Fold 1 cup mashed or chopped ripe bananas into the prepared batter.

Blueberry: Stir 1 cup fresh or frozen, thawed blueberries into the prepared batter.

Cinnamon Nut: Before adding the liquid ingredients to the batter, stir 1 teaspoon ground cinnamon and ½ cup finely chopped almonds, pecans, or walnuts into the mix.

EASY ENTERTAINING

The best parties are those in which the host or hostess feels relaxed and confident, and doesn't have to disappear into the kitchen for hours at a time. Plan a party where you will feel the most comfortable, and guests will follow suit. The Quick Cook keeps some of these ideas in mind for making a successful party without the hassles. Skillful menu planning, time-saving techniques, and easy presentation ideas all add up to a good time for everyone—and that includes the host.

MENU PLANNING

1 The golden rule: Don't make everything from scratch yourself. Plan to make some of the food, the main dish and dessert, for example, then purchase cheese and crackers, bread, and a couple of side dishes from the deli counter at the supermarket.

2 Choose recipes in which you can do some of the work ahead of time, rather than all at the last minute. For example, you can't toss a salad ahead of time, but you can certainly rinse and tear the lettuce and chop all the extras that go in it, then store the ingredients in plastic bags or containers in the refrigerator.

3 There is no substitute for lists. Take out a pen and paper and write out the menu, the shopping list, and a reminder of anything that can be made ahead. This will go a long way toward avoiding any last-minute panics.

4 Work out a time schedule. Organize your time so you will know in which order to prepare the food. This way you will avoid, say, chopping nuts or whipping cream when you could be enjoying a drink with your friends.

5 Plan the meal according to your own equipment and service rather than borrowing and improvising to accommodate the menu. For example, if you've got no soup bowls and two dozen salad plates, don't go through the trouble of borrowing; opt for serving salad instead. Make things easy on yourself.

WHAT KIND OF PARTY?

Buffets are always easier on the host than a sit-down meal. The atmosphere tends to be more casual, and the food can be laid out all at once. On the other hand, if you prefer the intimacy of a sit-down meal, just remember to keep the courses simple enough that they can flow from the kitchen without too much last-minute attention from you. In either case, have the buffet or table set as thoroughly as possible before guests arrive.

Another kind of party can be a life-saver for the Quick Cook: a cooking party, in which the guests cook their food themselves. If the size of your kitchen allows it, have an omelet party or a pizza party; you provide the ingredients and set them out in bowls, then let your guests create their own concoctions. A simpler variation, in which there is no cooking involved, is to have a sundae party with a selection of ice creams and imaginative toppings spread out buffet-style.

NO-COOK PARTY FOOD

Scout your supermarket for interesting foods that will round out your own cooking, especially when it comes to appetizers and desserts. Here are a few suggestions:

APPETIZERS
• A tray of olives and crudités, some almonds or a mixture of party nuts
• Salami rolled up with cheese inside, or Prosciutto with melon

IMAGINATIVE CONTAINERS

If you want a change from standard bowls or dishes, experiment with some of these creative containers:

Fruit salads Cut a large cantaloupe or honeydew in half horizontally and remove a ¼-inch slice from the top and bottom so that both halves will stand upright. Scoop out the seeds and discard. Scoop out about half of the flesh for a small bowl shape.

Dips Cut off the top third of a red cabbage. Using a small curved knife, scoop out enough of the cabbage to leave about a 1½-inch shell. Cut a thin slice off the base so it will stand upright.

Salads Hollow out tomatoes, cucumbers, or avocado halves.

• Prepared dips or package mixes with fresh vegetable strips, toasted sliced pita bread, and bread sticks
• A wedge of cheese laid out with a bunch of grapes and a basket of crackers

DESSERTS
• A cake, pie, or fruit tart from the bakery, served with coffee
• Plain cookies with sliced fresh fruit
• The most chocolatey truffles you can find

Menus

Good food need not be fussy food. The Quick Cook can give a buffet supper, an afternoon tea, or a Sunday brunch—no need to forgo get-togethers because time is short. The key is in advance planning and presenting food attractively. All the menus on these pages have been created with a combination of recipes from this book and some store-bought items.

WINTER SUPPER FOR FOUR

ASSORTED CRACKERS WITH CHEESE
CHICKEN PROVENÇAL, PAGE 138
RICE PILAF, PAGE 236
PECAN TARTLETS, PAGE 387

◆

• Arrange the cheese and crackers on a large platter garnished with grape clusters.
• Prepare the rice pilaf the morning of the party, then reheat.
• Bake the pecan tartlets the day before the party; store them at room temperature. If desired, serve them with scoops of vanilla ice cream.

SUNDAY BRUNCH

EGGS WITH CREAM CHEESE AND LOX, PAGE 255
ROASTED RED POTATOES, PAGE 277
MELON FRUIT SALAD, PAGE 308
WARM CROISSANTS AND ASSORTED MUFFINS
ORANGE JUICE

◆

• If orange juice will be made from a frozen concentrate, make it the day before and refrigerate. Pour it into a jug and stir before serving.
• Prepare the melon salad the day before, cover, and refrigerate.
• Place warm croissants and muffins in baskets lined with cloth napkins or tea towels. Serve them with sweet butter made by mixing fruit preserve into softened butter or margarine.

PATIO PARTY

TORTILLA CHIPS WITH TOMATO SALSA
CALIFORNIA BURGERS, PAGE 183
CORN ON THE COB
MISSISSIPPI MUD PIE, PAGE 360

◆

• Serve chips and salsa on a festive platter.
• Husk the corn on the cob the day before, wrap the corn, and refrigerate.
• Prepare the hamburger patties the day before, wrap and refrigerate. If you prefer, grill the burgers on the barbecue.
• Prepare the mud pie the day before and freeze. Let the pie stand for a few minutes to soften before serving.

CASUAL LUNCH FOR FOUR

CHICKEN CLUB, PAGE 64
DELI PASTA SALAD
CHEESECAKE CUPS, PAGE 373

◆

• Prepare the ingredients that fill the sandwiches the morning of the party, then reheat the chicken and bacon before assembling. Save toasting the bread and assembling the sandwiches until just before serving.
• To serve the pasta salad, line a shallow salad bowl with large lettuce leaves. Gently toss the salad, then spoon it on top of the lettuce. Garnish with tomato wedges or black olives.
• Prepare the cheesecake cups the day before, cover, and refrigerate.

Afternoon Tea Party

OPEN-FACED CUCUMBER TEA SANDWICHES, PAGE 58
PEAR AND PROSCIUTTO SANDWICHES, PAGE 65
ASSORTED BAKERY COOKIES AND PASTRIES
CHOCOLATE-DIPPED STRAWBERRIES, PAGE 350

◆

• Prepare the cucumber topping and cut the bread for the tea sandwiches the morning of the party. Assemble them just before serving.
• Prepare the pear sandwiches shortly before serving; if you prefer, cut them into quarters for easier handling.
• Make the cookies and pastries look special by arranging them decoratively on platters lined with paper doilies, or in a shallow basket lined with a linen cloth.
• Offer two or three choices of teas.
• Prepare the chocolate-dipped strawberries the morning of the party, and refrigerate.

Candlelight Dinner for Two

ASPARAGUS DIJONNAISE, PAGE 272
BAKERY ROLLS
SALMON VÉRONIQUE, PAGE 105
PACKAGED RICE MIX
BAKERY CHOCOLATE MOUSSE CAKE

◆

• Halve the Asparagus Dijonnaise recipe in order to serve two. Cook the asparagus the morning of the dinner, wrap it in plastic, and refrigerate. Prepare the sauce just before serving.
• Serve the rolls with softened butter mixed with finely chopped fresh parsley.
• Halve the Salmon Véronique recipe. Prepare the salmon just before serving.
• The rice mix may also be prepared in the morning, then sealed and refrigerated. Add a few drops of water to the rice before reheating on the stove or in the microwave.
• To serve the mousse cake, place a slice of cake on each dessert plate, then pour some cream around each slice.

Italian Dinner for Four

BRUSCHETTA, PAGE 53
SPAGHETTI TUSCAN STYLE, PAGE 230
GREEN SALAD
GORGONZOLA CHEESE WITH RIPE PEARS
AFTER-DINNER CHOCOLATES

◆

• The pasta and the sauce may be made the day before the dinner (see page 212), then reheated just before serving.
• Purchase pre-washed and torn salad leaves from the supermarket salad bar. Add croutons, sliced radishes, and artichoke hearts, then toss with a prepared creamy Italian dressing.
• For an authentic touch, place a wedge of Parmesan cheese on the table with a cheese grater, and let guests grate their own cheese.
• The gorgonzola may be substituted with another mild blue cheese if your store doesn't carry it. The cheese and fruit should be served at room temperature for the best flavor.
• Arrange the chocolates on a pretty plate; offer them with coffee.

After-Theater Supper

SPINACH SALAD WITH ORANGES, PAGE 294
CHEESE FONDUE, PAGE 268
BAKERY FRUIT TART

◆

• Rinse the spinach and slice the oranges for the salad the morning of the supper. Wrap them separately and refrigerate.
• Prepare the salad dressing in the morning; shake it well just before serving.
• Grate the cheese for the fondue and mix it with the dry ingredients the day before. Wrap and refrigerate.
• Prepare an assortment of bread cubes and fresh vegetables for the fondue in the morning. Wrap each tightly and refrigerate.
• Garnish the tart with fresh mint sprigs and sweetened whipped cream or frozen whipped topping, thawed.

APPETIZERS AND SNACKS

BAKED STUFFED MUSHROOMS (PAGE 41)

APPETIZERS

These hors d'oeuvres and first courses make quick work of
preparing party food, so you have more time for friends.

BITE-SIZE CRUSTLESS QUICHES

MAKES

One Piece: **Calories** 37 **Protein** 2g **Carbohydrates** Trace **Fat** 3g **Cholesterol** 45mg **Sodium** 75mg

1 **tablespoon butter or
margarine**

½ **cup finely chopped red
bell pepper**

¼ **cup chopped green onion
(white and green parts)**

3 **large eggs**

2 **tablespoons milk**

2 **ounces Cheddar cheese,
coarsely grated (½ cup)**

¼ **teaspoon salt**

⅛ **teaspoon ground black
pepper**

 PREPARATION TIME
10 MINUTES

COOKING TIME
20 MINUTES

SERVING SUGGESTION *These bite-size quiches are easier to handle
than slices of a large quiche—making them ideal finger food.*

1 Preheat the oven to 425°F. Grease one tray of 24 mini muffin-pan
cups (1¾- by 1-inch). In a small saucepan, melt butter over moderate
heat. Add bell pepper and onion; sauté until soft, about 5 minutes.
Remove the pan from the heat and let the mixture cool slightly.

2 In a medium-size bowl, combine eggs, milk, cheese, salt, and pepper.
Stir in the bell pepper and onions. Spoon about 1 tablespoon of the
mixture into each muffin cup. (The mixture will fill 18 to 22 cups.)

3 Bake until the centers are set, 8 to 10 minutes. Let the quiches cool
for 1 minute. Using a knife, loosen the quiches around the edges and
remove from the cups. Arrange them on a platter, and serve.

CAVIAR CORN CAKES

MAKES

One Piece: **Calories** 83 **Protein** 3g **Carbohydrates** 8g **Fat** 5g **Cholesterol** 41mg **Sodium** 164mg

1 **cup buttermilk baking mix
(Bisquick)**

1 **large egg**

½ **cup milk**

1 **cup fresh or frozen corn
kernels, thawed if frozen**

2 **tablespoons yellow
cornmeal**

2 **tablespoons (¼ stick)
butter or margarine,
melted**

6 **tablespoons sour cream**

1 **jar (2 ounces) red salmon
caviar**

Chopped chives (optional)

PREPARATION TIME
5 MINUTES

COOKING TIME
16 MINUTES

SERVING SUGGESTION *As an alternative, serve these corn cakes with
whipped cream cheese and a small slice of smoked salmon.*

1 In a medium-size bowl, combine baking mix with egg and milk to
form a batter. Stir in corn kernels, cornmeal, and melted butter.

2 Lightly oil a griddle or large skillet. Heat over moderate heat until a
drop of water sizzles on the surface. Drop 1 tablespoonful of batter
onto the griddle to make a 2-inch corn cake, making several at a time.

3 Cook the corn cakes until the undersides are golden brown, about
2 minutes. Turn the cakes over and continue cooking until the second
side is firm. Transfer the corn cakes to a large platter. Repeat to cook
the remaining batter. (The batter makes 16 to 19 cakes.)

4 Top each corn cake with 1 teaspoon sour cream and ½ teaspoon
caviar; garnish with chives, if desired, and serve.

BITE-SIZE CRUSTLESS QUICHES (RIGHT) AND CAVIAR CORN CAKES ▶

DEVILED EGGS

One Piece: **Calories** 64 **Protein** 3g **Carbohydrates** 0g **Fat** 5g **Cholesterol** 108mg **Sodium** 55mg

8 **large eggs**

¼ **cup mayonnaise or sour cream**

1 **teaspoon Dijon mustard**

¼ **teaspoon curry powder**

Salt and ground white pepper to taste

Paprika (optional)

Parsley sprigs (optional)

 PREPARATION TIME
20 MINUTES

 COOKING TIME
25 MINUTES

SERVING SUGGESTION *Add variety to these perennial favorites by garnishing them with crumbled bacon or sliced olives.*

1 In a small saucepan, place eggs; cover them with cold water. Bring the water to a boil over high heat. Remove the saucepan from the heat and let the eggs stand, covered, for 15 minutes.

2 Drain the eggs and rinse them with cold water. Leaving the eggs in the pan, cover them with cold water and let them stand for about 5 minutes. Shell the eggs and cut them in half lengthwise. Remove the yolks and set the whites on a baking sheet covered with a sheet of paper towels.

3 In a small bowl, using the back of a fork, mash the yolks. Stir in mayonnaise, mustard, and curry powder; season with salt and pepper. Fit a pastry bag with a large star tip and fill it with the yolk mixture. Pipe the mixture into the egg cavities.

4 Carefully transfer the eggs to a serving platter. Sprinkle the yolks with paprika and garnish the platter with tiny sprigs of parsley, if desired. Serve immediately or refrigerate until ready to serve.

Shelf Magic

These quick appetizers make a pair of light snacks for a casual get-together. Serve them warm, and watch them disappear.

FRIED TORTELLINI

In a medium-size skillet, heat **2 tablespoons olive oil.** Add **one 9-ounce package fresh, uncooked, cheese-filled tortellini.** Fry them until they are crisp and golden, 5 to 7 minutes, turning them frequently so they cook evenly. Drain the tortellini briefly on paper towels. Place them in a serving bowl, and toss them gently with **2 tablespoons grated Parmesan cheese.** Serve immediately, passing toothpicks on the side.
SERVES 4

TORTILLA CHIPS

Preheat the oven to 350°F. With **2 tablespoons oil,** brush a light coating of oil on one side of each of **twelve 8-inch flour or corn tortillas.** Stack the tortillas greased side up; using a sharp knife, cut the stack into eighths. Separate the tortilla pieces; arrange them greased side up on two lightly oiled baking sheets. Bake the chips until they are crisp and lightly browned, about 10 minutes. Serve with **fresh tomato salsa.**
SERVES 6

CHEDDAR QUESADILLAS

CHEDDAR QUESADILLAS

MAKES 16

One Piece: **Calories** 152 **Protein** 5g **Carbohydrates** 11g **Fat** 11g **Cholesterol** 15mg **Sodium** 172mg

- 4 **tablespoons vegetable oil, divided**
- 8 **small flour tortillas (7 or 8 inches in diameter)**
- 8 **ounces Cheddar cheese, coarsely grated (2 cups), divided**
- 1 **can (4 ounces) chopped green chilies, drained, divided**
- 1 **small ripe avocado**
- 1/3 **cup prepared thick-style tomato salsa**

 PREPARATION TIME
6 MINUTES

 COOKING TIME
25 MINUTES

FOOD NOTE Queso *is the Spanish word for cheese—which gives these traditional Tex-Mex appetizers their irresistible flavor.*

1 In a large skillet or griddle, heat 1 tablespoon oil over moderate heat. Put one flour tortilla in the skillet and sprinkle it with 1/2 cup cheese and one-quarter of the green chilies. Place another tortilla on top and press it gently to seal the tortillas together.

2 Cook the tortilla sandwich or quesadilla, turning it once with a broad spatula, until the cheese begins to melt, about 5 minutes. Transfer the quesadilla to a cutting board and cut it into four wedges. Repeat to cook the remaining quesadillas.

3 Transfer the quesadillas to a serving platter. Peel and pit avocado, and cut it into 16 thin slices. Garnish each quesadilla wedge with the avocado and about 1 teaspoon of tomato salsa. Serve immediately.

PIZZA PITA TRIANGLES

PIZZA PITA TRIANGLES

MAKES

One Piece: **Calories** 66 **Protein** 3g **Carbohydrates** 5g **Fat** 3g **Cholesterol** 9mg **Sodium** 156mg

- 4 **ounces small mushrooms**
- 2 **ounces thinly sliced pepperoni**
- 1 **small red onion**
- 2 **whole-wheat pita breads (about 6 inches in diameter)**
- 2 **tablespoons chopped fresh basil (or 2 teaspoons dried basil leaves, crumbled)**
- 4 **ounces mozzarella cheese, coarsely grated (1 cup)**
- 2 **tablespoons grated Parmesan cheese**

**PREPARATION TIME
20 MINUTES**

**COOKING TIME
10 MINUTES**

COOK'S TIP *If you prefer to make these ahead, cover and refrigerate them before they are cooked then bake just before serving.*

1 Preheat the oven to 425°F. Slice mushrooms; cut pepperoni into matchstick-size strips. Thinly slice onion and separate the rings.

2 Using a sharp knife, carefully cut each pita bread around the edges to split it into two layers. Place the pita halves, cut sides up, on an ungreased baking sheet. Scatter an equal amount of the mushrooms, pepperoni, onion, and basil over the pita halves. Sprinkle them with the grated mozzarella and Parmesan cheeses.

3 Bake until the cheese is melted, 10 to 12 minutes. Cut each pita into 4 wedges, arrange them on a platter, and serve immediately.

CHEDDAR CHEESE FRITTERS

MAKES 12

One Piece: **Calories** 99 **Protein** 4g **Carbohydrates** 9g **Fat** 5g **Cholesterol** 29mg **Sodium** 138mg

1 cup all-purpose flour
1 teaspoon baking powder
1/4 teaspoon salt
1/8 teaspoon cayenne pepper
1 large egg
1/2 cup milk, divided
4 ounces sharp Cheddar cheese, coarsely grated (1 cup)
Vegetable oil for frying

 PREPARATION TIME
6 MINUTES

 COOKING TIME
19 MINUTES

COOK'S TIP *Be sure the cooking oil is at the correct temperature before you begin frying the fritters, so they turn out light and crispy.*

1 In a medium-size bowl, using a wire whisk, combine flour, baking powder, salt, and cayenne pepper until well mixed. Form a well in the center and crack egg open into the well.

2 Pour 1/4 cup of the milk into the well in the flour mixture; stir until it is smooth. Add just enough of the remaining milk until the mixture is soft enough to drop from a spoon. Stir in the grated Cheddar cheese until the batter is well mixed.

3 In a large saucepan or deep fryer, heat 2 inches of oil to 375°F. Drop tablespoonfuls of the mixture, 6 to 8 at a time, into the hot oil and fry until golden brown on all sides, 1 to 2 minutes. Drain the fritters on paper towels, transfer them to a platter, and serve immediately.

BAKED STUFFED MUSHROOMS

MAKES  24

One Piece: **Calories** 30 **Protein** Trace **Carbohydrates** 2g **Fat** 2g **Cholesterol** 5mg **Sodium** 45mg

24 2-inch mushrooms (about 1 pound)
1 tablespoon olive oil
2 tablespoons (1/4 stick) butter or margarine
3 tablespoons finely chopped green onion
1/3 cup packaged plain bread crumbs
2 tablespoons chopped parsley
1/8 teaspoon ground white pepper
2 ounces feta cheese, crumbled (1/2 cup)
Parsley sprigs

PREPARATION TIME
20 MINUTES

COOKING TIME
15 MINUTES

COOK'S TIP *Chop the mushroom stems in a food processor to prepare these party appetizers even more quickly.*

1 Preheat the oven to 450°F. Remove the stems from mushrooms. Finely chop enough of the stems to measure 3/4 cup; set aside. Place the mushroom caps and oil in a large bowl; toss to coat evenly. Arrange the mushroom caps, stemless ends up, on a jelly-roll pan and set them aside.

2 In a medium-size saucepan, melt butter over moderate heat. Add green onion and sauté until soft, about 2 minutes. Add the chopped mushroom stems and sauté until tender, about 2 more minutes. Stir in bread crumbs, parsley, and pepper until well mixed. Remove the saucepan from the heat.

3 Stir cheese into the crumb mixture. Spoon about 1 teaspoon of the mixture into each mushroom cap. Bake the stuffed mushrooms until they are heated through and lightly browned, about 10 minutes. Transfer the mushrooms to a serving platter. Garnish each with a tiny sprig of parsley, and serve.

DILLED MEATBALLS

MAKES

One Piece: **Calories** 32 **Protein** 2g **Carbohydrates** Trace **Fat** 2g **Cholesterol** 8mg **Sodium** 54mg

1 **pound ground turkey**

1 **cup fresh bread crumbs**

1 **tablespoon grated onion**

1 **tablespoon snipped dill (or 1 teaspoon dill weed)**

½ **teaspoon salt**

¼ **teaspoon ground white pepper**

2 **tablespoons (¼ stick) butter or margarine**

1 **tablespoon vegetable oil**

1 **teaspoon cornstarch**

½ **cup plus 1 tablespoon canned reduced-sodium chicken broth, divided**

½ **cup sour cream**

Additional snipped dill or dill weed (optional)

 PREPARATION TIME
15 MINUTES

COOKING TIME
25 MINUTES

COOK'S TIP *The meatballs can be made a day ahead, if your schedule allows. Serve them chilled or reheated, with toothpicks.*

1 In a medium-size bowl, combine turkey, bread crumbs, onion, dill, salt, and pepper. Shape the turkey mixture into ¾-inch balls, making 42 to 46 meatballs.

2 In a large skillet, heat butter and oil over moderate heat until butter is melted. Cook half the meatballs until they are well browned on all sides, about 10 minutes. Using a slotted spoon, transfer them to a bowl. Repeat to cook the remaining meatballs; add them to the bowl.

3 In a cup, mix cornstarch with 1 tablespoon chicken broth until smooth; set the mixture aside. Gradually stir the remaining chicken broth into the drippings in the skillet; bring the mixture to a boil.

4 Add the cornstarch mixture to the broth in the skillet, stirring until it is smooth and slightly thickened. Return the meatballs and any accumulated juices to the skillet and bring to a boil.

5 Stir sour cream into the meatballs. (Do not boil.) Remove the skillet from the heat. Transfer the meatballs and sauce to a chafing dish or serving bowl. Sprinkle with dill, if desired, and serve.

BROILED CHICKEN NUGGETS

MAKES

One Piece: **Calories** 27 **Protein** 3g **Carbohydrates** 0g **Fat** 1g **Cholesterol** 12mg **Sodium** 45mg

4 **skinless, boneless chicken-breast halves (about 1½ pounds)**

⅓ **cup butter or margarine**

3 **cloves garlic, finely chopped**

1 **teaspoon paprika**

1 **teaspoon dried tarragon, crumbled**

½ **teaspoon salt**

⅛ **teaspoon ground black pepper**

Watercress (optional)

 PREPARATION TIME
6 MINUTES

COOKING TIME
10 MINUTES

1 Preheat the broiler. Cut each chicken breast in half lengthwise, then cut each half into 6 chunks. Set them aside. In a medium-size saucepan, melt butter over moderate heat. Add garlic and sauté for 15 seconds. Remove the saucepan from the heat.

2 Add paprika, tarragon, salt, and pepper to the garlic butter. Add the chicken and stir until it is coated with the garlic mixture.

3 Arrange the chicken in a single layer on the rack over a broiler pan. Broil the pieces 4 inches from the heat until the chicken is lightly browned, about 4 minutes. Turn the pieces over and continue broiling until tender, about 1 more minute.

4 Mound the chicken pieces on a serving platter and surround them with watercress sprigs, if desired. Serve with toothpicks.

DILLED MEATBALLS (RIGHT) AND ROAST BEEF CANAPÉS

Roast Beef Canapés

MAKES

One Piece: **Calories** 85 **Protein** 4g **Carbohydrates** 5g **Fat** 6g **Cholesterol** 9mg **Sodium** 105mg

8 ounces thinly sliced rare roast beef

2 tablespoons olive oil

1 tablespoon red-wine vinegar

1 tablespoon snipped chives or dill

¼ teaspoon salt

1 loaf French bread (about 16 by 3 inches)

½ cup mayonnaise

24 small strips pimiento or roasted red pepper

Chive or dill sprigs (optional)

PREPARATION TIME
20 MINUTES

COOKING TIME
0 MINUTES

SERVING SUGGESTION *Instead of French bread, try serving these canapés on mini bagels, sliced in half and toasted.*

1 Cut beef slices crosswise into 2-inch-wide strips. In a bowl, combine oil, vinegar, chives, and salt until well mixed. Add the beef slices and toss to coat thoroughly with the oil mixture. Let it stand for about 10 minutes to marinate.

2 Meanwhile, slice French bread into 24 ¼-inch-thick slices. Spread one side of each bread slice with 1 teaspoon mayonnaise.

3 Top the mayonnaise with the roast-beef strips, folding them to fit neatly on the bread. Garnish the top of each canapé with a pimiento strip and a piece of chive or dill, if desired.

4 Arrange the canapés on a platter and serve immediately, or cover and refrigerate until ready to serve.

PARMESAN PITA CHIPS

MAKES 48

One Piece: **Calories** 42 **Protein** 1g **Carbohydrates** 4g **Fat** 2g **Cholesterol** 3mg **Sodium** 60mg

6 pita breads (about 6 inches in diameter)

¼ cup (½ stick) butter or margarine

¼ cup olive oil

1 clove garlic, finely chopped

½ teaspoon dried savory or thyme leaves, crumbled

⅓ cup grated Parmesan cheese

PREPARATION TIME
15 MINUTES

COOKING TIME
10 MINUTES

FOOD NOTE *These homemade chips are tastier than any cheese-flavored chips you can buy—they'll quickly become a family favorite.*

1 Preheat the oven to 425°F. Using a sharp knife, cut each pita bread into quarters; cut through the middle and split each quarter into two, for a total of 48 pieces. Lay the pieces cut-side up on an ungreased baking sheet.

2 In a small saucepan, heat butter and oil over moderate heat. Add garlic and savory; sauté for 15 seconds. Remove the butter mixture from the heat. Brush the mixture over the cut side of the pita pieces. Sprinkle grated cheese evenly over the pita pieces.

3 Bake the pita until the pieces are crisp and lightly browned, about 10 minutes. Transfer the chips to a rack to let them cool, and serve. If not serving immediately, store the chips in an airtight container.

HERBED YOGURT DIP

 5

One Tablespoon: **Calories** 28 **Protein** Trace **Carbohydrates** 1g **Fat** 2g **Cholesterol** 2mg **Sodium** 24mg

2 tablespoons chopped green-onion tops or chives

2 tablespoons chopped parsley

1 tablespoon chopped fresh tarragon or snipped dill

1 clove garlic

1 container (8 ounces) plain low-fat yogurt

¼ cup mayonnaise

Salt and ground black pepper to taste

PREPARATION TIME
10 MINUTES

COOKING TIME
0 MINUTES

COOK'S TIP *This low-fat dip pairs wonderfully with Parmesan Pita Chips (above) or assorted raw vegetables.*

1 Using an electric blender or food processor fitted with the chopping blade, process green onion, parsley, tarragon, and garlic to a paste-like consistency. Add yogurt and mayonnaise; using a rubber spatula, stir to blend well.

2 Season the yogurt dip with salt and pepper; transfer it to a small bowl, and serve. (Makes 1¼ cups.)

VARIATION: YOGURT CREAM-CHEESE DIP

One Tablespoon: **Calories** 36 **Protein** Trace **Carbohydrates** Trace **Fat** 3g **Cholesterol** 11mg **Sodium** 31mg

In a medium-size bowl, using an electric mixer or wooden spoon, beat **one 8-ounce package cream cheese,** *at room temperature, until smooth. Add* **½ cup plain low-fat yogurt** *with* **⅛ teaspoon carraway seeds, ground cumin seeds, or ground fennel seeds;** *beat until well blended. Season and serve as in Step 2, above. (Makes 1½ cups.)*

SMOKED SALMON PÂTÉ

Smoked Salmon Pâté

One Tablespoon: **Calories** 21 **Protein** 2g **Carbohydrates** 0g **Fat** 2g **Cholesterol** 5mg **Sodium** 64mg

4 **ounces sliced smoked salmon**

4 **ounces light cream cheese, softened**

1 **tablespoon lime juice**

1 **tablespoon chopped fresh chives**

1 **tablespoon snipped dill (or 1 teaspoon dill weed)**

Ground black pepper to taste

Dill sprigs (optional)

PREPARATION TIME
22 MINUTES

COOKING TIME
0 MINUTES

SERVING SUGGESTION *This hors d'oeuvre is delicious served on party-size pieces of pumpernickel bread or water crackers. Place the serving bowl in the refrigerator while preparing the pâté; it will help the pâté stay cool much longer.*

1 Cut salmon into narrow strips. Using an electric blender or a food processor fitted with the chopping blade, process the salmon, cream cheese, lime juice, chives, and dill until fairly smooth.

2 Season the salmon pâté with pepper and spoon it into a small serving bowl. Cover and refrigerate for 15 minutes or until ready to serve. Garnish with dill, if desired. (Makes 1⅓ cups.)

BLUE CHEESE DIP

One Tablespoon: **Calories** 61 **Protein** 1g **Carbohydrates** 0g **Fat** 6g **Cholesterol** 9mg **Sodium** 98mg

½ cup mayonnaise

½ cup sour cream

4 ounces blue cheese, crumbled (1 cup)

2 to 4 tablespoons milk

1 teaspoon Worcestershire sauce

¼ teaspoon dry mustard

Dash hot red pepper sauce

PREPARATION TIME
27 MINUTES

COOKING TIME
0 MINUTES

SERVING SUGGESTION *Serve this dip with assorted cut vegetables, such as cauliflower florets, sliced zucchini, and bell-pepper sticks.*

1 In a small bowl, combine mayonnaise, sour cream, blue cheese, 2 tablespoons milk, Worcestershire sauce, mustard, and red pepper sauce. Stir in more milk if the dip is too thick.

2 Cover the bowl with plastic wrap and refrigerate the dip for about 20 minutes. Just before serving, spoon the dip into a bowl, and serve. (Makes 1½ cups.)

CHILI GUACAMOLE

One Tablespoon: **Calories** 18 **Protein** 0g **Carbohydrates** 1g **Fat** 2g **Cholesterol** 0mg **Sodium** 11mg

1 large ripe avocado

1 ripe plum tomato

1 fresh or canned pickled jalapeño pepper

1 tablespoon lime or lemon juice

¼ cup canned chopped green chilies

1 tablespoon chopped fresh cilantro (optional)

½ teaspoon hot red pepper sauce

Salt and ground black pepper to taste

PREPARATION TIME
10 MINUTES

COOKING TIME
0 MINUTES

SERVING SUGGESTION *This robust dip goes best with crispy tortilla chips. It tastes great on burgers, too.*

1 Cut avocado in half, remove the pit, and peel. Finely chop tomato; core, seed, and finely chop jalapeño pepper.

2 In a large bowl, using a potato masher or fork, mash the avocado with lime juice until it is fairly smooth. Stir in the chopped tomato and jalapeño pepper, green chilies, cilantro if desired, and pepper sauce.

3 Season the mixture with salt and pepper. Transfer the guacamole to a small bowl, and serve. (Makes 1¾ cups.)

TIME SAVERS

APPETIZERS

• When you're making creamy dips, buy whipped cream cheese—you will not need to take time to soften it before mixing it with the remaining ingredients.

• Crumbled bacon pieces can be made ahead to use as toppings on various appetizers. Cook the bacon, let it cool, and crumble it. Refrigerate it in a sealed plastic bag for up to a week.

• To clean mushrooms quickly and keep them fresh for crudités, dip a cloth into lemon juice and use it to wipe away the dirt, leaving the mushrooms clean and impervious to discoloration.

START WITH CRACKERS AND CHIPS

An attractively arranged variety of crackers and chips is always a hit at parties, especially when they're paired with a colorful selection of dips. Here are some irresistible dips to serve as appetizers at your next party. The recipes can easily be halved or doubled.

◄ **CHUNKY SALSA** In a medium-size bowl, combine **4 medium-size tomatoes**, peeled and diced, **½ cup chopped yellow onion**, **½ cup chopped celery**, **¼ cup chopped green pepper**, **one 4-oz. can mild chopped green chilies**, drained, and **1 Tbsp. chopped cilantro**, if desired. In a small bowl, combine **¼ cup olive oil**, **2 Tbsp. red-wine vinegar, 1 tsp. mustard seed, 1 tsp. salt, a pinch pepper, ¼ tsp. chili powder**, and **hot red pepper sauce** to taste. Pour oil mixture over vegetables and toss until coated. Cover salsa and chill at least 25 minutes or until ready to serve. Serve with **tortilla chips.** Makes 4 cups

► **HOT ARTICHOKE DIP** Preheat oven to 350°F. Chop **one 9-oz. package frozen artichoke hearts**, thawed and drained. Place them in a bowl and add **½ cup plain yogurt, ½ cup mayonnaise**, and **1 cup grated Parmesan cheese**; mix well. Spoon the mixture into a 1-quart casserole and sprinkle with **paprika**; bake for 30 minutes. Serve hot or cold with **crackers.** Makes 2 cups

► **SPICY VEGETABLE DIP** In a small bowl, cover **¼ cup seedless raisins** with hot water and let stand for 10 minutes. Meanwhile, in a blender or food processor, combine **1 cup cottage cheese, 2 Tbsp. cider vinegar, ½ small yellow onion**, coarsely chopped, **1 tsp. chili powder, ½ tsp. curry powder, ½ tsp. salt** and **⅛ tsp. ground black pepper**. Blend or process until smooth. If mixture is too thick for dipping, add **1 Tbsp. raisin water or milk**. Drain raisins and stir them into the cheese mixture. Chill dip for at least 20 minutes or until ready to serve. Serve with **crackers or cut raw vegetables.** Makes 1½ cups

◄ HOT CRAB DIP In the bottom portion of a double boiler, bring water to a simmer. Meanwhile, in the top portion of the double boiler, combine **two 8-oz. packages cream cheese**, softened, **½ cup half-and-half or milk**, **¼ cup chopped green onions**, **1½ Tbsp. horseradish**, **2 tsp. Worcestershire sauce**, and **salt and ground black pepper** to taste. Cook for 10 minutes. Do not allow water to boil. Stir in **12 oz. imitation crabmeat** and **2 Tbsp. white wine**. Continue cooking for 10 minutes. Spoon mixture into a small serving dish and serve immediately with **crackers.** Makes 4 cups

► HOT MEXICAN DIP Preheat oven to 350°F. In a 12-inch skillet, sauté **8 oz. lean ground beef, 1 small onion**, chopped, and **½ small red pepper**, seeded and chopped, until beef is lightly browned, about 7 minutes. Drain if necessary and stir in **one 1.25-oz. package taco seasoning mix**; cook for 1 minute. Add **one 16-oz. can refried beans** to meat mixture and mix thoroughly. Spoon mixture into a 1½-quart casserole, spreading it evenly. Layer **½ cup sour cream, one 4-oz. can chopped green chilies**, drained, **½ cup grated Monterey Jack cheese**, and **½ cup grated Cheddar cheese** over the meat mixture. Bake until hot and bubbly, 25 to 30 minutes. Serve with **tortilla chips.** Makes 4 cups

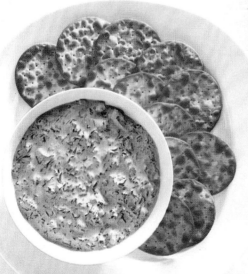

◄ SPINACH DIP In a large bowl, combine **two 10-oz. packages frozen chopped spinach**, thawed and drained, and **one 4-oz. package blue cheese**, crumbled. Stir in **one 8-oz. can sliced water chestnuts**, drained and coarsely chopped, **½ cup chopped celery**, **¾ cup chopped red pepper**, **½ cup chopped green onion**, and **one-half .65-oz. package garlic dressing mix**. In a small bowl, combine **2 cups sour cream** and **1 cup mayonnaise**. Gradually stir sour cream mixture into spinach mixture until ingredients are easy to spread. If desired, spoon dip into a **hollowed-out whole pumpernickel bread or hollowed-out red cabbage.** Makes 6 cups

HOT SHRIMP DIP

One Tablespoon: **Calories** 53 **Protein** 2g **Carbohydrates** Trace **Fat** 5g **Cholesterol** 22mg **Sodium** 171mg

1 tablespoon butter or margarine

1 tablespoon sliced almonds

1/2 small yellow onion, finely chopped

1 package (5 ounces) frozen cooked tiny shrimp

1 package (8 ounces) cream cheese, softened

2 teaspoons lemon juice

1 teaspoon prepared white horseradish

1/2 teaspoon Worcestershire sauce

Salt and ground white pepper to taste

 PREPARATION TIME
6 MINUTES

COOKING TIME
12 MINUTES

COOK'S TIP *This dip is also delicious chilled: Cover the bowl with plastic wrap and refrigerate it until ready to serve. Corn chips, tortilla chips, or raw vegetables all go well with it.*

1 In a medium-size saucepan, melt butter over moderate heat. Add almonds and sauté until golden brown, about 3 minutes. Using a slotted spoon, transfer the almonds to a small bowl.

2 Add onion to the remaining butter in the saucepan; sauté until soft, about 3 minutes. Stir in frozen shrimp and cook just until it is thawed and nearly all of the juices have evaporated, about 8 minutes. Stir in cream cheese, lemon juice, horseradish, and Worcestershire sauce. Cook until just heated through.

3 Season the hot shrimp dip with salt and pepper. Transfer it to a serving bowl, sprinkle with the almonds, and serve. (Makes 1 1/4 cups.)

VEGETABLE ANTIPASTO

One Serving: **Calories** 159 **Protein** 2g **Carbohydrates** 9g **Fat** 13g **Cholesterol** 0mg **Sodium** 139mg

1/4 cup olive oil

3 tablespoons red-wine vinegar

1/2 teaspoon dried oregano, crumbled

1/4 teaspoon salt

1/8 teaspoon ground black pepper

1 clove garlic, finely chopped

1 small eggplant (about 12 ounces)

2 small zucchini (about 12 ounces)

1 large red or yellow bell pepper

1 ounce Parmesan cheese, shaved (1/4 cup)

 PREPARATION TIME
15 MINUTES

COOKING TIME
15 MINUTES

1 Preheat the broiler. In a small bowl, combine oil, vinegar, oregano, salt, pepper, and garlic.

2 Cut eggplant crosswise into 1/4-inch-thick slices. Place the eggplant slices in a single layer on the rack over a broiler pan. Brush with some of the oil mixture. Broil the eggplant about 4 inches from the heat until lightly browned and tender, about 8 minutes, turning once and brushing with more of the oil mixture.

3 Meanwhile, cut zucchini lengthwise into thin slices. Core and seed bell pepper and cut it into 1-inch-wide strips.

4 Transfer the broiled eggplant slices to a plate. Place the zucchini and peppers on the broiler rack. Brush them with some of the oil mixture. Broil the zucchini and peppers until lightly browned on one side, about 3 minutes. Turn them over, brush them with more of the oil mixture, and broil 3 more minutes.

5 Arrange the vegetables on four serving plates and drizzle them with any remaining oil mixture. Top each with some shaved Parmesan cheese, and serve immediately.

MELON WITH PROSCIUTTO

MELON WITH PROSCIUTTO

One Serving: **Calories** 112 **Protein** 6g **Carbohydrates** 10g **Fat** 7g **Cholesterol** 20mg **Sodium** 26mg

½ **small honeydew melon, chilled**

½ **large cantaloupe, chilled**

8 **ounces thinly-sliced prosciutto**

Freshly ground black pepper

Mint sprigs (optional)

 PREPARATION TIME
20 MINUTES

COOKING TIME
0 MINUTES

FOOD NOTE *Prosciutto is famous for its delicately smoky flavor, which is due to the long time it is allowed to mature. It's the perfect contrast to ripe, sweet melon.*

1 Cut honeydew and cantaloupe lengthwise into ½-inch-thick, wedge-shaped slices (about 12 slices each). Cut off the rind. On 8 serving plates, alternately arrange the melon slices.

2 Cut each slice of prosciutto lengthwise in half. Loosely roll up each slice of prosciutto in a cone shape to resemble a rose; arrange the prosciutto roses in the center of the melon and cantaloupe slices. (Alternatively, place the prosciutto loosely among the melon slices.) Sprinkle with pepper, garnish with mint, if desired, and serve.

MARINATED VEGETABLES

One Serving: **Calories** 155 **Protein** 3g **Carbohydrates** 11g **Fat** 13g **Cholesterol** 0mg **Sodium** 481mg

- **2 large carrots (about 8 ounces)**
- **½ small head cauliflower (about 12 ounces)**
- **1 jar (6 ounces) marinated artichoke hearts**
- **½ cup pitted black olives**
- **2 tablespoons lemon juice**
- **1 tablespoon extra-virgin olive oil**
- **1 teaspoon Worcestershire sauce**
- **Salt and ground black pepper to taste**
- **1 tablespoon chopped parsley**

PREPARATION TIME **5 MINUTES**

COOKING TIME **10 MINUTES**

SERVING SUGGESTION *This refreshing antipasto platter makes an ideal opener to an Italian-style meal.*

1 In a large skillet, bring 1 inch of water to a boil over high heat. Meanwhile, peel carrots and cut them diagonally into ¼-inch-thick slices. Add the carrots to the boiling water. Reduce the heat to moderate, cover, and cook until the carrots are almost crisp-tender, about 2 minutes.

2 Trim cauliflower and cut it into florets. Add the cauliflower florets to the carrots in the skillet; continue cooking the vegetables about 3 more minutes.

3 Drain the vegetables and rinse them with cold water. Transfer them to a large bowl. Stir in artichoke hearts with their marinade, olives, lemon juice, olive oil, and Worcestershire sauce. Season the vegetables with salt and pepper, and toss gently.

4 Spoon the vegetables into a serving bowl and sprinkle them with parsley. Serve them warm, or cover and refrigerate to serve cold later.

BRUSCHETTA

One Serving: **Calories** 330 **Protein** 8g **Carbohydrates** 47g **Fat** 12g **Cholesterol** 1mg **Sodium** 423mg

- **5 tablespoons olive oil, divided**
- **1 tablespoon finely chopped white onion or shallots**
- **½ cup fresh basil, coarsely chopped**
- **½ teaspoon lemon juice**
- **6 ripe plum tomatoes (about 12 ounces)**
- **Salt and ground black pepper to taste**
- **2 cloves garlic, slivered**
- **8 ¾-inch-thick slices Italian bread**
- **Basil leaves (optional)**

PREPARATION TIME **22 MINUTES**

COOKING TIME **7 MINUTES**

COOK'S TIP *Garlic can be slivered or crushed and stored for a couple of weeks. Add some olive oil, place it in a tightly lidded jar, and keep it in the refrigerator.*

1 In a small bowl, combine 3 tablespoons olive oil, onion, basil, and lemon juice. Chop tomatoes into ¼ inch pieces; add them to the oil mixture. Season the mixture with salt and pepper; set it aside.

2 In a small skillet, heat the remaining 2 tablespoons oil over moderate heat. Add garlic and sauté until golden, about 1 minute. Discard the garlic from the oil.

3 Toast bread slices; arrange two pieces of toast on each of four serving plates. Brush the garlic-flavored oil over each slice. Using a slotted spoon, place an equal amount of the tomato mixture on each slice. Garnish each serving with basil leaves, if desired, and serve.

SNACKS

Whether you want a casual family meal, a brown bag lunch, or just a quick bite to eat, choose from these savory snacks.

SPICED NUTS

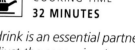

One Serving: **Calories** 220 **Protein** 6g **Carbohydrates** 7g **Fat** 20g **Cholesterol** 5mg **Sodium** 116mg

- **2 tablespoons (¼ stick) butter or margarine**
- **1 cup pecan halves**
- **1 cup whole almonds**
- **1 cup dry-roasted unsalted peanuts**
- **1 tablespoon Worcestershire sauce**
- **1 teaspoon chili powder**
- **½ teaspoon garlic salt**
- **¼ teaspoon cayenne pepper**

 PREPARATION TIME 2 MINUTES

COOKING TIME 32 MINUTES

SERVING SUGGESTION *A cooling drink is an essential partner to this hot and spicy nut mix. You can adjust the seasoning to your taste.*

1 Preheat the oven to 300°F. In a 13- by 9-inch baking pan, place butter; set the pan in the oven to melt the butter. Remove the pan from the oven; add pecans, almonds, peanuts, and Worcestershire sauce to the melted butter. Stir until well mixed.

2 Bake the nut mixture until it is toasted, stirring occasionally, about 30 minutes. Remove the nuts from the oven and sprinkle the mixture evenly with chili powder, garlic salt, and cayenne pepper. Toss until well mixed.

3 Transfer the warm nuts to a bowl and serve immediately, or let cool and store them at room temperature in an airtight container until ready to serve. (Makes 3 cups.)

HERBED POPCORN–CEREAL MIX

One Serving: **Calories** 199 **Protein** 6g **Carbohydrates** 19g **Fat** 12g **Cholesterol** 12mg **Sodium** 224mg

- **¼ cup (½ stick) butter or margarine**
- **1 tablespoon Worcestershire sauce**
- **1 tablespoon dried basil or oregano, crumbled**
- **Dash hot red pepper sauce**
- **4 cups bite-size corn, wheat, or rice cereal squares**
- **1 cup pretzel rings or small pretzels**
- **1 cup unsalted peanuts**
- **4 cups popped popcorn**

 **PREPARATION TIME** 5 MINUTES

 COOKING TIME 28 MINUTES

SERVING SUGGESTION *Serve this savory popcorn mix as a backyard snack or a bite while watching late-night TV.*

1 Preheat the oven to 300°F. In a 13- by 9-inch baking pan, place butter; set the pan in the oven to melt the butter. Remove the pan from the oven; stir Worcestershire sauce, basil, and pepper sauce into the melted butter.

2 Add cereal squares, pretzels, and peanuts; toss to coat well. Bake for 15 minutes, stirring occasionally.

3 Stir popcorn into the cereal mixture and bake until heated through, about 10 more minutes. Pour the cereal mix into a large bowl and serve immediately, or let them cool and store at room temperature in an airtight container. (Makes 10 cups.)

CRISP POTATO SKINS

MAKES

One Piece: **Calories** 47 **Protein** Trace **Carbohydrates** 4g **Fat** 3g **Cholesterol** 4mg **Sodium** 14mg

4 large baking potatoes, unpeeled

2 tablespoons (¼ stick) butter or margarine

2 tablespoons vegetable oil

Salt and ground black pepper to taste

Sour cream (optional)

Snipped chives (optional)

PREPARATION TIME
5 MINUTES

COOKING TIME
20 MINUTES

COOK'S TIP *The potato pulp scooped out of the skins shouldn't be wasted—save it to make mashed potatoes later.*

1 Rinse and dry potatoes. Using a fork, pierce the potatoes several times. Microwave the potatoes on high power until tender, 20 to 25 minutes, rotating the potatoes several times during cooking.

2 Meanwhile, in a small saucepan, heat butter and oil over low heat until the butter melts. Remove the pan from the heat.

3 Remove the potatoes from the oven and let them cool slightly; preheat the broiler. Cut the baked potatoes lengthwise in half and scoop out all but about ¼ inch of the potato pulp on the inside. (Reserve the potato pulp for another use, if desired.)

4 Cut the potato skins lengthwise in half again. Place them on the rack over a broiler pan, cut surfaces up. Brush each with the oil mixture. Broil the potato skins 4 inches from the heat until crisp and browned, about 4 minutes. Transfer the potato skins to a platter; serve them with sour cream and chives, if desired.

HAM ROLLS

MAKES

One Piece: **Calories** 35 **Protein** 2g **Carbohydrates** Trace **Fat** 3g **Cholesterol** 11mg **Sodium** 135mg

1 small cucumber, unpeeled

1 package (8 ounces) cream cheese, softened

2 tablespoons coarse-grained prepared mustard

1 tablespoon snipped dill (or 1 teaspoon dill weed)

8 rectangular slices (about 8 ounces) boiled ham

PREPARATION TIME
44 MINUTES

COOKING TIME
0 MINUTES

1 Cut unpeeled cucumber in half lengthwise. Using a spoon, scoop out and discard the seeds. Cut the seeded cucumber lengthwise into about eight ½-inch-thick strips.

2 In a medium-size bowl, combine cream cheese and mustard until blended. Stir in dill until well mixed. Spread about 2 tablespoons of the cream-cheese mixture evenly over each slice of ham, spreading it all the way to the edges.

3 Place a cucumber strip on one short edge of one ham slice. Trim the ends of the cucumber strip so it is even with the ham slice. Roll up the cucumber in the cheese-coated ham. Repeat with the remaining cucumber and ham slices. Refrigerate the rolls for 20 minutes.

4 Using a serrated knife, carefully cut the chilled ham rolls crosswise into four 1-inch-thick slices. Arrange the ham-roll slices on a serving platter, and serve.

GRILLED EGGPLANT SANDWICHES

GRILLED EGGPLANT SANDWICHES

One Serving: **Calories** 381 **Protein** 17g **Carbohydrates** 20g **Fat** 26g **Cholesterol** 54mg **Sodium** 372mg

- 1 **large eggplant (about 1½ pounds)**
- ¼ **cup all-purpose flour**
- ¼ **teaspoon salt**
- ¼ **cup vegetable oil, divided**
- 8 **ounces mozzarella cheese, cut into 8 slices**
- 4 **large slices ripe tomato**
- 8 **anchovy fillets**
- 1 **tablespoon chopped parsley**

 PREPARATION TIME
10 MINUTES

 COOKING TIME
10 MINUTES

SERVING SUGGESTION *This filling snack can easily become a meal with a crisp salad of curly lettuce, red onion, and crumbled feta.*

1 Slice unpeeled eggplant crosswise into eight ½-inch-thick slices. In a pie plate, combine flour and salt. Dip eggplant slices in the flour mixture to coat evenly.

2 In a large skillet or griddle, heat 2 tablespoons oil over moderate heat. Working in batches, add the eggplant and cook until tender and browned on both sides, about 2 minutes each side, adding more oil of necessary. Remove the eggplant slices and drain on paper towels.

3 On each of four eggplant slices, place a slice of cheese, a tomato slice, and two anchovies; top with the remaining slices of cheese. Cover with the remaining eggplant slices.

4 Return the skillet or griddle to moderate heat; cook the eggplant sandwiches until the cheese melts slightly, about 3 minutes, turning once. Transfer the eggplant sandwiches to serving plates, sprinkle with parsley, and serve immediately.

Open-Faced Cucumber Tea Sandwiches

MAKES

One Piece: **Calories** 39 **Protein** 2g **Carbohydrates** 4g **Fat** 2g **Cholesterol** 5mg **Sodium** 70mg

½ **small cucumber**

4 **ounces cream cheese, softened**

1 **teaspoon finely chopped chives or green onion top**

Salt and ground white pepper to taste

6 **slices firm whole-wheat bread**

24 **thin slices unpeeled cucumber**

 PREPARATION TIME
15 MINUTES

COOKING TIME
0 MINUTES

1 Peel ½ small cucumber; cut it in half lengthwise and discard the seeds. Finely chop the cucumber and let it drain. (It should make ¼ cup.) In a small bowl, mix the chopped cucumber with cream cheese and chives. Season the mixture with salt and pepper.

2 Using a sharp knife, trim the crusts from bread slices. Spread one side of each slice with some of the cream-cheese mixture. Cut each bread slice into quarters.

3 Top each bread square with a cucumber slice. Arrange the tea sandwiches on a platter, and serve immediately.

Pineapple Cheese Bagels

One Serving: **Calories** 667 **Protein** 20g **Carbohydrates** 96g **Fat** 25g **Cholesterol** 60mg **Sodium** 773mg

2 **cans (8 ounces each) sliced pineapple in juice**

1 **container (8 ounces) whipped cream cheese**

3 **tablespoons raisins**

4 **large pumpernickel bagels (or plain bagels)**

3 **tablespoons toasted sliced almonds**

 PREPARATION TIME
13 MINUTES

COOKING TIME
5 MINUTES

1 Place 2 tablespoons juice from pineapple in a medium-size bowl and set aside. Drain the pineapple slices and pat them dry on paper towels; set aside. Stir cream cheese and raisins into the reserved pineapple juice until well mixed.

2 Cut each bagel in half horizontally and toast in a toaster or toaster oven. Spread the cut surfaces of the bagels with an equal amount of the cheese mixture. Top each with a pineapple slice and some almonds. Serve immediately.

Peanut Butter–Banana Sandwiches

One Serving: **Calories** 435 **Protein** 13g **Carbohydrates** 60g **Fat** 19g **Cholesterol** 0mg **Sodium** 396mg

½ **cup creamy or chunky peanut butter**

2 **tablespoons orange marmalade or apricot preserves**

8 **slices whole-grain bread**

3 **medium-size ripe bananas**

 PREPARATION TIME
10 MINUTES

COOKING TIME
8 MINUTES

1 In a small bowl, combine peanut butter and orange marmalade until well mixed. In a toaster or toaster oven, toast bread. Meanwhile, peel bananas and cut them in half lengthwise. Cut each banana piece in half crosswise.

2 Spread the peanut butter mixture on each slice of toast. Top four slices of toast with three banana pieces each and cover with the remaining toast. Cut each sandwich in half diagonally, and serve.

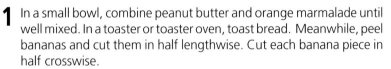

OPEN-FACED SMOKED TURKEY SANDWICHES

OPEN-FACED SMOKED TURKEY SANDWICHES ❙❨4❩❙

One Serving: **Calories** 367 **Protein** 13g **Carbohydrates** 38g **Fat** 18g **Cholesterol** 35mg **Sodium** 755mg

8 ½-inch-thick diagonal slices Italian bread

1 tablespoon olive or vegetable oil

2 small ripe tomatoes

½ bunch watercress

6 ounces thinly sliced smoked turkey

3 to 4 tablespoons mayonnaise, divided

PREPARATION TIME
10 MINUTES

COOKING TIME
4 MINUTES

SERVING SUGGESTION *With a spoonful of macaroni salad on the side, these sandwiches provide a satisfying lunch.*

1 Preheat the oven to 400°F. Brush each slice of bread with some olive oil. Place the bread on a baking sheet and bake until golden brown, 4 to 5 minutes.

2 Meanwhile, using a sharp knife, cut tomatoes crosswise into thin slices. Rinse and dry watercress; cut off and discard the thick lower stems of the watercress sprigs.

3 Top each slice of toast with an equal amount of smoked turkey, folding or cutting the turkey to fit if necessary. Spoon a dollop of mayonnaise on top of each turkey slice and arrange two or three slices of tomato over the mayonnaise. Garnish each open-faced sandwich with a sprig of watercress.

4 If desired, cover a serving platter with the remaining watercress, and arrange the open-faced sandwiches on top. Garnish the platter with any leftover tomato slices, and serve immediately.

SALMON-STUFFED CROISSANTS

One Serving: **Calories** 376 **Protein** 17g **Carbohydrates** 28g **Fat** 22g **Cholesterol** 50mg **Sodium** 959mg

4 **large croissants**

3 **ounces cream cheese, softened**

1 **tablespoon snipped fresh dill (or 1 teaspoon dill weed)**

1 **teaspoon lemon juice**

8 **ounces thinly sliced smoked salmon**

Coarsely ground black pepper

Dill sprigs (optional)

 PREPARATION TIME
10 MINUTES

COOKING TIME
3 MINUTES

SERVING SUGGESTION *A salad of melons, strawberries, and oranges makes a fresh accompaniment to these brunch sandwiches.*

1 Preheat the oven or a toaster oven to 400°F. Place croissants on a small baking sheet and bake until warmed, about 3 minutes.

2 Meanwhile, in a small bowl, combine cream cheese, dill, and lemon juice until the mixture is very soft. Using a serrated knife, cut each croissant in half horizontally. Spread the bottom halves with the cream-cheese mixture.

3 Cover the cream-cheese mixture with smoked salmon. Sprinkle the salmon with pepper and garnish with dill, if desired. Cover the croissant sandwiches with their top halves, and serve immediately.

CHICKEN SALAD PITAS

One Serving: **Calories** 572 **Protein** 24g **Carbohydrates** 40g **Fat** 36g **Cholesterol** 66mg **Sodium** 928mg

4 **pita breads (6 inches in diameter)**

2 **cans (5 ounces each) chunk chicken, chilled**

⅔ **cup mayonnaise**

½ **cup chopped celery**

½ **cup coarsely grated carrots**

Salt and ground black pepper to taste

2 **small ripe tomatoes**

½ **small cucumber**

2 **cups alfalfa sprouts**

PREPARATION TIME
7 MINUTES

COOKING TIME
10 MINUTES

1 Preheat the oven to 350°F. Wrap pita breads tightly in aluminum foil and warm them in the oven while preparing the other ingredients, about 10 minutes.

2 Drain chicken. In a medium-size bowl, combine the chicken, mayonnaise, celery, and carrots. Season the chicken mixture with salt and pepper. Cut tomatoes into wedges; slice cucumber.

3 Cut each pita in half and open up the pockets. Fill the pockets with the chicken mixture, tomatoes, cucumber slices, and alfalfa sprouts. Serve immediately.

TIME SAVERS

FREEZING SANDWICHES Many sandwiches can be frozen ahead, minimizing last-minute preparations. For best results, use dense breads, such as whole wheat, which won't become soggy when thawed. Spread the bread with butter or peanut butter to prevent the filling from soaking into the bread. (Spreads to avoid are salad dressing and mayonnaise.) Freeze no longer than two weeks.

Start with a Pizza Crust

Make one of these creative pizzas for party food or a satisfying snack. If you'd like to make your own crust, turn to the recipes on page 26. Otherwise, choose one of the many ready-made pizza crusts available. Each of these toppings makes enough for one large or four small pizzas.

◀ **SESAME SPINACH PIZZA** In a medium-size saucepan, heat **2 Tbsp. vegetable oil**; sauté **½ cup chopped onion** until soft, about 5 minutes. Add **one 10-oz. pack frozen chopped spinach.** Cover and cook over moderate heat until thawed and cooked through, about 5 minutes, stirring occasionally. Stir in **1 cup cottage cheese** and **4 oz. crumbled feta cheese.** Season with **salt** and **ground black pepper**. Spoon onto **pizza crust** and sprinkle with **1 Tbsp. sesame seeds**, if desired. Bake at 400°F until topping is bubbly and crust is golden, 25 to 30 minutes.

▶ **HAM AND CHEESE PIZZA** Strain **one 14-oz. can crushed tomatoes** and spread it over the pizza base. Thinly slice **6 oz. ham or salami** and sprinkle the meat over the top. Slice **8 oz. mozzarella cheese** and arrange over the meat. Bake at 400°F until topping is bubbly and crust is golden, 25 to 30 minutes.

◀ **ITALIAN SAUSAGE PIZZA** Remove the casings from **1 lb. hot Italian sausage**. Place sausage in a skillet and brown, stirring to break into pieces. Drain fat. Strain **one 14-oz. can crushed tomatoes**. Spoon over **pizza crust**. Spread sausage over it and sprinkle with **Parmesan cheese**. Bake at 400°F until topping is bubbly and crust is golden, 25 to 30 minutes.

► **TUNA AND ONION PIZZA** Strain **one 14-oz. can crushed tomatoes** and spread over pizza base. Drain and flake **two 6 ⅛-oz. cans tuna packed in water,** and sprinkle over the tomato. Sprinkle with **1 tsp. dried thyme**. Season with **ground black pepper** and sprinkle with **½ cup grated Parmesan cheese**. Bake until topping is bubbly and crust is golden, 25 to 30 minutes.

◄ **SOUTHWESTERN BEEF PIZZA** In a large skillet, brown **1 lb. ground beef**. Add **½ cup spaghetti sauce, ½ cup frozen peas**, and **½ cup frozen corn**. Add **½ tsp. red pepper flakes**, or to taste. Cook for 10 minutes, stirring occasionally. Spoon onto pizza base and top with **½ cup chopped cilantro**, if desired. Sprinkle with **½ cup grated Monterey Jack cheese**. Cook at 400°F until topping is bubbly and crust is golden, 25 to 30 minutes.

◄ **SPICY MUSHROOM PIZZA** In a medium-size skillet, cook **4 slices bacon**. Meanwhile, in a large skillet, heat **2 Tbsp. vegetable oil**. Add **1 lb. sliced mushrooms** and cook, stirring occasionally, until soft, about 5 minutes. Add **2 Tbsp. Worcestershire sauce, 2 Tbsp. soy sauce**, and **1 Tbsp. Dijon mustard**. Continue cooking over moderate heat until the sauce thickens, 5 to 10 minutes. Slice **4 green onions**. Add the green part to the mushroom mixture. Spoon the mushroom mixture onto **pizza crust** and sprinkle with the white part of the onion. Thinly slice bacon crosswise. Top mushrooms with bacon. Bake at 400°F until topping is bubbly and crust is golden, 25 to 30 minutes.

CHICKEN CLUB

CHICKEN CLUB

One Serving: **Calories** 525 **Protein** 26g **Carbohydrates** 45g **Fat** 27g **Cholesterol** 57mg **Sodium** 833mg

8 **slices bacon**

2 **boneless, skinless chicken-breast halves (about 6 ounces each)**

8 **slices firm white bread**

4 **slices firm whole-wheat bread**

6 **tablespoons mayonnaise**

8 **curly lettuce leaves**

8 **large slices ripe tomato**

   Ground black pepper to taste

 PREPARATION TIME
10 MINUTES

COOKING TIME
15 MINUTES

COOK'S TIP *If you prefer another version of this favorite standard, substitute turkey breast cutlets for the chicken.*

1 In a large skillet, cook bacon over moderate heat until crisp, about 5 minutes. Drain on paper towels and cut each slice in half crosswise. Cook chicken breasts in the bacon drippings until juices run clear when pierced with a fork, about 3 minutes on each side. Transfer the chicken breasts to a plate and slice crosswise.

2 Meanwhile, in a toaster or toaster oven, lightly toast the white and whole-wheat breads. Spread each slice of toast with mayonnaise. Arrange half of lettuce and all of the bacon halves on four of the white-bread slices. Top with half of tomato slices. Cover the tomato with the whole-wheat slices.

3 Top each whole-wheat slice with some chicken; season with pepper. Top with the remaining tomato slices, lettuce, and white bread. Cut the sandwiches on a diagonal, and serve immediately.

CALIFORNIA BLT

One Serving: **Calories** 439 **Protein** 14g **Carbohydrates** 39g **Fat** 26g **Cholesterol** 22mg **Sodium** 711mg

- **12 slices bacon**
- **4 pita breads (6 inches in diameter)**
- **3 tablespoons mayonnaise**
- **2 cups shredded romaine lettuce leaves**
- **1 large ripe tomato, diced**
- **1 small avocado, sliced**

PREPARATION TIME
10 MINUTES

COOKING TIME
5 MINUTES

1 In a large skillet, cook bacon over moderate heat until crisp, about 5 minutes. Drain on paper towels and cut each slice in half crosswise.

2 Cut each pita in half and open up the pockets. Spread the inside surface of each pocket with some mayonnaise. Fill the pockets with lettuce, tomato, avocado slices, and the bacon. Serve immediately.

SCRAMBLED-EGG SANDWICHES

One Serving: **Calories** 545 **Protein** 18g **Carbohydrates** 34g **Fat** 38g **Cholesterol** 265mg **Sodium** 1184mg

- **⅓ cup mayonnaise**
- **1 tablespoon Dijon mustard**
- **4 poppy-seed rolls or buns, split and toasted**
- **4 large eggs**
- **¼ teaspoon salt**
- **¼ teaspoon ground black pepper**
- **2 tablespoons (¼ stick) butter or margarine**
- **1 stalk celery, sliced**
- **4 slices American cheese**
- **4 slices ripe tomato**

PREPARATION TIME
10 MINUTES

COOKING TIME
14 MINUTES

1 In a cup or small bowl, combine mayonnaise and mustard. Spread the mayonnaise mixture over cut surfaces of rolls. Place the bottom halves on a serving platter, and set the top halves aside.

2 In a medium-size bowl, beat eggs with salt and pepper. In a large skillet, melt butter over moderate heat. Add celery and sauté until soft, about 2 minutes. Stir in the eggs and cook, stirring occasionally, until the eggs are almost set. Remove the skillet from the heat and spoon the eggs over the bottom halves of the rolls.

3 Top each with a slice of cheese and tomato. Cover with the top halves of the rolls, and serve immediately.

PEAR AND PROSCIUTTO SANDWICHES

One Serving: **Calories** 431 **Protein** 21g **Carbohydrates** 38g **Fat** 22g **Cholesterol** 56mg **Sodium** 1567mg

- **1 ripe Bosc pear**
- **1 tablespoon lemon juice**
- **8 slices pumpernickel bread**
- **3 tablespoons coarse-grained prepared mustard**
- **8 ounces thinly sliced prosciutto, trimmed of all fat (or smoked ham)**
- **4 ounces creamy blue cheese (Saga Blue or Bleu de Bresse), cut into pieces**

PREPARATION TIME
15 MINUTES

COOKING TIME
0 MINUTES

1 Remove the core from unpeeled pear and cut the pear lengthwise into thin slices. In a small bowl, toss the pear slices in lemon juice and set them aside.

2 Spread bread slices thinly with mustard. On four of the bread slices, arrange half of prosciutto. Sprinkle cheese over the prosciutto; top with the remaining prosciutto and the drained pear slices.

3 Cover each sandwich with the remaining bread slices, mustard side down. Cut each sandwich in half, and serve immediately.

Tuna Muffin Melts

One Serving: **Calories** 621 **Protein** 38g **Carbohydrates** 29g **Fat** 39g **Cholesterol** 63mg **Sodium** 967mg

2 **cans (6 ⅛ ounces each) tuna packed in water**

⅔ **cup mayonnaise**

½ **cup sliced celery**

¼ **cup chopped red bell pepper or pimiento**

Dash hot red pepper sauce

4 **English muffins**

4 **ounces Jarlsberg or Swiss cheese, sliced**

Red bell pepper or pimiento strips (optional)

PREPARATION TIME
10 MINUTES

COOKING TIME
5 MINUTES

SERVING SUGGESTION *Make a quick supper out of these simple tuna melts, and round them out with some sliced raw vegetables.*

1 Preheat the broiler. Drain tuna thoroughly. In a medium-size bowl, combine tuna, mayonnaise, sliced celery, chopped bell pepper, and hot pepper sauce.

2 Split each muffin in half horizontally. Place the muffins, split surfaces up, on the rack of a broiler pan. Broil the muffins about 4 inches from the heat until lightly browned.

3 Remove the muffins from the broiler and spread each with an equal amount of the tuna mixture. Top the tuna with a slice of cheese. Return the muffins to the broiler and continue broiling until the cheese melts.

4 Transfer the muffins to a serving platter; garnish each with a few bell pepper strips, if desired. Serve immediately.

Stacked Sandwich Loaf

One Serving: **Calories** 622 **Protein** 23 **Carbohydrates** 64g **Fat** 32g **Cholesterol** 32mg **Sodium** 1938mg

2 **cups spinach or arugula**

¼ **cup pitted black olives**

¼ **cup pimiento-stuffed green olives**

2 **tablespoons parsley**

2 **tablespoons olive oil**

1 **tablespoons red-wine vinegar**

½ **teaspoon dried oregano, crumbled**

1 **round loaf sourdough bread (about 7 ½ inches in diameter)**

2 **medium-size ripe tomatoes, sliced**

3 **ounces provolone cheese, sliced**

3 **ounces hard salami, thinly sliced**

PREPARATION TIME
15 MINUTES

COOKING TIME
0 MINUTES

1 Rinse and dry spinach thoroughly; remove the tough stems, and set the spinach aside. Using a blender or food processor fitted with the chopping blade, coarsely chop black and green olives with parsley, oil, vinegar, and oregano. Set the mixture aside.

2 Using a serrated knife, horizontally cut through bread to remove the top third of the loaf. Scoop out the center of the loaf and the top piece, leaving a 1-inch-thick shell. (Freeze the bread dough for crumbs, if desired.)

3 Into the hollowed-out loaf, spoon most of the olive mixture, spreading it evenly over the inside. Into the center, layer half of the spinach, half of the tomatoes, all of the cheese, and salami; continue with the remaining spinach and tomatoes. Spread the remaining olive mixture on the inside of the top piece of the loaf.

4 Cover the loaf with the top piece of the bread and press firmly. Place the sandwich loaf on a cutting board; using a serrated knife, cut it into quarters. Serve immediately.

FRENCH-TOASTED SANDWICHES

FRENCH-TOASTED SANDWICHES

One Serving: **Calories** 669 **Protein** 34g **Carbohydrates** 28g **Fat** 47g **Cholesterol** 270mg **Sodium** 1246mg

3 **large eggs**

³/₄ **cup milk**

¹/₂ **teaspoon dry mustard**

8 **ounces sliced Swiss cheese**

8 **slices day-old white or rye bread**

4 **ounces thinly sliced boiled ham**

3 **or 4 tablespoons butter or margarine, divided**

¹/₄ **cup mayonnaise**

1 **tablespoon finely chopped chives or green onion top**

1 **tablespoon Dijon mustard**

1 **teaspoon paprika**

 PREPARATION TIME
20 MINUTES

COOKING TIME
17 MINUTES

FOOD NOTE *This sizzling ham-and-cheese sandwich is better known in France as* Croque Monsieur.

1 Preheat the oven to 250°F. In a shallow dish or pie plate, beat eggs well. Stir in milk and dry mustard until well blended.

2 Arrange half of the cheese slices on four slices bread, cutting the cheese to fit if necessary. Top the cheese slices with ham slices and the remaining cheese, and cover with the remaining bread. Carefully dip each sandwich in the egg mixture; using a spatula, turn the sandwich over to soak both slices of bread.

3 In a large skillet or griddle, melt 1 tablespoon butter over moderately low heat. Cook the sandwiches two at a time, turning once, until lightly browned on both sides, 3 to 4 minutes each side. Add more butter as needed. Keep the cooked sandwiches warm in the oven while cooking the remaining sandwiches.

4 In a small bowl, combine mayonnaise, chives, mustard, and paprika. Top the sandwiches with a spoonful of the mayonnaise mixture, and serve immediately.

BEAN TOSTADAS

BEAN TOSTADAS

One Serving: **Calories** 446 **Protein** 20g **Carbohydrates** 54g **Fat** 18g **Cholesterol** 25mg **Sodium** 832mg

Vegetable oil

8 **corn tortillas**

1 **small yellow onion, chopped**

1 **can (15 or 16 ounces) refried beans**

1 **can (4 ounces) chopped green chilies, drained**

4 **ounces mild Cheddar or Monterey Jack cheese, coarsely grated (1 cup), divided**

2 **cups shredded lettuce**

¼ **cup red radish slices**

¼ **cup sliced pitted black olives**

¾ **cup prepared chunky tomato salsa**

 PREPARATION TIME
15 MINUTES

 COOKING TIME
28 MINUTES

COOK'S TIP *You can skip Step 1 completely if you purchase prepared tostada shells; wrap them in foil and warm them in the oven.*

1 In a large skillet, heat ¼ inch vegetable oil over moderately high heat. Add tortillas, one at a time, and fry until crisp on both sides, about 2 minutes, turning once. Drain the fried tortilla, or tostada shell, on paper towels and repeat to fry the remaining tortillas.

2 Drain all but 2 tablespoons of oil from the skillet. Add chopped onion and sauté over moderate heat until soft, about 5 minutes. Stir in beans and chilies; cook until the beans are heated through, 1 to 2 minutes. Stir half of the cheese into the beans until melted. Remove the bean mixture from the heat.

3 Spread the bean mixture on the tostada shells. Top each with some shredded lettuce, radishes, olives, the remaining cheese, and salsa. Serve immediately.

KNACKWURST REUBEN

One Serving: **Calories** 669 **Protein** 29g **Carbohydrates** 25g **Fat** 51g **Cholesterol** 110mg **Sodium** 1810mg

1 pound knackwurst (4 sausages)

¹⁄₃ cup prepared Thousand Island dressing

4 oval slices dark rye or pumpernickel bread

1 can (8 ounces) sauerkraut, drained and rinsed

4 slices Swiss cheese (about 6 ounces)

Dill pickles (optional)

PREPARATION TIME **6 MINUTES**

COOKING TIME **9 MINUTES**

1 Preheat the broiler. Without cutting all the way through, slice each knackwurst almost in half lengthwise. Place the split sausages, cut sides down, on the greased rack over a broiler pan. Broil them 4 inches from the heat until lightly browned, about 6 minutes, turning once during broiling.

2 Meanwhile, spread Thousand Island dressing on one side of each bread slice. Place one sausage, cut side up, on each slice of bread. Top each with one-fourth of the sauerkraut and a slice of cheese.

3 Return the sandwiches to the broiler and broil until the cheese melts, about 1 minute. Transfer the sandwiches to serving plates and serve with pickles, if desired.

ROAST BEEF BUNS

One Serving: **Calories** 294 **Protein** 19g **Carbohydrates** 40g **Fat** 7g **Cholesterol** 33mg **Sodium** 466mg

4 sesame-seed buns or rolls

6 ounces deli-prepared coleslaw

1 tablespoon prepared white horseradish, drained

8 ounces thinly sliced rare roast beef

¹⁄₄ cup red radish slices

Red radishes with their leaves (optional)

PREPARATION TIME **15 MINUTES**

COOKING TIME **2 MINUTES**

1 Preheat the broiler or a toaster oven to top brown. Using a serrated knife, cut each bun in half horizontally. Place the buns, cut sides up, on a small baking sheet and broil 4 inches from the heat until lightly browned, about 2 minutes.

2 In a small bowl, combine coleslaw and horseradish. On the bottom half of the buns, spread a ¹⁄₄-inch-thick layer of the coleslaw mixture. Top with roast beef, folding or cutting to fit on the bun.

3 Over the roast beef, spoon a little more coleslaw and arrange a layer of radish slices; add the top part of the buns. Place the beef buns on serving plates, garnish with whole radishes, if desired, and serve.

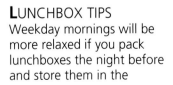

TIME SAVERS

LUNCHBOX TIPS
Weekday mornings will be more relaxed if you pack lunchboxes the night before and store them in the refrigerator. For the freshest sandwiches, pack lettuce and tomatoes separately from the bread and add them just before eating.

Avoid chilling foods—such as cookies and crackers—that lose their crispness when chilled. Add them to the lunchbox in the morning.

SLOPPY-JOE CORN CAKES

One Serving: **Calories** 469 **Protein** 27g **Carbohydrates** 42g **Fat** 23g **Cholesterol** 85mg **Sodium** 1098mg

2 tablespoons vegetable oil

1 small yellow onion, chopped

1 small green bell pepper, cored, seeded, and chopped

1 pound lean ground beef or ground turkey

1½ teaspoons ground cumin

½ teaspoon garlic powder

1 cup ketchup

1 cup diced fresh or canned tomatoes

Salt and ground black pepper to taste

4 toaster corn cakes or 2 (4- by 2-inch) pieces cornbread, split

 PREPARATION TIME
8 MINUTES

COOKING TIME
22 MINUTES

COOK'S TIP *If you prefer more traditional sloppy joes, replace the corn cakes with toasted hamburger buns.*

1 In a large skillet, heat oil over moderate heat. Add chopped onion and bell pepper; sauté until soft, about 5 minutes. Stir in ground beef, cumin, and garlic powder; cook until the meat is lightly browned, about 7 minutes.

2 Remove the skillet from the heat and drain any excess drippings from the beef mixture. Return the skillet to the heat and stir ketchup and tomatoes into the beef mixture; bring to a boil. Reduce the heat to low. Cook the mixture for 5 more minutes, stirring constantly. Season with salt and pepper. Remove the meat mixture from the heat.

3 In a toaster or toaster oven, toast corn cakes. Place the cakes on serving plates; top each with an equal amount of the beef mixture, and serve immediately.

CRUSTY DOGS

MAKES

One Piece: **Calories** 176 **Protein** 4g **Carbohydrates** 10g **Fat** 13g **Cholesterol** 28mg **Sodium** 404mg

1 package (15 ounces) refrigerated ready-to-bake pie crusts

¼ cup prepared mustard

1 package (16 ounces) frankfurters (10)

1 large egg

1 tablespoon water

Sesame or poppy seeds (optional)

Additional prepared mustard (optional)

 PREPARATION TIME
13 MINUTES

 COOKING TIME
22 MINUTES

SERVING SUGGESTION *These hot-dog snacks make a warm and tasty treat for kids. Serve them with a bowl of canned vegetable soup for a filling and wholesome lunch.*

1 Preheat the oven to 400°F. Unwrap pie crusts according to package directions. Using a rubber spatula, spread the crusts lightly with mustard. Cut each crust into 10 wedges.

2 Cut each frankfurter in half crosswise. Place a frankfurter half on the wide end of each wedge-shaped piece of crust. Roll up the crust with the frankfurter to the opposite pointed end. Place the crust-wrapped frankfurter, pointed-end down, on a baking sheet. Repeat to wrap the remaining frankfurters.

3 In a cup, combine egg with water. Brush the crust-wrapped frankfurters with the egg mixture. Sprinkle with sesame or poppy seeds, if desired. Bake the hot dogs until lightly browned, 20 to 25 minutes. Transfer the crusty dogs to a warm platter and serve with additional prepared mustard on the side, if desired.

SOUPS

NEW ENGLAND CLAM CHOWDER (PAGE 87)

FIRST-COURSE SOUPS

Served with a sandwich or as the opener to a ready-made meal, these quick starter soups will add a touch of homemade goodness.

MIDDLE EASTERN TOMATO SOUP

One Serving: **Calories** 238 **Protein** 9g **Carbohydrates** 40g **Fat** 5g **Cholesterol** 2mg **Sodium** 792mg

- 1 **tablespoon olive oil**
- 1 **small zucchini, julienned**
- ½ **cup bulgur**
- 4 **cups canned reduced-sodium chicken broth**
- 2 **teaspoons dried mint, crumbled**
- 2 **large ripe tomatoes (about 1 pound), skinned and chopped (or one 16-ounce can chopped tomatoes, drained)**
- 1 **green onion, julienned**
- 2 **pita breads, toasted and cut into 6 triangles each**

 PREPARATION TIME **12 MINUTES**   COOKING TIME **19 MINUTES**

FOOD NOTE *Be sure to use bulgur, not uncooked cracked wheat, to make this easy soup, since bulgur cooks relatively quickly. Mixed greens and toasted pita bread make natural accompaniments.*

1 In a medium-size saucepan, heat oil over moderate heat. Add zucchini and sauté for 2 minutes. Add bulgur and stir to coat with oil. Add broth and mint; bring the mixture to a boil over high heat. Reduce the heat to low, cover, and simmer for 5 minutes.

2 Stir chopped tomatoes into the bulgur mixture. Cover the pan and simmer the mixture 5 more minutes. Serve the soup garnished with onion, and with toasted pita triangles on the side.

EASY MUSHROOM SOUP

One Serving: **Calories** 135 **Protein** 5g **Carbohydrates** 13g **Fat** 8g **Cholesterol** 20mg **Sodium** 392mg

- 2 **tablespoons (¼ stick) butter or margarine**
- 1 **large yellow onion, finely chopped**
- ½ **cup chopped green bell pepper**
- 1 **small clove garlic, finely chopped**
- 4 **ounces mushrooms, sliced (1½ cups)**
- 2 **tablespoons all-purpose flour**
- 2 **cups canned reduced-sodium chicken broth**
- ½ **cup milk**
  Salt and ground black pepper to taste
- 1 **tablespoon chopped parsley**

PREPARATION TIME **17 MINUTES**   COOKING TIME **20 MINUTES**

DIET NOTE *This simple starter soup will easily suit vegetarians if the chicken broth is replaced by vegetable broth, made with vegetable stock cubes and boiling water. Either base combines deliciously with the earthy flavor of mushrooms.*

1 In a large saucepan, melt butter over moderate heat. Add onion, bell pepper, and garlic; sauté until the onion is soft, stirring occasionally, about 5 minutes. Stir in mushrooms and sauté until they are just wilted, about 3 minutes.

2 Stir flour into the mushroom mixture until well mixed. Add chicken broth and bring the mixture to a boil over high heat, stirring until thickened, about 5 minutes.

3 Reduce the heat to moderate. Add milk and season with salt and pepper. Heat the soup, stirring frequently, until it is hot but not boiling. Stir in parsley and serve immediately.

LEEK AND POTATO SOUP

LEEK AND POTATO SOUP

One Serving: **Calories** 166 **Protein** 3g **Carbohydrates** 23g **Fat** 7g **Cholesterol** 19mg **Sodium** 353mg

- **2 tablespoons (¼ stick) butter or margarine**
- **2 medium-size leeks, white part only, sliced and rinsed**
- **1 small yellow onion, chopped**
- **1 large (12 ounces) baking potato, peeled and diced**
- **2 cups water**
- **½ cup milk**
- **½ teaspoon salt**
- **1 tablespoon chopped fresh chives**
- **Ground black pepper to taste**

 PREPARATION TIME
10 MINUTES

 COOKING TIME
30 MINUTES

COOK'S TIP *Based on the classic soup called vichyssoise, this soup is just as delicious served cold. If it thickens too much upon chilling, dilute it with a little milk.*

1 In a large saucepan, melt butter over moderate heat. Add leeks, onion, and potato; sauté for 5 minutes, stirring occasionally. Add water; cover the pan and bring the mixture to a boil over high heat. Reduce the heat; still covered, simmer the soup until the potatoes are soft, about 15 minutes.

2 Using a food processor or electric blender, purée the soup, half at a time, until smooth. Pour the soup into a medium-size saucepan.

3 Stir in milk and salt. Reheat the soup over moderate heat until it is hot but not boiling. Ladle the soup into individual bowls. Sprinkle each serving with an equal amount of chives and a pinch of black pepper. Serve immediately.

GREEN PEA SOUP

One Serving: **Calories** 69 **Protein** 4g **Carbohydrates** 9g **Fat** Trace **Cholesterol** Trace **Sodium** 446mg

4 cups vegetable broth (made with vegetable stock cubes and water)

2 cups frozen green peas

1 small head Boston lettuce, cored, halved, and cut into shreds (about 6 cups)

3 green onions, chopped

½ teaspoon dried tarragon, crumbled

¼ teaspoon ground white pepper

Salt to taste

Croutons (optional)

PREPARATION TIME 10 MINUTES

COOKING TIME 28 MINUTES

SERVING SUGGESTION *This chill-warming, low-calorie soup goes well in a mug next to a ham sandwich on whole-wheat bread.*

1 In a large saucepan, combine broth, peas, lettuce, onions, and tarragon; bring to a boil over high heat. Reduce the heat, cover, and simmer for 5 minutes.

2 Using a food processor or electric blender, purée the soup, one-third at a time. Pour the soup into a medium-size saucepan. Reheat over moderate heat until the soup is hot but not boiling.

3 Stir in pepper and season with salt. Ladle the soup into bowls and top each serving with a few croutons, if desired. Serve immediately.

PENNSYLVANIA DUTCH DUMPLING SOUP

One Serving: **Calories** 135 **Protein** 6g **Carbohydrates** 20g **Fat** 4g **Cholesterol** 68mg **Sodium** 315mg

3 cups canned reduced-sodium chicken broth or beef broth

3 cups water

2 cups fresh or frozen corn kernels

For the dumplings

⅔ cup all-purpose flour

½ teaspoon salt

2 large eggs

PREPARATION TIME 5 MINUTES

COOKING TIME 25 MINUTES

1 In a large saucepan, bring chicken broth, water, and corn kernels to a boil over high heat.

2 Meanwhile, to make the dumplings, in a small bowl, combine flour and salt. In another small bowl, whisk eggs thoroughly. Stir the eggs into the flour mixture until a soft dough forms. Dip a serving teaspoon into cold water; spoon up some of the dough and, using a knife, push off ½-teaspoon-size pieces of the dough into the boiling broth.

3 Reduce the heat; cover and simmer the soup until the dumplings are puffy and cooked through, about 15 minutes. Serve immediately.

VARIATION: MEATBALL SOUP

One Serving: **Calories** 111 **Protein** 8g **Carbohydrates** 7g **Fat** 6g **Cholesterol** 25mg **Sodium** 140mg

*Cook the soup as in Step 1 above. To make meatballs instead of dumplings, soak **2 slices whole-wheat bread** in water or extra broth. Squeeze nearly dry and cut into pieces. In a food processor or electric blender, combine the bread, **4 ounces lean ground beef**, **1 tablespoon minced onion**, **1 teaspoon chopped parsley**, **a pinch cayenne pepper**, **a dash soy sauce** and **1 large egg**. Purée until smooth. Form the meat into 1-inch balls. Drop the meatballs into the boiling soup; simmer until cooked through, 10 to 15 minutes.*

CAULIFLOWER YOGURT SOUP

One Serving: **Calories** 188 **Protein** 9g **Carbohydrates** 17g **Fat** 11g **Cholesterol** 27mg **Sodium** 411mg

- 1 **bag (20 ounces) frozen cauliflower**
- 2¼ **cups water**
- 2 **tablespoons (¼ stick) butter or margarine**
- 2 **tablespoons slivered almonds**
- 1 **small yellow onion, chopped**
- 1 **tablespoon all-purpose flour**
- ½ **teaspoon salt**
- ½ **teaspoon sugar**
- ⅛ **teaspoon ground nutmeg**
- 1 **cup plain low-fat yogurt**
- 1 **cup milk**
- **Chopped parsley**

 PREPARATION TIME
10 MINUTES

COOKING TIME
32 MINUTES

SERVING SUGGESTION *Save a bit of yogurt to swirl into each serving. This elegant soup makes a fine opener to roast chicken or lamb.*

1 In a large saucepan, combine cauliflower and water; bring the mixture to a boil over high heat. Reduce the heat to low; cover and simmer until the cauliflower is soft, 6 to 8 minutes. Over a medium-size bowl, drain the cauliflower and reserve 2 cups of the cooking water. Remove the cauliflower from the pan and set aside.

2 In the same saucepan, melt butter over moderate heat. Add almonds and sauté until brown, 1 to 2 minutes. Using a slotted spoon, remove the almonds and set aside. Add onion to the remaining butter in the pan and sauté over moderate heat until soft, about 5 minutes.

3 Stir in flour, salt, sugar, and nutmeg. Stir in reserved cooking water and continue cooking until the soup is thickened and bubbly. Remove the pan from the heat and stir in the cauliflower.

4 Using a food processor or electric blender, purée the cauliflower mixture with the yogurt, combining one-third of each at a time.

5 Pour the soup into a medium-size saucepan; stir in milk. Over moderate heat, reheat the soup until hot but not boiling. Ladle the soup into bowls. Sprinkle each serving with some almonds and a pinch of parsley, and serve immediately.

QUICK BORSCHT

One Serving: **Calories** 126 **Protein** 3g **Carbohydrates** 9g **Fat** 9g **Cholesterol** 19mg **Sodium** 332mg

- 1 **can (8¼ ounces) sliced beets, undrained**
- 1 **cup canned reduced-sodium chicken broth**
- ¾ **cup sour cream, divided**
- 2 **tablespoons lemon juice**
- 2 **tablespoons chopped yellow onion**
- 2 **teaspoons sugar, or to taste**
- ½ **teaspoon dill weed**
- **Salt to taste**

PREPARATION TIME
7 MINUTES

COOKING TIME
5 MINUTES

1 Using a food processor or electric blender, purée sliced beets with their liquid for 1 minute.

2 Add broth, ½ cup sour cream, lemon juice, onion, sugar, and dill to the beets. Season with salt and purée the mixture until it is smooth, stopping occasionally to scrape the sides of the container with a rubber spatula.

3 Pour the soup into a medium-size saucepan and heat gently over moderate heat until it is hot but not boiling, about 5 minutes. Ladle the soup into bowls and swirl a dollop of the remaining sour cream into each serving. Serve immediately.

SPICY CREAM OF CARROT SOUP

One Serving: **Calories** 114 **Protein** 4g **Carbohydrates** 14g **Fat** 5g **Cholesterol** 11mg **Sodium** 362mg

- **3 to 3½ cups canned reduced-sodium chicken broth, divided**
- **4 medium-size carrots, sliced**
- **1 medium-size yellow onion, cut into thick slices**
- **1 medium-size stalk celery, sliced**
- **3 tablespoons long-grain white rice**
- **½ teaspoon sugar**
- **⅛ teaspoon cayenne pepper, or to taste**
- **½ cup milk**
- **½ cup sour cream**
- **Salt to taste**
- **Diced pimientos (optional)**

 PREPARATION TIME
10 MINUTES

 COOKING TIME
32 MINUTES

DIET NOTE *This healthy soup is rich in vitamin A, the nutrient essential for strong bones, good vision and healthy skin. Enjoy it immediately off the stove or chilled and served cold. Either way, it makes a zesty first course or sandwich accompaniment.*

1 In a large saucepan, combine 3 cups of broth, carrots, onion, celery, rice, sugar, and cayenne pepper. Cover and bring to a boil over high heat. Reduce the heat to low and simmer until the rice and carrots are tender, 15 to 20 minutes.

2 Stir milk and sour cream into the carrot mixture. Using a food processor or electric blender, purée the soup, half at a time, until it is smooth. If a thinner soup is desired, blend in ½ cup of additional chicken broth.

3 Return the soup to a medium-size saucepan. Stir in salt and additional cayenne pepper, if desired. Reheat the soup over moderate heat until it is hot but not boiling. Ladle the soup into bowls and top each serving with a few pimientos, if desired. Serve immediately.

Shelf Magic

Two fruit blender soups for two seasons—one a warming, wintery combination of pumpkin and peaches, the other a cool and summery blueberry and sour cream starter. Both can be done in less than 15 minutes.

PUMPKIN-PEACH BISQUE

In a food processor or electric blender, purée **one 16-ounce can sliced cling peaches packed in juice**, undrained, until smooth. In a medium-size saucepan, combine the peach purée with **one 16-ounce can pumpkin, one 14½-ounce can chicken broth, ½ teaspoon dried thyme leaves**, and **⅛ teaspoon ground white pepper**. Bring the mixture to a boil over moderately high heat, stirring occasionally. Stir in **¾ cup milk** and continue cooking until heated through.
SERVES 4

COOL BLUEBERRY SOUP

Place **one 16-ounce package frozen blueberries**, partially thawed, into the container of a food processor or electric blender. Add **⅔ cup sour cream, ⅓ cup orange juice**, and **3 or 4 tablespoons sugar**. Purée the mixture until it is smooth, occasionally scraping the sides of the container with a rubber spatula. Pour the cold soup directly from the processor container into the serving bowls and garnish each dish with **2 or 3 very thin lemon slices**. Serve immediately.
SERVES 4

Vegetable Consommé

One Serving: **Calories** 44 **Protein** 2g **Carbohydrates** 5g **Fat** 2g **Cholesterol** 5mg **Sodium** 810mg

- 6 **sprigs parsley**
- 2 **cloves garlic**
- 2 **bay leaves**
- 1 **teaspoon black pepper-corns**
- 1 **tablespoon butter or margarine**
- 1 **medium-size leek, white part only, sliced and rinsed**
- 4 **cups water**
- 2 **vegetable stock cubes**
- 2 **medium-size stalks celery**
- 2 **medium-size carrots, peeled**
- 4 **ounces snow peas**

PREPARATION TIME
6 MINUTES

COOKING TIME
20 MINUTES

SERVING SUGGESTION *This light starter soup makes an elegant introduction to a main dish of beef or poultry. It's best served in shallow bowls so that the colorful vegetables are most visible.*

1 Using string and a piece of cheesecloth, tie parsley, garlic, bay leaves, and peppercorns tightly together to form a small packet.

2 In a large saucepan, melt butter over low heat. Add leek and sauté until soft, about 5 minutes. Add water, stock cubes, and the herb and spice packet. Increase the heat to high, cover, and bring to a boil.

3 Meanwhile, cut celery and carrots into matchstick-size strips. Add the vegetables to the boiling consommé. Reduce the heat to moderate and simmer until the vegetables are just tender, 5 to 8 minutes.

4 Meanwhile, trim snow peas and slice them into thirds lengthwise, if desired. Remove and discard the herb and spice packet from the consommé. Stir in the snow peas and cook for 1 minute. Ladle the soup into bowls and serve immediately.

START WITH A STOCK

Stocks form the flavorful base of most soups—and having a supply on hand makes it easy to put together a quick, tasty, and healthy meal. Start with a few cups of canned or homemade stock (see pages 22 to 24). Allowing about one cup per person, add one or several ingredients. Let the food in your refrigerator and the staples in your cupboard be your guide. Don't be afraid to experiment with a variety of flavors and textures. Always bring the stock to a rolling boil and skim off any foam (from homemade stocks) before adding the other ingredients. Each of the following recipes makes four servings.

◄ **VEGETABLE AND PASTA SOUP** In a large saucepan, boil **4 cups vegetable stock**. Slice **2 or 3 mushrooms** and ¼ **leek**; peel and dice **1 small tomato**. Add ¼ **cup pastina** (tiny pasta shapes) to the boiling stock and simmer until the pasta is partially cooked, about 4 minutes. Add the vegetables and continue to simmer until the vegetables are crisp-tender. Stir in **1 Tbsp. chopped parsley**; season with **salt and pepper**. Serve with **crackers.**

► **ORIENTAL-STYLE FISH SOUP** In a medium-size sauce-pan, boil **4 cups fish or vegetable stock**. Slice **4 green onions**, finely chop **1 small clove garlic**, and peel and finely chop **½-inch piece ginger root**. Add the onions, garlic, ginger, **1 tsp. soy sauce**, and **1 tsp. chili flakes** to the boiling stock. Add **½ cup cooked chopped shrimp or one 6 ½-oz can chopped clams**, drained. Simmer 2 minutes. Garnish with **cilantro.**

◄ **SHREDDED-SPINACH SOUP** In a medium-size sauce-pan, boil **4 cups vegetable stock**. Roll **1 cup tender spinach leaves** into a cigar shape, and cut the leaves crosswise into very thin strips. Add the spinach to the boiling stock and simmer 1 minute. Season with **salt, pepper**, and a **pinch of nutmeg**. Sprinkle with **toasted slivered almonds.**

◄ **HAM AND CHEESE SOUP** In a large saucepan, boil **4 cups beef stock**. Slice **1 stalk celery**, cube **2 slices cooked ham**, and dice **2 ounces mozzarella cheese**. Add the celery to the boiling stock; simmer 1 to 2 minutes. Add the ham and cook 1 minute. Season with **salt and pepper**. Place some cheese in each serving bowl and ladle the soup over it. Garnish with **croutons** and **fresh basil.**

► **LIMA BEAN SOUP** In a large saucepan, boil **4 cups chicken stock**. Chop **1 medium-size yellow onion**; slice **2 bratwurst** or other mild cooked sausage. Add the onion and sausage to the boiling stock. Add **one 16-ounce can lima beans**, drained, and **1 crushed clove garlic**. Simmer until the onion is tender and the sausage is warmed through, about 5 minutes. Season with **salt and pepper.**

◄ **CHICKEN SOUP** In a large saucepan, boil **4 cups chicken stock**. Thinly slice **1 small carrot, ½ small leek**, and **1 small stalk celery**. Cut **1 small skinned and boned chicken breast** into thin slices. Add it to the boiling stock and simmer for 2 minutes. Add the vegetables and simmer until the chicken is cooked through and the vegetables are crisp-tender, 2 to 3 minutes. Season with **salt and pepper.**

INGREDIENTS TO ADD TO STOCKS

BEEF STOCK	CHICKEN & VEGETABLE STOCKS	FISH STOCK
Sliced sausage	Croutons	Cooked fish or seafood
Cubed cheese	Toasted nuts	Fresh herbs
Diced potato	Diced chicken	Soy sauce
Canned beans	Shredded greens	Oriental vegetables
Noodles or pasta		Toasted sesame seeds

MAIN-COURSE SOUPS

Hearty and delicious, these easy soups need only a tossed salad and a basket of warm bread to round out the meal.

CREAMY PEANUT SOUP

One Serving: **Calories** 361 **Protein** 14g **Carbohydrates** 25g **Fat** 23g **Cholesterol** 9mg **Sodium** 599mg

- 1 **tablespoon vegetable oil**
- 1 **medium-size yellow onion, finely chopped**
- 1 **clove garlic, finely chopped**
- 2 **medium-size all-purpose potatoes, peeled and chopped**
- 2 **medium-size carrots, sliced**
- 1 **medium-size stalk celery, sliced**
- 3½ **cups canned reduced-sodium chicken broth**
- ½ **cup smooth peanut butter**
- ¼ **teaspoon cayenne pepper**
- ¼ **cup sour cream**

PREPARATION TIME
12 MINUTES

COOKING TIME
30 MINUTES

FOOD NOTE *Rich in protein, peanut butter is the unlikely ingredient that makes this soup so tasty and filling. Vegetable broth made with stock cubes and water may be substituted for the chicken broth, if you prefer to make a vegetarian soup.*

1 In a large saucepan, heat oil over moderate heat. Add onion and garlic; sauté for 1 minute. Stir in potatoes, carrots, and celery. Add broth and bring to a boil over high heat. Reduce the heat; cover and simmer until the vegetables are tender, about 15 minutes.

2 Remove the soup from the heat. Stir in peanut butter and cayenne pepper until well mixed. Using a food processor or electric blender, purée the soup, half at a time, until smooth.

3 Return the soup to a medium-size saucepan. Reheat over moderate heat until it is hot but not boiling. Ladle the soup into bowls and swirl a spoonful of sour cream into each serving. Serve immediately.

TIME SAVERS

SOUP

- If your soup has too much liquid for the proportion to solid ingredients, press a large strainer into the saucepan and hold it over the solid ingredients. Ladle off the excess liquid that filters into the strainer.

- Make fast use of excess broth—freeze it in an ice cube tray for the future. You can use it to add flavor to rice, pasta, or vegetables.

- A hand-held blender is a great gadget for puréeing soups. It allows you to blend the soup directly in the pan instead of transferring it to a blender container.

- To thicken the liquid in chunky soups quickly, lay a slice of toasted French bread on the bottom of each serving bowl, then add the soup. The bread absorbs the liquid and disintegrates into the soup, making it thick.

- Quickly preheat bowls or mugs in order to keep hot soups hot. An easy way to warm the dishes is to fill them with boiling water and let them stand for a few minutes while you finish preparing the soup.

- Soups make great do-ahead meals—most taste even better a couple of days after they're made. Chill them in airtight containers and simply reheat.

CHEDDAR CHEESE SOUP

One Serving: **Calories** 483 **Protein** 21g **Carbohydrates** 29g **Fat** 33g **Cholesterol** 102mg **Sodium** 803mg

2 stalks celery, sliced

1 small green bell pepper, cored, seeded, and chopped

2 medium-size carrots, diced

1 cup chopped cauliflower

2 cups canned reduced-sodium chicken broth

4 tablespoons (½ stick) butter or margarine

½ cup all-purpose flour

3 cups milk

6 ounces sharp Cheddar cheese, coarsely grated (1½ cups)

1 teaspoon Worcestershire sauce

Paprika

 PREPARATION TIME
12 MINUTES

COOKING TIME
15 MINUTES

SERVING SUGGESTION *Turn this popular Midwestern soup into a complete meal by matching it with a mixed green salad topped with raisins and chopped nuts.*

1 In a large saucepan, combine celery, bell pepper, carrots, cauliflower, and broth; bring to a boil over high heat. Reduce the heat; cover and simmer until the vegetables are tender, about 10 minutes.

2 Meanwhile, in a medium-size saucepan, melt butter over moderate heat. Stir in flour and cook until just bubbly, about 1 minute. Remove the pan from the heat. Using a wire whisk, gradually stir in milk.

3 Cook the milk mixture over moderate heat, stirring constantly, until slightly thickened, about 5 minutes. (Do not boil.) Stir in cheese until it is just melted and smooth.

4 Stir the cheese mixture and Worcestershire sauce into the vegetable mixture until it is thoroughly mixed. Ladle the soup into bowls and sprinkle each serving with a pinch of paprika. Serve immediately.

FRENCH ONION SOUP

One Serving: **Calories** 352 **Protein** 13g **Carbohydrates** 37g **Fat** 18g **Cholesterol** 49mg **Sodium** 743mg

3 tablespoons butter or margarine

4 large yellow onions, sliced

1 tablespoon all-purpose flour

2 cups canned beef broth

2 cups water

1 teaspoon Worcestershire sauce

4 ½-inch-thick slices French bread

4 slices Swiss cheese (about 1 ounce each)

 PREPARATION TIME
8 MINUTES

 COOKING TIME
27 MINUTES

COOK'S TIP *A glass of dry red wine added to the broth creates an even richer flavor in this comforting classic.*

1 In a large saucepan, melt butter over moderate heat. Add onions and cook, covered, 10 minutes, shaking the pan frequently to prevent them from sticking. Stir in flour until well mixed.

2 Add broth, water, and Worcestershire sauce. Bring to a boil over high heat. Reduce the heat; cover and simmer until the onions are very soft, about 10 minutes.

3 Meanwhile, preheat the broiler. Place bread on a baking sheet and toast it on both sides. Cover each slice of bread with a slice of cheese. Return it to the oven and broil until the cheese is just browned and melted, a few seconds.

4 Place a cheese-topped slice of bread in each serving bowl. Ladle the soup over the bread and serve immediately.

BACON AND CORN CHOWDER

BACON AND CORN CHOWDER

One Serving: **Calories** 276 **Protein** 13g **Carbohydrates** 31g **Fat** 10g **Cholesterol** 28mg **Sodium** 311mg

3 slices bacon, cut into ½-inch pieces

1 large yellow onion, chopped

2 medium-size all-purpose potatoes, peeled and diced

1½ cups canned reduced-sodium chicken broth

1½ cups fresh or frozen corn kernels

3 cups milk

Salt and ground white pepper to taste

Chopped parsley

 **PREPARATION TIME**
15 MINUTES

COOKING TIME
30 MINUTES

SERVING SUGGESTION *This Western chowder goes well with quick quesadillas—slices of Monterey Jack cheese melted between two flour tortillas. Simpler yet, serve it with crispy tortilla chips.*

1 In a large saucepan, fry bacon pieces until crisp, about 4 minutes. Using a slotted spoon, remove the bacon and let it drain on a paper towel. Pour off all but 1 tablespoon of the drippings from the pan.

2 Add onion and sauté until soft, about 5 minutes. Add potatoes and broth and bring to a boil over high heat. Reduce the heat; cover and simmer until the potatoes are very soft, about 10 minutes.

3 Stir in corn kernels and milk. Heat the soup over moderate heat until just hot but not boiling. Season with salt and pepper. Ladle the soup into bowls and top each serving with some bacon and a pinch of chopped parsley. Serve immediately.

PUGET SOUND FISH CHOWDER

PUGET SOUND FISH CHOWDER

One Serving: **Calories** 355 **Protein** 24g **Carbohydrates** 26g **Fat** 17g **Cholesterol** 85mg **Sodium** 164mg

- **2** tablespoons (¼ stick) butter or margarine
- **1** medium-size yellow onion, chopped
- **1½** cups water
- **1** large (12 ounces) baking potato, scrubbed, unpeeled, diced
- **½** teaspoon salt
- **¼** teaspoon ground white pepper
- **1** pound salmon fillets or steaks, skinned, boned and cut into 1-inch chunks
- **2** cups milk
- **2** teaspoons snipped fresh dill or chopped parsley

 PREPARATION TIME
7 MINUTES

 COOKING TIME
31 MINUTES

FOOD NOTE *This chowder from the Pacific Northwest tastes best with fresh salmon. But since that's not always available, one 16-ounce can of salmon, drained, may be substituted.*

1 In a large saucepan, melt butter over moderate heat. Add onion and sauté until soft, stirring occasionally, about 5 minutes.

2 Add water, potato, salt, and pepper; increase the heat to high and bring the mixture to a boil. Reduce the heat to low. Cover and simmer the soup until the potato pieces are fork-tender, about 10 minutes.

3 Increase the heat to high and again bring the soup to a boil. Stir in salmon. Reduce the heat and cook until the fish flakes easily when tested with a fork, 3 to 5 minutes. Stir in milk; continue cooking the soup until it is heated through but not boiling. Sprinkle with dill or parsley, and serve immediately.

SOUTH OF THE BORDER CHOWDER

One Serving: **Calories** 200 **Protein** 10g **Carbohydrates** 24g **Fat** 7g **Cholesterol** 20mg **Sodium** 361mg

- 2 **tablespoons (¼ stick) butter or margarine**
- 1 **small yellow onion, chopped**
- 1 **tablespoon all-purpose flour**
- 2 **cups canned reduced-sodium chicken broth**
- 2 **small zucchini, diced (about 2 cups)**
- 2 **cups fresh or frozen corn kernels**
- ¼ **cup canned chopped green chilies**
- ¼ **teaspoon ground black pepper**
- 1 **cup milk**
- 2 **ounces Monterey Jack cheese, coarsely grated (½ cup)**

PREPARATION TIME
5 MINUTES

COOKING TIME
17 MINUTES

COOK'S TIP *Corn is a staple of the Mexican diet. In winter, frozen or canned corn may be used to make this main-dish soup, but in summer, try making it with fresh corn cut right off the cob: Using a sharp knife, slice along the rows of kernels, letting the corn fall onto a plate. With the dull side of the knife, press along the rows, catching the juice and heart of the kernels.*

1 In a large saucepan, melt butter over moderate heat. Add onion and sauté until soft, about 5 minutes. Stir in flour until well mixed.

2 Stir in broth, zucchini, corn, chilies, and pepper. Bring the mixture to a boil over high heat, stirring occasionally. Reduce the heat; cover and simmer for 5 minutes.

3 Add milk; stirring frequently, heat the soup over moderate heat until it is hot but not boiling. Ladle the soup into bowls and top each serving with an equal amount of grated cheese. Serve immediately.

NEW ENGLAND CLAM CHOWDER

One Serving: **Calories** 326 **Protein** 17g **Carbohydrates** 21g **Fat** 19g **Cholesterol** 71mg **Sodium** 398mg

- 1½ **ounces salt pork, diced (about ¼ cup)**
- 1 **medium-size yellow onion, chopped**
- ¼ **cup chopped celery**
- 2 **medium-size all-purpose potatoes (about 12 ounces), peeled and diced**
- 1 **bottle (8 ounces) clam juice**
- ½ **cup water**
- 1 **cup cooked clams, chopped (or two 6½-ounce cans chopped clams, drained)**
- 1½ **cups milk**
- 1 **cup half-and-half**
- ⅛ **teaspoon ground white pepper**
- **Salt to taste**

PREPARATION TIME
15 MINUTES

COOKING TIME
28 MINUTES

1 In a large saucepan, cook salt pork over moderate heat until it is lightly browned. Add onion and celery; sauté until the onion is soft, about 5 minutes. Stir in potatoes, clam juice, and water. Cover and bring to a boil over high heat. Reduce the heat and simmer the potatoes until they are fork-tender, about 10 minutes.

2 Stir clams, milk, half-and-half, and pepper into the potato mixture; season with salt. Continue cooking over moderate heat until the soup is hot but not boiling. Serve immediately.

MICROWAVE VERSION

In a microwave-safe, 4-quart casserole, microwave salt pork on high power for 3 minutes, uncovered, stirring once. Add onion and celery; cook on high, covered, until they are tender, about 3 minutes, stirring once. Stir in potatoes, clam juice, and water; cook on high until the potatoes are tender, 7 to 9 minutes. Stir in clams, milk, half-and-half, and pepper; season with salt. Cook on medium power, covered, until very hot, 5 to 7 minutes, stirring once during cooking.

CREOLE SHRIMP SOUP

One Serving: **Calories** 160 **Protein** 14g **Carbohydrates** 12g **Fat** 7g **Cholesterol** 125mg **Sodium** 371mg

- **1 bag (12 ounces) frozen, uncooked, shelled, and deveined shrimp**
- **1 medium-size white onion**
- **1 medium-size green bell pepper**
- **1 can (14½ or 16 ounces) whole, peeled tomatoes**
- **2 tablespoons (¼ stick) butter or margarine**
- **1 teaspoon finely chopped parsley**
- **½ teaspoon dried thyme leaves, crumbled**
- **1 small bay leaf**
- **¼ teaspoon hot red pepper sauce (or to taste)**
- **2½ teaspoons all-purpose flour**
- **1½ cups water**
- **Salt to taste**

**PREPARATION TIME
17 MINUTES**

**COOKING TIME
19 MINUTES**

FOOD NOTE *For this Louisiana favorite, add as much hot red pepper sauce as your taste buds will allow. Although frozen shrimp works fine, the flavor of fresh will reward you. Serve the soup with a loaf of crusty bread on the side.*

1 Thaw shrimp by placing it in a colander under lukewarm running water. Meanwhile, finely chop onion; seed and coarsely chop bell pepper. Coarsely chop tomatoes, reserving the liquid.

2 In a large saucepan, melt butter over moderate heat. Add the onion and sauté until soft, about 5 minutes. Stir in the green pepper, parsley, thyme, bay leaf, and hot pepper sauce; sauté for 1 minute. Stir in flour until well mixed.

3 Add the tomatoes with their liquid, and water; bring the mixture to a boil over high heat. Reduce the heat, cover, and simmer for 5 minutes. Add the shrimp and continue simmering, covered, until the shrimp is cooked through, about 5 more minutes. Discard the bay leaf; season the soup with salt to taste. Ladle the soup into bowls and serve immediately.

HEARTY VEGETABLE SOUP

One Serving: **Calories** 284 **Protein** 17g **Carbohydrates** 36g **Fat** 8g **Cholesterol** 0mg **Sodium** 267mg

- **2 tablespoons olive oil**
- **1 medium-size yellow onion, chopped**
- **1 stalk celery, chopped**
- **1 large carrot, chopped**
- **1 cup dried split red lentils, rinsed and sorted**
- **2 cups vegetable broth (made with vegetable stock cubes and water)**
- **2 cups water**
- **1 bay leaf**
- **½ teaspoon dried thyme leaves, crumbled**
- **1 medium-size ripe tomato, seeded and chopped**
- **1 green onion, thinly sliced**

**PREPARATION TIME
8 MINUTES**

**COOKING TIME
30 MINUTES**

FOOD NOTE *Split red lentils cook quickly and give the soup the body it needs to become a filling main dish. It's best not to skimp on the bay leaf and thyme in this recipe—the lentils absorb the flavors of the herbs beautifully.*

1 In a large saucepan, heat oil over moderate heat. Add chopped onion, celery, and carrot; sauté for 1 minute. Stir in lentils, vegetable broth, water, bay leaf, and thyme.

2 Bring the mixture to a boil over high heat. Reduce the heat; cover and simmer until the vegetables are tender, about 15 minutes.

3 Stir in chopped tomato. Continue cooking, covered, until the lentils are tender, about 10 minutes. Discard the bay leaf. Ladle the soup into bowls and sprinkle each serving with an equal amount of sliced green onion. Serve immediately.

CREOLE SHRIMP SOUP ▶

CHICKEN VEGETABLE SOUP

One Serving: **Calories** 361 **Protein** 30g **Carbohydrates** 33g **Fat** 12g **Cholesterol** 91mg **Sodium** 621mg

3 **tablespoons butter or margarine**

3 **medium-size all-purpose potatoes (about 1 pound), peeled and cut into 1-inch chunks**

8 **ounces carrots, sliced**

3 **green onions, sliced diagonally into ½-inch lengths, white and green parts divided**

2 **tablespoons all-purpose flour**

½ **teaspoon sugar**

¼ **teaspoon dried tarragon, crumbled**

⅛ **teaspoon ground black pepper**

4 **cups canned reduced-sodium chicken broth**

8 **ounces boneless, skinless chicken breasts, cut into ½-inch pieces**

 PREPARATION TIME
12 MINUTES

COOKING TIME
30 MINUTES

1 In a large saucepan, melt butter over moderate heat. Add potatoes and carrots; stir to coat the vegetables with butter. Add white part of onions and sauté for 1 minute.

2 Add flour, sugar, tarragon, and pepper to vegetables; stir to combine. Add broth and bring to a boil over high heat.

3 Reduce the heat; add chicken; cover and simmer until the vegetables are tender and the chicken is cooked through, about 20 minutes. Stir in green part of onions and serve immediately.

MICROWAVE VERSION

In a microwave-safe, 3-quart casserole, microwave butter on high power, covered, until melted, about 1 minute. Stir in potatoes, carrots, and white part of onions; cook on high, covered, until tender, about 8 minutes. Stir in flour, sugar, tarragon, and pepper; cook on high, covered, for 1 minute. Stir in broth. Stir in chicken; cook on high, covered, until chicken is cooked through, 8 to 10 minutes, stirring twice during cooking.

Shelf Magic

Both of these main dishes make use of easy packaged soups. With only a few added ingredients, they quickly become as good as homemade.

CRAB NOODLE SOUP

In a large saucepan, bring **4 ½ cups water** and the seasoning packet from **one of two 3-ounce packages chicken-flavored ramen noodle soup** to a boil. Add the noodles from both packages and **one 6-ounce package frozen snow peas.**

Cook, stirring frequently, until the noodles are soft and the peas are thawed, about 3 minutes. Add **8 ounces imitation crabmeat.** Continue cooking until the soup is just heated through, and serve.
SERVES 4

CHICKEN CHOWDER

In a medium-size saucepan, bring **1 cup water** and **one 10-ounce package frozen mixed vegetables** to a boil over high heat. Stir in **two 10 ¾-ounce cans condensed reduced-sodium cream of chicken soup, 1 ½ cups milk,** and **one 5-ounce can white chicken packed in water,** drained. Bring the mixture to a boil over moderately high heat, stirring occasionally. Pour into bowls and serve immediately, with **breadsticks or crackers** on the side.
SERVES 4

QUICK VEGETABLE BEEF SOUP

QUICK VEGETABLE BEEF SOUP

One Serving: **Calories** 194 **Protein** 19g **Carbohydrates** 18g **Fat** 5g **Cholesterol** 37mg **Sodium** 850mg

1 **pound lean ground beef**

1 **medium-size yellow onion, sliced**

4 **cups canned beef broth**

1 **can (14½ or 16 ounces) stewed tomatoes**

1 **package (16 ounces) frozen mixed vegetables (such as broccoli, carrots, and cauliflower)**

1 **cup fresh or frozen corn kernels**

½ **teaspoon dried basil, crumbled**

Salt and ground black pepper to taste

PREPARATION TIME
3 MINUTES

COOKING TIME
35 MINUTES

COOK'S TIP *Be sure to taste the soup before adding any salt—canned beef broth is particularly salty and you will probably not need to add more. Because it freezes well and can be quickly reheated, this is an excellent meal to make ahead.*

1 In a large saucepan, cook ground beef and sliced onion over moderate heat, stirring occasionally, until the beef is well browned and the onion is tender, about 10 minutes.

2 Stir in broth, stewed tomatoes, mixed vegetables, corn, and basil; season with salt and pepper. Cover and bring to a boil over high heat.

3 Reduce the heat to low; simmer until the vegetables are tender, stirring occasionally, 10 to 15 minutes. Serve immediately.

TORTELLINI MINESTRONE

One Serving: **Calories** 233 **Protein** 12g **Carbohydrates** 32g **Fat** 7g **Cholesterol** 30mg **Sodium** 935mg

- 2 **tablespoons (¼ stick) butter or margarine**
- 1 **medium-size red onion, sliced**
- 2 **small yellow squash (about 8 ounces), sliced**
- 1 **clove garlic, chopped**
- 5 **cups canned beef broth**
- 2 **ounces day-old Italian bread, cubed (about 2 cups)**
- 8 **ounces refrigerated or frozen meat-filled tortellini**
- 1 **package (10 ounces) frozen chopped broccoli, partially thawed under warm running water**
- **Salt and ground black pepper to taste**
- 12 **cherry tomatoes, halved**

PREPARATION TIME **6 MINUTES**

COOKING TIME **28 MINUTES**

FOOD NOTE *Tortellini are the round pockets of pasta filled with ground meat or ricotta cheese. This meal-in-a-bowl makes use of the fresh tortellini available in the refrigerator section of most supermarkets. The cheese-filled ones may be used in place of the meat-filled if you prefer. This soup thickens as it stands—add a bit more broth if a thinner soup is desired.*

1 In a large saucepan, melt butter over moderate heat. Add sliced onion and sauté until soft, about 5 minutes. Stir in squash and garlic; sauté for 2 minutes.

2 Add broth and bread. Increase the heat to high, cover, and bring to a boil over high heat, stirring occasionally. Reduce the heat to low and simmer the soup for 2 to 3 minutes.

3 Add tortellini and simmer for 7 minutes. Increase the heat to high and bring the soup to a boil. Add broccoli and cook until it is tender, 3 to 4 minutes. Season the soup with salt and pepper, stir in cherry tomatoes, and serve immediately.

HUNGARIAN CABBAGE SOUP

One Serving: **Calories** 254 **Protein** 18g **Carbohydrates** 14g **Fat** 15g **Cholesterol** 57mg **Sodium** 921mg

- ½ **teaspoon caraway seeds**
- 1½ **teaspoons paprika**
- ½ **cup sour cream**
- 2 **tablespoons (¼ stick) butter or margarine**
- 1 **large yellow onion, finely chopped**
- 4 **cups canned beef broth**
- 8 **ounces baked ham, diced**
- **Salt and ground black pepper to taste**
- ½ **small head cabbage, cored and cut into shreds (about 6 cups)**
- 1 **tablespoon chopped parsley**

PREPARATION TIME **12 MINUTES**

COOKING TIME **17 MINUTES**

DIET NOTE *Cabbage offers a wealth of healthy benefits—it provides a rich source of vitamin A for healthy skin and vision, vitamin C for cell growth, and fiber for proper digestion. Here cabbage is paired with ham in a satisfying main-dish soup.*

1 Using a mortar or rolling pin, crush caraway seeds. In a small bowl, combine the caraway seeds, paprika, and sour cream; refrigerate until the soup is ready to serve.

2 In a large saucepan, melt butter over moderate heat. Add onion and sauté until soft, stirring occasionally, about 5 minutes.

3 Add broth and ham; season with salt and pepper. Bring to a boil over high heat. Reduce the heat; stir in cabbage and continue cooking the soup until the cabbage is crisp-tender, about 5 minutes. Stir in parsley. Ladle the soup into bowls and top each serving with a dollop of the sour-cream mixture. Serve immediately.

GOULASH SOUP

One Serving: **Calories** 197 **Protein** 5g **Carbohydrates** 14g **Fat** 14g **Cholesterol** 16mg **Sodium** 358mg

- 2 **tablespoons vegetable oil**
- 1 **small yellow onion, chopped**
- 2 **small Jerusalem artichokes (or 1 medium-size all-purpose potato), peeled and diced**
- 1 **small carrot, sliced**
- 1 **clove garlic, finely chopped**
- 2 **knackwurst, sliced**
- 1½ **teaspoons paprika**
- ½ **teaspoon dill weed**

  Salt and ground black pepper to taste
- 4 **cups water**
- 1 **can (14½ or 16 ounces) whole, peeled tomatoes, drained and coarsely chopped**
- ½ **cup medium-width egg noodles**

PREPARATION TIME
10 MINUTES

COOKING TIME
35 MINUTES

1 In a large saucepan, heat oil over moderate heat. Add onion, Jerusalem artichokes, carrot, and garlic; sauté gently until the onions are soft, stirring occasionally, about 10 minutes.

2 Add knackwurst, paprika, and dill to the vegetables; season with salt and pepper. Stir until well mixed.

3 Add water and tomatoes to knackwurst mixture; bring to a boil over high heat. Reduce the heat; cover and simmer for 10 minutes.

4 Increase the heat to high and return the soup to a boil. Stir in noodles; continue cooking until the noodles are just tender, about 5 minutes. Serve immediately.

MICROWAVE VERSION

In a microwave-safe, 4-quart casserole, microwave oil, onion, artichokes, carrot, and garlic on high power, covered, until tender, about 5 minutes, stirring once. Stir in knackwurst, paprika, and dill; cook on high, uncovered, for 1 minute. Add water and chopped tomatoes; cook on high, covered, until boiling, 8 to 13 minutes. Stir in noodles; cook on high, uncovered, until tender, 5 to 7 minutes.

BEAN AND HAM SOUP

One Serving: **Calories** 231 **Protein** 19g **Carbohydrates** 31g **Fat** 4g **Cholesterol** 22mg **Sodium** 850mg

- 2 **slices bacon**
- 1 **large yellow onion, chopped**
- 2 **medium-size carrots, peeled and sliced**
- 4 **cups water**
- 2 **cans (19 ounces each) white kidney beans (cannellini) (or two 16-ounce cans navy beans), drained and rinsed, divided**
- 1 **can (8 ounces) tomato sauce**
- 8 **ounces baked ham, cubed**
- 1 **bay leaf**

  Salt and ground black pepper to taste

PREPARATION TIME
7 MINUTES

COOKING TIME
36 MINUTES

1 In a large saucepan, cook bacon over moderately high heat until it is lightly browned on both sides. Using a slotted spoon, remove the bacon and drain it on a paper towel. Reduce the heat to moderate. Add chopped onion and sliced carrots to the remaining drippings in the pan and sauté for 5 minutes.

2 Stir in water, half of the beans, the tomato sauce, ham, and bay leaf. Increase the heat to high, cover, and bring the soup to a boil. Reduce the heat to low; still covered, simmer the soup 20 to 25 minutes, stirring occasionally.

3 Discard the bay leaf. Stir in the remaining beans, and season with salt and pepper. Increase the heat to high and bring the soup to a boil. Ladle the soup into bowls and crumble an equal amount of the bacon on top of each serving. Serve immediately.

IBERIAN POTATO SOUP

IBERIAN POTATO SOUP

One Serving: **Calories** 320 **Protein** 13g **Carbohydrates** 17g **Fat** 22g **Cholesterol** 40mg **Sodium** 942mg

- 2 **tablespoons olive oil**
- 1 **large yellow onion, chopped**
- 2 **cloves garlic, finely chopped**
- 2 **medium-size baking potatoes (about 12 ounces), peeled and diced**
- 3 **cups canned reduced-sodium chicken broth**
- 1 **bay leaf**
- 2 **chorizo sausages (or 8 ounces kielbasa)**
- 2 **cups thinly sliced kale (hard stems removed)**

PREPARATION TIME
12 MINUTES

COOKING TIME
32 MINUTES

FOOD NOTE *Chorizo sausage is the spicy ingredient that gives this soup its Spanish flavor. Kielbasa makes a fine substitute, but since it's milder, you may wish to add a pinch of cayenne pepper.*

1 In a large saucepan, heat oil over moderate heat. Add onion and garlic; sauté for 2 minutes. Stir in potatoes. Add broth and bay leaf; cover and bring to a boil over high heat. Reduce the heat to low and simmer until the potatoes are very tender, 18 to 20 minutes.

2 Meanwhile, cut sausage into ½-inch slices. When the soup is finished simmering, discard the bay leaf. Using the back of a fork, mash some of the potatoes in the soup to thicken it slightly, if desired.

3 Stir in sausage and kale. Continue cooking the soup until the sausage is heated through, about 5 minutes. Serve immediately.

CHINESE CHICKEN SOUP

One serving: **Calories** 130 **Protein** 18g **Carbohydrates** 7g **Fat** 3g **Cholesterol** 37mg **Sodium** 881mg

8 ounces boneless, skinless chicken breasts

2 tablespoons dry sherry (not cooking sherry)

4 cups canned reduced-sodium chicken broth

4 ounces mushrooms, sliced

1 teaspoon minced fresh ginger (or ⅛ teaspoon ground ginger)

1 tablespoon light soy sauce

3 green onions, sliced diagonally ½ inch thick

¼ pound Chinese cabbage (Napa variety), sliced into shreds ½ inch thick

½ cup canned whole water chestnuts, thinly sliced

 PREPARATION TIME
18 MINUTES

COOKING TIME
13 MINUTES

FOOD NOTE *Although you can use canned, sliced water chestnuts, they usually are not thin enough for this recipe. It's better to buy the whole ones and slice them yourself. The result is a more delicate soup with some of the favorite flavors of Asia.*

1 Cut chicken crosswise into ¼-inch-thick slices. In a medium-size bowl, combine the chicken and dry sherry; let it stand about 10 minutes to marinate.

2 Meanwhile, in a large saucepan, combine chicken broth, sliced mushrooms, minced ginger, and soy sauce; bring the mixture to a boil over high heat.

3 Add the chicken and cook for 1 minute. Stir in onions, cabbage, and water chestnuts. Cook until the cabbage is just crisp-tender, about 5 minutes. Serve immediately.

PORK EGG DROP SOUP

One Serving: **Calories** 474 **Protein** 28g **Carbohydrates** 11g **Fat** 35g **Cholesterol** 177mg **Sodium** 575mg

2 ½-inch-thick pork loin rib chops (about 1¼ pounds)

1 tablespoon vegetable oil

2 cups canned beef broth

2 cups water

3 green onions, sliced

½ cup canned sliced bamboo shoots, drained

1 tablespoon minced fresh ginger (or 1 teaspoon ground ginger)

1 package (10 ounces) frozen peas

2 large eggs

Salt to taste

 PREPARATION TIME
11 MINUTES

COOKING TIME
32 MINUTES

FOOD NOTE *For authenticity of flavor, the pungent taste of fresh ginger is preferred over dried. But if fresh ginger isn't available, don't let that stop you from enjoying this Chinese classic.*

1 Bone pork chops and set the bones aside. Trim and discard any visible fat from the chops. Cut the pork into strips. In a 5-quart Dutch oven, heat oil over high heat. Add the pork and the bones; sauté until the meat is well browned, 8 to 10 minutes.

2 Add beef broth, water, green onions, bamboo shoots, and minced ginger to the pork. Cover and bring the mixture to a boil over high heat. Reduce the heat to low and simmer the soup for 10 minutes. Meanwhile, to thaw peas, place them in a colander under warm running water for about 2 minutes.

3 Discard the pork bones. Add the peas to the soup; increase the heat and cook until the peas are tender, about 4 minutes.

4 In a small bowl, beat eggs. Slowly stir the eggs into the soup and cook until they are just set. Remove the pan from the heat, season the soup with salt, and serve immediately.

FISH AND SHELLFISH

AMERASIAN SHRIMP (PAGE 122)

FISH

From catfish to swordfish, bakes to brochettes, fish is a natural for the quick cook's repertoire. It's also one of the healthiest sources of protein you'll find.

HERBED BAKED WHOLE FISH

One Serving: **Calories** 447 **Protein** 46g **Carbohydrates** 3g **Fat** 27g **Cholesterol** 93mg **Sodium** 115mg

¹/₃ cup fresh basil (do not use dried)

¹/₃ cup parsley, lightly packed (do not use dried)

1 clove garlic

¹/₃ cup olive oil

Salt and ground black pepper to taste

¹/₂ cup sour cream

1 teaspoon dried rosemary, crumbled

2 whole red snappers or sea bass (about 1¹/₂ pounds each), dressed

Lime slices (optional)

Additional fresh herbs (optional)

 PREPARATION TIME **10 MINUTES**

COOKING TIME **25 MINUTES**

SERVING SUGGESTION *Serve this fish with boiled new potatoes—the herbed sour-cream sauce goes deliciously with both.*

1 Preheat the oven to 350°F. With heavy-duty aluminum foil, line a baking pan large enough to hold the fish.

2 Using a food processor or electric blender, purée basil, parsley, and garlic with olive oil. Season the mixture with salt and pepper. Stir 2 tablespoons of the herb mixture into sour cream; cover and refrigerate the sauce until the fish is ready to serve. Add rosemary to the remaining herb mixture and continue to purée for 1 minute.

3 Using a sharp knife, make three shallow diagonal slashes on each side of both fish. Using your fingers, work the herb mixture into the slashes and cavity of each fish. Carefully place the fish on the prepared baking pan.

4 Bake the fish, uncovered, until it flakes easily when tested with a fork, about 20 minutes. Using the foil to lift it, transfer the fish to a serving platter. Cut away the foil and discard. Garnish the fish with lime slices and additional herbs, if desired, and serve it immediately with the chilled herbed sour-cream sauce on the side.

TIME SAVERS

FISH

• The quickest way to estimate the cooking time for any fish is to calculate 10 minutes for every inch of thickness. Lay the fish on the counter and measure the fish at its thickest part. This estimate applies to any cooking method.

• Save time on cleanup when you are baking, roasting, or broiling fish by lining the cooking pan with aluminum foil before preparing the fish. Also, spray the broiling rack with nonstick cooking spray to prevent the meat from sticking to the rack and making a mess.

• When fish is being fried, it will cook faster and taste better if you cook only one or two pieces at a time. If the pan is overloaded, the cold fish will greatly reduce the temperature of the oil. The fish will not only become greasy and soggy, it will also take longer to cook.

TROUT WITH MUSHROOM SAUCE

One Serving: **Calories** 538 **Protein** 52g **Carbohydrates** 17g **Fat** 29g **Cholesterol** 163mg **Sodium** 572mg

⅓ **cup all-purpose flour**

½ **teaspoon salt**

¼ **teaspoon ground black pepper**

4 **brook or rainbow trout (about 8 ounces each), dressed, with heads and tails left on**

4 **slices bacon, cut into 1-inch pieces**

2 **tablespoons (¼ stick) butter or margarine**

1 **medium-size yellow onion, chopped**

8 **ounces small mushrooms, halved**

1 **cup milk**

1 **tablespoon chopped parsley**

 PREPARATION TIME **11 MINUTES**

 COOKING TIME **34 MINUTES**

1 On a sheet of wax paper, combine flour, salt, and pepper; set 2 teaspoons of the flour mixture aside. Rinse trout but do not pat dry. Roll the fish in the remaining flour mixture until they are well coated.

2 In a large skillet, cook bacon over moderately low heat until it is crisp. Using a spatula, remove the bacon and drain it on paper towels.

3 In the remaining bacon fat, fry the trout, two at a time, until they are well browned on both sides, 5 to 6 minutes on each side. Transfer the trout to a serving platter and keep it warm. Repeat to cook the remaining trout.

4 In the same skillet, melt butter over moderate heat. Add onion and sauté for 3 minutes. Add mushrooms and sauté until wilted. Stir in the reserved flour mixture until well mixed. Gradually stir milk into the mushroom-flour mixture and cook, stirring, until the mixture boils and thickens slightly.

5 Spoon some of the mushroom sauce over the trout. Pour the remaining sauce into a serving bowl. Sprinkle the trout with the bacon pieces and parsley and serve, passing the sauce separately.

PAN-FRIED TROUT WITH LEMON BUTTER

One Serving: **Calories** 564 **Protein** 60g **Carbohydrates** 5g **Fat** 31g **Cholesterol** 196mg **Sodium** 439mg

¼ **cup all-purpose flour**

½ **teaspoon salt**

¼ **teaspoon ground black pepper**

4 **brook or rainbow trout (about 8 ounces each), dressed, with heads removed**

 Vegetable oil for frying

¼ **cup (½ stick) butter or margarine**

1 **tablespoon lemon juice**

8 **lemon slices**

 Chopped parsley (optional)

 PREPARATION TIME **10 MINUTES**

 COOKING TIME **27 MINUTES**

COOK'S TIP *This is the classic way to serve fresh, succulent trout— the lemon butter brings out the mild flavor of the fish.*

1 On a sheet of wax paper, combine flour, salt, and pepper. Rinse trout and pat dry. Roll the fish in the flour mixture until they are well coated.

2 In a large skillet, pour enough oil to cover the bottom to a depth of about ¼ inch. Over moderate heat, heat the oil until it is hot. Add the trout, two at a time, and fry until well browned on both sides, 6 to 7 minutes on each side. Transfer the trout to serving plates and keep them warm. Repeat to cook the remaining two trout.

3 Meanwhile, in a small saucepan, melt butter and cook until lightly browned, about 1 minute. Stir in lemon juice. Pour an equal amount of the lemon butter over each trout; place lemon slices on the side. Garnish with parsley, if desired, and serve immediately.

TUNA CAKES WITH CUCUMBER-YOGURT SAUCE

Tuna Cakes with Cucumber-Yogurt Sauce

One Serving: **Calories** 232 **Protein** 28g **Carbohydrates** 9g **Fat** 8g **Cholesterol** 103mg **Sodium** 535mg

1 **medium-size cucumber**

1¼ **teaspoons salt, divided**

2 **cans (6⅛ ounces each) tuna packed in water, drained and flaked**

½ **cup packaged plain bread crumbs**

½ **cup thinly sliced green onion**

1 **large egg**

2 **tablespoons mayonnaise**

¼ **teaspoon ground black pepper**

½ **cup plain yogurt**

1 **tablespoon snipped fresh dill (or 1 teaspoon dill weed)**

Additional salt and ground black pepper to taste

1 **tablespoon vegetable oil**

Fresh dill sprigs (optional)

PREPARATION TIME
30 MINUTES

COOKING TIME
4 MINUTES

COOK'S TIP *This recipe makes enough for four first-course servings, but it can easily be doubled to make enough for a main dish.*

1 Peel cucumber; cut it in half lengthwise, seed, and coarsely grate it. Place the grated cucumber in a strainer; sprinkle it with 1 teaspoon salt and toss. Place the strainer over a bowl and set it aside for about 15 minutes to let the cucumber drain.

2 Meanwhile, in a large bowl, combine tuna, bread crumbs, onions, egg, mayonnaise, pepper, and ¼ teaspoon salt until well mixed. Shape the tuna mixture into four 1-inch-thick cakes.

3 Rinse the grated cucumber under cold water; drain and squeeze it to remove the excess moisture. In a small bowl, combine the cucumber with yogurt and dill, season with salt and pepper. Cover and refrigerate the mixture until ready to serve.

4 In a large skillet, heat oil over moderate heat. Add the tuna cakes and cook until they are browned on both sides, about 2 minutes on each side. Transfer to individual serving plates and garnish with fresh dill sprigs, if desired. Serve immediately with the cucumber sauce.

BAKED TUNA WITH BROCCOLI

One Serving: **Calories** 377 **Protein** 35g **Carbohydrates** 21g **Fat** 18g **Cholesterol** 55mg **Sodium** 614mg

- **2 packages (10 ounces) frozen broccoli spears**
- **3 tablespoons butter or margarine**
- **¼ cup slivered blanched almonds**
- **¼ cup all-purpose flour**
- **¼ teaspoon salt**
- **⅛ teaspoon ground black pepper**
- **2 cups milk**
- **2 cans (6 ⅛ ounces each) tuna packed in water, drained and flaked**
- **Paprika**

 PREPARATION TIME
10 MINUTES

COOKING TIME
27 MINUTES

SERVING SUGGESTION *A chopped salad of Bibb lettuce, avocado, and tomato would make a refreshing accompaniment to this easy and economical main dish.*

1 Preheat the oven to 350°F. Grease an 12- by 8-inch baking dish. Partially thaw broccoli under warm running water or in the microwave oven just until the spears can easily be separated.

2 Meanwhile, in a large saucepan, melt butter over moderate heat. Add almonds and sauté until lightly browned, about 1½ minutes. Blend in flour, salt, and pepper. Gradually add milk and cook, stirring constantly, until the mixture thickens, 4 to 5 minutes. Remove the almond sauce from the heat.

3 Pat the broccoli dry; arrange the floret end of each spear down the long sides of the prepared baking dish, with the stems turned toward the center of the dish. Place tuna over the broccoli stems in the center of the dish. Pour the almond sauce over the tuna.

4 Cover the dish with aluminum foil and bake until the broccoli is tender, 20 to 25 minutes. Uncover, sprinkle with paprika, and serve.

BLACKENED CATFISH

One Serving: **Calories** 322 **Protein** 32g **Carbohydrates** 5g **Fat** 19g **Cholesterol** 130mg **Sodium** 1293mg

- **2 tablespoons paprika**
- **2 teaspoons salt**
- **2 teaspoons onion powder**
- **2 teaspoons garlic powder**
- **1½ teaspoons ground black pepper**
- **1 teaspoon cayenne pepper**
- **1 teaspoon dried thyme leaves, crumbled**
- **1 teaspoon dried oregano, crumbled**
- **¼ cup (½ stick) unsalted butter or margarine**
- **4 catfish fillets (about 6 ounces each)**
- **4 lemon wedges**

 PREPARATION TIME
5 MINUTES

COOKING TIME
12 MINUTES

COOK'S TIP *The secret to the popular Cajun dish of blackened fish is to use a cast-iron skillet and fry the fish only when the pan is very hot.*

1 In a pie plate or shallow dish, combine paprika, salt, onion and garlic powders, black and cayenne peppers, thyme, and oregano. Melt butter and pour it into another shallow dish.

2 Heat a large skillet until very hot. Dip fish fillets into the melted butter, then into the paprika mixture, until they are coated on both sides. Place the fillets, two at a time, into the hot skillet and cook each side until blackened, 2 to 3 minutes.

3 Transfer fillets to a serving platter and keep them warm. Repeat to cook the remaining two fillets. Serve the catfish immediately, with lemon wedges on the side.

PECAN FRIED CATFISH

PECAN FRIED CATFISH

One Serving: **Calories** 485 **Protein** 34g **Carbohydrates** 15g **Fat** 31g **Cholesterol** 166mg **Sodium** 439mg

¹/₃ **cup ground pecans**

¹/₃ **cup yellow cornmeal**

3 **tablespoons all-purpose flour**

¹/₂ **teaspoon salt**

¹/₄ **teaspoon cayenne pepper**

1 **large egg**

1 **tablespoon water**

4 **catfish fillets (about 6 ounces each)**

3 **tablespoons vegetable oil, divided**

2 **tablespoons (¹/₄ stick) butter or margarine, divided**

Lemon wedges

 PREPARATION TIME
15 MINUTES

COOKING TIME
14 MINUTES

SERVING SUGGESTION *Serve this crispy catfish with buttered green beans sprinkled with extra chopped pecans.*

1 On a sheet of wax paper, combine pecans and cornmeal. On another sheet of wax paper, combine flour, salt, and cayenne pepper. In a pie plate or shallow dish, combine egg and water.

2 Dredge each fillet in the flour mixture, shaking off the excess. Dip the floured fillets into the egg mixture, then coat each one with the pecan-cornmeal mixture.

3 In a large skillet, heat half of the oil and half of the butter over moderate heat. Add two fillets and fry until golden brown on both sides, about 3 to 4 minutes on each side.

4 Transfer the fillets to a serving platter and keep them warm. Repeat to cook the remaining fillets using the remaining oil and butter. Serve immediately, with lemon wedges on the side.

FOIL-WRAPPED CATFISH

One Serving: **Calories** 280 **Protein** 32g **Carbohydrates** 3g **Fat** 14g **Cholesterol** 99mg **Sodium** 369mg

2 tablespoons dry sherry

2 tablespoons vegetable oil

1 tablespoon chopped green onion top

1 tablespoon soy sauce

¼ teaspoon ground ginger

4 catfish fillets (about 6 ounces each)

1 small tomato, thinly sliced

1 small zucchini, thinly sliced

 PREPARATION TIME
13 MINUTES

COOKING TIME
15 MINUTES

1 Preheat the oven to 450°F. In a small bowl, combine sherry, oil, onion, soy sauce, and ginger. Cut out four 12-inch squares of heavy-duty aluminum foil or oven-safe parchment paper.

2 Place a catfish fillet in the center of each square. Divide tomato and zucchini slices among the four fillets. Spoon the sherry mixture over each fillet and fold each foil or paper diagonally in half to form a triangle. Crimp the edges to seal tightly.

3 Place the packets on a baking sheet. Bake until the fish flakes easily when the packets are opened and the fish is tested with a fork, 15 to 20 minutes. Transfer the fish and vegetables to individual serving plates and serve immediately.

TERIYAKI SALMON

One Serving: **Calories** 430 **Protein** 57g **Carbohydrates** 4g **Fat** 19g **Cholesterol** 156mg **Sodium** 896mg

3 tablespoons soy sauce

1 tablespoon lime juice

2 teaspoons sugar

1 teaspoon Oriental sesame oil

½ teaspoon ground ginger

4 1-inch-thick, center-cut salmon steaks (about 10 ounces each)

Lime slices (optional)

 PREPARATION TIME
12 MINUTES

COOKING TIME
10 MINUTES

1 Preheat the broiler. In a large shallow dish, combine soy sauce, lime juice, sugar, sesame oil, and ginger. Add salmon steaks and turn them in the mixture until they are well coated. Set aside for 10 minutes to marinate, turning once.

2 Place the salmon steaks on the rack over a broiler pan. Broil 4 inches from the heat for 5 minutes. Turn the salmon and baste it with any leftover marinade. Continue broiling until the fish flakes easily when tested with a fork, 5 to 7 more minutes. Garnish with lime slices, if desired, and serve immediately.

TIME SAVERS

FROZEN FISH
If you don't have time to thaw frozen fish overnight in the refrigerator, use the microwave to do the job, keeping these two simple pointers in mind:

Carefully follow the oven-manufacturer's instructions for defrosting cuts of fish. Different microwave ovens have a wide variety of cooking time and temperature requirements.

It is always better to stop the defrosting process too early rather than too late. You can finish off the thawing by gently running cool water over the parts of the fish that are still frozen.

SALMON VÉRONIQUE

Salmon Véronique

One Serving: **Calories** 428 **Protein** 48g **Carbohydrates** 11g **Fat** 18g **Cholesterol** 96mg **Sodium** 135mg

1 **cup water**

⅓ **cup dry white wine**

1 **small onion, sliced**

1 **clove garlic, halved**

1 **bay leaf**

½ **cup seedless green or red grapes**

4 **red salmon fillets (about 6 ounces each)**

1 **tablespoon butter or margarine**

1 **tablespoon all-purpose flour**

¼ **cup half-and-half**

Salt and ground white pepper to taste

1 **tablespoon chopped walnuts (optional)**

Small clusters of grapes (optional)

PREPARATION TIME
5 MINUTES

COOKING TIME
21 MINUTES

FOOD NOTE *Created at the Ritz hotel in Paris, the Véronique method combines the sweet taste of grapes with fish; here it makes an elegant treatment for salmon. Serve it with brown rice and lemon.*

1 In a large skillet, bring water, wine, onion, garlic and bay leaf to a boil over a high heat. Reduce the heat to low, cover the pan, and simmer the liquid for 5 minutes. Meanwhile, cut each grape in half.

2 Add salmon to the liquid. Return to a boil and poach the fish, covered, until the fish is firm and it flakes easily when tested with a fork, 8 to 10 minutes. Transfer the fish to a serving platter and keep it warm. Strain the poaching liquid into a measuring cup.

3 In the same skillet, melt butter over moderate heat. Add flour and cook until bubbly. Whisk in ¾ cup of the strained poaching liquid and bring it to a boil, stirring constantly. Add the grapes and half-and-half, and heat through (do not boil). Season with salt and pepper.

4 Spoon the sauce over the salmon. Sprinkle with walnuts and garnish with grape clusters, if desired. Serve immediately.

SALMON-STUFFED FLOUNDER

One Serving: **Calories** 279 **Protein** 33g **Carbohydrates** 1g **Fat** 15g **Cholesterol** 97mg **Sodium** 230mg

- 3 tablespoons mayonnaise
- 1 heaping tablespoon minced yellow onion
- 2 teaspoons Dijon mustard
- 1 teaspoon dried tarragon, crumbled
- ¼ teaspoon ground black pepper
- ½ cup watercress leaves
- 8 ounces red salmon steak or thick fillet, skinned and boned
- 4 flounder fillets (about 4 ounces each)
- 2 teaspoons butter or margarine, cut into small pieces
  Pinch paprika

PREPARATION TIME 18 MINUTES

COOKING TIME 20 MINUTES

SERVING SUGGESTION *This light springtime dish pairs well with fresh steamed asparagus topped with a dollop of extra mayonnaise, or brown rice mixed with sautéed slivered almonds.*

1 Preheat the oven to 375°F. Grease a 10- by 6-inch baking dish. In a small bowl, combine mayonnaise, onion, mustard, tarragon, and pepper. Rinse watercress leaves and pat them dry on paper towels. Cut salmon into four thick strips.

2 Spread some of the mayonnaise mixture on the dark side of each flounder fillet. Cover each fillet with an even layer of watercress leaves. Place a strip of salmon across one end of each flounder fillet and roll each one up.

3 Place the stuffed fillets, seam sides down, in the prepared baking dish. Dot the fillets with butter and sprinkle with paprika. Cover the dish with aluminum foil and bake just until the fish flakes easily when tested with a fork, 20 to 25 minutes. Transfer the cooked fillets to a warm serving platter, and serve immediately.

FISH AND POTATO PIE

One Serving: **Calories** 316 **Protein** 25g **Carbohydrates** 24g **Fat** 13g **Cholesterol** 86mg **Sodium** 374mg

- 1 pound all-purpose potatoes, unpeeled, cut into ¼-inch-thick slices
- ¼ cup (½ stick) butter or margarine
- 2 cloves garlic, finely chopped
- 2 tablespoons chopped parsley
- ⅛ teaspoon cayenne pepper
- ¼ teaspoon salt
- 1 pound flounder, orange roughy, or catfish fillets
- 3 tablespoons packaged plain bread crumbs

PREPARATION TIME 10 MINUTES

COOKING TIME 25 MINUTES

1 In a large saucepan, cook potatoes in boiling water until they are almost fork-tender, about 10 minutes. Meanwhile, in a small saucepan, melt butter over moderate heat. Add chopped garlic and cook for 10 seconds. Remove the pan from the heat and stir in parsley and cayenne pepper. Cut fish into 1-inch slices.

2 Preheat the oven to 400°F. Grease a 9-inch pie plate. Drain the parboiled potatoes and lay them in the pie plate. Brush the potatoes with some of the parsley butter and sprinkle salt over them.

3 Arrange the fish slices over the potatoes and brush them with some more of the parsley butter. Cover the dish with aluminum foil and bake for 15 minutes.

4 Stir bread crumbs into the remaining parsley butter. Uncover the fish and sprinkle it with the crumb mixture. Continue baking the fish, uncovered, until the top is golden brown and crisp, about 10 more minutes. Serve immediately.

Variations on the basic Baked Fish

Baked fish is simpler to make than you may think, and the rewards are great. It creates a mouth-watering main dish, and, since it is low in fat, fish offers one of the healthiest sources of protein you can find. You can enjoy the fish on its own with a squeeze of lemon, but its delicate taste goes best with a flavorful sauce.

Once the fish is in the oven, begin preparing one of these easy sauces to serve on the side. The sauces aren't limited to this basic recipe—they will work just as well with whole fish or fish steaks, and are delicious on barbecued seafood. The fish and sauces each make four servings.

BASIC BAKED FISH FILLETS Select **3- to 4-lb. salmon, bass, or red snapper fillets**. Preheat the oven to 400°F. Lay out a piece of aluminum foil large enough to wrap the fish completely. Brush the foil with **olive or vegetable oil**. Lay the fillets in the center of the foil. Brush the fish with more oil. Season fish with **salt and pepper**, and place a few **thin lemon slices** between the fillets. Wrap the foil loosely around the fish, sealing the foil securely so the juices do not evaporate.

Bake the fish 10 minutes for each inch of the fillets' total thickness. The fish should flake easily when tested with a fork.

Using a spatula, lift the fish onto a serving platter. Garnish the platter with **additional thin lemon slices**, and **watercress or dill**, if desired. Serve the fish with one of the following sauces.

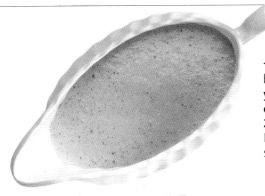

◄ GREEN SAUCE Using a food processor or electric blender, combine **½ cup mayonnaise, ½ cup plain yogurt, 2 Tbsp. snipped dill or 1 tsp. dill weed, 2 Tbsp. chopped green onion top, 2 Tbsp. chopped parsley, 2 tsp. red-wine vinegar,** and **¼ tsp. dried tarragon.** Process or blend all ingredients until smooth, occasionally stopping to scrape the sides of the container.

◄ MUSHROOM TOMATO SAUCE In a medium-size saucepan, melt **1 Tbsp. butter** over moderate heat. Add **4 oz. sliced mushrooms, 2 Tbsp. finely chopped onion,** and **1 clove garlic, chopped.** Sauté mushroom mixture until soft, about 5 minutes. Stir in **one 14½-oz. can whole tomatoes with their juice** and **½ tsp. dried rosemary.** Bring the mixture to a boil, cover, and cook for 10 minutes, stirring occasionally.

► CUCUMBER DILL SAUCE In a medium-size bowl, thoroughly combine **¾ cup finely chopped seeded unpeeled cucumber, ½ cup sour cream, 2 Tbsp. mayonnaise, 2 tsp. finely chopped yellow onion, ½ tsp. grated lemon peel,** and **½ tsp. dill weed.** Season with **salt and ground white pepper.**

▼ SPICY TOMATO SAUCE In a medium-size bowl, combine **1 cup ketchup, 1 to 2 Tbsp. prepared horseradish, 1 Tbsp. lemon juice, ¼ tsp. Worcestershire sauce,** and **a few drops hot red pepper sauce** until well mixed.

▼ MUSTARD ONION SAUCE In a medium-size saucepan, melt **2 Tbsp. butter or margarine** over moderate heat. Add **1 medium-size yellow onion, sliced,** and sauté until soft, about 5 minutes. Stir in **1 Tbsp. all-purpose flour** until well mixed. Add **¾ to 1 cup fish stock or chicken broth,** and **1 Tbsp. prepared mustard.** Season with salt and pepper. Cook, stirring constantly, until slightly thickened, about 2 to 3 minutes.

FLOUNDER WITH CAPER SAUCE

One Serving: **Calories** 271 **Protein** 32g **Carbohydrates** 7g **Fat** 11g **Cholesterol** 89mg **Sodium** 367mg

¼ **cup all-purpose flour**

¼ **teaspoon salt**

⅛ **teaspoon ground black pepper**

4 **flounder fillets (about 6 ounces each)**

2 **tablespoons olive oil, divided**

1 **tablespoon butter or margarine, divided**

½ **cup water**

¼ **cup lemon juice**

1 **teaspoon Worcestershire sauce**

1 **tablespoon capers, rinsed**

Lemon slices (optional)

 PREPARATION TIME
10 MINUTES

COOKING TIME
11 MINUTES

SERVING SUGGESTION *Complement this slightly tangy fish dish with broiled tomato halves sprinkled with Parmesan cheese, and a glass of crisp white wine.*

1 On a sheet of wax paper, combine flour, salt, and pepper. Dredge each fillet in the flour mixture, shaking off the excess.

2 In a large skillet, heat half of the oil and half of the butter over moderate heat. Add two fillets and fry until they are golden brown on both sides, about 2 minutes on each side. Transfer to serving plates and keep them warm. Repeat to cook the remaining fillets, using the remaining oil and butter.

3 Pour water, lemon juice, and Worcestershire sauce into the skillet. Bring the mixture to a boil over high heat. Reduce the heat to moderate and simmer the sauce until it is slightly thickened, about 2 minutes. Stir in capers.

4 Pour an equal amount of the sauce over each fillet, garnish with lemon slices, if desired, and serve immediately.

BROILED FLOUNDER WITH MUSTARD

One Serving: **Calories** 213 **Protein** 32g **Carbohydrates** Trace **Fat** 8g **Cholesterol** 84mg **Sodium** 226mg

4 **flounder fillets (about 6 ounces each)**

1 **tablespoon vegetable oil**

Pinch ground black pepper

2 **tablespoons mayonnaise**

1 **tablespoon Dijon mustard**

2 **teaspoons finely chopped parsley**

4 **lime wedges**

 PREPARATION TIME
5 MINUTES

COOKING TIME
3 MINUTES

COOK'S TIP *Mild and delicate, these thin flatfish fillets cook so quickly that they do not need to be turned during broiling. Watch them carefully to avoid overcooking. Although flounder is generally available, fillets of sole may be substituted.*

1 Preheat the broiler. Cover the rack of a broiler pan with aluminum foil. Brush flounder fillets with oil on both sides; place them on the foil. Sprinkle the fillets with pepper.

2 In a small bowl, combine mayonnaise, mustard, and parsley. Brush or spread the mixture evenly over the fillets.

3 Broil the fillets 3 to 4 inches from the heat until they are golden brown on top and the fish flakes easily when tested with a fork, about 3 minutes. Transfer to serving plates and serve immediately, with lime wedges on the side.

BROCHETTES OF SWORDFISH

One Serving: **Calories** 332 **Protein** 35g **Carbohydrates** 9g **Fat** 17g **Cholesterol** 66mg **Sodium** 423mg

1½ **pounds thickly sliced swordfish steaks**

3 **tablespoons olive oil**

1 **tablespoon red-wine vinegar**

2 **cloves garlic, finely chopped**

1 **teaspoon paprika**

½ **teaspoon salt**

½ **teaspoon dried thyme leaves, crumbled**

¼ **teaspoon ground black pepper**

1 **large green bell pepper**

1 **large red onion (about 8 ounces)**

PREPARATION TIME
25 MINUTES

COOKING TIME
6 MINUTES

SERVING SUGGESTION *Serve these skewers of vegetables and swordfish on a bed of white rice. In the summer, try barbecuing them.*

1 Skin and bone swordfish if necessary. Cut the swordfish into 1- to 1¼-inch cubes. In a bowl, combine oil, vinegar, garlic, paprika, salt, thyme, and pepper. Add the fish cubes and toss until they are well coated. Let stand 10 minutes to marinate.

2 Meanwhile, core and seed bell pepper. Cut the pepper into 1¼-inch squares. Cut onion in half, and cut each half into sixths; separate the onion layers. Toss the pepper and onion pieces in the marinade with the fish cubes to coat.

3 Preheat the broiler. On four long metal skewers, thread alternate pieces of the fish, pepper, and onion until all of the pieces are used. Arrange the brochettes on the rack over a broiler pan and brush them with the remaining marinade.

4 Broil the brochettes 4 inches from the heat for 3 minutes. Turn the brochettes and continue broiling until the fish is just tender but still firm, about 3 more minutes. Serve immediately.

BAKED COD OVER RICE

One Serving: **Calories** 947 **Protein** 47g **Carbohydrates** 162g **Fat** 8g **Cholesterol** 88mg **Sodium** 352mg

1 **cup long-grain white rice**

1 **package (10 ounces) frozen green peas**

4 **cod fillets (about 6 ounces each)**

¼ **cup dry white wine**

1 **tablespoon lemon juice**

2 **tablespoons (¼ stick) butter or margarine, cut into small pieces**

2 **large ripe plum tomatoes, chopped**

½ **teaspoon dried thyme leaves, crumbled**

¼ **teaspoon salt**

¼ **teaspoon ground black pepper**

	PREPARATION TIME **10 MINUTES**		COOKING TIME **22 MINUTES**

FOOD NOTE *Fresh tomatoes, white wine, and thyme make a colorful and appetizing sauce for lean and delicate cod. If cod isn't available, scrod or flounder can be substituted.*

1 Preheat the oven to 450°F. Grease a 12- by 8-inch baking dish. In two separate saucepans, prepare rice and peas according to their package directions.

2 Meanwhile, place cod fillets in a single layer in the prepared dish. Drizzle the fillets with wine and lemon juice. Dot with butter and sprinkle with tomatoes, thyme, salt, and pepper. Bake until the cod flakes easily when tested with a fork, 8 to 10 minutes.

3 Drain the cooked peas and rice. Stir the peas into the rice. Spoon the rice and peas onto a serving platter or individual plates. Spoon the fillets and their juices over the rice mixture and serve immediately.

HADDOCK CREOLE

One Serving: **Calories** 210 **Protein** 23g **Carbohydrates** 14g **Fat** 7g **Cholesterol** 80mg **Sodium** 402mg

1 **pound frozen haddock or pollock fillet**

1 **small celery stalk**

1 **small yellow onion**

1 **clove garlic**

1 **small green bell pepper**

2 **tablespoons (¼ stick) butter or margarine**

2 **tablespoons all-purpose flour**

1 **can (14½ or 16 ounces) stewed tomatoes**

2 **tablespoons water**

½ **teaspoon sugar**

1 **bay leaf**

Celery leaves for garnish (optional)

	PREPARATION TIME **8 MINUTES**		COOKING TIME **30 MINUTES**

1 Place frozen haddock in a heavy-duty plastic food-storage bag, and seal the bag tightly. Place the wrapped haddock in a large pan containing very hot water; thaw the fish until it can be cut through. (Alternatively, thaw the fish in a microwave oven.)

2 Meanwhile, chop celery, onion, and garlic. Core and seed bell pepper and cut it into strips.

3 In a large skillet, melt butter over moderately high heat and cook until lightly browned. Add the chopped celery, onion and garlic and sauté until lightly browned, about 5 minutes.

4 Stir flour into celery mixture until well mixed. Stir in tomatoes, water, sugar, and bay leaf; bring to a boil, stirring occasionally. Reduce the heat to low; simmer for 5 to 10 minutes, stirring occasionally.

5 Using a sharp knife, cut the fish crosswise into four pieces. Place the fish in the simmering tomato mixture. Add the pepper strips and cover the skillet. Cook the fish until it flakes easily when tested with a fork and it is cooked in the center, 12 to 15 minutes. Discard the bay leaf and garnish with celery leaves, if desired. Serve immediately.

STIR-FRIED FISH WITH VEGETABLES

One Serving: **Calories** 321 **Protein** 23g **Carbohydrates** 14g **Fat** 19g **Cholesterol** 77mg **Sodium** 66mg

1 **pound grouper, halibut, striped bass, or orange roughy fillets**

2 **tablespoons cornstarch, divided**

¼ **cup canned reduced-sodium chicken broth**

2 **tablespoons dry sherry**

2 **tablespoons soy sauce**

1 **teaspoon sugar**

4 **tablespoons vegetable oil, divided**

4 **green onions, cut into 1-inch lengths**

2 **cups sliced mushrooms**

1 **cup diagonally sliced celery**

1 **can (8 ounces) sliced water chestnuts, drained**

2 **cloves garlic, finely chopped**

 PREPARATION TIME **15 MINUTES**

 COOKING TIME **9 MINUTES**

COOK'S TIP *As with most stir-fried dishes, most of the cook's time is spent cutting rather than cooking. If the vegetables are prepared ahead and refrigerated, the dish can be done in less than 15 minutes.*

1 Cut the fillets crosswise into ½-inch-wide strips. In a medium-size bowl, toss the fish strips with 1 tablespoon cornstarch until well mixed. In a small bowl, combine the remaining 1 tablespoon of cornstarch, broth, sherry, soy sauce, and sugar. Set aside.

2 In a large skillet or wok, heat 2 tablespoons of oil over high heat. Add the fish, making sure all the strips are in contact with the pan. Fry the strips until lightly browned, about 3 minutes, using a spatula to turn the fish carefully. Transfer the fish to a plate and keep it warm.

3 Heat the remaining 2 tablespoons of oil in the skillet. Add onions, mushrooms, celery, water chestnuts and garlic; stir fry just until the vegetables are wilted, 2 to 3 minutes. Stir in the cornstarch mixture and bring to a boil. Continue boiling for 1 minute.

4 Return the fish to the skillet. Remove the pan from heat, toss the fish and vegetables gently, and serve immediately.

BROILED MARINATED FISH STEAKS

One Serving: **Calories** 398 **Protein** 43g **Carbohydrates** 1g **Fat** 22g **Cholesterol** 85mg **Sodium** 330mg

¼ **cup vegetable oil**

¼ **cup dry white wine**

1 **teaspoon grated lemon peel**

2 **tablespoons lemon juice**

1 **tablespoon chopped parsley**

1 **teaspoon dried thyme leaves, crumbled**

¼ **teaspoon salt**

4 **¾-inch-thick swordfish, halibut, or tuna steaks (about 6 ounces each)**

 PREPARATION TIME **25 MINUTES**

 COOKING TIME **8 MINUTES**

FOOD NOTE *Swordfish is a dense, firm fish with a delicate flavor that benefits from marinating, and this lemon-wine mixture suits it perfectly. Since the marinade is acidic, be sure to use a glass or porcelain dish (not metal) for marinating.*

1 In a large shallow glass dish, combine vegetable oil, wine, lemon peel, lemon juice, parsley, thyme, and salt. Place fish steaks in the wine mixture. Turn to coat the fish, cover, and marinate for 20 minutes at room temperature.

2 Preheat the broiler. Place the marinated fish steaks on the rack over a broiler pan. Broil them 4 inches from the heat for 3 minutes. Turn the steaks over and continue broiling just until the fish is lightly browned and flakes easily when tested with a fork, about 5 more minutes. Serve immediately.

WEST COAST SEAFOOD STEW

WEST COAST SEAFOOD STEW

One Serving: **Calories** 251 **Protein** 27g **Carbohydrates** 10g **Fat** 9g **Cholesterol** 68mg **Sodium** 499mg

1 medium-size yellow onion

2 cloves garlic

1 small green bell pepper

1 pound monkfish or halibut

3 tablespoons olive oil

1 cup sliced mushrooms

1 can (14 1/2 or 16 ounces) whole, peeled tomatoes, undrained

1 can (8 ounces) tomato sauce

1 cup water

1/2 cup dry white wine

1 bay leaf

12 littleneck clams (or one 10-ounce can whole clams, drained)

8 ounces cooked crabmeat or imitation crabmeat chunks

PREPARATION TIME
15 MINUTES

COOKING TIME
27 MINUTES

SERVING SUGGESTION *Pass around a loaf of warm sourdough bread with this robust stew of monkfish, clams, and crabmeat.*

1 Slice onion and chop garlic; core, seed, and coarsely chop bell pepper. Cut monkfish or halibut into medium-size chunks.

2 In a large saucepan or kettle, heat oil over moderate heat. Add the onion, bell pepper, mushrooms, and garlic; sauté for 5 minutes. Stir in tomatoes and their liquid, tomato sauce, water, wine, and bay leaf.

3 Increase the heat to high; bring to a boil, stirring to break up the tomatoes. Reduce the heat to low, cover, and simmer for 10 minutes.

4 (If you are using canned clams, skip Step 4 and add them with the crabmeat in Step 5.) Meanwhile, scrub fresh clams under cold running water to remove any sand. Add the fresh clams to the tomato mixture. Cover the pan, increase the heat to high and bring to a boil.

5 Add the monkfish chunks. Reduce the heat to moderate; simmer until the clams open and the fish flakes easily, about 5 more minutes. Stir in crabmeat and heat through. Discard the bay leaf, and serve.

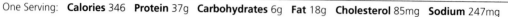

BAKED CRUMB-TOPPED HALIBUT

One Serving: **Calories** 346 **Protein** 37g **Carbohydrates** 6g **Fat** 18g **Cholesterol** 85mg **Sodium** 247mg

- ¼ **cup (½ stick) butter or margarine**
- 2 **1-inch-thick halibut steaks (12 to 14 ounces each)**
- 2 **tablespoons sesame seeds**
- 1 **cup fresh bread crumbs**
- 1 **tablespoon chopped fresh thyme leaves (or 1 teaspoon dried thyme)**
- ¼ **teaspoon ground black pepper**
  Thyme sprigs (optional)

 PREPARATION TIME
5 MINUTES

 COOKING TIME
26 MINUTES

COOK'S TIP *Fresh bread crumbs can be made by processing pieces of bread in the blender. In a pinch, use packaged bread crumbs.*

1 Preheat the oven to 350°F. Grease a 9-inch square baking dish. In a small saucepan, melt butter over moderate heat. Remove the pan from the heat. Place fish steaks in the prepared baking dish and brush them with some of the melted butter.

2 Bake the fish steaks for 10 minutes. Meanwhile, in the saucepan with the remaining butter, sauté sesame seeds over moderate heat for 3 minutes, taking care not to burn the butter. Add bread crumbs, thyme, and pepper; mix well.

3 Sprinkle the fish steaks with the crumb mixture. Continue to bake the fish until it flakes easily when tested with a fork, about 15 minutes. Cut each steak in half, place them on serving plates, and garnish with thyme sprigs, if desired. Serve immediately.

FILLET OF SOLE AMANDINE

One Serving: **Calories** 279 **Protein** 23g **Carbohydrates** 7g **Fat** 15g **Cholesterol** 62mg **Sodium** 257mg

- ¼ **cup all-purpose flour**
- ¼ **teaspoon salt**
- ¼ **teaspoon ground black pepper**
- 4 **sole fillets (about 4 ounces each)**
- 2½ **tablespoons vegetable oil, divided**
- 3 **tablespoons sliced almonds**
- 2 **tablespoons (¼ stick) butter or margarine**
- ½ **cup dry white wine or cooking sherry**
- 2 **tablespoons chopped parsley**

 PREPARATION TIME
4 MINUTES

COOKING TIME
21 MINUTES

1 On a sheet of wax paper, combine flour, salt, and pepper. Dredge each fillet in the flour mixture, shaking off the excess. Transfer the fillets to a plate and set aside.

2 In a large skillet (preferably with nonstick coating), heat ½ tablespoon of vegetable oil over moderate heat. Add almonds and sauté until lightly browned, 2 to 3 minutes. Using a slotted spoon, transfer the almonds to a bowl and set aside.

3 Add the remaining oil and butter to the skillet and heat over moderately high heat. Add two fillets; fry them until they are golden brown on both sides, about 3 minutes for each side. Transfer the fish to individual serving plates and keep them warm. Repeat to cook the remaining two fillets.

4 Stir wine or sherry into the pan drippings and bring the mixture to a boil. Continue boiling until the sauce is slightly thickened, about 4 minutes. Spoon an equal amount of the sauce over each fillet, sprinkle the sauce with the toasted almonds and chopped parsley, and serve immediately.

SPINACH-WRAPPED FILLET OF SOLE

SPINACH-WRAPPED FILLET OF SOLE

One Serving: **Calories** 210 **Protein** 32g **Carbohydrates** 1g **Fat** 7g **Cholesterol** 97mg **Sodium** 191mg

4 **sole fillets (about
  6 ounces each)**

4 **teaspoons lemon juice**

2 **tablespoons (¼ stick)
  butter or margarine,
  softened**

1 **teaspoon dried tarragon,
  crumbled**

¼ **teaspoon ground white
  pepper**

12 **large spinach leaves**

4 **lemon wedges**

**PREPARATION TIME
15 MINUTES**

**COOKING TIME
10 MINUTES**

SERVING SUGGESTION *Make this low-calorie main dish even more
nutritious by adding a colorful mix of sautéed vegetables on the side.*

1 Drizzle each fillet with 1 teaspoon lemon juice. Dot with butter and
sprinkle with tarragon and pepper. Fold the fillets crosswise in half
and arrange them on a heatproof plate.

2 Into a stockpot, place 1 inch of water and a steaming rack or several
custard cups; bring the water to a boil over high heat. Reduce the
heat to moderately low to bring the water to a simmer.

3 Set the plate with the fish onto the steaming rack or on top of the
custard cups. Cover the pan and steam the fish for 5 to 7 minutes.
Meanwhile, remove the large, tough stems from spinach leaves.

4 Wrap each fillet in three layers of spinach leaves and secure with
toothpicks. Return them to the steamer and cook until the leaves are
wilted but still bright green, about 2 minutes. Serve the wrapped
fillets immediately, with lemon wedges on the side.

SHELLFISH

Among the wealth of seafood at the fish counter is shellfish,
here lending its flavors to a range of easy dishes.

PEPPERED TARRAGON SHRIMP SCAMPI

One Serving: **Calories** 218 **Protein** 18g **Carbohydrates** 5g **Fat** 14g **Cholesterol** 145mg **Sodium** 187mg

1 medium-size red bell
  pepper

2 cloves garlic

2 tablespoons olive oil

12 ounces large uncooked
   shelled and deveined
   shrimp, thawed if frozen

3 tablespoons lemon juice

2 tablespoons (¼ stick)
  butter or margarine

1 teaspoon dried tarragon,
  crumbled

⅛ teaspoon crushed red
  pepper flakes, or to taste

  Salt to taste

2 tablespoons chopped
  parsley

  Cooked long-grain white
  rice (optional)

	PREPARATION TIME **7 MINUTES**		COOKING TIME **5 MINUTES**

COOK'S TIP *Shrimp are at their best when only just cooked through, so take care not to keep them on the stove any longer than necessary. Be sure to heat the oil before adding the shrimp so they can cook as quickly as possible.*

1 Core and seed bell pepper and cut it into ¼-inch-wide strips. Peel and finely chop garlic.

2 In a large skillet or wok, heat oil over moderately high heat. Add shrimp, the bell pepper, and the chopped garlic; sauté until the shrimp turn pink, 2 to 3 minutes.

3 Add lemon juice, butter, tarragon, and pepper flakes to the shrimp and pepper mixture. Cook until the butter melts, stirring constantly, about 1 minute. Season with salt and sprinkle with parsley. Place the shrimp on a warm serving platter. Serve with hot white rice on the side, if desired.

SHRIMP IN TOMATO-WINE SAUCE

One Serving: **Calories** 361 **Protein** 22g **Carbohydrates** 42g **Fat** 10g **Cholesterol** 190mg **Sodium** 441mg

1 cup long-grain white rice

2 medium-size tomatoes

¾ cup canned reduced-
  sodium chicken broth

¼ cup dry white wine

1 tablespoon cornstarch

3 tablespoons butter or
  margarine

12 ounces large uncooked
   shelled and deveined
   shrimp, thawed if frozen

1 tablespoon capers, rinsed
  and drained

	PREPARATION TIME **2 MINUTES**		COOKING TIME **20 MINUTES**

1 Prepare rice according to package directions. Meanwhile, cut tomatoes into ½-inch pieces. In a small bowl, combine chicken broth, wine, and cornstarch.

2 In a large skillet, melt butter over moderately high heat. Add shrimp and sauté until they begin to turn pink, about 2 minutes.

3 Add the cornstarch mixture to the shrimp in the skillet, stirring thoroughly. Bring the mixture to a boil, stirring constantly; continue boiling until the sauce thickens. Add the chopped tomatoes and rinsed capers to the shrimp; continue cooking until the tomatoes are just heated through.

4 Transfer the cooked rice to a serving bowl; pour the shrimp and sauce over the rice and serve immediately.

CURRIED SHRIMP

CURRIED SHRIMP

One Serving: **Calories** 227 **Protein** 22g **Carbohydrates** 10g **Fat** 11g **Cholesterol** 185mg **Sodium** 417mg

1	**small yellow onion**
1	**clove garlic**
2	**tablespoons (¼ stick) butter or margarine**
1	**tablespoon vegetable oil**
12	**ounces large uncooked shelled and deveined shrimp, thawed if frozen**
1	**tablespoon all-purpose flour**
2	**teaspoons curry powder**
1	**cup plain low-fat yogurt**
	Salt and ground black pepper to taste
	Cooked long-grain white rice (optional)
	Chopped parsley

 PREPARATION TIME
5 MINUTES

COOKING TIME
11 MINUTES

SERVING SUGGESTION *Long-grain white rice can be left to cook while you prepare the shrimp. Serve warm pita bread on the side.*

1 Slice onion; finely chop garlic. In a large skillet, heat butter and oil over moderate heat. Add the onion and sauté until soft, about 5 minutes. Add the garlic and sauté for 2 more minutes.

2 Using paper towels, pat shrimp dry. Place the shrimp in a medium-size bowl and sprinkle flour and curry powder over them. Toss to coat. Add the shrimp to the skillet and cook until they begin to turn pink, stirring constantly, 2 minutes.

3 Reduce the heat to low and stir in yogurt. Heat until the mixture becomes bubbly, about 1 minute. Season with salt and pepper. Serve over rice, if desired, and garnish with parsley.

PAPRIKA SHRIMP

One Serving: **Calories** 385 **Protein** 23g **Carbohydrates** 12g **Fat** 25g **Cholesterol** 217mg **Sodium** 294mg

1 small yellow onion

8 ounces mushrooms

2 tablespoons (¼ stick) butter or margarine

12 ounces large uncooked shelled and deveined shrimp, thawed if frozen

1 tablespoon vegetable oil

2 tablespoons all-purpose flour

2 teaspoons paprika

¾ cup dry white wine

¾ cup half-and-half

½ cup sour cream

4 to 6 drops hot red pepper sauce

Salt to taste

Parsley sprigs (optional)

Cooked long-grain white rice (optional)

PREPARATION TIME
5 MINUTES

COOKING TIME
15 MINUTES

COOK'S TIP *If there's no time to thaw the shrimp before cooking them, sauté them in the melted butter over moderate heat for about 2½ minutes or until they turn pink.*

1 Chop onion and slice mushrooms. In a large skillet, melt butter over moderately high heat. Add shrimp and sauté until they turn pink, about 2 minutes. Transfer the shrimp to a bowl and set it aside.

2 Add oil to the skillet and heat over moderate heat. Add the onion and sauté until soft, about 5 minutes. Add the mushrooms; cover and cook until wilted, about 4 minutes, stirring occasionally.

3 Stir flour and paprika into the mushroom mixture until well mixed. Gradually stir in wine. Bring the mixture to a boil, stirring constantly, until the sauce thickens. Stir in half-and-half until the mixture is hot but not boiling.

4 Reduce the heat to low; stir in sour cream, pepper sauce, and the sautéed shrimp. Cook, stirring gently, about 1 minute. Season with salt. Transfer the shrimp to a serving bowl; garnish them with parsley and serve with rice, if desired.

BEER-COOKED SHRIMP

One Serving: **Calories** 195 **Protein** 25g **Carbohydrates** 8g **Fat** 5g **Cholesterol** 221mg **Sodium** 293mg

1 bottle (12 ounces) beer

8 black peppercorns

3 celery tops

2 sprigs parsley

½ lemon

1 bay leaf

1 pound jumbo or very large shrimp in their shells

1 tablespoon olive oil

1 tablespoon all-purpose flour

2 tablespoons prepared horseradish

1 tablespoon hot red pepper sauce

PREPARATION TIME
8 MINUTES

COOKING TIME
12 MINUTES

1 In a large saucepan, combine beer, peppercorns, celery tops, parsley sprigs, lemon, and bay leaf. Bring the mixture to a boil over high heat. Add shrimp and return the beer mixture to a boil. Remove the pan from the heat.

2 Using a strainer placed over a measuring cup, strain ½ cup of the cooking liquid, and discard the rest. Cover the shrimp and set the pan aside for 5 minutes.

3 In a small saucepan, heat oil over moderate heat. Stir in flour until blended. Gradually stir in the strained shrimp liquid and bring it to a boil, stirring constantly. Stir in horseradish and pepper sauce.

4 Transfer the cooked shrimp to a warm serving platter. Serve immediately, passing the beer sauce separately.

SHRIMP AND VEGETABLE STIR-FRY

One Serving: **Calories** 256 **Protein** 21g **Carbohydrates** 14g **Fat** 13g **Cholesterol** 129mg **Sodium** 510mg

12 ounces large uncooked shelled and deveined shrimp, thawed if frozen

2 tablespoons dry sherry

¾ cup canned reduced-sodium chicken broth, divided

1 tablespoon soy sauce

2 teaspoons cornstarch

½ teaspoon sugar

1 clove garlic

1 medium-size yellow onion

8 ounces green beans

2 tablespoons vegetable oil

1 teaspoon finely chopped ginger (or ¼ teaspoon ground ginger)

¼ cup roasted cashews

 PREPARATION TIME **20 MINUTES**

COOKING TIME **11 MINUTES**

1 In a medium-size bowl, combine shrimp and sherry; toss to coat evenly. Set the shrimp aside for 15 to 20 minutes to marinate, turning them occasionally.

2 Meanwhile, in a cup or small bowl, combine ¼ cup broth, soy sauce, cornstarch, and sugar; set aside. Finely chop garlic, cut onion into 1-inch pieces, and cut green beans into 2-inch lengths; set aside.

3 In a wok or large skillet, heat oil over high heat. Add the garlic and ginger; stir-fry a few seconds. Add the shrimp and stir-fry until they turn pink, 2 to 3 minutes. Using a slotted spoon, transfer the shrimp to a bowl and set them aside.

4 Reheat the wok or skillet over moderate heat. Add the onion, green beans, and the remaining ½ cup of chicken broth. Cover and cook the vegetables until they are crisp-tender, about 6 minutes.

5 Add the cornstarch mixture to the vegetables and cook until it is thickened and bubbly, about 30 seconds. Stir in the shrimp and cook until just heated through. Transfer to a serving dish, sprinkle with cashews, and serve immediately.

AMERASIAN SHRIMP

One Serving: **Calories** 188 **Protein** 17g **Carbohydrates** 9g **Fat** 9g **Cholesterol** 129mg **Sodium** 562mg

¼ cup ketchup

2 tablespoons Worcester-shire sauce

2 teaspoons soy sauce

2 teaspoons brandy or dry sherry

1 teaspoon sugar

3 to 4 drops hot red pepper sauce

2 cloves garlic

2 green onions

2 tablespoons vegetable oil

12 ounces large uncooked shelled and deveined shrimp, thawed if frozen

Cooked long-grain white rice (optional)

 PREPARATION TIME **6 MINUTES**

COOKING TIME **4 MINUTES**

COOK'S TIP *For best results, pat the shrimp dry with a paper towel before adding them to the skillet. This prevents them from spattering in the oil at such a high temperature.*

1 In a cup or small bowl, combine ketchup, Worcestershire sauce, soy sauce, brandy, sugar, and hot red pepper sauce. Set the mixture aside. Finely chop garlic and cut green onions into ¼-inch lengths.

2 In a large skillet or wok, heat oil over high heat. Add the chopped garlic, cut green onions, and shrimp; stir-fry until the shrimp turn pink, about 2 minutes.

3 Stir the ketchup mixture into the shrimp and bring the mixture to a boil. Place the shrimp on a warm serving platter over hot white rice, if desired, and serve immediately.

COQUILLES ST. JACQUES

COQUILLES ST. JACQUES

One Serving: **Calories** 373 **Protein** 27g **Carbohydrates** 19g **Fat** 19g **Cholesterol** 90mg **Sodium** 360mg

- 3 **tablespoons butter or margarine, divided**
- ½ **cup fresh bread crumbs**
- 1 **medium-size yellow onion, sliced**
- 1 **pound large sea scallops**
- 8 **ounces mushrooms, sliced**
- 3 **tablespoons all-purpose flour**
- ½ **cup dry white wine**
- ½ **cup water**
- ¾ **cup half-and-half**
- 2 **ounces Swiss or Jarlsberg cheese, coarsely grated (½ cup)**

PREPARATION TIME
10 MINUTES

 COOKING TIME
17 MINUTES

FOOD NOTE Coquilles St. Jacques *simply means scallops; here they are baked with a cheese topping. Serve them with steamed broccoli.*

1 Preheat the broiler. Grease four individual 8- to 10-ounce broiler-safe baking dishes. In a large skillet, melt 1 tablespoon of butter over moderate heat. Pour the butter into a small bowl; stir in bread crumbs. Set the buttered crumbs aside.

2 In the skillet, heat the remaining 2 tablespoons of butter over low heat. Add onion; sauté until soft, 5 minutes. Increase the heat to moderate. Stir in scallops and mushrooms; sauté for 5 minutes.

3 Add flour to the scallops and mix well. Gradually stir in wine and water. Bring the mixture to a boil, stirring constantly, until the sauce thickens, 2 to 3 minutes. Stir in half-and-half; heat the mixture until it is hot but not boiling. Remove the skillet from the heat.

4 Divide the scallop mixture among the baking dishes. Sprinkle each serving with an equal amount of cheese and top the cheese with the buttered crumbs. Broil 4 inches from the heat until lightly browned on top, 1 to 2 minutes. Serve immediately.

STIR-FRIED SCALLOPS WITH VEGETABLES

One Serving: **Calories** 296 **Protein** 28g **Carbohydrates** 13g **Fat** 15g **Cholesterol** 50mg **Sodium** 509mg

¼ cup vegetable oil

1 pound bay scallops or small sea scallops

4 green onions, cut into 1½-inch lengths

2 cloves garlic, chopped

4 small carrots, thinly sliced

½ cup water

1 tablespoon cornstarch

1 tablespoon soy sauce

4 ounces snow peas, trimmed

 PREPARATION TIME **10 MINUTES**

 COOKING TIME **8 MINUTES**

SERVING SUGGESTION *Complete this quick main dish with a steaming dish of egg noodles tossed with butter and ground pepper.*

1 In a large skillet or wok, heat oil over high heat. Add scallops and stir-fry until they just turn opaque, about 2 minutes. Using a slotted spoon, transfer the scallops to a bowl and set them aside.

2 Reduce the heat to moderate. Add onions, garlic, and carrots to the skillet. Stir-fry the vegetables until they are softened but not browned, about 1 minute.

3 Add water to the skillet; reduce the heat to low. Cover the skillet and continue cooking the vegetables until the carrots are crisp-tender, about 2 minutes. Meanwhile, in a cup, combine cornstarch and soy sauce until the mixture is smooth.

4 Increase the heat to moderate; stir the cornstarch mixture into the carrots. Add snow peas and bring the mixture to a boil, stirring constantly. Return the scallops and any accumulated juices to the skillet and cook until the scallops are heated through, about 1 minute. Serve immediately.

STEAMED SPICY SCALLOPS

One Serving: **Calories** 149 **Protein** 20g **Carbohydrates** 7g **Fat** 4g **Cholesterol** 37mg **Sodium** 737mg

2 medium-size carrots, julienned

1 stalk celery, julienned

1 green onion, julienned

1 teaspoon seasoned salt

1 teaspoon dried tarragon, crumbled

⅛ teaspoon cayenne pepper

1 pound bay scallops or small sea scallops

1 tablespoon olive or vegetable oil

 PREPARATION TIME **11 MINUTES**

 COOKING TIME **13 MINUTES**

1 In a steamer or large stockpot, bring 1 to 1½ inches of water to a boil over high heat. Place the carrots, celery, and onion strips in a pie plate or dish with a 1-inch lip, which will fit inside the steamer.

2 Place a wire rack or several custard cups in the steamer to prop up the plate. Place the plate of vegetables on the rack. Steam the vegetables, covered, until the carrots are crisp-tender, 2 to 3 minutes.

3 Meanwhile, in a cup, combine salt, tarragon, and cayenne pepper. In a medium-size bowl, place scallops and oil; toss to coat. Sprinkle the scallops with the salt mixture and toss again to coat evenly.

4 Heap the scallops on top of the vegetables in the steamer. Cover and steam the scallops and vegetables until the scallops are just firm and white, 3 to 5 minutes. Serve immediately.

SCALLOP KEBABS WITH ORANGE SAUCE

One Serving: **Calories** 259 **Protein** 22g **Carbohydrates** 15g **Fat** 13g **Cholesterol** 68mg **Sodium** 439mg

3 small zucchini

1 pound large sea scallops

12 medium-size mushroom caps

For the orange sauce

¼ cup (½ stick) butter or margarine

1 cup orange juice

1 tablespoon grated orange peel (or 1 teaspoon dried orange peel)

1½ teaspoons cornstarch

1 teaspoon dried thyme leaves, crumbled

¼ teaspoon salt

 PREPARATION TIME **14 MINUTES** COOKING TIME **20 MINUTES**

1 Preheat the broiler. In a large saucepan, bring 2 inches of water to a boil over high heat. Meanwhile, cut zucchini into 1-inch-thick slices. Add the zucchini to the boiling water and cook for 2 minutes. Drain the zucchini and set the pan aside.

2 To make the sauce, in a medium-size saucepan, melt butter over moderate heat. Stir in orange juice, orange peel, cornstarch, thyme, and salt. Bring the mixture to a boil and cook until it is slightly thickened, 5 to 6 minutes. Remove the pan from the heat and keep the sauce warm.

3 Divide the zucchini, scallops, and mushroom caps into four equal amounts; thread them alternately onto four 12-inch metal skewers. Brush the kebabs with ½ cup of the sauce. Broil them 4 inches from the heat until they are lightly browned, 6 to 7 minutes, turning once during cooking. Serve immediately with the remaining sauce.

DEVILED CRAB

One Serving: **Calories** 329 **Protein** 18g **Carbohydrates** 22g **Fat** 18g **Cholesterol** 170mg **Sodium** 404mg

¼ cup (½ stick) butter or margarine

1 medium-size yellow onion, chopped

½ cup chopped green bell pepper

2 tablespoons all-purpose flour

1¼ cups milk

2 large egg yolks

2 teaspoons prepared mustard

1 tablespoon Worcestershire sauce

12 ounces crabmeat, flaked

1 cup fresh bread crumbs

 PREPARATION TIME **10 MINUTES**   COOKING TIME **20 MINUTES**

1 Preheat the oven to 400°F. In a medium-size saucepan, melt butter over moderate heat. Pour half of the butter into a small bowl and set it aside. Add onion and green pepper to the remaining butter in the saucepan and sauté until soft, about 5 minutes.

2 Stir flour into the onion mixture until well mixed. Gradually stir in milk. Cook, stirring constantly, until the mixture thickens. Remove the pan from the heat.

3 One at a time, add egg yolks to the milk mixture, stirring well after each yolk has been added. Add mustard and Worcestershire sauce; stir thoroughly. Return the pan to moderate heat and cook 1 minute. Remove the pan from the heat; stir in crabmeat until well mixed.

4 Stir bread crumbs into the melted butter in the small bowl. Spoon the crab mixture into four 5½-inch shallow oven-safe dishes. Sprinkle an equal amount of the buttered crumbs over each dish. Bake until the crab is heated through and the crumb topping is golden brown, about 10 minutes. Serve immediately.

CRAB CAKES

CRAB CAKES

One Serving: **Calories** 465 **Protein** 18g **Carbohydrates** 25g **Fat** 33g **Cholesterol** 100mg **Sodium** 1411mg

½ cup packaged plain bread crumbs

½ cup mayonnaise

1 large egg

1 tablespoon lemon juice

½ teaspoon dry mustard

Dash hot red pepper sauce

1 pound crabmeat, flaked

¼ cup finely chopped celery

3 tablespoons chopped parsley (or 1 tablespoon parsley flakes)

1 tablespoon finely chopped yellow onion

2 tablespoons vegetable oil, divided

2 tablespoons (¼ stick) butter, divided

Lime wedges

 PREPARATION TIME
13 MINUTES

 COOKING TIME
16 MINUTES

SERVING SUGGESTION *With a fresh green salad and a glass of white wine, these crab cakes make a delicious lunch or light supper. Imitation crabmeat works beautifully in the recipe.*

1 In a large bowl, combine bread crumbs, mayonnaise, egg, lemon juice, mustard, and pepper sauce until well mixed. Stir in crabmeat, celery, parsley, and onion.

2 Divide the mixture into eight ⅓-cup portions; shape each portion into a ½-inch-thick cake. In a large skillet, heat 1 tablespoon oil with 1 tablespoon butter over moderate heat.

3 Fry four of the cakes until they are golden on both sides, 3 to 4 minutes on each side. Transfer the cakes to a serving platter and cover to keep them warm. Wipe the skillet with a paper towel and repeat to cook the remaining crab cakes in the remaining oil and butter. Arrange the crab cakes on a warm serving platter. Serve immediately with lime wedges on the side.

Scalloped Oysters with Clams

One Serving: **Calories** 390 **Protein** 11g **Carbohydrates** 23g **Fat** 29g **Cholesterol** 97mg **Sodium** 603mg

1 small yellow onion

½ pint shucked oysters (or one 8-ounce can whole oysters)

¼ cup half-and-half

1 teaspoon Worcestershire sauce

½ cup (1 stick) butter or margarine

1 cup saltine-cracker crumbs (about 30 crackers)

½ cup fresh bread crumbs

2 tablespoons chopped parsley

1 can (6 ½ ounces) chopped clams, drained

 PREPARATION TIME
10 MINUTES

COOKING TIME
35 MINUTES

1 Preheat the oven to 375°F. Lightly grease a 10- by 6-inch baking dish. Chop onion. Reserving ¼ cup of the liquor, drain oysters. In a small bowl, combine the reserved oyster liquor, half-and-half, and Worcestershire sauce. Set the mixture aside.

2 In a medium-size saucepan, melt butter over moderate heat. Add the onion and sauté until it begins to soften, about 3 minutes. Stir in cracker crumbs, bread crumbs, and parsley.

3 Spoon half of the crumb mixture into the prepared baking dish. Arrange the drained oysters and clams over the crumbs. Top with the remaining crumb mixture. Pour the half-and-half mixture over the top layer. Bake, uncovered, until heated through, 20 to 25 minutes.

Clam Patties

One Serving: **Calories** 317 **Protein** 26g **Carbohydrates** 16g **Fat** 16g **Cholesterol** 166mg **Sodium** 323mg

2 cans (6 ½ ounces each) chopped clams, drained

2 large eggs

1 cup saltine-cracker crumbs (about 30 crackers)

2 tablespoons finely chopped green onion top

1 tablespoon lemon juice

½ teaspoon dried thyme leaves, crumbled

3 tablespoons vegetable oil

Lemon slices (optional)

Tartar sauce (optional)

 PREPARATION TIME
10 MINUTES

COOKING TIME
7 MINUTES

1 In a medium-size bowl, combine clams, eggs, cracker crumbs, green onion top, lemon juice, and thyme.

2 In a large skillet, heat oil over moderate heat. Spoon the clam mixture into four mounds in the skillet. Using a spatula, flatten each mound to a ½-inch-thick patty. Cook the clam patties until browned on both sides, about 3 minutes for each side.

3 Transfer the clam patties to a warm serving platter and garnish them with lemon slices, if desired. Serve immediately, passing prepared tartar sauce separately, if desired.

Time Savers

SHRIMP
A package of shelled, frozen shrimp will keep in the freezer for up to a year. If you don't have time to thaw the shrimp in the refrigerator, you can cook them frozen as long as they're not being deep-fried. Cook the shrimp at a slightly lower temperature than the recipe calls for, and cook them slightly longer—about 1¼ times as long as you would thawed shrimp.

POULTRY

ORANGE-GLAZED BARBECUE CHICKEN (PAGE 134)

CHICKEN

The all-time favorite fowl appears in a mouth-watering selection of fast and economical dishes. However you serve it, chicken pleases friends and family.

BUFFALO CHICKEN WINGS

One Serving: **Calories** 767 **Protein** 44g **Carbohydrates** 8g **Fat** 62g **Cholesterol** 160mg **Sodium** 536mg

2 **pounds chicken wings (approximately 12 wings)**

Vegetable oil for frying

¼ **cup (½ stick) butter or margarine**

1 **tablespoon hot red pepper sauce**

1 **small bunch celery**

For the blue cheese dip

½ **cup sour cream**

½ **cup mayonnaise**

1 **ounce blue cheese, crumbled (¼ cup)**

2 **tablespoons chopped parsley**

½ **teaspoon Worcestershire sauce**

  PREPARATION TIME
9 MINUTES

 COOKING TIME
25 MINUTES

FOOD NOTE *This sensational appetizer originated in Buffalo, New York. Dip the hot chicken in the cool blue cheese dip, and wash it all down with a tall beer or soft drink.*

1 Cut the tips off chicken wings and discard (or freeze to use in soup stock). Split the remaining part of each wing at the joint into 2 pieces. In a large saucepan, heat 2 inches of oil over moderate heat to 375°F. Add half of the wing pieces and fry them until they are golden brown, 12 to 15 minutes.

2 Meanwhile, make the blue cheese dip. In a small bowl, combine sour cream, mayonnaise, crumbled blue cheese, chopped parsley, and Worcestershire sauce until well mixed. Cover the dip and refrigerate it until the chicken is ready to serve.

3 Drain the first batch of fried wings on a baking sheet lined with paper towels, keeping them warm. Repeat to fry the second half of the wings. Meanwhile, in a small saucepan, melt butter over low heat and stir in red pepper sauce. Cut celery into 4-inch-long sticks.

4 Drizzle or toss the drained chicken wings with the pepper-sauce mixture. Arrange the wings and celery sticks on a platter. Serve the chicken and celery, passing the blue cheese dip separately.

TIME SAVERS

POULTRY
• For a quick glaze for chicken or turkey, brush the pieces with a mixture of prepared barbecue sauce and a tablespoon or two of orange juice. This glaze goes particularly well on broiled or barbecued chicken.

• Prepared teriyaki sauce makes the quickest marinade for chicken or turkey, and it's always easy to keep a bottle on the shelf. For best results in the shortest time, cut the boned meat into pieces to soak in more of the marinade, then stir-fry.

• It is worth investing in some poultry shears for cutting up whole chicken; they go through joints, bones, and meat easily. This will save the extra expense of buying pre-cut poultry. The shears are available in most kitchen-supply stores.

PARSLEY MUSTARD CHICKEN

One Serving: **Calories** 845 **Protein** 108g **Carbohydrates** 4g **Fat** 42g **Cholesterol** 345mg **Sodium** 481mg

- **1 chicken (about 3¼ pounds), cut into serving pieces**
- **1 tablespoon butter or margarine**
- **2 tablespoons finely chopped yellow onion**
- **1 clove garlic, finely chopped**
- **½ cup fresh bread crumbs**
- **2 tablespoons finely chopped parsley**
- **¼ cup mayonnaise**
- **2 teaspoons Dijon mustard**

PREPARATION TIME
10 MINUTES

COOKING TIME
28 MINUTES

FOOD NOTE *In France, a preparation of parslied crumbs is called* persillade. *It complements chicken perfectly, as would a side dish of steamed broccoli or cauliflower florets.*

1 Preheat the broiler. Arrange chicken pieces, skin side down, on the rack over a broiler pan. Broil the chicken 5 inches from the heat until lightly browned and almost tender, about 20 minutes.

2 Meanwhile, in a small saucepan, melt butter over moderate heat. Add onion and garlic; sauté until soft, about 5 minutes. Stir in bread crumbs and parsley. Remove the pan from the heat and set it aside. In a cup, combine mayonnaise and mustard.

3 Turn the chicken pieces over and continue broiling until they are tender, about 5 more minutes.

4 Spread or brush the mayonnaise mixture over the top of the chicken pieces. Sprinkle or pat the parsley mixture onto the chicken pieces. Continue broiling the chicken until the crumb coating is golden brown, about 3 minutes. Serve immediately.

TANGY BROILED CHICKEN

One Serving: **Calories** 755 **Protein** 108g **Carbohydrates** 13g **Fat** 28g **Cholesterol** 329mg **Sodium** 1437mg

- **1 chicken (about 3¼ pounds), cut into quarters**
- **¼ teaspoon each salt and ground black pepper**
- **⅔ cup ketchup**
- **2 tablespoons soy sauce**
- **1 clove garlic, finely chopped**
- **½ teaspoon ground ginger**
- **¼ teaspoon dry mustard**
  Parsely sprigs (optional)

PREPARATION TIME
5 MINUTES

COOKING TIME
35 MINUTES

1 Preheat the broiler. Arrange chicken quarters, skin side down, on the rack over a broiler pan. Season the chicken with salt and pepper. Broil the chicken 5 inches from the heat until lightly browned and almost tender, about 20 minutes.

2 Meanwhile, in a small saucepan, combine ketchup, soy sauce, garlic, ginger, and mustard. Bring the mixture to a boil over moderate heat, stirring occasionally.

3 Turn the chicken over and continue broiling for 5 minutes. Brush the chicken generously with some of the ketchup mixture; continue broiling until the sauce on the chicken is bubbly and lightly browned, about 2 minutes, taking care not to burn it.

4 Place the chicken on a warm serving platter, and pour any remaining sauce over it. Garnish the chicken with sprigs of parsley, if desired, and serve immediately.

CHICKEN TACOS

CHICKEN TACOS

One Serving: **Calories** 409 **Protein** 34g **Carbohydrates** 34g **Fat** 18g **Cholesterol** 78mg **Sodium** 957mg

1 tablespoon vegetable oil

1 medium-size yellow onion, chopped

1 pound ground chicken

1 tablespoon all-purpose flour

1 can (4 ounces) chopped green chilies, undrained

1 teaspoon chili powder

½ teaspoon dried oregano

½ teaspoon salt

8 taco shells

2 ounces Monterey Jack cheese with jalapeño peppers, coarsely grated (½ cup)

1 to 1½ cups shredded iceberg lettuce

⅔ cup prepared tomato salsa

PREPARATION TIME
8 MINUTES

COOKING TIME
14 MINUTES

SERVING SUGGESTION *This Mexican-style favorite goes naturally with refried beans. For a lighter touch, serve it with a green salad tossed with chopped tomatoes and avocado.*

1 In a large skillet, heat oil over moderate heat. Add onion and sauté until soft, about 5 minutes. Increase the heat to moderately high and add ground chicken. Cook the chicken until lightly browned, stirring frequently, about 3 minutes.

2 Sprinkle flour over the chicken mixture and stir until blended. Stir in undrained chopped green chilies, chili powder, oregano, and salt; continue cooking, stirring occasionally, for 5 minutes. Remove the chicken mixture from the heat.

3 Spoon the chicken mixture into taco shells. Sprinkle each with grated cheese and top and with some shredded lettuce. Spoon salsa over the lettuce and serve immediately.

133

ORANGE-GLAZED BARBECUE CHICKEN

One Serving: **Calories** 677 **Protein** 56g **Carbohydrates** 49g **Fat** 29g **Cholesterol** 173mg **Sodium** 219mg

½ **cup orange marmalade**

⅓ **cup firmly packed dark brown sugar**

⅓ **cup orange juice**

¼ **cup red-wine vinegar**

1 **tablespoon Dijon mustard**

½ **teaspoon ground ginger**

2 **cloves garlic, finely chopped**

1 **tablespoon plus 2 teaspoons vegetable oil**

1 **chicken (about 3¼ pounds), cut into serving pieces**

	PREPARATION TIME		COOKING TIME
	5 MINUTES		**38 MINUTES**

1 Preheat the oven to 425°F. In a small bowl, combine marmalade, brown sugar, orange juice, vinegar, mustard, ginger, garlic, and 2 teaspoons oil. Set the mixture aside.

2 In a large oven-safe skillet, heat the remaining 1 tablespoon of oil over moderately high heat. Cook the chicken until lightly browned on all sides, about 8 minutes. Drain the fat; add the marmalade mixture to the skillet and bring it to a boil.

3 Transfer the skillet to the oven. Bake until the chicken juices run clear, about 15 minutes for white meat, 30 minutes for dark. Skim the fat from the sauce. Transfer the chicken to a warm platter, spoon the sauce over it, and serve.

MICROWAVE VERSION

Omit vegetable oil and add 2 tablespoons all-purpose flour to the list of ingredients. Remove the skin from chicken pieces. In a microwave-safe 13- by 9-inch baking dish, combine brown sugar and flour until well mixed. Add marmalade, orange juice, vinegar, mustard, ginger, and garlic; mix well. Add the chicken pieces and toss to coat with the marmalade mixture. Arrange the chicken in a single layer in the dish, with the thickest part of the pieces around the sides of the dish, and the narrowest parts toward the center.

Cover the baking dish with plastic wrap vented at one corner. Microwave the chicken on high power for 9 minutes. Spoon some sauce over each piece. Replace the cover, rotate the dish halfway, and microwave on high until the chicken juices run clear, 9 to 12 more minutes.

TIME SAVERS

QUICK-COOKED CHICKEN
If you need cooked chicken for a salad or other recipe, poach it on the stove or in the microwave. For two cups of cooked chicken, you will need two 6-ounce skinned and boned breasts.

To cook the chicken conventionally, place the breasts in a large skillet with 1⅓ cups water or broth. Bring to a boil, then reduce the heat and simmer, covered, for 12 to 14 minutes, or until the chicken is tender and cooked through.

To microwave the chicken, wrap each breast in a double length of paper towels. Moisten with water and place them on a microwave-safe plate. Cook on high power for 4 to 5 minutes. Let the chicken stand for 3 minutes before cutting.

CRUSTY OVEN-BAKED CHICKEN

CRUSTY OVEN-BAKED CHICKEN

One Serving: **Calories** 341 **Protein** 42g **Carbohydrates** 6g **Fat** 16g **Cholesterol** 133mg **Sodium** 373mg

¼ **cup (½ stick) butter or margarine**

1 **clove garlic, finely chopped**

1 **cup fresh bread crumbs**

3 **tablespoons grated Parmesan cheese**

1 **tablespoon finely chopped parsley**

½ **teaspoon dried marjoram, crumbled**

¼ **teaspoon dried thyme leaves, crumbled**

⅛ **teaspoon ground black pepper**

4 **large boneless, skinless chicken-breast halves (about 1½ pounds)**

 PREPARATION TIME **10 MINUTES**

 COOKING TIME **28 MINUTES**

SERVING SUGGESTION *A crisp green salad with cucumber and snow peas makes a light accompaniment to this crunchy chicken.*

1 Preheat the oven to 400°F. Lightly grease a baking sheet. In a small saucepan, melt butter over moderate heat. Add garlic and sauté for 10 seconds. Remove the pan from the heat.

2 On a sheet of wax paper, combine bread crumbs, cheese, parsley, marjoram, thyme, and pepper. One at a time, dip chicken breasts into the garlic butter, letting the excess drain back into the saucepan. Roll the chicken breasts in the crumb mixture, coating them evenly. Pat the crumb mixture onto the chicken to make it stick, if necessary.

3 Arrange the chicken pieces in a single layer on the prepared baking sheet. Pat any remaining crumbs onto the top surface of the chicken breasts and drizzle them with any remaining garlic butter. Bake until the chicken is lightly browned and cooked through, about 25 to 30 minutes. Serve immediately.

HONEY-GLAZED CHICKEN WITH ORANGES

One Serving: **Calories** 571 **Protein** 52g **Carbohydrates** 51g **Fat** 18g **Cholesterol** 148mg **Sodium** 141mg

4 **chicken-breast halves with wings (about 3 pounds)**

1/3 **cup honey**

1/3 **cup apricot preserves**

2 **tablespoons orange juice**

1 **tablespoon lemon juice**

1 **teaspoon ground ginger**

2 **navel oranges**

Pinch salt

Watercress sprigs (optional)

 PREPARATION TIME
5 MINUTES

COOKING TIME
29 MINUTES

SERVING SUGGESTION *On the side, toss steamed green beans with lemon juice, melted butter, and chopped parsley.*

1 Preheat the broiler. Cut chicken wings off the breasts. Arrange the chicken breasts and wings, skin side down, on the rack over a broiler pan. Broil the chicken 5 inches from the heat until lightly browned, about 15 minutes.

2 Meanwhile, in a small bowl, combine honey, apricot preserves, orange juice, lemon juice, and ginger. Brush the chicken with some of the honey mixture and broil 1 more minute.

3 Turn the chicken over and continue broiling until the chicken is tender, about 10 minutes. Meanwhile, using a sharp knife, cut all the peel off oranges. Cut the peeled oranges crosswise into 1/2-inch-thick slices. Add the oranges to the broiler pan with the chicken. Season the chicken with salt.

4 Brush the orange slices and chicken with the remaining honey mixture and continue broiling until the chicken is lightly browned and the orange slices are glazed, about 2 more minutes. Arrange the chicken and oranges on a warm serving platter, garnish with watercress, if desired, and serve.

SAVORY PAN-FRIED CHICKEN BREASTS

One Serving: **Calories** 453 **Protein** 44g **Carbohydrates** 15g **Fat** 24g **Cholesterol** 150mg **Sodium** 321mg

1/2 **cup ground pecans**

1/3 **cup packaged plain bread crumbs**

1 **teaspoon dried sage, crumbled**

1/4 **teaspoon salt**

1/4 **teaspoon cayenne pepper**

1/4 **cup all-purpose flour**

1 **large egg**

2 **tablespoons water**

4 **large boneless, skinless chicken-breast halves (about 1 1/2 pounds)**

3 **tablespoons vegetable oil**

Pecan halves (optional)

 PREPARATION TIME
10 MINUTES

COOKING TIME
8 MINUTES

FOOD NOTE *Enjoy this easy Southern-style chicken, coated with the distinctive taste and delightful crunch of pecans.*

1 On a large sheet of wax paper, combine ground pecans, bread crumbs, sage, salt, and cayenne pepper. On another sheet of wax paper, place flour. In a pie plate, beat egg with 2 tablespoons water. Coat each chicken breast first with the flour, then the egg mixture, then the pecan mixture.

2 In a large skillet, heat oil over moderately high heat. Add the chicken; cook until the pieces are golden brown on both sides, 3 to 4 minutes on each side. Transfer the chicken to a warm platter. Garnish with pecan halves, if desired, and serve.

CHICKEN PROVENÇAL

CHICKEN PROVENÇAL

One Serving: **Calories** 336 **Protein** 19g **Carbohydrates** 11g **Fat** 25g **Cholesterol** 80mg **Sodium** 628mg

2 tablespoons olive oil

4 whole chicken legs (about 2 pounds)

1 medium-size yellow onion

2 cloves garlic

½ teaspoon saffron threads (optional)

1 cup canned reduced-sodium chicken broth

½ cup dry white wine

1 can (14½ or 16 ounces) whole, peeled tomatoes, drained and halved

1 teaspoon dried rosemary, crumbled

1 bay leaf

2 small zucchini

½ cup small pitted black olives

Salt and ground black pepper to taste

 PREPARATION TIME
5 MINUTES

 COOKING TIME
40 MINUTES

FOOD NOTE *Olive oil, tomatoes, garlic, and olives are all typical of Provence cuisine and give this dish a truly Mediterranean savor.*

1 In a 5-quart Dutch oven or a large, deep skillet, heat oil over moderate heat. Add chicken and cook until well browned on all sides, about 15 minutes. Meanwhile, cut onion into 8 wedges; finely chop garlic.

2 Transfer the chicken to a plate; drain all but 2 tablespoons of the drippings. Combine the onion, garlic, and saffron if desired, in the Dutch oven; sauté for 3 minutes.

3 Add broth and wine to the onion mixture. Increase the heat to high and bring the mixture to a boil. Stir in tomatoes, rosemary, and bay leaf. Add the chicken; cover the Dutch oven, reduce the heat to moderate, and cook for 10 minutes.

4 Meanwhile, slice zucchini. Stir the zucchini and olives into the chicken and cook for 5 minutes. Uncover the pan and continue cooking until the chicken juices run clear, about 5 more minutes. Season the mixture with salt and pepper, discard the bay leaf, and serve.

SPICED CHICKEN

One Serving: **Calories** 454 **Protein** 33g **Carbohydrates** 15g **Fat** 29g **Cholesterol** 38mg **Sodium** 415mg

½ teaspoon salt

½ teaspoon ground black pepper

½ teaspoon ground cinnamon

½ teaspoon ground cloves

4 chicken legs, cut into thighs and drumsticks (about 2 pounds)

1½ tablespoons vegetable oil

1 medium-size yellow onion

1 stalk celery

2 tablespoons raisins

¾ cup orange juice, divided

2 teaspoons cornstarch

¼ cup slivered almonds

Salt to taste

PREPARATION TIME
5 MINUTES

COOKING TIME
30 MINUTES

1 In a small bowl or cup, combine salt, pepper, cinnamon, and cloves. Sprinkle chicken pieces on all sides with the spice mixture. In a large skillet, heat oil over moderately high heat. Add the chicken pieces and cook until lightly browned on one side, about 10 minutes.

2 Meanwhile, slice onion and celery. Turn the chicken pieces over; add the onion and celery to the skillet. Cook the chicken until the second side is browned, about 5 minutes.

3 Add raisins and ½ cup orange juice to the chicken mixture. Reduce the heat to moderately low, cover the skillet, and cook the chicken until tender, 15 minutes.

4 Meanwhile, in a cup, combine cornstarch and the remaining ¼ cup orange juice. Stir the cornstarch mixture and almonds into the chicken mixture. Bring the sauce to a boil and cook until thickened, 1 to 2 more minutes; season with salt. Transfer the chicken to a serving platter, pour the sauce over it, and serve.

PAPRIKA CHICKEN

One Serving: **Calories** 423 **Protein** 34g **Carbohydrates** 12g **Fat** 27g **Cholesterol** 105mg **Sodium** 480mg

2 tablespoons vegetable oil

4 large chicken-breast halves (about 2½ pounds)

2 medium-size yellow onions

1 medium-size green bell pepper

1 can (14½ or 16 ounces) whole, peeled tomatoes

2 tablespoons paprika

½ cup canned reduced-sodium chicken broth

½ cup sour cream

Salt and ground black pepper to taste

Chopped parsley (optional)

PREPARATION TIME
5 MINUTES

COOKING TIME
35 MINUTES

1 In a large skillet, heat oil over moderate heat. Add chicken breasts and cook until well browned on all sides, about 15 minutes. Meanwhile, coarsely chop onions. Core and seed bell pepper, and cut it into strips. Drain and chop tomatoes.

2 Transfer the chicken to a plate. Drain all but 2 tablespoons of the drippings in the pan. Stir in the chopped onions and pepper strips; sauté until they begin to soften, 3 minutes.

3 Add tomatoes, paprika, and chicken broth to the skillet; increase the heat to high and bring the mixture to a boil.

4 Return the chicken to the pan; reduce the heat to low, cover the skillet, and simmer the chicken and vegetables until they are tender and cooked through, about 10 minutes.

5 Stir sour cream into the chicken mixture and cook until just heated through (do not boil). Season the chicken with salt and pepper, sprinkle with parsley, if desired, and serve.

BROILED LIME CHICKEN

One Serving: **Calories** 368 **Protein** 51g **Carbohydrates** 2g **Fat** 16g **Cholesterol** 151mg **Sodium** 284mg

2 ½ **pounds chicken, cut into serving pieces**

2 **large limes**

1 **tablespoon butter or margarine**

2 **cloves garlic, finely chopped**

1 **teaspoon cracked black pepper**

1 **teaspoon dried basil, crumbled**

¼ **teaspoon salt**

 PREPARATION TIME
5 MINUTES

COOKING TIME
25 MINUTES

1 Preheat the broiler. Arrange chicken pieces, skin side down, on the rack over a broiler pan. Broil the chicken 5 inches from the heat until lightly browned on one side, about 20 minutes.

2 Meanwhile, finely grate only the green part of the lime peel to make about 1 teaspoon of lime zest. Cut the limes in half and squeeze them to extract ¼ cup lime juice.

3 In a small saucepan, melt butter over low heat. Add garlic and cook for 10 seconds. Remove the pan from the heat and stir in the lime zest and juice, pepper, basil, and salt. Brush the chicken pieces with some of the lime mixture.

4 Turn the chicken pieces over; brush them with more of the lime mixture. Continue broiling until the chicken is tender, 5 to 10 more minutes, brushing frequently with the lime mixture. Transfer the chicken to a platter, and serve immediately.

DEVILED DRUMSTICKS

One Serving: **Calories** 501 **Protein** 44g **Carbohydrates** 70g **Fat** 26g **Cholesterol** 142mg **Sodium** 874mg

2 **tablespoons vegetable oil**

12 **chicken drumsticks (about 3 pounds)**

2 **medium-size yellow onions, sliced**

⅓ **cup prepared steak sauce**

⅓ **cup plus 1 tablespoon water**

3 **tablespoons light brown sugar**

2 **tablespoons prepared mustard**

½ **teaspoon salt**

2 **teaspoons cornstarch**

1 **small green onion**

 PREPARATION TIME
5 MINUTES

 COOKING TIME
35 MINUTES

1 In a 12-inch skillet (preferably with nonstick coating), heat oil over moderately high heat. Add chicken drumsticks and cook until well browned on all sides, about 15 minutes.

2 Move the drumsticks to one side of the skillet. Add sliced onions and sauté for 3 minutes.

3 In a small bowl, combine steak sauce, ⅓ cup water, brown sugar, mustard, and salt until well mixed. Pour the sauce over the drumsticks and onions in the skillet. Reduce the heat to low, cover, and simmer the drumsticks until they are tender, 10 to 15 minutes.

4 Meanwhile, in a cup, combine 1 tablespoon water and cornstarch; set aside. Diagonally slice green onion into ½-inch pieces.

5 Using a slotted spoon, transfer the drumsticks to a warm serving platter. Increase the heat to moderate, and stir the cornstarch mixture into the skillet. Bring the mixture to a boil and cook the sauce until thickened. Pour the sauce over the chicken, sprinkle the green onion over it, and serve.

CHICKEN WITH APPLE RINGS

CHICKEN WITH APPLE RINGS

One Serving: **Calories** 396 **Protein** 41g **Carbohydrates** 27g **Fat** 14g **Cholesterol** 119mg **Sodium** 376mg

- ¼ **cup all-purpose flour**
- ¼ **teaspoon each salt and ground black pepper**
- 4 **large boneless, skinless chicken-breast halves (about 1½ pounds)**
- 2 **tablespoons (¼ stick) butter or margarine, divided**
- 2 **Granny Smith apples, unpeeled, cored and cut into ¼-inch-thick rings**
- 1 **tablespoon vegetable oil**
- ½ **cup canned reduced-sodium chicken broth**
- ¼ **cup half-and-half**
- ½ **teaspoon dried thyme leaves, crumbled**
- ½ **cup apple juice**
- 1 **teaspoon cornstarch**

PREPARATION TIME
5 MINUTES

COOKING TIME
15 MINUTES

SERVING SUGGESTION *Serve a dish of steamed new potatoes with butter and chopped parsley alongside this quick entrée.*

1 On a sheet of wax paper, combine flour, salt, and pepper. Dip chicken breasts into the flour until well coated, shaking off the excess.

2 In a large skillet, heat 1 tablespoon butter over moderate heat. Add apple rings and cook for 3 minutes, turning once, until slightly softened. Using a slotted spoon, transfer the apples to a bowl and keep them warm.

3 In the same skillet, heat 1 more tablespoon butter and 1 tablespoon oil over moderate heat. Add the chicken breasts; cook until golden brown on both sides, 2 to 3 minutes on each side. Using a slotted spoon, transfer the chicken to a warm serving platter.

4 Add chicken broth, half-and-half, and thyme to the skillet; bring the mixture to a boil. In a cup, combine apple juice and cornstarch. Stir the cornstarch mixture into the broth mixture. Return the sauce to a boil, stirring constantly. Cook until thickened and bubbly, about 1 minute. Pour the sauce over the chicken, top with apples, and serve.

START WITH A ROAST CHICKEN

A roast chicken makes a healthy start to a quick and nourishing meal. It is just as at home in salads and sandwiches as in hot meals like curry and tostadas. In fact, you will probably think of many more variations to add to the ideas you find here.

Start with a whole, fully cooked 3½-pound roast chicken. Of course you can cook your own (see page 25), but supermarkets are stocking delicious cooked ones these days, making things quite a bit easier. Remove the skin and bones from the chicken before beginning the recipe. Each recipe makes enough to serve four.

▼ **SPINACH CHICKEN SALAD** Shred the meat of **1 roast chicken**; chop **2 large tomatoes**, and slice **8 oz. Swiss or mozzarella cheese** into thin strips. Line a platter with **5 oz. spinach leaves**. In a small bowl, mix **½ cup vegetable oil, 3 Tbsp. Dijon mustard**, and **2 Tbsp. red-wine vinegar**. Arrange chicken, tomatoes, and cheese strips over spinach. Pour some of the dressing over salad; pass remaining dressing on the side.

▲ **CHICKEN-CHUTNEY CROISSANTS** Shred the meat of **1 roast chicken**. In a large bowl, combine chicken, **1 cup thinly sliced celery, ⅓ cup mayonnaise, 2 Tbsp. chopped chutney, 1 tsp. finely grated onion**, and **¾ tsp. salt**. Split **4 croissants** in half horizontally. Spoon an equal amount of the mixture into each croissant.

▼ **BARBECUED CHICKEN SLOPPY JOES** Shred the meat of **1 roast chicken**. Preheat the broiler. In a large saucepan, melt **2 Tbsp. butter or margarine** over moderate heat. Add **1 medium-size yellow onion**, chopped, and **1 large green bell pepper**, diced. Sauté until soft, about 5 minutes. Stir in chicken and **1 cup prepared barbecue sauce**. Bring mixture to a boil, stirring frequently. Split and toast **4 hamburger buns**. Spoon the chicken mixture over the buns and sprinkle with **½ cup grated Cheddar cheese**. Place under the broiler until cheese melts.

◀ **CHICKEN-FETA SALAD** Shred the meat of **1 roast chicken**. Preheat the oven to 400°F. In a small baking pan, spread **¼ cup walnut pieces** and bake until toasted, about 5 minutes. Meanwhile, in a large salad bowl, combine **2 medium-size heads Bibb lettuce**, torn into small pieces, chicken, and **3 oz. feta cheese**, crumbled. Top salad with toasted walnuts and **1 tomato**, chopped. Gently toss with **prepared vinaigrette salad dressing.**

▶ **CHICKEN TOSTADAS** Shred the meat of **1 roast chicken**. In a small saucepan, heat **one 16-oz. can refried beans** until hot. In a medium-size saucepan, heat chicken and **1 cup prepared tomato salsa** until hot. On each of **8 tostada shells**, spread one-eighth of the refried beans. Top with one-eighth of the shredded chicken mixture. Garnish with **shredded lettuce, avocado slices**, and **sour cream.**

◀ **CURRIED CHICKEN** Chop the meat of **1 roast chicken**. In a medium-size saucepan, melt **2 Tbsp. butter**. Add **1 small yellow onion**, chopped, and **2 tsp. curry powder**; cook until onion is soft, about 5 minutes. Stir in **2 Tbsp. all-purpose flour** and **½ tsp. salt**; cook 1 minute. Gradually stir in **¾ cup milk**. Cook, stirring constantly, until sauce is thickened and bubbly, about 5 minutes. Stir in chicken; heat through. Serve over **cooked white rice.**

CHICKEN BREASTS WITH PEPPER SAUCE

One Serving: **Calories** 292 **Protein** 41g **Carbohydrates** 8g **Fat** 9g **Cholesterol** 99mg **Sodium** 264mg

- ¼ **cup all-purpose flour**
- ¼ **teaspoon ground black pepper**
- 4 **large boneless, skinless chicken-breast halves (about 1½ pounds)**
- 2 **tablespoons vegetable oil**
- 1 **cup canned reduced-sodium chicken broth**
- ½ **teaspoon dried basil or oregano, crumbled**
- ½ **cup diced red bell pepper**
- ½ **cup diced green bell pepper**
- 2 **tablespoons dry white wine or water**
- 1 **teaspoon cornstarch**

 PREPARATION TIME
14 MINUTES

COOKING TIME
15 MINUTES

DIET NOTE *Bell peppers are a good source of vitamin A, which is needed for healthy skin. This low-calorie dish is as appealing to the eye as it is to the taste; complement it with glass of white wine.*

1 On a sheet of wax paper, combine flour and pepper. Dip chicken breasts in the flour mixture until well coated, shaking off the excess.

2 In a large skillet, heat oil over moderately high heat. Add the chicken; cook until golden brown, 2 to 3 minutes on each side. Transfer the chicken to a warm serving platter, cover, and keep them warm.

3 Wipe out the skillet with paper towels. Add broth and basil to the skillet; bring the mixture to a boil. Add red and green peppers, and cook for 3 minutes.

4 Meanwhile, in a cup, combine wine and cornstarch; stir the wine mixture into the broth mixture in the skillet. Bring to a boil, stirring constantly. Continue cooking until thickened, about 2 minutes. Spoon the sauce over the chicken and serve.

Shelf Magic

Easy and economical canned chicken is the basis of these two refreshing salads. With a loaf of French bread on the side, each makes a terrific entrée for a cool lunch or light supper.

CHICKEN COLESLAW

In a medium-size mixing bowl, combine **3 cups shredded cabbage, 1 medium-size red or green apple**, peeled (if desired) and chopped, and **½ cup coleslaw salad dressing**. Stir in **two 5-ounce cans white chunk chicken packed in water**, drained.

Toss the coleslaw lightly until it is just combined. Cover the bowl and place it in the freezer for 5 minutes to chill slightly. Spoon the coleslaw onto cold salad plates, and serve immediately.
SERVES 3

CHINESE CHICKEN SALAD

In a large bowl, combine **two 5-ounce cans white chunk chicken packed in water**, drained, **one 8-ounce can sliced water chestnuts**, drained, **4 green onions**, julienned, **1 red bell pepper**, thinly sliced, **8 ounces bean sprouts, 2 tablespoons sesame seeds**, and **1 cup canned dried chow mein noodles**.

Toss the salad with **½ cup Oriental-style salad dressing** and a handful of **cashew nuts**. Serve immediately.
SERVES 3

MUSHROOM CHICKEN

One Serving: **Calories** 308 **Protein** 30g **Carbohydrates** 11g **Fat** 15g **Cholesterol** 95mg **Sodium** 324mg

¼ **cup all-purpose flour**

¼ **teaspoon each salt and ground black pepper**

4 **large chicken-breast halves (about 2 ½ pounds), skinned**

2 **tablespoons butter or margarine, divided**

1 **tablespoon vegetable oil**

8 **ounces mushrooms**

4 **green onions**

⅓ **cup canned reduced-sodium chicken broth**

¼ **cup dry white wine**

½ **cup half-and-half**

PREPARATION TIME 15 MINUTES

COOKING TIME 16 MINUTES

1 On a sheet of wax paper, combine flour, salt, and pepper. Dip chicken in the flour mixture until well coated, shaking off the excess. Reserve the remaining flour mixture.

2 In a large skillet, heat 1 tablespoon butter and oil over moderate heat. Add the chicken and cook until it is golden brown on both sides, about 3 minutes on each side. Meanwhile, cut mushrooms into quarters and set aside. Cut green tops of onions into 1-inch lengths; chop the white parts. (Keep white and green parts separate.)

3 Transfer the chicken to a plate. Add the remaining 1 tablespoon of butter to the skillet. Add the quartered mushrooms and sauté until wilted, about 3 minutes. Stir in chicken broth, wine, and the white part of the onions; bring the mixture to a boil.

4 Return the chicken to the skillet; reduce the heat to low, cover the skillet, and cook until the chicken is tender, about 5 minutes. Meanwhile, in a cup or small bowl, whisk half-and-half with 1 teaspoon of the flour mixture.

5 Transfer the chicken to a warm serving platter and keep it warm. Stir the half-and-half mixture and green onion tops into the mushroom sauce in the skillet. Cook, stirring constantly, until the sauce is thickened and bubbly, about 1 minute. Spoon the mushroom sauce over the chicken and serve.

MUSTARD CHICKEN

One Serving: **Calories** 147 **Protein** 28g **Carbohydrates** 3g **Fat** 2g **Cholesterol** 68mg **Sodium** 438mg

¼ **cup lemon juice**

2 **teaspoons Worcestershire sauce**

¼ **teaspoon salt**

¼ **teaspoon cayenne pepper**

4 **large boneless, skinless chicken-breast halves (about 1 ½ pounds)**

¼ **cup coarse-grained prepared mustard**

PREPARATION TIME 15 MINUTES

COOKING TIME 16 MINUTES

1 In a medium-size bowl, combine lemon juice, Worcestershire sauce, salt, and cayenne. Add the chicken and turn it to coat evenly. Let the chicken stand for 10 minutes to marinate.

2 Preheat the broiler. Drain the chicken and arrange the pieces on the rack over a broiler pan. Brush or spread half of the mustard on top of the chicken. Broil the chicken 5 inches from the heat until golden brown on one side, about 8 minutes.

3 Turn the chicken breasts over and spread them with the remaining mustard. Continue broiling the chicken until tender and cooked through, 5 to 8 minutes. Serve immediately.

SOUTHWESTERN CHICKEN ROLLS

SOUTHWESTERN CHICKEN ROLLS

One Serving: **Calories** 461 **Protein** 47g **Carbohydrates** 9g **Fat** 26g **Cholesterol** 156mg **Sodium** 445mg

4 large boneless, skinless chicken-breast halves (about 1½ pounds)

¼ teaspoon salt

4 ounces Monterey Jack cheese with jalapeño peppers

⅓ cup packaged plain bread crumbs

2 to 3 tablespoons all-purpose flour

1 large egg

1 tablespoon milk

¼ cup vegetable oil

Prepared tomato salsa (optional)

PREPARATION TIME
11 MINUTES

COOKING TIME
25 MINUTES

SERVING SUGGESTION *A salad of sliced avocados and chopped tomatoes, drizzled with vinaigrette, pairs with these chicken rolls.*

1 Preheat the oven to 400°F. Place the chicken breasts between sheets of wax paper or plastic wrap; using a mallet, pound each piece until it is about ¼-inch thick. Sprinkle the chicken breasts with salt.

2 Cut cheese into 4 strips. Place one strip of cheese in the center of each chicken breast. Fold the sides of the chicken over the cheese to enclose completely. Secure with wooden toothpicks, if necessary.

3 On two separate sheets of wax paper, place bread crumbs and 2 tablespoons flour. In a pie plate, combine egg with milk. Coat the chicken rolls first with the flour, then with the egg mixture, then with the bread crumbs.

4 In an oven-safe skillet, heat oil over moderate heat. Cook the chicken rolls until lightly browned on all sides, 5 minutes. Place the skillet in the oven and bake until the chicken feels firm to the touch, 15 to 20 minutes. Remove the toothpicks. Serve with salsa, if desired.

BRAISED CHICKEN WITH VEGETABLES

BRAISED CHICKEN WITH VEGETABLES

One Serving: **Calories** 481 **Protein** 23g **Carbohydrates** 48g **Fat** 22g **Cholesterol** 80mg **Sodium** 550mg

2 tablespoons vegetable oil

4 whole chicken legs (about 2 pounds)

1 pound small red potatoes

4 large carrots

2 small yellow onions

1½ cups canned reduced-sodium chicken broth

½ teaspoon dried thyme leaves, crumbled

¼ teaspoon ground black pepper

2 tablespoons water

2 teaspoons cornstarch

1 cup frozen green peas, partially thawed

 PREPARATION TIME
5 MINUTES

 COOKING TIME
35 MINUTES

SERVING SUGGESTION *Flavor a loaf of French bread with garlic butter, made by sautéing chopped garlic and parsley in butter.*

1 In a 5-quart Dutch oven or stockpot, heat oil over moderate heat. Add chicken legs and brown well on all sides, about 15 minutes.

2 Meanwhile, cut unpeeled potatoes into quarters. Peel and cut carrots into 1-inch chunks. Peel and cut onions in half. Transfer the chicken to a plate; drain all but 1 tablespoon of the oil. Add the potatoes, carrots, and onions to the pan; sauté for 3 minutes.

3 Add chicken broth, thyme leaves, and pepper to the potato mixture. Increase the heat to high and bring the mixture to a boil. Return the chicken to the pan. Reduce the heat to low, cover, and simmer until the chicken juices run clear, about 15 minutes. Using a slotted spoon, transfer the chicken and vegetables to a platter, keeping them warm.

4 In a cup, combine water and cornstarch; stir it into the liquid in the pan. Increase the heat to high; add peas and cook until the mixture thickens, about 3 minutes. Pour the sauce over the chicken and serve.

148

TERIYAKI CHICKEN WITH BROCCOLI

One Serving: **Calories** 255 **Protein** 30g **Carbohydrates** 15g **Fat** 9g **Cholesterol** 68mg **Sodium** 783mg

- **1 pound boneless, skinless chicken breasts**
- **¼ cup prepared teriyaki sauce**
- **¼ cup orange juice**
- **1 teaspoon cornstarch**
- **½ teaspoon ground ginger**
- **2 tablespoons vegetable oil**
- **2 cups small broccoli florets**
- **1 can (8 ounces) sliced water chestnuts, drained**
- **Hot cooked rice or chow mein noodles (optional)**

PREPARATION TIME	COOKING TIME
8 MINUTES	**8 MINUTES**

COOK'S TIP *You can use fresh snow peas instead of the broccoli florets if you prefer. Either way, this light and flavorful stir-fry goes well with white rice or noodles.*

1 Cut chicken breasts into 1¼ -inch pieces; set the chicken aside. In a small bowl, combine teriyaki sauce, orange juice, cornstarch, and ginger; set the mixture aside.

2 In a wok or large skillet, heat oil over high heat. Add the chicken pieces and stir-fry until they are lightly browned, about 3 minutes. Using a slotted spoon, transfer the chicken to a bowl, leaving the drippings in the wok. Reduce the heat to moderate. Add broccoli to the skillet and stir-fry 1 minute.

3 Stir the teriyaki mixture and pour it into the wok with the broccoli. Cook the mixture, stirring constantly, until it is thickened and bubbly, about 1 minute. Add water chestnuts and the cooked chicken with any accumulated juices; continue cooking until heated through. Serve over hot cooked rice or chow mein noodles, if desired.

ORIENTAL CHICKEN

One Serving: **Calories** 330 **Protein** 34g **Carbohydrates** 6g **Fat** 16g **Cholesterol** 115mg **Sodium** 693mg

- **1 tablespoon vegetable oil**
- **8 large chicken thighs (about 2¼ pounds), skinned**
- **½ cup canned reduced-sodium chicken broth, divided**
- **¼ cup dry sherry**
- **1 clove garlic, sliced**
- **½ teaspoon ground ginger**
- **1 package (6 ounces) frozen snow peas**
- **2 tablespoons soy sauce**
- **2 teaspoons cornstarch**
- **½ teaspoon sugar**
- **Pinch red pepper flakes**

PREPARATION TIME	COOKING TIME
5 MINUTES	**28 MINUTES**

1 In a large skillet, heat oil over moderately high heat. Add chicken thighs and cook, turning occasionally, until they are well browned on all sides, about 15 minutes.

2 Add ¼ cup chicken broth, sherry, garlic, and ginger to the skillet; bring the mixture to a boil. Place frozen snow peas on top of the chicken. Reduce the heat to low and cover the skillet. Simmer the chicken and snow peas for 10 minutes, stirring occasionally to break the snow peas apart.

3 Meanwhile, in a cup or small bowl, combine soy sauce, cornstarch, sugar, red pepper flakes, and the remaining ¼ cup chicken broth. Stir the mixture thoroughly to dissolve the cornstarch.

4 Increase the heat to moderately high; stir the cornstarch mixture into the chicken and snow peas. Cook the mixture, stirring occasionally, until the thighs are tender and the sauce thickens, about 2 minutes. Transfer to a warm platter and serve.

Tarragon Chicken

One Serving: **Calories** 557 **Protein** 65g **Carbohydrates** 22g **Fat** 22g **Cholesterol** 196mg **Sodium** 605mg

1 tablespoon vegetable oil

1 tablespoon butter or margarine

1 chicken (about 3¼ pounds), cut into serving pieces

1 pound carrots

1 cup canned reduced-sodium chicken broth, divided

1 teaspoon dried tarragon, crumbled

¼ teaspoon salt

¼ teaspoon ground black pepper

1 teaspoon cornstarch

1 cup watercress sprigs (1 bunch)

PREPARATION TIME **5 MINUTES**

COOKING TIME **32 MINUTES**

1 In a 5-quart Dutch oven, heat oil and butter over moderate heat. Add chicken pieces and cook until well browned on all sides, about 15 minutes. Meanwhile, peel carrots, if desired, and cut them into 1½-inch sticks.

2 Add ⅔ cup chicken broth, the carrot sticks, tarragon, salt, and pepper to the chicken; bring the mixture to a boil. Reduce the heat to low; cover and simmer the chicken until tender, about 15 minutes. Meanwhile, in a cup, combine the remaining ⅓ cup chicken broth and cornstarch until the mixture is smooth.

3 Using a slotted spoon, transfer the chicken and carrots to a serving platter and keep them warm. Stir the cornstarch mixture and watercress into the Dutch oven. Increase the heat to moderate; cook the sauce until it is thickened and bubbly, about 2 minutes. Pour the sauce over the chicken and serve.

Hawaiian Chicken

One Serving: **Calories** 517 **Protein** 55g **Carbohydrates** 14g **Fat** 26g **Cholesterol** 181mg **Sodium** 187mg

1 chicken (about 3¼ pounds), cut into quarters

1 tablespoon butter or margarine

2 teaspoons cornstarch

1 can (8 ounces) pineapple slices in juice, undrained

1 tablespoon light brown sugar

1 teaspoon parsley flakes

½ teaspoon ground ginger

¼ teaspoon dry mustard

Salt and ground black pepper to taste

PREPARATION TIME **3 MINUTES**

COOKING TIME **30 MINUTES**

1 Preheat the broiler. Arrange chicken quarters, skin side down, on the rack over a broiler pan. Broil the chicken 5 inches from the heat until lightly browned and almost tender, 15 to 20 minutes.

2 Meanwhile, in a small saucepan, melt butter over moderate heat. Stir in cornstarch until blended. Add juice drained from pineapple slices to the cornstarch mixture and cook it until thickened and bubbly, about 45 seconds.

3 Stir brown sugar, parsley, ginger, and mustard into the pineapple sauce; remove the pan from the heat. Season the sauce with salt and ground black pepper.

4 Brush the chicken with some of the pineapple sauce and broil 2 more minutes. Turn the chicken over and continue broiling for 5 minutes.

5 Brush the chicken generously with more of the pineapple sauce and top the quarters with pineapple slices. Continue broiling until the sauce on the chicken is bubbly and the pineapple slices are glazed, about 4 minutes. Place the chicken and pineapple on a warm platter, and serve immediately.

CREAMY CHICKEN AND GRAPES

CREAMY CHICKEN AND GRAPES

One Serving: **Calories** 354 **Protein** 41g **Carbohydrates** 8g **Fat** 15g **Cholesterol** 117mg **Sodium** 276mg

2 tablespoons vegetable oil

4 large boneless, skinless chicken-breast halves (about 1½ pounds)

1 tablespoon butter or margarine

1 small yellow onion, finely chopped

1 teaspoon cornstarch

½ cup dry white wine

½ cup half-and-half

½ cup seedless green or red grapes, halved

Salt and ground black pepper to taste

PREPARATION TIME
10 MINUTES

COOKING TIME
12 MINUTES

SERVING SUGGESTION *For an elegant but easy side dish, cook brown rice in canned chicken broth, and mix in some sautéed mushrooms and chopped red onion.*

1 In a large skillet, heat oil over moderately high heat. Add chicken and cook until golden brown on both sides, 2 to 3 minutes on each side. Transfer the chicken to a plate and set it aside.

2 Reduce the heat to moderate and add butter to the skillet. Add onion and sauté for 3 minutes. In a cup, combine cornstarch and wine. Add the wine mixture to the skillet and cook, stirring continuously, until the mixture is thickened and bubbly, about 1 minute. Stir in half-and-half and grapes; cook 1 minute.

3 Return the chicken and any accumulated juices to the skillet. Cook until heated through. Season with salt and pepper, and serve.

CHICKEN SATAY WITH PEANUT SAUCE

One Serving: **Calories** 424 **Protein** 41g **Carbohydrates** 10g **Fat** 25g **Cholesterol** 96mg **Sodium** 835mg

½ teaspoon ground cumin

¼ teaspoon salt

3 tablespoons vegetable oil, divided

3 tablespoons lemon juice, divided

4 large boneless, skinless chicken-breast halves (about 1½ pounds)

1 medium-size yellow onion, sliced

½ cup water

2 tablespoons soy sauce

¼ teaspoon garlic powder

⅓ cup creamy peanut butter

Cilantro sprigs (optional)

PREPARATION TIME	COOKING TIME
11 MINUTES	**11 MINUTES**

FOOD NOTE *Traditional Thai satay has the meat skewered and grilled over a charcoal fire, then dipped into the peanut sauce just before eating. Try cooking the chicken breasts in this easy variation over the barbecue.*

1 Preheat the broiler. In a large bowl, combine cumin, salt, 2 table-spoons oil, and 2 tablespoons lemon juice. Add chicken breasts and turn to coat evenly. Let the chicken stand 10 minutes to marinate.

2 Meanwhile, in a medium-size saucepan, heat 1 tablespoon oil over moderate heat. Add onion and sauté until golden, about 7 minutes. Stir in water, soy sauce, garlic powder, and 1 tablespoon lemon juice. Bring the mixture to a boil.

3 Remove the pan from the heat. Using a wire whisk, beat in peanut butter until it is melted. Cover the pan and set the peanut sauce aside.

4 Arrange the chicken breasts on the rack over a broiler pan. Broil the chicken 4 inches from the heat for 4 minutes. Turn the chicken and continue broiling until it is tender, 2 to 5 more minutes. Transfer the chicken to a warm platter and garnish with cilantro, if desired. Serve it with the warm peanut sauce on the side.

BRAISED ITALIAN-STYLE CHICKEN

One Serving: **Calories** 418 **Protein** 34g **Carbohydrates** 18g **Fat** 24g **Cholesterol** 93mg **Sodium** 564mg

2 tablespoons olive oil

4 large chicken-breast halves (about 2½ pounds)

8 ounces mushrooms

2 cloves garlic

1 package (9 ounces) frozen cut green beans

1 cup prepared plain spaghetti sauce

1 cup canned reduced-sodium chicken broth

¼ teaspoon red pepper flakes

PREPARATION TIME	COOKING TIME
2 MINUTES	**35 MINUTES**

1 In a 5-quart Dutch oven or a large, deep skillet, heat oil over moderate heat. Add chicken breasts and cook until well browned on all sides, about 15 minutes.

2 Meanwhile, cut mushrooms into quarters; finely chop garlic. Transfer the chicken to a plate and set it aside. Pour off all but 1 tablespoon of the oil from the pan. Stir in the mushrooms, garlic, and frozen beans; sauté for 3 minutes.

3 Add spaghetti sauce, chicken broth, and pepper flakes. Increase the heat to high and bring the mixture to a boil. Return the chicken to the Dutch oven. Reduce the heat to low, cover, and simmer until the chicken and beans are tender, about 15 minutes. Place the chicken on a warm platter and serve.

CHICKEN AND SQUASH KEBABS

Chicken and Squash Kebabs

One Serving: **Calories** 372 **Protein** 33g **Carbohydrates** 16g **Fat** 20g **Cholesterol** 129mg **Sodium** 467mg

2 **medium-size yellow squash**

2 **medium-size zucchini**

6 **boneless, skinless chicken thighs (about 1¼ pounds)**

3 **tablespoons butter or margarine**

3 **cloves garlic, finely chopped**

6 **tablespoons lemon juice**

2 **tablespoons light brown sugar**

½ **teaspoon salt**

 PREPARATION TIME
8 MINUTES

 COOKING TIME
20 MINUTES

SERVING SUGGESTION *White rice cooked with a handful of blanched almonds and raisins sets off this low-calorie dish.*

1 Preheat the broiler. In a large saucepan, bring 2 inches of water to a boil over high heat. Meanwhile, cut yellow squash and zucchini into 1-inch-thick slices. Add the vegetables to the boiling water and cook until just softened, about 2 minutes.

2 Meanwhile, cut each boned chicken thigh into four chunks. In a medium-size saucepan, melt butter over moderate heat. Add garlic and sauté 10 seconds. Remove the pan from the heat and stir in lemon juice, brown sugar, and salt until well mixed.

3 Drain the vegetables. Add the vegetables and chicken to the butter mixture. Toss until well mixed. On four 12-inch metal skewers, alternately thread the chicken and vegetables, reserving any of the remaining butter mixture.

4 Broil the kebabs 4 inches from the heat until lightly browned, 6 to 8 minutes, turning the kebabs occasionally and brushing them with more of the butter mixture. Serve immediately.

OREGANO LEMON CHICKEN

One Serving: **Calories** 463 **Protein** 33g **Carbohydrates** 2g **Fat** 35g **Cholesterol** 158mg ·**Sodium** 325mg

8 **large chicken thighs (about 2 pounds)**

2 **teaspoons dried oregano leaves, crumbled**

¼ **teaspoon each salt and ground black pepper**

2 **tablespoons olive oil**

2 **tablespoons lemon juice**

1 **tablespoon Worcester-shire sauce**

 PREPARATION TIME
10 MINUTES

COOKING TIME
35 MINUTES

1 Preheat the oven to 450°F. In a 13- by 9-inch baking pan, arrange chicken thighs in a single layer, skin side down.

2 In a small bowl, combine oregano, salt, and pepper. Whisk in oil, lemon juice, and Worcestershire sauce. Drizzle half of the mixture over the chicken. Bake the chicken for 20 minutes.

3 Drain the excess fat from the chicken. Turn the chicken over and brush on the remaining oregano-oil mixture. Continue baking until the chicken thighs are tender and the juices run clear, about 15 minutes, and serve.

CHICKEN IN RED WINE

One Serving: **Calories** 827 **Protein** 73g **Carbohydrates** 15g **Fat** 45g **Cholesterol** 232mg **Sodium** 230mg

1 **chicken (about 3 ¼ pounds), cut into serving pieces**

Pinch salt and ground black pepper

⅓ **cup all-purpose flour, divided**

3 **tablespoons vegetable oil, divided**

8 **ounces small mushrooms**

8 **small white onions (about 4 ounces), peeled**

2 **cloves garlic, finely chopped**

1½ **cups dry red wine (such as Burgundy)**

1 **teaspoon dried thyme leaves (do not crumble)**

1 **bay leaf**

1 **tablespoon butter or margarine, softened**

2 **tablespoons chopped parsley**

PREPARATION TIME
11 MINUTES

COOKING TIME
34 MINUTES

1 Sprinkle the chicken pieces with salt and pepper. On a sheet of wax paper, place ¼ cup flour. Dip the chicken in the flour until well coated, shaking off the excess.

2 In a 5-quart Dutch oven, heat 2 tablespoons oil over moderately high heat. Add the chicken pieces, skin side down, to cover the bottom of the pan without crowding. Cook until the skin side is lightly browned, 5 to 7 minutes. Transfer the chicken pieces to a bowl and set it aside; discard the drippings.

3 In the same Dutch oven, heat the remaining 1 tablespoon oil over moderately high heat. Add mushrooms and onions; sauté until the vegetables are lightly browned, about 3 minutes. Stir in garlic; add wine, thyme, and bay leaf.

4 Return the chicken and any accumulated juices to the pan. Bring the mixture to a boil. Reduce the heat to low, cover, and cook the chicken until tender, 15 to 20 minutes. Meanwhile, in a cup, mix butter and the reserved flour into a paste.

5 Using a slotted spoon, transfer the chicken, mushrooms, and onions to a serving platter. Discard the bay leaf. Increase the heat to high and stir the flour paste into the remaining liquid. Bring the mixture to a boil, stirring constantly, and cook until slightly thickened. Pour some of the sauce over the chicken and sprinkle it with parsley. Serve, passing the extra sauce separately.

STIR-FRIED CHICKEN WITH ALMONDS

STIR-FRIED CHICKEN WITH ALMONDS

One Serving: **Calories** 380 **Protein** 32g **Carbohydrates** 21g **Fat** 20g **Cholesterol** 66mg **Sodium** 867mg

1 **pound boneless, skinless chicken breasts**

2 **cloves garlic**

8 **ounces green beans**

4 **large carrots**

1½ **cups canned reduced-sodium chicken broth, divided**

2 **tablespoons soy sauce**

4 **teaspoons cornstarch**

1 **teaspoon Oriental sesame oil**

3 **tablespoons vegetable oil**

⅓ **cup blanched whole almonds**

 PREPARATION TIME
15 MINUTES

 COOKING TIME
12 MINUTES

SERVING SUGGESTION *Serve this stir-fry with hot egg noodles tossed with a dash of soy sauce and Oriental sesame oil.*

1 Cut chicken into ½-inch-wide strips. Finely chop garlic. Cut green beans into 2-inch lengths. Peel carrots and slice them diagonally.

2 In a cup, combine ½ cup broth, soy sauce, cornstarch, and sesame oil; set aside. In a wok or large skillet, heat oil over high heat. Add almonds and sauté until lightly browned, 1 to 2 minutes. Using a slotted spoon, transfer the almonds to a medium-size bowl; set aside.

3 Add the chicken strips to the wok; stir-fry until lightly browned. Using a slotted spoon, add the chicken to the almonds.

4 Reduce the heat to moderate. Add the chopped garlic to the wok and stir-fry 10 seconds. Stir in the green beans, carrots, and remaining 1 cup chicken broth. Cover the pan and cook the vegetables until crisp-tender, about 5 minutes.

5 Stir the cornstarch mixture and add it to the vegetables; cook until the sauce is thickened and bubbly, about 1 minute. Stir in the chicken and almonds. Cook until just heated through, and serve immediately.

VARIATIONS ON THE BASIC CHICKEN BREAST

A flavorful sauce turns the everyday chicken breast into an elegant main dish. Start with the basic recipe for broiled chicken breasts, below, taking special care not to overcook them—they should be tender and juicy. Then pour on a sweet or savory sauce from the group at the right. Add a salad and rice or potatoes, and you have the makings of a memorable dinner party. Each recipe makes four servings.

BASIC BROILED CHICKEN BREASTS Preheat the broiler. In a medium-size bowl, place **4 large skinless, boneless chicken-breast halves** (about 6 ounces each); toss with **1 Tbsp. melted butter** and **¼ tsp. each salt and ground black pepper.** Arrange chicken on the rack over a broiler pan.

Broil the chicken 4 inches from the heat until lightly browned, 7 to 8 minutes. Meanwhile, prepare one of the sauces. Turn the chicken and continue broiling until tender and lightly browned, 4 to 7 more minutes. Place chicken on a warm serving platter and pour the sauce over it. Serve immediately.

► **CHEESE SAUCE** In a saucepan, melt **2 Tbsp. butter**. Stir in **1/4 cup chopped green onions**; cook for 1 minute. Stir in **2 Tbsp. all-purpose flour**; gradually stir in **1 1/4 cups milk**. Cook, stirring, until sauce thickens. Stir in **3/4 cup grated sharp Cheddar cheese**, **1/2 tsp. Dijon mustard**, and **1/2 tsp. paprika**; cook until cheese is just melted and smooth.

► **MUSHROOM SAUCE** In a saucepan, melt **2 Tbsp. butter**. Add **4 oz. sliced mushrooms**; sauté until tender. Stir in **2 Tbsp. all-purpose flour**. Gradually stir in **1 cup canned chicken broth**. Cook, stirring, until sauce thickens. Stir in **1 tsp. dried thyme leaves, crumbled**; season with **salt and pepper**.

► **SPICED CRANBERRY SAUCE** In a saucepan, combine **1 cup whole-berry cranberry sauce**, **1 tsp. dry mustard**, **1/2 tsp. Worcestershire sauce**, **1/8 tsp. ground ginger**, and **3 or 4 drops hot red pepper sauce**. Bring to a boil over moderate heat. In a cup, mix **1 Tbsp. cornstarch** with **2 Tbsp. water**. Stir mixture into sauce; boil for 1 minute.

◄ **HONEY MUSTARD SAUCE** In a blender, combine **1/4 cup coarse-grained prepared mustard** with **1/4 cup honey**, **2 Tbsp. ketchup**, and **6 Tbsp. olive oil** until well blended. Season the sauce with **salt and pepper to taste**.

◄ **CURRY SAUCE** In a saucepan, melt **2 Tbsp. butter or margarine** over moderate heat. Add **1 small yellow onion, sliced**; sauté until soft. Stir in **2 Tbsp. all-purpose flour** and **1 tsp. curry powder**. Gradually stir in **1 cup canned chicken broth** and **1/4 cup half-and-half**. Cook, stirring, until sauce thickens. Season the sauce with **salt and pepper to taste**.

TURKEY AND CORNISH GAME HENS

The quick cook's repertoire can even include these
surprisingly easy ideas for turkey and Cornish game hens.

TURKEY BREAST WITH MUSHROOMS

One Serving: **Calories** 306 **Protein** 28g **Carbohydrates** 9g **Fat** 18g **Cholesterol** 88mg **Sodium** 416mg

4 large turkey-breast cutlets
(about 1 pound)

¼ cup all-purpose flour

½ teaspoon salt

¼ teaspoon ground black
pepper

3 tablespoons vegetable oil,
divided

2 tablespoons (¼ stick)
butter or margarine

8 ounces mushrooms, sliced

1 clove garlic, finely
chopped

¼ cup canned reduced-
sodium chicken broth

1 tablespoon chopped
parsley

 PREPARATION TIME
9 MINUTES

COOKING TIME
15 MINUTES

SERVING SUGGESTION *For an easy side dish, prepare a packaged
stove-top stuffing mix; roll the cooked stuffing into 2-inch balls,
brush with oil, and bake at 400°F until browned, about 10 minutes.*

1 Place turkey cutlets between sheets of wax paper or plastic wrap;
using a mallet, pound each piece until it is about ¼ inch thick. On
another sheet of wax paper, combine flour, salt, and pepper. Dip the
cutlets in the flour mixture until well coated, shaking off the excess.

2 In a large skillet, heat 2 tablespoons oil over moderately high heat.
Add enough turkey cutlets to cover the bottom of the skillet without
crowding. Cook until golden brown on both sides, 2 to 3 minutes on
each side. Transfer the cutlets to a warm serving platter.

3 Add another tablespoon of oil to the skillet, cook the remaining
cutlets, and transfer to the platter.

4 In the same skillet, melt butter over moderate heat. Add mushrooms
and garlic; sauté for 5 minutes. Add broth and bring the mixture to
a boil, stirring and scraping the bottom of the skillet. Spoon the
mushroom mixture over the turkey, sprinkle with parsley, and serve.

*Fresh ground turkey is a low-fat alternative to ground beef. Use it to make this
quick and tasty microwave supper.*

TURKEY AND RICE CASSEROLE

In a 1½-quart microwave-safe casserole,
crumble **8 ounces ground turkey**. Add
½ cup chopped green bell pepper. Cover
and microwave on high power until meat is
browned, 3 to 5 minutes, stirring once.
Drain. Stir in **one 15-ounce jar pizza sauce**,

**1 cup quick-cooking rice, one 8-ounce can
kidney beans**, drained, and **¼ cup water**.
Cook on high, covered, until rice is tender,
3 to 5 minutes, stirring once. Sprinkle with
½ cup grated Monterey Jack cheese.
SERVES 4

TURKEY À LA SUISSE

One Serving: **Calories** 422 **Protein** 36g **Carbohydrates** 25g **Fat** 18g **Cholesterol** 192mg **Sodium** 541mg

¼ **cup all-purpose flour**

1½ **teaspoons lemon-pepper seasoning**

¼ **teaspoon ground nutmeg**

2 **large eggs**

1 **tablespoon water**

1 **cup packaged plain bread crumbs**

8 **small turkey-breast cutlets (about 1 pound)**

2 **tablespoons butter or margarine**

1 **tablespoon vegetable oil**

2 **large slices boiled ham, each cut into 4 pieces**

2 **large slices Swiss cheese, each cut into 4 pieces**

Chopped parsley (optional)

 PREPARATION TIME **15 MINUTES**

COOKING TIME **6 MINUTES**

COOK'S TIP *Using packaged sliced ham and Swiss cheese allows you to bring this supper to the table in less than half an hour. Be sure to cook larger cutlets longer than the time specified here.*

1 On a sheet of wax paper, combine flour, lemon-pepper seasoning, and nutmeg. In a pie plate, beat eggs with water. On another sheet of wax paper, place the bread crumbs.

2 Dip turkey cutlets in the flour mixture until well coated, shaking off the excess. Dip the floured slices into the egg mixture, then coat them with the crumbs. In a large skillet, heat butter and oil over moderate heat. Add the turkey cutlets and cook until golden brown on one side, 2 to 3 minutes.

3 Turn the turkey cutlets over and top each first with a piece of ham, then a piece of cheese. Cover the pan and continue cooking until the cheese begins to melt, about 2 more minutes. Transfer the turkey to a warm serving platter, sprinkle with chopped parsley, if desired, and serve immediately.

TURKEY PATTIES DIJON

One Serving: **Calories** 414 **Protein** 32g **Carbohydrates** 23g **Fat** 20g **Cholesterol** 86mg **Sodium** 663mg

1 **small green onion**

1¼ **pounds ground turkey**

¼ **teaspoon salt**

¼ **teaspoon dried tarragon, crumbled**

1 **tablespoon butter or margarine**

¼ **cup Dijon mustard**

¼ **cup dry white wine, canned reduced-sodium chicken broth, or water**

2 **cloves garlic, finely chopped**

4 **large, 1-inch-thick slices French or Italian bread**

1 **small ripe tomato, cut into 8 wedges**

 PREPARATION TIME **6 MINUTES**

COOKING TIME **10 MINUTES**

1 Keeping the white and green parts separate, finely chop green onion. In a medium-size bowl, combine turkey, the white part of the onion, salt, and tarragon. Shape the turkey mixture into four oval patties, each about ½ inch thick, to fit the French bread.

2 In a large skillet, melt butter over moderately high heat. Add the turkey patties and cook until they are lightly browned on both sides, about 3 minutes on each side.

3 Transfer the turkey patties to a plate. Stir mustard, white wine, and garlic into the skillet. Bring the mixture to a boil, stirring and scraping the bottom of the skillet. Return the turkey patties to the skillet and coat them with the mustard mixture. Toast the bread slices.

4 Place a slice of toast on each serving plate. Place a patty on each slice of toast and spoon the remaining sauce over each. Garnish each serving with two tomato wedges and the chopped green part of the onion. Serve immediately.

SPICED TURKEY BURGERS

SPICED TURKEY BURGERS

One Serving: **Calories** 365 **Protein** 30g **Carbohydrates** 26g **Fat** 16g **Cholesterol** 75mg **Sodium** 527mg

1¼ **pounds ground turkey**

2 **tablespoons finely chopped onion**

2 **tablespoons chopped parsley**

¼ **teaspoon each salt and ground black pepper**

¼ **teaspoon each ground coriander, ground cumin, and curry powder**

1 **tablespoon vegetable oil**

4 **hamburger buns**

1 **cup alfalfa sprouts or shredded lettuce**

1 **ripe tomato, sliced**

PREPARATION TIME
10 MINUTES

COOKING TIME
6 MINUTES

SERVING SUGGESTION *Add crunch to these burgers with a basket of potato or tortilla chips, or a crisp salad.*

1 In a medium-size bowl, combine turkey, onion, parsley, salt, pepper, coriander, cumin, and curry powder. Shape the turkey mixture into four patties, each about ½ inch thick.

2 In a large skillet, heat oil over moderately high heat. Add the turkey patties and cook until browned on both sides and cooked through, about 3 minutes on each side.

3 Meanwhile, toast hamburger buns. Place a turkey patty in each bun; top each with some alfalfa sprouts or lettuce and slices of tomato. Serve immediately with mustard and ketchup, if desired.

TURKEY PICCATA

One Serving: **Calories** 303 **Protein** 32g **Carbohydrates** 12g **Fat** 14g **Cholesterol** 175mg **Sodium** 356mg

- 2 **large eggs**
- 1 **tablespoon water**
- 2 **cups fresh bread crumbs**
- 8 **small turkey-breast cutlets (about 1 pound)**
- 2 **tablespoons (¼ stick) butter or margarine, divided**
- 1 **tablespoon vegetable oil**
- ¾ **cup canned reduced-sodium chicken broth**
- 2 **tablespoons lemon juice**
- 4 **lemon slices**

PREPARATION TIME
15 MINUTES

COOKING TIME
10 MINUTES

FOOD NOTE *The lemony sauce gives tangy flavor to this Italian-inspired dish. Tender turkey breasts are used here, but you may substitute veal if you prefer.*

1 In a pie plate, beat eggs with water. On a sheet of wax paper, place bread crumbs. Dip turkey cutlets first in the egg mixture, then in the crumbs, coating them evenly.

2 In a large skillet, heat butter and oil over moderate heat. Add the turkey cutlets and cook until golden brown on both sides, 2 to 3 minutes on each side. Transfer the turkey to a plate.

3 Stir chicken broth and lemon juice into the drippings in the skillet, stirring and scraping the bottom of the skillet. Bring the mixture to a boil; cook the mixture, stirring constantly, until it is slightly thickened, about 1 minute.

4 Return the turkey to the skillet and continue cooking until the slices are heated through. Arrange the turkey and sauce on a warm platter, top with lemon slices, and serve.

ITALIAN-STYLE TURKEY SAUSAGES

One Serving: **Calories** 340 **Protein** 27g **Carbohydrates** 14g **Fat** 20g **Cholesterol** 75mg **Sodium** 589mg

- 1¼ **pounds ground turkey**
- ½ **cup fresh bread crumbs**
- 1 **teaspoon Italian herb seasoning**
- 2 **cloves garlic, finely chopped**
- ¼ **teaspoon salt**
- 1 **small green bell pepper**
- 2 **tablespoons olive or vegetable oil, divided**
- 1 **cup prepared plain spaghetti sauce**
- 4 **hero rolls, split, or hot cooked spaghetti (optional)**

PREPARATION TIME
10 MINUTES

COOKING TIME
12 MINUTES

1 In a medium-size bowl, combine ground turkey, bread crumbs, Italian seasoning, garlic, and salt. Divide the turkey mixture into 8 portions and roll each portion into the shape of a sausage link about 4 inches long and 1 inch thick. Core and seed bell pepper, and cut it into ¼-inch-wide strips.

2 In a large skillet, heat 1 tablespoon oil over moderately high heat. Add turkey sausages and cook until firm and lightly browned, carefully turning them to brown evenly, about 6 minutes. Transfer the sausages to a plate. Wipe out the skillet with paper towels.

3 Heat the remaining 1 tablespoon of oil in the skillet. Add pepper strips and sauté until just wilted, about 2 minutes. Stir in spaghetti sauce and bring to a boil. Return the sausages to the skillet and heat through. Serve the sausages and sauce in hero rolls or over cooked spaghetti, if desired.

SESAME TURKEY AND ASPARAGUS

SESAME TURKEY AND ASPARAGUS

One Serving: **Calories** 293 **Protein** 32g **Carbohydrates** 6g **Fat** 16g **Cholesterol** 79mg **Sodium** 312mg

2 tablespoons Oriental sesame oil

1 tablespoon soy sauce

1 teaspoon honey

¼ teaspoon ground cumin

1 pound turkey tenderloin or cutlets, cut into strips

1 pound small asparagus

1 tablespoon sesame seeds

2 tablespoons vegetable oil

Salt and ground black pepper to taste

PREPARATION TIME
18 MINUTES

COOKING TIME
9 MINUTES

SERVING SUGGESTION *Turkey goes Asian in this easy stir-fry dish. Serve it with a packaged herbed or fried rice.*

1 In a large bowl, combine sesame oil, soy sauce, honey, and cumin. Add turkey and turn to coat evenly. Let the turkey marinate for 15 minutes. Meanwhile, trim the bottom ends off asparagus and discard. Cut the asparagus diagonally into 2-inch lengths.

2 In a wok or large skillet, heat sesame seeds over moderate heat until browned, stirring constantly. Transfer to a bowl and set aside.

3 Increase the heat to high. Add vegetable oil to the wok; add the turkey and stir-fry for 5 minutes. Add the asparagus and cook, stirring constantly, until the asparagus is crisp-tender, 2 to 4 minutes. Season the turkey and asparagus with salt and pepper. Transfer to a serving dish, sprinkle with the toasted sesame seeds, and serve.

TURKEY CUTLETS MILANO

TURKEY CUTLETS MILANO

One Serving: **Calories** 324 **Protein** 29g **Carbohydrates** 11g **Fat** 18g **Cholesterol** 27mg **Sodium** 384mg

2 tablespoons all-purpose flour

¼ teaspoon each salt and ground black pepper

4 large turkey-breast cutlets (about 1 pound)

4 tablespoons olive or vegetable oil, divided

1 small yellow onion, chopped

¼ cup dry white wine

1 jar (6 ounces) marinated artichoke hearts, drained

1 cup chopped fresh or well-drained canned plum tomatoes

½ teaspoon dried basil, crumbled

 PREPARATION TIME
6 MINUTES

 COOKING TIME
20 MINUTES

SERVING SUGGESTION *For an authentic Italian taste, team these cutlets with pasta tossed with butter and chopped fresh herbs.*

1 On a sheet of wax paper, combine flour, salt, and pepper. Dip turkey cutlets in the flour mixture until well coated, shaking off the excess.

2 In a large skillet, heat 2 tablespoons oil over moderately high heat. Add enough turkey cutlets to cover the bottom of the skillet without crowding. Cook the cutlets until golden brown on both sides, 2 to 3 minutes on each side. Transfer the cutlets to a warm serving platter.

3 Add another tablespoon of oil to the skillet, cook the remaining turkey cutlets, and transfer them to the platter.

4 In the same skillet, heat 1 tablespoon oil over moderate heat. Add onion and sauté until soft, about 5 minutes. Add wine and bring the mixture to a boil, stirring and scraping the bottom of the skillet. Stir in artichokes, tomatoes, and basil. Bring the mixture to a boil. Pour the sauce over the turkey cutlets and serve.

CHEESE-STUFFED TURKEY ROLLS

One Serving: **Calories** 342 **Protein** 33g **Carbohydrates** 13g **Fat** 18g **Cholesterol** 79mg **Sodium** 679mg

- **1 package (4 ounces) soft garlic-and-herb cheese**
- **1 ounce mozzarella cheese, coarsely grated (¼ cup)**
- **4 large turkey-breast cutlets (about 1 pound)**
- **2 tablespoons (¼ stick) butter or margarine**
- **⅓ cup packaged seasoned bread crumbs**
- **1 clove garlic, finely chopped**
- **1 can (8 ounces) tomato sauce**
- **1 teaspoon dried oregano, crumbled**
- **Salt and ground black pepper to taste**

PREPARATION TIME
7 MINUTES

COOKING TIME
30 MINUTES

1 Preheat the oven to 375°F. Lightly grease a 9-inch square baking pan. In a medium-size bowl, combine the cheeses. Spread an equal amount of the cheese mixture down the center of each turkey cutlet. Roll up the cutlets, jelly-roll style, and secure each of them with a wooden toothpick.

2 In a small saucepan, melt butter over low heat. Remove the pan from the heat. On a sheet of wax paper, place bread crumbs. Dip the turkey rolls in the melted butter, then coat them with the crumbs. Set the saucepan with the remaining butter aside.

3 Arrange the breaded cutlet rolls 1 inch apart in the prepared baking pan. Bake the cutlets, uncovered, until they are just golden brown, 25 to 30 minutes.

4 In the saucepan with the remaining butter, sauté garlic over low heat for 10 seconds. Stir in tomato sauce and oregano; season with salt and pepper. Bring the sauce to a boil. Place the turkey rolls on a warm serving platter, pour the sauce over them, and serve.

HERBED TURKEY MARSALA

One Serving: **Calories** 282 **Protein** 29g **Carbohydrates** 13g **Fat** 11g **Cholesterol** 63mg **Sodium** 339mg

- **¼ cup all-purpose flour**
- **½ teaspoon ground sage**
- **½ teaspoon salt**
- **¼ teaspoon ground black pepper**
- **8 small turkey-breast cutlets (about 1 pound)**
- **2 tablespoons vegetable oil**
- **1 tablespoon butter or margarine**
- **1 medium-size red onion, sliced**
- **4 ounces mushrooms, cut into quarters**
- **¼ cup Marsala**
- **¼ cup water**

 PREPARATION TIME
10 MINUTES

COOKING TIME
15 MINUTES

FOOD NOTE *Turkey cutlets are an excellent alternative to veal, and more economical. Here they are covered with a simple sauce of onions, mushrooms, and Marsala wine.*

1 On a sheet of wax paper, combine flour, sage, salt, and pepper. Dip turkey cutlets in the flour mixture until they are well coated, shaking off the excess flour.

2 In a large skillet, heat oil over moderately high heat. Add the turkey cutlets and cook until they are golden brown on both sides, 2 to 3 minutes on each side. Transfer the turkey to a plate and set it aside.

3 In the same skillet, melt butter over moderate heat. Add onion and mushrooms; sauté until soft, about 5 minutes. Add Marsala and water; bring the mixture to a boil, stirring and scraping the bottom of the skillet. Return the turkey to the skillet, cover, and cook until the turkey is heated through. Serve immediately.

CORNISH HENS WITH VEGETABLES

One Serving: **Calories** 320 **Protein** 23g **Carbohydrates** 18g **Fat** 19g **Cholesterol** 119mg **Sodium** 381mg

2 Rock Cornish hens (about 1³/₄ pounds each), thawed if frozen

2 tablespoons (¼ stick) butter or margarine

4 medium-size carrots

1 medium-size yellow onion

1 bay leaf

½ teaspoon dried rosemary, crumbled

1¼ cups canned reduced-sodium chicken broth, divided

1 package (9 ounces) frozen cut green beans

2 tablespoons all-purpose flour

Salt and ground black pepper to taste

 PREPARATION TIME
3 MINUTES

 COOKING TIME
40 MINUTES

1 Cut each hen in half lengthwise. In a 5-quart Dutch oven or a large, deep skillet, melt butter over moderate heat. Place the hens, skin side down, in the skillet and cook until they are lightly browned on both sides, 10 to 15 minutes. Meanwhile, peel carrots and cut them into 1-inch lengths. Slice onion.

2 Drain the fat from the Dutch oven, if desired. Add the carrots, onion, bay leaf, rosemary, and 1 cup chicken broth to the Dutch oven. Bring the mixture to a boil over high heat. Reduce the heat to moderately low, cover, and simmer the hens and vegetables for 5 minutes. Meanwhile, partially thaw beans by rinsing them under hot water.

3 Stir the green beans into the Dutch oven and continue cooking the hens until they are tender and cooked through, about 15 minutes. In a small bowl or cup, combine flour and ¼ cup chicken broth until the mixture is completely smooth.

4 Transfer the hens to a serving platter and keep them warm. Gradually stir the flour mixture into the liquid in the Dutch oven. Cook, stirring constantly, until the sauce boils and thickens. Discard the bay leaf; season the sauce with salt and pepper. Spoon the sauce over the hens, and serve immediately.

BROILED CORNISH HENS

One Serving: **Calories** 486 **Protein** 66g **Carbohydrates** 13g **Fat** 23g **Cholesterol** 218mg **Sodium** 426mg

2 Rock Cornish hens (about 1³/₄ pounds each), thawed if frozen

2 tablespoons (¼ stick) butter or margarine

1 tablespoon lemon juice

1 tablespoon Worcester-shire sauce

½ teaspoon dried tarragon, crumbled

½ teaspoon dried thyme leaves, crumbled

¼ teaspoon salt

PREPARATION TIME
5 MINUTES

COOKING TIME
35 MINUTES

1 Preheat the broiler. Cut each hen in half lengthwise. Place the hens, skin side down, on the rack over a broiler pan. Broil the hens 5 inches from the heat until they are lightly browned on one side and almost tender, about 20 minutes.

2 Meanwhile, in a small saucepan, melt butter over moderate heat. Remove the pan from the heat and stir in lemon juice, Worcestershire sauce, tarragon, thyme, and salt.

3 Brush the hens with some of the butter mixture. Turn them over and broil 5 minutes. Brush them with more of the butter mixture and continue broiling them until they are tender, about 10 more minutes. Place the hens on a warm platter, pour the pan drippings over them, and serve immediately.

BRAISED HENS SOUTHERN STYLE

Braised Hens Southern Style

One Serving: **Calories** 890 **Protein** 110g **Carbohydrates** 25g **Fat** 37g **Cholesterol** 337mg **Sodium** 518mg

2 **Rock Cornish hens (about 1³/₄ pounds each), thawed if frozen**

¹/₄ **cup all-purpose flour**

¹/₄ **teaspoon each salt and ground black pepper**

¹/₄ **teaspoon curry powder**

1 **tablespoon butter or margarine**

2 **tablespoons vegetable oil**

1 **can (16 ounces) sliced cling peaches in extra-light syrup**

¹/₂ **cup canned reduced-sodium chicken broth**

¹/₄ **cup lemon juice**

¹/₄ **cup pecan halves**

Chopped parsley (optional)

PREPARATION TIME
5 MINUTES

COOKING TIME
35 MINUTES

SERVING SUGGESTION *Continue the Southern theme of these juicy hens with a basket of warm cornbread on the side.*

1 Cut each hen into quarters. On a sheet of wax paper, combine flour, salt, pepper, and curry powder. Dip the hen quarters into the flour mixture until well coated, shaking off the excess.

2 In a large skillet, heat butter and oil over moderate heat. Place the hen quarters, skin side down, in the skillet; cook until browned on both sides, about 15 minutes. Reserving the liquid, drain canned peaches.

3 Transfer the hen quarters to a plate. Add the peach liquid, chicken broth, and lemon juice to the skillet. Bring the mixture to a boil, stirring and scraping the bottom of the skillet. Continue to boil the sauce until it is reduced by half, about 5 minutes.

4 Return the hen quarters with any accumulated juices to the skillet; cover and cook until they are tender, about 10 minutes. Add the peach slices and pecans to the skillet and heat through. Transfer to a warm platter, sprinkle with parsley, if desired, and serve.

BAKED CORNISH HENS WITH RICE PILAF

One Serving: **Calories** 486 **Protein** 25g **Carbohydrates** 48g **Fat** 23g **Cholesterol** 119mg **Sodium** 657mg

2 tablespoons (¼ stick) butter or margarine

1 tablespoon lemon juice

2 Rock Cornish hens (about 1¾ pounds each), thawed if frozen

½ teaspoon paprika

½ teaspoon salt

¼ teaspoon ground black pepper

Green grapes (optional)

For the rice pilaf

1 small yellow onion

1 tablespoon vegetable oil

1 cup long-grain white rice

¼ cup golden raisins

1 can (13¾ or 14½ ounces) reduced-sodium chicken broth

1 tablespoon chopped parsley

 PREPARATION TIME
3 MINUTES

COOKING TIME
35 MINUTES

1 Preheat the oven to 375°F. Place butter and lemon juice in a 13- by 9-inch baking pan and melt the butter in the oven while it is preheating. Meanwhile, cut each hen in half lengthwise. In a cup, mix paprika, salt, and pepper; rub the mixture over the hens.

2 Remove the baking pan from the oven and place the hens, skin side down, in the pan. Bake the hens for 20 minutes.

3 Meanwhile, prepare rice pilaf. Chop onion. In a medium-size saucepan, heat oil over moderate heat. Add the onion and sauté until soft, about 5 minutes. Stir in rice and raisins until well mixed; add broth. Increase the heat to high and bring the mixture to a boil. Reduce the heat to low, cover, and simmer the rice mixture until tender, about 15 minutes. Using a fork, stir in parsley.

4 Brush the hens with the pan drippings and turn the pieces over. Continue baking the hens until they are golden brown and tender, 15 to 20 more minutes. Place the hens with the pan drippings and rice pilaf on a warm serving platter. Garnish with green grapes, if desired, and serve immediately.

Shelf Magic

Sliced turkey doesn't have to sit between two cold slices of bread. If you keep a couple of packages in the refrigerator, you can whip up one of these delicious lunches in the same amount of time it takes to make a sandwich.

BARBECUE TURKEY BUNS

Cut **two 6-ounce packages turkey luncheon meat** into strips. In a medium-size saucepan, stir together the turkey strips and **¾ cup prepared barbecue sauce**. Cook, stirring, over moderately high heat until heated through, about 5 minutes.

To serve, place **1 cup shredded cabbage** on the bottom halves of **4 hamburger buns**. Spoon the turkey over them, replace the tops, and serve immediately.
SERVES 4

TURKEY AND GRAPE SALAD

Cut **two 6-ounce packages turkey luncheon meat** into strips. In a large mixing bowl, combine **½ cup sour cream**, **¼ cup mayonnaise**, **1 tablespoon thawed orange juice concentrate**, and **1 tablespoon chopped walnuts**. Stir in **3 stalks celery**, sliced, and **1 cup seedless red grapes**, and the turkey; toss lightly. Arrange **4 lettuce leaves** on salad plates. Spoon the salad on top of the lettuce, and serve immediately.
SERVES 4

MEAT

BEEF STEAK CAJUN STYLE (PAGE 172)

BEEF

Beef is America's most popular meat—it is the basis of a robust range of nourishing classics from chili to ribs, hamburgers to steaks, and many more.

BARBECUED SHORT RIBS

One Serving: **Calories** 696 **Protein** 66g **Carbohydrates** 42g **Fat** 29g **Cholesterol** 181mg **Sodium** 1539mg

4 pounds beef short ribs, cut into serving-size pieces

Unseasoned meat tenderizer

1 tablespoon vegetable oil

1 medium-size yellow onion, chopped

1½ cups ketchup

¼ cup firmly packed light brown sugar

2 tablespoons prepared white horseradish

1 teaspoon Worcestershire sauce

½ teaspoon salt

1 tablespoon chopped parsley

 PREPARATION TIME
6 MINUTES

 COOKING TIME
30 MINUTES

SERVING SUGGESTION *These ribs are delicious served with piping hot corn on the cob or a refreshing macaroni salad from the deli section. Save preparation time by asking the butcher to cut the ribs into serving-size pieces for you.*

1 Preheat the broiler. Sprinkle short ribs with meat tenderizer according to package directions. Place the ribs on the rack over a broiler pan. Broil the ribs 5 inches from the heat, turning occasionally, until they are fork-tender, about 20 minutes.

2 Meanwhile, in a small saucepan, heat oil over moderate heat. Add onion and sauté until soft, about 5 minutes. Stir in ketchup, sugar, horseradish, Worcestershire sauce, and salt; bring the mixture to a boil, stirring occasionally. Reduce the heat to low, cover, and simmer the barbecue sauce for 10 minutes.

3 Brush the ribs with some of the barbecue sauce. Continue broiling 10 more minutes, turning the ribs over and brushing them once more during broiling so they are well coated. Transfer the ribs to a warm platter, sprinkle with chopped parsley, and serve.

Shelf Magic

Marinated vegetable salads are often found in the deli section of the supermarket. If you need a substitute, use shredded lettuce.

DELI-BEEF SANDWICH

Cut a thin slice off the top of each of **four 6-inch French-style rolls**. Hollow out the bottoms, leaving about a ½-inch shell. Spread the cavity of each roll with a small spoonful of **Dijon mustard**. Divide **8 ounces thinly sliced cooked beef** among the roll shells; pile the meat inside each cavity. Drain **1 pint marinated mixed-vegetable salad**. Fill each roll with one-fourth of the salad; top with **sliced Swiss cheese**. Cover with roll tops; serve.
SERVES 4

Beef Steak Cajun Style

One Serving: **Calories** 437 **Protein** 54g **Carbohydrates** 1g **Fat** 23g **Cholesterol** 16mg **Sodium** 196mg

1 **1-inch-thick beef top round steak (about 1½ pounds)**

2 **tablespoons olive oil**

2 **cloves garlic, finely chopped**

1 **teaspoon chili powder**

½ **teaspoon ground cumin**

½ **teaspoon dried thyme leaves, crumbled**

¼ **teaspoon cayenne pepper**

2 **tablespoons (¼ stick) butter or margarine**

1 **tablespoon finely chopped parsley**

PREPARATION TIME
25 MINUTES

COOKING TIME
15 MINUTES

1 Trim and discard any excess fat from steak. Place the steak in a shallow glass dish. In a small bowl, combine oil, garlic, chili powder, cumin, thyme, and cayenne pepper. Brush the oil mixture on both sides of the steak. Let it stand at room temperature for 15 minutes to marinate. Meanwhile, preheat the broiler.

2 Place the marinated steak on the rack over a broiler pan. Broil the steak 4 inches from the heat for 10 minutes. Turn the steak over and continue broiling until it reaches the desired degree of doneness, about 5 minutes for rare.

3 Transfer the steak to a carving board with a well to catch the juices. Dot the steak with pieces of butter; let it stand for several minutes to allow the juices to settle. Slice the steak crosswise into thin strips. Transfer it to a warm serving platter. Pour any accumulated juices over the steak, sprinkle with parsley, and serve.

Beef Stroganoff

One Serving: **Calories** 270 **Protein** 28g **Carbohydrates** 8g **Fat** 14g **Cholesterol** 76mg **Sodium** 291mg

1½ **pounds boneless beef sirloin steak**

1 **tablespoon butter or margarine**

1 **tablespoon vegetable oil**

1 **medium-size yellow onion, sliced**

8 **ounces small mushrooms, halved**

1 **teaspoon cornstarch**

1 **cup canned beef broth, divided**

¼ **cup sour cream**

Salt and ground black pepper to taste

1 **tablespoon chopped parsley**

Hot cooked noodles (optional)

PREPARATION TIME
10 MINUTES

COOKING TIME
20 MINUTES

1 Trim and discard any excess fat from steak. Cut the steak into strips about 2 inches long and ½ inch wide. In a large skillet, heat butter and oil over high heat. Add the steak strips and quickly brown the steak on all sides. Using a slotted spoon, transfer the strips to a bowl, cover, and keep them warm.

2 Reduce the heat to moderately low. Add sliced onion to the remaining drippings in the skillet and sauté until soft, about 5 minutes. Add halved mushrooms to the skillet and cook until they are just tender, about 5 minutes.

3 In a cup or small bowl, combine cornstarch with some of the beef broth; stir it into the mushroom mixture until well mixed. Gradually stir in the remaining broth. Bring the mixture to a boil, stirring constantly. Continue cooking until the sauce is slightly thickened, about 2 minutes.

4 Stir sour cream into the sauce and season it with salt and pepper. Remove the pan from the heat. Stir the steak strips and any accumulated juices into the sauce; sprinkle with parsley. Serve immediately over noodles, if desired.

BROCCOLI-GINGER BEEF

BROCCOLI-GINGER BEEF

One Serving: **Calories** 398 **Protein** 30g **Carbohydrates** 36g **Fat** 17g **Cholesterol** 68mg **Sodium** 1031mg

- ⅓ **cup plus 1 tablespoon reduced-sodium soy sauce**
- 1½ **tablespoons cornstarch**
- 4½ **tablespoons honey**
- 1½ **tablespoons dry sherry**
- 1 **½-inch-thick boneless beef sirloin steak (about 1 pound)**
- 3 **tablespoons vegetable oil**
- 1 **tablespoon slivered fresh ginger**
- 4 **cups broccoli florets**
- ½ **cup water**
- 1 **can (8 ounces) sliced water chestnuts or bamboo shoots, drained**
- ⅓ **cup sliced green onions**
  Salt to taste

PREPARATION TIME
11 MINUTES

COOKING TIME
10 MINUTES

FOOD NOTE *A combination of ginger and water chestnuts gives this beef stir-fry a distinctly Far Eastern flavor. It goes well with steamed rice or Chinese noodles.*

1 In a cup, combine soy sauce, cornstarch, honey, and sherry. Trim and discard any excess fat from steak. Cut the beef lengthwise into 2 strips, then crosswise into ½-inch-thick slices.

2 In a wok or 5-quart Dutch oven, heat oil over high heat. Add ginger and stir-fry for 1 minute. Add the beef slices and stir-fry until they are well browned, about 3 minutes. Using a slotted spoon, transfer the beef and ginger to a bowl and set them aside.

3 Reduce the heat to moderate. Add broccoli and water to the wok. Cover and cook until the broccoli is crisp-tender, about 3 minutes. Add water chestnuts, green onions, and the soy-sauce mixture to the broccoli; bring to a boil. Continue cooking, stirring constantly, until the mixture is thickened, about 2 minutes.

4 Return the beef and any accumulated juices to the broccoli mixture; stir to combine. Season with salt, if desired, and serve immediately.

GINGERED BEEF KEBABS

One Serving: **Calories** 266 **Protein** 26g **Carbohydrates** 15g **Fat** 12g **Cholesterol** 61mg **Sodium** 322mg

1½ pounds boneless beef sirloin (about 1¼ inches thick)

¼ cup lemon juice

1 tablespoon honey

1 tablespoon soy sauce

1 teaspoon ground ginger

2 cloves garlic, finely chopped

1 large green bell pepper

1 large red bell pepper

1 medium-size red onion

2 tablespoons vegetable oil

PREPARATION TIME
25 MINUTES

COOKING TIME
8 MINUTES

1 Trim and discard any excess fat from sirloin. Cut the beef into 1¼-inch cubes. In a large bowl, combine lemon juice, honey, soy sauce, ginger, and chopped garlic; mix thoroughly. Add the beef cubes and toss to coat evenly. Let them stand at room temperature for 15 minutes to marinate.

2 Meanwhile, core, seed, and cut bell peppers into 1¼-inch pieces. Cut red onion into 8 wedges.

3 Preheat the broiler. On four metal skewers, alternately thread the beef cubes and the vegetable pieces, reserving the marinade. Place the skewers on the rack over a broiler pan. Brush the kebabs on all sides with vegetable oil.

4 Broil the kebabs 4 inches from the heat for 5 minutes. Turn the kebabs and brush them with some of the reserved marinade. Continue broiling the kebabs until the beef is cooked to the desired degree of doneness, about 3 minutes for medium-rare. Transfer the kebabs to a warm platter and serve.

CHICKEN-FRIED STEAK WITH GRAVY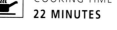

One Serving: **Calories** 422 **Protein** 41g **Carbohydrates** 11g **Fat** 23g **Cholesterol** 145mg **Sodium** 530mg

2 large eggs

2 tablespoons water

⅓ cup all-purpose flour

½ teaspoon salt

¼ teaspoon ground black pepper

4 beef cube steaks (tenderized round steak, about 4 ounces each)

¼ cup (½ stick) butter or margarine, divided

1 cup milk

PREPARATION TIME
3 MINUTES

COOKING TIME
22 MINUTES

1 In a pie plate, beat eggs with water. On a sheet of wax paper, combine flour, salt, and pepper. Dip steaks first in the egg mixture, then in the flour mixture, shaking them gently to remove the excess flour. Reserve the remaining flour mixture.

2 In a large skillet, melt 2 tablespoons butter over moderate heat. Add two steaks and cook until they are golden brown on both sides, 3 to 4 minutes on each side. Transfer the steaks to a warm serving platter, cover, and keep them warm.

3 Add another tablespoon of butter to the skillet and cook the remaining two steaks. Transfer them to the serving platter, cover, and keep them warm.

4 Add the remaining butter to the skillet. Stir in the reserved flour mixture until smooth. Gradually add milk; bring the mixture to a boil, stirring constantly. Cook until the gravy thickens, about 5 minutes. Pour the gravy over the steaks, and serve immediately.

BURGUNDY BEEF

Burgundy Beef

One Serving: **Calories** 261 **Protein** 26g **Carbohydrates** 8g **Fat** 11g **Cholesterol** 69mg **Sodium** 217mg

4 small ½-inch-thick beef top loin steaks (about 6 ounces each)

1 tablespoon butter or margarine

1 tablespoon vegetable oil

1 medium-size yellow onion, sliced

1 tablespoon all-purpose flour

⅔ cup Burgundy (or other red wine)

⅔ cup canned beef broth

1 teaspoon sugar

½ teaspoon ground black pepper

PREPARATION TIME
10 MINUTES

COOKING TIME
20 MINUTES

SERVING SUGGESTION *A baked potato with sour cream and bacon offsets the hearty flavor of the steaks; garnish with watercress.*

1 Trim and discard any excess fat from steaks. In a large skillet, heat butter and oil over moderately high heat. Add the steaks and cook until they are well browned on both sides and cooked to the desired degree of doneness, about 5 minutes on each side for medium-rare. Transfer the steaks to a serving platter, cover, and keep them warm.

2 Add onion to the remaining drippings in the skillet; sauté until soft, about 5 minutes. Add flour and stir until well mixed.

3 Add Burgundy, broth, sugar, and pepper to the onion mixture; bring to a boil, stirring constantly. Continue cooking until thickened and bubbly, 2 to 3 minutes. Spoon the sauce over the steaks, and serve.

175

BEEF FAJITAS

One Serving: **Calories** 535 **Protein** 32g **Carbohydrates** 52g **Fat** 24g **Cholesterol** 79mg **Sodium** 597mg

- 1 **pound beef flank steak or skirt steak**
- ¼ **cup lime juice**
- ½ **teaspoon salt**
- ½ **teaspoon garlic powder**
- ½ **teaspoon ground black pepper**
- 1 **large red bell pepper**
- 1 **medium-size green bell pepper**
- 1 **medium-size white or yellow onion**
- 8 **small (7- or 8-inch) flour tortillas**
- 2 **tablespoons vegetable oil**
- ½ **cup sour cream**
  Prepared tomato salsa (optional)

PREPARATION TIME
25 MINUTES

COOKING TIME
16 MINUTES

FOOD NOTE Fajita *is the Spanish word for "little belt" or "sash," and this dish is so called because skirt steak resembles a cummerbund. Serve the meat with hot tortillas and cool salsa.*

1 Preheat the oven to 350°F. Trim and discard any excess fat from steak. In a large plastic food-storage bag or shallow glass dish, place the steak. Sprinkle it on all sides with lime juice, salt, garlic powder, and pepper. Let the steak stand at room temperature for 15 to 20 minutes to marinate.

2 Meanwhile, core, seed, and cut bell peppers into strips; slice the onion. Wrap flour tortillas in aluminum foil and heat in the oven until warmed, about 15 minutes.

3 In a large skillet, heat vegetable oil over moderately high heat. Add the marinated beef; cook it until one side is well browned, about 5 minutes. Turn the steak over and continue cooking it to the desired degree of doneness, about 5 more minutes for medium-rare. Transfer the steak to a carving board, cover it with aluminum foil to keep it warm, and set it aside.

4 Reduce the heat to moderate. Add the onion and bell peppers to the skillet. Cook the vegetables, stirring occasionally, until they are crisp-tender, about 5 minutes. Remove the pan from the heat and cover it to keep warm.

5 Cut the steak crosswise into thin slices. Place an equal amount of the the beef slices and vegetables on each tortilla. Top each filling with a dollop of sour cream, and salsa if desired. Roll the tortillas up and place them on serving plates. Serve immediately.

TIME SAVERS

MAKE-AHEAD BURGERS
With a little planning ahead, you can cook up a platter of hamburgers in minutes:

Shape ground meat into ½-inch-thick patties (about 4 ounces each). Stack the patties, placing two pieces of wax paper between each patty. Put the patties into a freezer container or sealed plastic bag and freeze.

To serve the burgers, remove the number of patties you need (the wax paper makes it easy to separate them). Place the burgers in a preheated skillet. Cook, covered, over medium-low heat, about 6 minutes on each side or to the desired degree of doneness. Season with salt and pepper.

FLANK STEAK WITH WATERCRESS SAUCE

One Serving: **Calories** 390 **Protein** 47g **Carbohydrates** 4g **Fat** 20g **Cholesterol** 151mg **Sodium** 317mg

1 **bunch watercress**

1 **tablespoon butter or margarine**

1 **tablespoon vegetable oil**

1 **small yellow onion, chopped**

1 **clove garlic, chopped**

1 **tablespoon all-purpose flour**

¾ **cup canned beef broth**

2 **teaspoons Worcestershire sauce**

1¼ **pounds beef flank steak**

   Salt and ground black pepper to taste

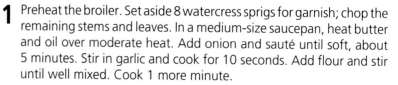

PREPARATION TIME
10 MINUTES

COOKING TIME
25 MINUTES

1 Preheat the broiler. Set aside 8 watercress sprigs for garnish; chop the remaining stems and leaves. In a medium-size saucepan, heat butter and oil over moderate heat. Add onion and sauté until soft, about 5 minutes. Stir in garlic and cook for 10 seconds. Add flour and stir until well mixed. Cook 1 more minute.

2 Gradually stir broth into the onions; bring the mixture to a boil, stirring constantly. Cook until slightly thickened, 2 to 3 minutes. Remove the pan from the heat. Stir in the chopped watercress and Worcestershire sauce. If desired, purée the watercress sauce in a blender or food processor until the mixture is fairly smooth. Cover the sauce and set it aside.

3 Using a sharp knife, score both sides of flank steak in a diamond pattern about ⅛ inch deep. Place the steak on the rack over a broiler pan. Broil the steak 3 inches from the heat for 5 minutes. Turn the steak and continue broiling it to the desired degree of doneness, about 5 minutes for rare.

4 Transfer the steak to a carving board with a well to catch the juices; let it stand for several minutes to let the juices settle. Sprinkle the steak with salt and pepper. Cut the steak crosswise into thin slices.

5 Transfer the slices to warm serving plates. Pour any accumulated juices and the watercress sauce over the steak, garnish with the reserved watercress sprigs, if desired, and serve immediately.

HERBED BEEF RIB STEAKS

One Serving: **Calories** 338 **Protein** 31g **Carbohydrates** 2g **Fat** 22g **Cholesterol** 91mg **Sodium** 134mg

4 **½-inch-thick beef rib steaks (about 6 ounces each)**

2 **tablespoons vegetable oil**

2 **tablespoons chopped mixed herbs (thyme, tarragon, and oregano)**

1 **tablespoon Worcestershire sauce**

½ **teaspoon ground black pepper**

2 **cloves garlic, finely chopped**

   Herb sprigs (optional)

PREPARATION TIME
20 MINUTES

COOKING TIME
10 MINUTES

1 Trim and discard any excess fat from steaks. In a shallow glass dish, combine oil, herbs, Worcestershire sauce, pepper, and garlic. Add the steaks and rub the herb mixture on both sides of each. Let the steaks stand at room temperature for 15 minutes to marinate. Meanwhile, preheat the broiler.

2 Place the steaks on the rack over a broiler pan. Broil the steaks 4 inches from the heat for 5 minutes. Turn the steaks over and continue broiling to the desired degree of doneness, about 5 more minutes for medium-rare. Place the steaks on a warm serving platter, garnish with fresh herbs, if desired, and serve.

CURRIED BEEF STEAK WITH HONEY

Curried Beef Steak With Honey

One Serving: **Calories** 347 **Protein** 38g **Carbohydrates** 11g **Fat** 17g **Cholesterol** 107mg **Sodium** 682mg

4 **³/₄-inch-thick beef tender-loin steaks (about 1¹/₂ pounds)**

¹/₄ cup reduced-sodium soy sauce

1 tablespoon curry powder

1 tablespoon vegetable oil

2 tablespoons honey

¹/₈ teaspoon ground black pepper

Fresh watercress sprigs (optional)

Hot cooked rice (optional)

 PREPARATION TIME
25 MINUTES

COOKING TIME
8 MINUTES

SERVING SUGGESTION *To make the rice more colorful, add some chopped bell pepper and a small pinch of saffron during cooking.*

1 Trim and discard any excess fat from steaks. In a shallow dish, combine soy sauce, curry powder, oil, honey, and pepper. Add the steaks to the soy-sauce mixture, turning them to coat evenly. Let the steaks stand at room temperature for 20 to 25 minutes to marinate, turning them occasionally. Meanwhile, preheat the boiler.

2 Reserving the marinade, place the steaks on the rack over a broiler pan. Broil the steaks 3 inches from the heat for 5 minutes. Turn the steaks and brush them with some of the marinade. Continue broiling to the desired degree of doneness, about 2 minutes for rare.

3 Transfer the steaks to serving plates. Garnish with watercress and serve with rice, if desired.

SPICY BEEF SIRLOIN WITH ARTICHOKES

One Serving: **Calories** 314 **Protein** 38g **Carbohydrates** 20g **Fat** 13g **Cholesterol** 106mg **Sodium** 474mg

- 4 **green onions**
- 1 **large red bell pepper**
- 1 **1-inch-thick boneless beef sirloin steak (about 1¼ pounds)**
- 1 **jar (6 ounces) marinated artichoke hearts**
- ¼ **cup water**
- 2 **tablespoons ketchup**
- 1 **tablespoon prepared steak sauce**
- 1 **teaspoon cornstarch**
- ½ **teaspoon Worcestershire sauce**

**PREPARATION TIME
7 MINUTES**

**COOKING TIME
10 MINUTES**

1 Cut green onions into 1-inch lengths. Seed bell pepper and cut it into 1-inch squares. Cut steak crosswise into thin slices. Pour the marinade from artichoke hearts into a small bowl; set the drained artichokes aside. In a cup, combine water, ketchup, steak sauce, cornstarch, and Worcestershire sauce.

2 Into a large skillet, pour 2 tablespoons of the reserved artichoke marinade, and heat it over moderately high heat. Add the bell pepper; cook until it is crisp-tender, stirring occasionally, about 2 minutes. Stir in the onions and cook for 1 minute. Using a slotted spoon, transfer the pepper and onions to a bowl and set it aside.

3 Pour the remaining marinade into the skillet; heat it until hot. Add the beef and cook until lightly browned. Transfer the beef to the bowl with the vegetables.

4 Stir the ketchup mixture into the skillet; bring the mixture to a boil, stirring constantly. Add the drained artichokes, the beef and vegetables, and any accumulated juices to the skillet; cook until just heated through. Transfer to a warm platter and serve immediately.

STIR-FRIED BEEF AND GREEN BEANS

One Serving: **Calories** 300 **Protein** 26g **Carbohydrates** 12g **Fat** 17g **Cholesterol** 66mg **Sodium** 402mg

- 1 **pound beef flank steak or boneless sirloin**
- 8 **ounces green beans**
- 1 **large yellow onion**
- 3 **tablespoons vegetable oil, divided**
- 1 **clove garlic, finely chopped**
- ½ **cup canned beef broth**
- 1 **tablespoon cornstarch**
- 1 **tablespoon soy sauce**
- 1 **tablespoon dry sherry**
- 1 **teaspoon ground ginger**
  Salt and ground white pepper to taste

 **PREPARATION TIME
13 MINUTES**

 **COOKING TIME
14 MINUTES**

1 Cut flank steak lengthwise in half; cut across the grain into thin slices. Trim and cut beans into 2-inch lengths. Slice onion.

2 In a wok or Dutch oven, heat 2 tablespoons oil over high heat. Add the beef and garlic; stir-fry the beef until browned, about 4 minutes. Using a slotted spoon, transfer the beef to a bowl and set it aside.

3 Add the remaining 1 tablespoon of oil to the wok and heat it until hot. Add the onion and stir-fry for 2 minutes. Add the green beans and broth. Reduce the heat to moderately high, cover the wok, and cook the beans until they are crisp-tender, about 5 to 7 minutes. Meanwhile, in a cup, combine cornstarch, soy sauce, sherry, and ginger.

4 Stir the cornstarch mixture into the beans. Cook until thickened and bubbly, about 30 seconds. Return the beef and any juices to the wok. Continue cooking until the beef is just heated through. Remove from the heat; season with salt and pepper, and serve.

PEPPER STEAK

PEPPER STEAK

One Serving: **Calories** 369 **Protein** 35g **Carbohydrates** 7g **Fat** 23g **Cholesterol** 123mg **Sodium** 123mg

2 tablespoons black peppercorns

1 1-inch-thick beef top
  round steak (about
  1 pound)

1 tablespoon butter or
  margarine

1 tablespoon vegetable oil

1 small yellow onion,
  chopped

1 cup half-and-half

  Salt to taste

PREPARATION TIME
5 MINUTES

COOKING TIME
18 MINUTES

SERVING SUGGESTION *A green salad and steamed asparagus pair well with this traditional steak, which is ready to cook in five minutes.*

1 Place peppercorns on a work surface or cutting board. Cover them with a paper towel and, using a rolling pin or mallet, crush the peppercorns into coarse pieces. Press the crushed peppercorns onto both sides of steak.

2 In a large skillet, heat butter and oil over moderately high heat. Add the steak and cook it for 5 minutes. Turn the steak over and continue cooking it to the desired degree of doneness, about 5 minutes for rare. Transfer the steak to a carving board with a well to catch the juices. Cover with aluminum foil to keep it warm.

3 Reduce the heat to moderate; add onion to the remaining drippings in the skillet. Sauté the onion until soft, about 5 minutes. Gradually stir in half-and-half. Cook the sauce, stirring constantly, until it thickens slightly, 2 to 3 minutes. Season the sauce with salt.

4 Cut the steak crosswise into thin slices; transfer it to a warm serving platter. Pour any accumulated juices and the onion sauce over the steak, and serve immediately.

Variations on the basic Hamburger

A thick, juicy hamburger is one of the quickest meals you can put together. Purists prefer their burgers of the most basic variety, adding only mustard, a tomato slice, and a lettuce leaf to adorn the flavor. But the fact is, once you've made the basic meat mixture, the possibilities have just begun for the myriad forms that burgers can take.

Prepare the basic hamburger mixture below, then look to the right for an international choice of treatments. Each recipe makes enough to serve four.

BASIC HAMBURGER In a medium-size bowl, combine **1¼ pounds lean ground beef** with **1 Tbsp. Worcestershire sauce** and **¼ tsp. each salt and ground black pepper**. Shape the beef mixture into four patties.

In a large skillet, heat **1 Tbsp. vegetable oil** over high heat. Add the beef patties and cook 2 minutes. Turn the patties over and continue cooking to the desired degree of doneness, about 3 minutes for medium-rare. Serve with the topping and bread of your choice.

► **CALIFORNIA BURGER** Prepare the **basic hamburger** patties and cook as directed. Cut each patty in half crosswise. Cut **4 pita breads** in half crosswise. Stuff the pocket of each pita with a patty half, **alfalfa sprouts, sliced avocado**, and **diced tomato**. In a small bowl, combine **½ cup mayonnaise** with **3 Tbsp. Thousand Island dressing**. Place some in each burger.

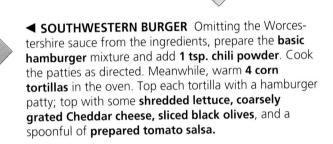

◄ **SOUTHWESTERN BURGER** Omitting the Worcestershire sauce from the ingredients, prepare the **basic hamburger** mixture and add **1 tsp. chili powder**. Cook the patties as directed. Meanwhile, warm **4 corn tortillas** in the oven. Top each tortilla with a hamburger patty; top with some **shredded lettuce, coarsely grated Cheddar cheese, sliced black olives**, and a spoonful of **prepared tomato salsa**.

► **BAVARIAN BURGER** Prepare the **basic hamburger** patties, adding **1 tsp. caraway seeds** to the meat mixture. Cook the patties as directed. Meanwhile, in a medium-size bowl, combine **2 cups thinly sliced green cabbage, 3 Tbsp. mayonnaise**, and **1 tsp. milk**. Spoon cabbage mixture on the bottom halves of **4 toasted split Kaiser rolls**. Place the patties on the cabbage, garnish with **pickle slices**, and cover with tops of rolls.

◄ **ITALIAN BURGER** Prepare the **basic hamburger** patties. Cook for 3 minutes, turn, then top each patty with one of **4 slices provolone cheese**. Cover the skillet and continue cooking until the cheese melts, about 2 minutes. Place burgers on **4 slices toasted Italian bread**. Top each with **rings of red onion** and **green bell pepper**, and some heated **pizza sauce**.

SALISBURY STEAK WITH WINE SAUCE

SALISBURY STEAK WITH WINE SAUCE

One Serving: **Calories** 548 **Protein** 46g **Carbohydrates** 9g **Fat** 36g **Cholesterol** 153mg **Sodium** 503mg

4 slices bacon

1 medium-size red bell pepper

8 ounces mushrooms, sliced

1 large yellow onion, sliced

1½ pounds lean ground beef

½ teaspoon salt

½ teaspoon cracked black pepper

⅓ cup Burgundy (or other red wine)

¼ teaspoon dried thyme leaves, crumbled

 PREPARATION TIME **15 MINUTES**

 COOKING TIME **16 MINUTES**

FOOD NOTE *This economical ground-beef dish is dressed up with a red-wine sauce topped with crumbled bacon.*

1 In a large skillet, cook bacon over moderately high heat until crisp and browned, about 5 minutes. Using a fork, transfer the bacon to paper towels and set it aside; reserve the drippings in the skillet.

2 Core and seed bell pepper; cut it into strips. Add mushrooms, onion, and the bell pepper strips to the drippings in the skillet. Cook, stirring frequently, until crisp-tender, about 4 minutes.

3 Meanwhile, shape ground beef into four oval steaks about ¾ inch thick. Sprinkle them on both sides with salt and pepper.

4 Transfer the vegetables to a warm serving platter, cover, and keep them warm. In the same skillet, cook the beef steaks until they are well browned, about 3 minutes on each side for medium. Place the steaks on top of the vegetable mixture, cover, and keep them warm.

5 Add wine and thyme leaves to the skillet; bring the mixture to a boil, stirring and scraping the bottom of the skillet. Pour the wine sauce over the steaks; crumble the bacon over the sauce, and serve.

CHILI WITH BEANS

One Serving: **Calories** 342 **Protein** 32g **Carbohydrates** 31g **Fat** 12g **Cholesterol** 85mg **Sodium** 1266mg

1 **pound extra-lean ground beef**

1 **large yellow onion, chopped**

2 **cloves garlic, chopped**

3 **to 4 teaspoons chili powder**

¾ **teaspoon salt**

½ **teaspoon dried oregano, crumbled**

¾ **teaspoon ground cumin**

1 **can (14½ or 16 ounces) stewed tomatoes**

1 **can (16 ounces) red kidney beans, drained and rinsed**

1 **can (8 ounces) tomato sauce**

2 **green onions, chopped**

PREPARATION TIME
7 MINUTES

COOKING TIME
30 MINUTES

1 In a large saucepan (preferably with nonstick coating), cook ground beef, onion, and garlic over moderate heat, stirring occasionally, until the meat is well browned, about 7 minutes. Drain off fat. Stir chili powder, salt, oregano, and cumin into the beef until well mixed.

2 Add stewed tomatoes and their juice, drained beans, and tomato sauce to the meat; bring the mixture to a boil. Reduce the heat to low, cover, and simmer for 20 minutes. Spoon the chili into bowls, sprinkle each serving with green onions, and serve.

VARIATION: CHILI WITH RICE

One Serving: **Calories** 438 **Protein** 30g **Carbohydrates** 51g **Fat** 13g **Cholesterol** 85mg **Sodium** 711mg

Add **1 cup long-grain white rice** *and* **one 14½-ounce can beef broth** *to the ingredients list; omit the salt, red kidney beans, and tomato sauce. Brown beef with onion and garlic as in Step 1 above. Stir rice, chili powder, oregano, and cumin into the beef mixture. Stir in stewed tomatoes and beef broth. Bring the mixture to a boil.*

Reduce the heat to low, cover, and simmer until the rice is tender and all of the liquid has been absorbed, 25 to 30 minutes. Spoon the chili into bowls, sprinkle each serving with green onions, and serve.

RUSSIAN-STYLE BEEF PATTIES

One Serving: **Calories** 611 **Protein** 41g **Carbohydrates** 13g **Fat** 43g **Cholesterol** 164mg **Sodium** 292mg

1½ **pounds lean ground beef**

1 **tablespoon butter or margarine**

2 **small green onions, finely chopped**

2 **tablespoons brandy**

1 **cup sour cream**

1 **can (16 ounces) mixed vegetables, drained**

Salt and ground black pepper to taste

PREPARATION TIME
4 MINUTES

COOKING TIME
13 MINUTES

1 Shape ground beef into four patties about ¾ inch thick. In a large skillet, melt butter over moderate heat. Add the beef patties and cook until they are well browned, about 3 minutes on each side for medium. Using a spatula, transfer the patties to a warm serving platter, cover, and keep them warm.

2 Add onions to the remaining drippings in the skillet; sauté until soft, about 2 minutes. Add brandy and cook for 1 minute. Reduce the heat to moderately low. Add sour cream and mixed vegetables; cook, stirring constantly, until the mixture is heated through. (Do not boil.)

3 Season the sauce with salt and pepper. Spoon the sauce onto the serving platter with the beef patties, and serve immediately.

SOUTHWEST CHILI CASSEROLE

One Serving: **Calories** 518 **Protein** 36g **Carbohydrates** 41g **Fat** 25g **Cholesterol** 30mg **Sodium** 1040mg

- 1 **pound lean ground beef**
- 1 **medium-size yellow onion, chopped**
- 2 **to 3 teaspoons chili powder**
- 1 **can (14½ or 16 ounces) diced tomatoes, drained**
- 1 **can (4 ounces) chopped green chilies, drained**
- 1 **can (16 or 17 ounces) corn kernels, drained**
- 4 **small (7- or 8-inch) flour tortillas**
- 4 **ounces Cheddar cheese, coarsely grated (1 cup)**
- **Fresh cilantro sprigs (optional)**

PREPARATION TIME
9 MINUTES

COOKING TIME
33 MINUTES

SERVING SUGGESTION *A salad of sliced tomatoes and chopped green onions accompanies this variation on the ever-popular chili.*

1 Preheat the oven to 375°F. Lightly grease a 1½-quart casserole. In a large skillet, cook ground beef and onion over moderate heat, stirring occasionally, until the meat is well browned, 6 to 7 minutes. Drain off fat if necessary.

2 Stir chili powder into the meat and continue cooking for 1 more minute. Add tomatoes, green chilies, and corn; bring the mixture to a boil. Remove the pan from the heat.

3 Line the bottom of the prepared casserole with one tortilla. Spoon one-fourth of the meat mixture, then one-fourth of the cheese over the tortilla. Repeat the layering, ending with meat, and reserving the last portion of the cheese. Cover the casserole and bake until bubbly and hot, 20 to 25 minutes.

4 Remove the cover from the casserole, top the meat with the reserved cheese, and continue baking the casserole until the cheese is melted, about 2 minutes. Garnish with cilantro, if desired, and cut into wedges before serving.

INDIVIDUAL MEAT LOAVES

One Serving: **Calories** 401 **Protein** 32g **Carbohydrates** 15g **Fat** 23g **Cholesterol** 151mg **Sodium** 641mg

- 1 **pound lean ground beef**
- ½ **cup packaged plain bread crumbs**
- 1 **small yellow onion, finely chopped**
- 1 **large egg**
- 2 **tablespoons chopped parsley**
- ½ **teaspoon salt**
- ½ **teaspoon dried oregano or basil, crumbled**
- ¼ **teaspoon ground black pepper**
- ¼ **cup ketchup**
- 2 **tablespoons water**
- **Parsley sprigs (optional)**

PREPARATION TIME
10 MINUTES

COOKING TIME
35 MINUTES

FOOD NOTE *This version of the childhood favorite cooks faster than a traditional meatloaf—so you can quickly satisfy that craving.*

1 Preheat the oven to 375°F. Grease a 12- by 8-inch baking pan. In a large bowl, using a fork, combine ground beef, bread crumbs, onion, egg, parsley, salt, oregano, and pepper. Shape the mixture into four 3½-inch-long loaves. Place the loaves in the prepared baking pan. Bake them for 25 minutes.

2 In a cup, combine ketchup and water. Brush the ketchup mixture over the meat loaves. Continue baking them until the juices run clear, about 10 more minutes, occasionally brushing them with more of the ketchup mixture. Transfer the loaves to a warm serving platter; garnish with parsley sprigs, if desired, and serve.

Sautéed Calf's Liver

One Serving: **Calories** 467 **Protein** 36g **Carbohydrates** 17g **Fat** 27g **Cholesterol** 405mg **Sodium** 503mg

1 large zucchini

3 tablespoons all-purpose flour

½ teaspoon salt

¼ teaspoon ground black pepper

4 ½-inch-thick slices calf's liver (about 4 ounces each)

¼ cup (½ stick) butter or margarine, divided

2 large white onions, sliced

⅓ cup dry red wine

PREPARATION TIME
5 MINUTES

COOKING TIME
25 MINUTES

1 Cut zucchini into 1½- by ½-inch strips; set aside. On a sheet of wax paper, combine flour, salt, and pepper. Coat liver slices with the flour mixture, shaking off the excess.

2 In a large skillet, melt 2 tablespoons butter or margarine over moderate heat. Add the zucchini and onions; sauté until both are tender, about 10 minutes. Transfer the onion mixture to a warm serving platter, cover, and keep it warm.

3 In the same skillet, melt 2 tablespoons butter over moderately high heat. Add the liver slices and sauté until they are lightly browned, about 5 minutes on each side for medium-rare.

4 Transfer the liver to the platter; cover, and keep it warm. Add wine to the skillet and bring it to a boil, stirring and scraping the bottom of the skillet. Pour the wine sauce over the liver, and serve.

Veal Parmigiana

One Serving: **Calories** 631 **Protein** 45g **Carbohydrates** 36g **Fat** 33g **Cholesterol** 201mg **Sodium** 1366mg

8 slices veal scaloppine (about 1¼ pounds)

1 large egg

3 tablespoons water

¼ cup all-purpose flour

¾ cup packaged seasoned bread crumbs

4 tablespoons olive oil, divided

2 cloves garlic, finely chopped

¼ cup dry white wine

2 cups prepared plain spaghetti sauce

4 ounces mozzarella cheese, cut into 8 slices

¼ cup grated Parmesan cheese

1 tablespoon finely chopped parsley

PREPARATION TIME
13 MINUTES

COOKING TIME
17 MINUTES

1 Using a mallet, pound each veal slice until it is about ⅛ inch thick. In a pie plate, combine egg with water. On each of two separate sheets of wax paper, place flour and bread crumbs. Coat the scaloppine first with the flour, then with the egg mixture, then the crumbs.

2 In a large skillet (preferably with nonstick coating), heat 2 tablespoons oil over moderately high heat. Add enough veal slices to cover the bottom of the skillet without crowding. Cook until they are lightly browned on both sides, about 1½ minutes on each side.

3 Transfer the cooked veal to a plate and keep warm. Add the remaining 2 tablespoons of oil to the skillet, cook the remaining veal slices, and transfer them to the plate.

4 Add garlic to the skillet; sauté 10 seconds. Add wine, stirring and scraping the skillet. Add spaghetti sauce; bring to a boil.

5 Return the veal and any accumulated juices to the skillet. Top each veal slice with a slice of mozzarella; sprinkle with Parmesan. Reduce the heat to low, cover, and cook until the cheeses are melted, about 5 minutes. Sprinkle the veal with parsley, and serve.

HERBED VEAL CHOPS

Herbed Veal Chops

One Serving: **Calories** 311 **Protein** 39g **Carbohydrates** 4g **Fat** 15g **Cholesterol** 163mg **Sodium** 171mg

- 2 **tablespoons olive oil**
- 1 **tablespoon butter or margarine**
- 2 **small green onions, finely chopped**
- 1 **tablespoon Dijon mustard**
- 1 **tablespoon chopped parsley**
- 1 **teaspoon dried tarragon or chervil, crumbled**
- 4 **³/₄-inch-thick veal chops (about 6 ounces each)**
- 12 **mushroom caps**
  Salt and ground black pepper to taste

 PREPARATION TIME
15 MINUTES

 COOKING TIME
12 MINUTES

SERVING SUGGESTION *Baby carrots make an ideal accompaniment to the full flavor of this veal dish.*

1 Preheat the broiler. In a small saucepan, heat oil and butter over moderate heat. Add green onions and sauté until soft, about 3 minutes. Remove the pan from the heat; stir in mustard, parsley, and tarragon until well mixed.

2 Place chops on the rack over a broiler pan. Brush them with some of the herb mixture. Broil 4 inches from the heat for 5 minutes.

3 Turn the chops over and arrange mushrooms caps, stem side down, around them on the broiler rack. Brush the chops and mushrooms with more of the herb mixture. Continue broiling the chops with the mushrooms until the mushrooms are tender, about 3 minutes. Transfer the mushrooms to a serving platter.

4 Brush the chops with more of the herb mixture; continue broiling them until the centers are light pink when cut near the bone, or they are cooked to the desired degree of doneness. Transfer the chops to the platter with the mushrooms, season them with salt and pepper, and serve immediately.

LAMB

Tender lamb is combined with the diverse flavors of herbs and fresh fruits. It makes a delicate and varied alternative to other meats, and can often be cooked more quickly.

BROILED LAMB CHOPS WITH MINT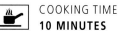

One Serving: **Calories** 468 **Protein** 33g **Carbohydrates** 10g **Fat** 33g **Cholesterol** 111mg **Sodium** 106mg

8 **½-inch-thick rib lamb chops (about 2 pounds)**

2 **large ripe tomatoes, halved**

3 **tablespoons olive oil**

2 **cloves garlic, chopped**

1 **tablespoon finely chopped fresh mint (or 1 teaspoon dried mint, crumbled)**

¼ **teaspoon ground black pepper**

Mint sprigs (optional)

Salt to taste

 PREPARATION TIME
20 MINUTES

 COOKING TIME
10 MINUTES

FOOD NOTE *The sweet taste of mint is the traditional partner for tender lamb, which is best served slightly rare.*

1 Trim and discard any excess fat from chops. Place the chops and tomato halves in a shallow glass dish. In a small bowl, combine oil, garlic, mint, and ground black pepper.

2 Brush the oil mixture on the cut surfaces of the tomatoes and both sides of the lamb chops. Let the tomatoes and chops stand at room temperature for at least 15 minutes to marinate. Meanwhile, preheat the broiler.

3 Place the chops on the rack over a broiler pan. Broil the chops 3 inches from the heat for 5 minutes. Turn the chops over and add the tomatoes to the broiler.

4 Continue broiling the chops to the desired degree of doneness, about 5 minutes for rare. (If the tomatoes begin to overcook before the chops are finished broiling, transfer them to a serving platter, cover, and keep them warm.)

5 Transfer the chops and tomatoes to a warm serving platter. Garnish with mint sprigs, if desired, season with salt, and serve.

TIME SAVERS

LAMB
• Add cooked ground lamb to a prepared tomato-based spaghetti sauce, and turn it into a quick main dish. Drain the meat well before you add it to the sauce. Heat the sauce through, and serve it over your choice of pasta.

• When cooking leftover meat, don't waste time by overcooking it. Since the meat has been cooked once, all you need to do is reheat it, which is best done in the microwave or using the stir-fry method. Mix in some fresh vegetables and herbs.

• Save preparation time by asking your butcher to cut the lamb or other meat into the size you need.

• Make a quick side dish for lamb by combining some applesauce with a small carton of plain yogurt.

BROCHETTES OF LAMB

BROCHETTES OF LAMB

One Serving: **Calories** 284 **Protein** 31g **Carbohydrates** 1g **Fat** 16g **Cholesterol** 101mg **Sodium** 212mg

1½ **pounds lamb center leg steaks**

2 **tablespoons vegetable oil**

1 **tablespoon red-wine vinegar**

2 **cloves garlic, finely chopped**

½ **teaspoon ground ginger**

½ **teaspoon turmeric**

½ **teaspoon ground cumin**

¼ **teaspoon cayenne pepper**

¼ **teaspoon salt**

   Hot cooked rice (optional)

   Lemon wedges (optional)

 PREPARATION TIME
30 MINUTES

COOKING TIME
15 MINUTES

FOOD NOTE *Turmeric, cumin, and cayenne give these kebabs their piquant flavor. A squeeze of lemon makes them even better.*

1 Trim and discard bones and any excess fat from lamb. Cut the lamb into 1¼-inch cubes. In a large bowl, combine oil, vinegar, garlic, ginger, turmeric, cumin, cayenne, and salt. Add the lamb and toss to coat. Let stand at room temperature for 15 minutes to marinate.

2 Preheat the broiler. On four short metal skewers, thread the lamb cubes. Place the skewers on the rack over a broiler pan. Broil the lamb 4 inches from the heat for 5 minutes. Turn the brochettes over and continue broiling them to the desired degree of doneness, about 10 minutes for medium-rare.

3 Transfer the lamb brochettes to a warm serving platter, adding rice, if desired. Garnish with lemon wedges, if desired, and serve.

Glazed Lamb Shoulder Chops

One Serving: **Calories** 414 **Protein** 44g **Carbohydrates** 13g **Fat** 19g **Cholesterol** 155mg **Sodium** 421mg

4 ¾-inch-thick lamb shoulder chops (about 8 ounces each)

¼ cup apple jelly

2 tablespoon dry white wine

1 clove garlic, finely chopped

½ teaspoon salt

¼ teaspoon ground black pepper

 PREPARATION TIME
3 MINUTES

 COOKING TIME
15 MINUTES

1 Preheat the broiler. Trim and discard any excess fat from chops. Place the chops on the rack over a broiler pan. Broil the chops 4 inches from the heat for 5 minutes.

2 Meanwhile, in a small saucepan, combine apple jelly, wine, garlic, salt, and pepper. Stirring occasionally, bring the mixture to a boil over moderate heat. When the jelly melts, remove the pan from the heat.

3 Brush both sides of the lamb chops with the warm jelly mixture. Continue broiling the chops, occasionally brushing them with more of the jelly mixture. Broil the chops until they are cooked to the desired degree of doneness, about 10 minutes for medium. Transfer to a warm platter and serve immediately.

Lamb-Stuffed Pita

One Serving: **Calories** 492 **Protein** 39g **Carbohydrates** 42g **Fat** 19g **Cholesterol** 106mg **Sodium** 738mg

1 pound ground lamb

½ cup fresh bread crumbs

1 clove garlic, finely chopped

1 teaspoon ground cumin

½ teaspoon salt

2 tablespoons chopped parsley

½ cup plain nonfat yogurt

½ teaspoon dill weed

4 pita breads

½ cucumber, peeled

2 small tomatoes

 PREPARATION TIME
20 MINUTES

COOKING TIME
8 MINUTES

COOK'S TIP *Make your own fresh bread crumbs in the blender, or—even quicker—use packaged bread crumbs. Either way, enjoy the Middle Eastern taste of these easy sandwiches.*

1 Preheat the broiler. In a large bowl, using an electric mixer, beat lamb, bread crumbs, garlic, cumin, and salt until the mixture is of a paste-like consistency. Beat in parsley. (Alternatively, using a food processor, break up a slice of bread into the container; add whole garlic clove and parsley leaves. Process until finely chopped. Add lamb, cumin, and salt; process until well mixed.)

2 Shape the lamb mixture into 4 patties about 1 inch thick. Lightly grease the rack over a broiler pan. Place the patties on the rack and broil them 4 inches from the heat for 5 minutes. Turn the patties over and continue broiling to the desired degree of doneness, about 3 minutes for medium. (The patties should not be served rare.)

3 Transfer the patties to a carving board; let stand for 5 minutes. In a small bowl, mix yogurt and dill weed. Cut pita breads in half crosswise and open each pocket. Thinly slice cucumber and tomatoes.

4 Cut each lamb patty crosswise into ¼-inch-thick strips. Fill each pita-bread pocket with an equal amount of the cucumber, tomato, and lamb. Top each with a spoonful of the yogurt sauce, and serve.

PORK AND SAUSAGE

These pork and sausage recipes include favorites like chops and stews, plus the cuisines of Europe and the Far East.

PORK À L'ORANGE

One Serving: **Calories** 289 **Protein** 22g **Carbohydrates** 19g **Fat** 15g **Cholesterol** 66mg **Sodium** 237mg

4 ½-inch-thick rib pork chops (about 6 ounces each)

1 tablespoon butter or margarine

1 tablespoon vegetable oil

2 medium-size navel oranges

3 green onions

½ cup canned reduced-sodium chicken broth

2 tablespoons ketchup

Salt and ground black pepper to taste

PREPARATION TIME
5 MINUTES

COOKING TIME
15 MINUTES

SERVING SUGGESTION *Serve the chops with tiny boiled potatoes sprinkled with lemon peel and chives.*

1 Trim and discard any excess fat from chops. In a large skillet, heat butter and oil over moderate heat. Add the chops and cook until they are browned, about 8 minutes.

2 Meanwhile, finely grate only the orange part of one orange peel; set the peel aside. Cut both ends off each orange; cut away the skin and pith, and cut each orange crosswise into six slices.

3 Turn the chops over and continue cooking until the juices run clear, about 4 more minutes. Meanwhile, coarsely chop green onions. In a cup, combine chicken broth and ketchup. Transfer the chops to a serving platter, cover, and keep them warm.

4 Add the onions to the remaining drippings in the skillet; sauté until they are just wilted, about 1 minute. Add the broth mixture and bring it to a boil, stirring constantly.

5 Add the orange slices and any accumulated meat juices to the sauce; season with salt and pepper. Spoon the sauce over the chops, garnish with the reserved orange peel, and serve immediately.

 *Shelf Magic*

Everyone knows that pork sausage makes a good breakfast, but few realize that it makes a fine supper as well. Try it in this one-skillet dish.

TEX-MEX RICE AND SAUSAGE

In a large skillet, brown **1 pound bulk pork sausage**; drain. Stir in **one 15-ounce can tomato sauce, one 11-ounce can whole-kernel corn**, drained, **½ cup water**, and **1 tablespoon chili powder**. Bring to a boil.

Stir in **1 cup quick-cooking rice**. Remove from the heat. Top with ¼ **cup grated Cheddar cheese**. Let stand, covered, until rice is tender, about 5 minutes. **SERVES 4**

GLAZED PORK SPARERIBS

One Serving: **Calories** 818 **Protein** 52g **Carbohydrates** 28g **Fat** 54g **Cholesterol** 216mg **Sodium** 330mg

4 pounds small pork spareribs, cut into 2-rib portions

½ cup apricot preserves

2 tablespoons lemon juice

1 teaspoon prepared mustard

½ teaspoon ground ginger

¼ teaspoon salt

 PREPARATION TIME **4 MINUTES**

 COOKING TIME **41 MINUTES**

1 In a large stockpot, place spareribs; add enough water to cover the meat. Cover the stockpot and bring the water to a boil over high heat. Uncover the pot and continue boiling for 5 minutes.

2 Meanwhile, in a small saucepan, combine apricot preserves, lemon juice, mustard, ginger, and salt. Bring the mixture to a boil, stirring constantly. Remove the saucepan from the heat.

3 Preheat the broiler. Drain the ribs thoroughly and place them on the rack over a broiler pan. Broil the ribs 4 inches from the heat for 5 minutes. Brush them with some of the apricot mixture and continue broiling 1 more minute.

4 Turn the ribs over, brush them with more of the apricot mixture, and continue broiling them until they are well glazed, 9 to 10 minutes. Serve immediately.

PORK CHOPS WITH APPLES

One Serving: **Calories** 338 **Protein** 20g **Carbohydrates** 13g **Fat** 23g **Cholesterol** 86mg **Sodium** 224mg

4 ½-inch-thick loin or center-cut pork chops (about 6 ounces each)

2 tablespoons olive oil

1 tablespoon finely chopped fresh thyme (or 1 teaspoon dried thyme leaves, crumbled)

¼ teaspoon salt

¼ teaspoon ground black pepper

1 large Granny Smith apple

1 tablespoon butter or margarine

1 teaspoon cornstarch

½ cup apple juice

⅓ cup half-and-half

 PREPARATION TIME **15 MINUTES**

 COOKING TIME **10 MINUTES**

1 Trim and discard any excess fat from chops. In a shallow glass dish, combine oil, thyme, salt, and pepper. Place the chops in the dish and brush the oil mixture on both sides. Let the chops stand at room temperature for 15 minutes to marinate. Meanwhile, quarter and core unpeeled apple and slice it thinly.

2 In a large skillet, cook the chops over moderately high heat until they are browned on one side, about 3 minutes. Turn the chops over and continue cooking until the juices run clear, about 3 more minutes. Transfer the chops to a warm serving platter, cover, and keep warm.

3 Reduce the heat to moderate. Add butter to the skillet. Add the apple slices and cook until they are golden, turning once, about 2 minutes. Using a slotted spoon, transfer the apple slices to the serving platter, cover, and keep them warm.

4 In a cup or small bowl, mix cornstarch, apple juice, and half-and-half until smooth. Stir the mixture into the remaining drippings in the skillet and bring to a boil. Continue cooking the sauce, stirring constantly, until it thickens slightly, 2 to 3 minutes. Pour the sauce over the pork chops and serve.

PORK WITH CUMBERLAND SAUCE

PORK WITH CUMBERLAND SAUCE

One Serving: **Calories** 277 **Protein** 20g **Carbohydrates** 16g **Fat** 14g **Cholesterol** 71mg **Sodium** 60mg

- **4** **½-inch-thick rib or loin pork chops (about 6 ounces each)**
- **1** **tablespoon vegetable oil**
- **¼** **cup red-currant jelly**
- **2** **tablespoons ruby port**
- **1** **teaspoon cornstarch**
- **1** **teaspoon finely grated lemon peel**
- **2** **teaspoons lemon juice**
  Lemon slices (optional)

PREPARATION TIME
5 MINUTES

COOKING TIME
15 MINUTES

SERVING SUGGESTION *For a simple side dish, steam yellow squash and zucchini, and toss it with butter and parsley.*

1 Trim and discard any excess fat from pork chops. In a large skillet, heat oil over moderate heat. Add the pork chops and cook, turning them occasionally, about 6 minutes or until the juices run clear.

2 Meanwhile, in a small saucepan, melt jelly over moderate heat. In a cup, mix port and cornstarch until smooth. Stir the mixture into the melted jelly. Cook until thickened and bubbly, stirring constantly, about 5 minutes. Stir in lemon peel and lemon juice.

3 Transfer the pork chops to a warm serving platter. Pour the sauce over the chops, garnish with lemon slices, if desired, and serve.

START WITH SMOKED HAM

If you keep a package of smoked ham steaks in the refrigerator, you can make any of these sumptuous dishes in a flash. The ham is fully cooked already, so you can use it in cold salads and sandwiches as well as in hot dishes. The smoky flavor of the ham is complemeted by both sweet fruits and crunchy vegetables; try some of these new ideas for a quick and hearty meal.

The smoked ham in these recipes can easily be replaced with boiled or baked ham for a more delicate flavor. Each of the following recipes makes four servings.

▶ **HAM PENNE** Cook **12 oz. dried penne** according to package directions. In a large skillet, melt **¼ cup butter** over moderate heat. Add **1 large yellow onion**, sliced, and **1½ cups broccoli florets**; sauté until crisp-tender. Stir in **3 Tbsp. all-purpose flour.** Gradually stir in **one 10¾-oz. can chicken broth**; bring to a boil. Add **2 cups julienned smoked ham**; thin the sauce slightly with **milk**. Top the pasta with the ham sauce.

◀ **HAM AND CANTALOUPE SALAD** In a large bowl, combine **2 cups diced smoked ham, ¼ cup chopped walnuts, ¼ cup sliced celery,** and **¼ cup mayonnaise.** Slice **2 medium-size cantaloupes** in half crosswise; scoop out the seeds. Place ¼ of the ham mixture into the cavity of each cantaloupe half, and serve.

▶ **WILD RICE AND HAM SALAD** Prepare **one 4.3-oz. package long-grain and wild rice** according to package directions. Set aside to cool slightly. In a large bowl, combine **2 cups diced smoked ham, 1 cup chopped red onion, 1 cup peeled, cubed jicama** (or sliced water chestnuts), and **¾ cup creamy Italian dressing**. Add the rice and toss to coat evenly. Serve warm or cold.

► **HAM WITH PEACH SAUCE** In a small bowl, drain syrup from **one 16-oz. can peach halves packed in extra-lite syrup**, reserving ½ cup syrup. Stir **1 tsp. cornstarch** into the reserved syrup. Fry **two 1-inch-thick slices smoked ham** in a skillet until lightly browned on both sides. Transfer ham to a serving platter. Add **½ cup orange juice, 1 Tbsp. light brown sugar, 2 tsp. prepared mustard**, and the syrup mixture to the skillet. Bring to a boil, stirring, until thickened. Add peaches; heat through. Pour sauce over ham.

◄ **HAM AND BRIE SANDWICHES** Thinly slice **2 small pears**; brush with **lemon juice**. Among four serving plates, divide **8 slices pumpernickel bread**. Spread bread equally with **8 oz. Brie cheese, 2 cups julienned smoked ham**, and 2 or 3 pear slices. Garnish with **chopped parsley**, if desired.

► **SKILLET POTATOES AND HAM** Peel **2 large baking potatoes**; cut into ¼-inch-thick slices. In a large skillet, boil potatoes until tender, about 5 minutes. In a medium-size saucepan, melt **3 Tbsp. butter** over moderate heat. Add **2 cups diced smoked ham** and **1 small green bell pepper**, diced. Sauté until lightly browned, about 6 minutes. Stir in **3 Tbsp. all-purpose flour**. Gradually stir in **1½ cups milk**; cook until sauce is thickened and bubbly. Drain potatoes; stir in ham mixture. Sprinkle **2 Tbsp. toasted bread crumbs** on top.

STIR-FRIED PORK

One Serving: **Calories** 508 **Protein** 34g **Carbohydrates** 31g **Fat** 29g **Cholesterol** 97mg **Sodium** 838mg

1 pound boneless pork shoulder or loin

¼ cup firmly packed light brown sugar

¼ cup reduced-sodium soy sauce

2 tablespoons cornstarch

4 medium-size carrots

4 ounces snow peas

¼ cup vegetable oil

¾ cup canned reduced-sodium chicken broth

¼ cup dry-roasted peanuts

PREPARATION TIME **18 MINUTES**

COOKING TIME **25 MINUTES**

SERVING SUGGESTION *Serve this stir-fry with fluffy white rice and you'll have a meal light enough for a summer supper.*

1 Trim and discard any excess fat from pork. Cut the pork into 1-inch cubes. In a large bowl, combine sugar, soy sauce, and cornstarch. Add the pork cubes and toss to coat evenly. Let the pork cubes stand at room temperature for 15 to 20 minutes to marinate.

2 Meanwhile, peel and diagonally cut carrots into ½-inch slices. Remove strings and tips from snow peas.

3 In a wok or large skillet, heat oil over moderately high heat. Using a slotted spoon, add the pork cubes; reserve the marinade. Cook the pork, stirring occasionally, until it is well browned, about 4 minutes.

4 Add the carrots and chicken broth to the wok. Reduce the heat to moderately low, cover the pan, and cook until the pork and carrots are tender, about 15 minutes.

5 Add the snow peas to the pork mixture and cook until crisp-tender, about 2 minutes. Increase the heat to moderate; stir in the reserved marinade, and cook, uncovered, until the sauce is thickened, about 2 minutes. Transfer the mixture to a serving dish, sprinkle with peanuts, and serve.

PORK STEAKS WITH MUSHROOM SAUCE
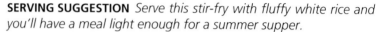

One Serving: **Calories** 414 **Protein** 41g **Carbohydrates** 13g **Fat** 21g **Cholesterol** 134mg **Sodium** 508mg

4 ½-inch-thick pork blade steaks or shoulder chops (about 6 ounces each)

1 tablespoon vegetable oil

1 medium-size yellow onion, sliced

1 can (10 ¾ ounces) condensed cream-of-mushroom soup

1 cup water

½ teaspoon dried thyme leaves, crumbed

1 teaspoon Worcestershire sauce

1 cup frozen green peas

PREPARATION TIME **5 MINUTES**

COOKING TIME **35 MINUTES**

1 Trim and discard any excess fat from steaks. In a large skillet, heat oil over moderately high heat. Add the steaks and cook until they are browned, about 3 minutes on each side. Transfer the steaks to a plate and set them aside. Drain all but 1 tablespoon of the drippings from the skillet.

2 Add onion to the skillet and sauté until soft, about 5 minutes. Reduce the heat to moderately low. Stir in undiluted soup, water, thyme, Worcestershire sauce, and peas. Bring the mixture to a boil.

3 Return the steaks and any accumulated juices to the sauce in the skillet. Cover and cook, stirring occasionally, until the steaks are cooked through, about 15 minutes.

CAROLINA-STYLE PORK

One Serving **Calories** 340 **Protein** 37g **Carbohydrates** 4g **Fat** 19g **Cholesterol** 111mg **Sodium** 102mg

2 tablespoons olive oil

2 tablespoons cider vinegar

2 teaspoons chili powder

1 teaspoon garlic powder

1 teaspoon ground cumin

1 teaspoon dry mustard

1 teaspoon honey

½ teaspoon ground black pepper

8 ¼-inch-thick boneless pork loin slices (about 1¼ pounds)

Salt to taste

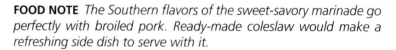

PREPARATION TIME **20 MINUTES**

COOKING TIME **9 MINUTES**

FOOD NOTE *The Southern flavors of the sweet-savory marinade go perfectly with broiled pork. Ready-made coleslaw would make a refreshing side dish to serve with it.*

1 In a l3- by 9-inch dish, combine oil, vinegar, chili, garlic, cumin, mustard, honey, and pepper. Coat each side of pork slices with the mixture. Let the pork stand at room temperature for 15 to 20 minutes to marinate. Meanwhile, preheat the broiler.

2 Using a fork, transfer the pork medallions to the rack over a broiler pan. Reserve the marinade. Broil the pork 3 inches from the heat for 5 minutes. Turn the pork over and brush with the marinade.

3 Continue broiling the pork until it is cooked through, 3 to 4 minutes. Transfer the pork to serving plates, season with salt, and serve.

PORK SAUTÉ WITH ASPARAGUS

One Serving: **Calories** 457 **Protein** 24g **Carbohydrates** 10g **Fat** 37g **Cholesterol** 101mg **Sodium** 188mg

3 tablespoons butter or margarine, divided

1 pound boneless pork tenderloin, trimmed and diagonally sliced ½ inch thick

1½ pounds asparagus

8 ounces mushrooms

1 medium-size red onion

⅓ cup canned reduced-sodium chicken broth

1 teaspoon cornstarch

½ teaspoon dried tarragon or thyme leaves, crumbled

¼ teaspoon ground black pepper

PREPARATION TIME **5 MINUTES**

COOKING TIME **15 MINUTES**

1 In a large skillet, melt 2 tablespoons butter over moderate heat. Add pork slices and cook until browned on both sides, about 2 minutes on each side. Meanwhile, cut off the top 4 inches of asparagus; discard the ends. Thickly slice mushrooms and thinly slice onion. Half fill a small saucepan with water and bring it to a boil.

2 Using a slotted spoon, transfer the pork slices to a warm serving platter, cover, and keep them warm. Add 1 tablespoon butter to the skillet; sauté the onion until it begins to soften, about 3 minutes. Add the mushrooms and cook until the mushrooms and onions are just soft, about 2 minutes.

3 Meanwhile, add the asparagus tips to the boiling water. Return the water to a boil. Cover the pan, remove it from the heat, and set aside.

4 In a cup, combine broth and cornstarch. Add the broth, tarragon, and pepper to the skillet. Bring the mixture to a boil. Cook, stirring constantly, until the broth is slightly thickened, about 1 minute.

5 Return the pork slices with any accumulated juices to the skillet. Stir to combine; transfer to the serving platter. Drain the asparagus, add it to the platter, and serve immediately.

PORK SCALOPPINE DIJON

Pork Scaloppine Dijon

One Serving: **Calories** 222 **Protein** 23g **Carbohydrates** Trace **Fat** 14g **Cholesterol** 87mg **Sodium** 154mg

4 **½-inch-thick boneless pork loin chops (about 4 ounces each)**

2 **tablespoons (¼ stick) butter or margarine, softened**

1 **tablespoon Dijon mustard**

1 **clove garlic, finely chopped**

1½ **teaspoons chopped dill (or ½ teaspoon dill weed)**

Salt and ground black pepper to taste

Fresh dill sprigs (optional)

PREPARATION TIME 15 MINUTES

COOKING TIME 5 MINUTES

SERVING SUGGESTION *This low-calorie dish remains so if you pair it with a green salad with croutons and shaved Parmesan.*

1 Preheat the broiler. Place pork chops between sheets of wax paper; using a mallet, pound each chop until it is about ¼ inch thick.

2 In a small bowl, mix butter, mustard, garlic and dill into a paste. Thinly spread the mustard mixture on one side of each pork chop. Place the pork, mustard side up, on the rack over a broiler pan. Broil the pork 3 inches from the heat until it is lightly browned, about 5 minutes.

3 Transfer the pork to a warm serving platter and pour any accumulated juices over it. Sprinkle the pork with salt and pepper, garnish it with fresh dill sprigs, if desired, and serve.

SKILLET BARBECUED PORK

One Serving: **Calories** 451 **Protein** 48g **Carbohydrates** 13g **Fat** 22g **Cholesterol** 162mg **Sodium** 655mg

1 tablespoon vegetable oil

4 ¹/₂-inch-thick pork shoulder steaks (about 8 ounces each)

1 small yellow onion, chopped

1 cup prepared barbecue sauce

1 large green bell pepper

4 lemon slices

 PREPARATION TIME **3 MINUTES**   COOKING TIME **42 MINUTES**

FOOD NOTE *Enjoy the flavors of the grill from the convenience of your kitchen. Use your favorite barbecue sauce, as hot as you like.*

1 In a large skillet (preferably with nonstick coating), heat oil over moderately high heat. Add pork steaks and cook until they are lightly browned on both sides, 2 to 3 minutes on each side. Reduce the heat to moderately low. Move the pork to one side of the skillet. Add onion and sauté until soft, about 5 minutes.

2 Stir barbecue sauce in with the pork and onion. Cover the pan and cook for 10 minutes. Reduce the heat to low; continue cooking until the meat is fork-tender, about 15 more minutes.

3 Meanwhile, core, seed, and cut green bell pepper into thin strips. Stir the bell pepper into the pork mixture, cover, and cook until crisp-tender, about 6 minutes.

4 Transfer the pork steaks and sauce to to serving plates, top each steak with a slice of lemon, and serve.

PORK WITH RHUBARB-ORANGE SAUCE

One Serving: **Calories** 562 **Protein** 26g **Carbohydrates** 25g **Fat** 40g **Cholesterol** 110mg **Sodium** 346mg

4 ¹/₂-inch-thick rib or loin pork chops (about 6 ounces each)

1 teaspoon dried rosemary, crumbled

¹/₂ teaspoon salt

¹/₄ teaspoon ground black pepper

2 tablespoons all-purpose flour

2 tablespoons vegetable oil

1¹/₂ cups sliced rhubarb

¹/₃ cup sugar

¹/₄ cup orange juice

1 tablespoon cornstarch

 PREPARATION TIME **7 MINUTES**   COOKING TIME **21 MINUTES**

1 Trim and discard any excess fat from pork chops. Sprinkle the chops on both sides with rosemary, salt, and pepper; dust them with flour, shaking off the excess.

2 In a large skillet, heat oil over moderately high heat. Add the chops and cook until they are well browned on one side, 6 to 7 minutes. Turn them over and reduce the heat to moderate; cook until the chops are cooked through, 6 to 7 more minutes. Transfer to a warm serving platter, cover, and keep them warm.

3 Add rhubarb and sugar to the same skillet. Cook over moderate heat until the rhubarb is soft, about 6 minutes, stirring constantly. In a cup, combine orange juice and cornstarch until smooth.

4 Stir the cornstarch mixture into the rhubarb and bring to a boil, stirring constantly. Continue cooking the rhubarb sauce until thickened, about 30 seconds. Pour the sauce over the pork chops, and serve immediately.

PORK TENDERLOIN WITH PINEAPPLE SALSA

PORK TENDERLOIN WITH PINEAPPLE SALSA

One Serving: **Calories** 420 **Protein** 20g **Carbohydrates** 8g **Fat** 34g **Cholesterol** 78mg **Sodium** 330mg

1¼ **pounds boneless pork tenderloin**

2 **tablespoons olive oil**

1 **teaspoon dried thyme leaves, crumbled**

½ **teaspoon salt**

¼ **teaspoon cayenne pepper**

1 **can (8 ounces) crushed pineapple packed in juice, drained**

¼ **cup finely chopped red onion**

1 **small red tomato, finely chopped**

1 **small jalapeño pepper, seeded and finely chopped**

¼ **cup chopped cilantro**

¾ **teaspoon ground cumin**

 PREPARATION TIME
20 MINUTES

COOKING TIME
8 MINUTES

FOOD NOTE *The tangy flavors of Hawaii are combined in pork and this unusual salsa. Try it on the barbecue in the summer.*

1 Preheat the broiler. Trim and discard any excess fat from pork. To butterfly the tenderloin, with a sharp knife placed along one long side of the meat, cut it horizontally almost to the opposite side. Open the meat like a book and press it flat.

2 Place the pork on the rack over a broiler pan. In a small bowl, combine oil, thyme, salt, and cayenne pepper. Brush both sides of the pork with the mixture. Broil the pork 4 inches from the heat for 5 minutes. Turn the meat over and continue broiling until it is just cooked but still moist, about 3 more minutes.

3 Meanwhile, in a small bowl, combine pineapple, onion, tomato, jalapeno pepper, cilantro, and cumin.

4 Transfer the pork to a carving board and let it stand for several minutes. Slice the pork across the grain. Place the pork slices on a warm serving platter, serve with the pineapple salsa on the side.

KIELBASA STEW

One Serving: **Calories** 512 **Protein** 21g **Carbohydrates** 36g **Fat** 31g **Cholesterol** 74mg **Sodium** 1325mg

- 1 **pound kielbasa sausage, cut into 1¼-inch chunks**
- 8 **small white onions, peeled**
- 8 **small red potatoes, quartered**
- 4 **medium-size carrots, cut into ½-inch-thick slices**
- 1 **teaspoon dried marjoram or thyme leaves, crumbled**
- 1 **bay leaf**
- 2 **cups water, divided**
- 1 **teaspoon cornstarch**
- 1 **cup frozen green peas or frozen cut green beans**
  Salt and ground black pepper to taste

PREPARATION TIME
10 MINUTES

COOKING TIME
35 MINUTES

SERVING SUGGESTION *This Polish-sausage stew only needs a basket of warm bread on the side to complete a nourishing meal.*

1 In a 5-quart Dutch oven or kettle, cook sausage pieces over moderate heat until they are browned on all sides, turning them frequently. Line a plate with paper towels; using a slotted spoon, transfer the sausage to the plate and set them aside.

2 Add onions, potatoes, and carrots to the remaining drippings in the Dutch oven; cook, stirring occasionally, until the vegetables are lightly browned, about 10 minutes.

3 Return the sausage to the Dutch oven; add marjoram, bay leaf and all but 1 tablespoon of water. Increase the heat to high and bring the mixture to a boil. Reduce the heat to low, cover, and cook until the potatoes and carrots are tender, about 20 minutes. Meanwhile, in a cup, mix 1 tablespoon water and cornstarch until smooth.

4 Stir the cornstarch mixture and frozen peas into the sausage mixture. Increase the heat to high and bring the stew to a boil, stirring constantly. Continue cooking for 5 more minutes or until the peas are tender. Discard the bay leaf, and serve.

PORK SAUSAGE STEW

One Serving: **Calories** 601 **Protein** 27g **Carbohydrates** 62g **Fat** 28g **Cholesterol** 71mg **Sodium** 1738mg

- 1 **pound bulk pork sausage**
- 1 **medium-size yellow onion, sliced**
- 1 **can (14½ or 16 ounces) diced tomatoes**
- 1 **can (8 ounces) corn kernels**
- 1 **can (8 ounces) tomato sauce**
- 1 **cup water**
- 2 **cups (about 4 ounces) elbow macaroni**
- 2 **cups thinly sliced green cabbage**
  Salt and ground black pepper to taste

PREPARATION TIME
4 MINUTES

COOKING TIME
21 MINUTES

COOK'S TIP *The recipe calls for elbow macaroni, but you may use any shape of pasta of a similar size.*

1 In a 5-quart Dutch oven or kettle, cook pork sausage and onion over moderately high heat until the pork is well browned and the onion is soft, about 7 minutes. Drain the excess fat.

2 Stir tomatoes with their juices, corn with its liquid, tomato sauce, and water into the pork mixture; bring to a boil. Stir in macaroni and cabbage; return the mixture to a boil.

3 Reduce the heat to low, cover, and simmer the mixture until the macaroni is tender and most of the liquid has been absorbed, 8 to 10 minutes. Season the stew with salt and pepper, and serve.

WHITE BEANS AND SAUSAGES

White Beans and Sausages

One Serving: **Calories** 503 **Protein** 23g **Carbohydrates** 24g **Fat** 34g **Cholesterol** 81mg **Sodium** 1486mg

- 1 tablespoon vegetable oil
- 1 medium-size yellow onion, halved and sliced
- 1 stalk celery, sliced
- 8 ounces kielbasa sausage
- 8 ounces sweet Italian sausage
- 1 can (14½ or 16 ounces) diced tomatoes
- 1 can (16 or 19 ounces) white kidney beans (cannellini), drained and rinsed
- 1 tablespoon firmly packed light brown sugar
- 2 tablespoons dry white wine
- ½ cup canned reduced-sodium chicken broth
- 1 teaspoon dried oregano, crumbled
- ¼ teaspoon each salt and ground black pepper

 PREPARATION TIME
15 MINUTES

 COOKING TIME
25 MINUTES

FOOD NOTE *This economical stove-top casserole will satisfy the most hearty appetites on a winter evening. It's filling enough to be a meal in itself, but adding a salad will stretch it even further.*

1 In a 5-quart Dutch oven or kettle, heat oil over moderate heat. Add onion and celery; sauté until they are soft, about 5 minutes.

2 Meanwhile, slice kielbasa diagonally; cut Italian sausage into 1-inch slices. In a large dry skillet, sauté kielbasa and Italian sausage until they are lightly browned, about 5 minutes. Drain off any excess fat. Line a plate with paper towels; transfer the sausage to the plate, and set them aside.

3 Stir tomatoes with their juice, beans, sugar, wine, chicken broth, oregano, salt, and pepper into the onion mixture. Increase the heat to high and bring the mixture to a boil.

4 Add the sausages to the tomato mixture; reduce the heat to low. Cover the pan and let simmer for 10 minutes. Uncover the pan and continue cooking the sausage mixture 5 more minutes. Spoon the beans and sausages into bowls and serve.

KIELBASA WITH CREAMY VEGETABLES

One Serving: **Calories** 773 **Protein** 24g **Carbohydrates** 59g **Fat** 50g **Cholesterol** 129mg **Sodium** 1417mg

4 cups water

1 pound kielbasa sausage

4 medium-size baking potatoes

1 cup frozen green peas

¼ cup (½ stick) butter or margarine

1 medium-size yellow onion, chopped

¼ cup all-purpose flour

1 cup half-and-half or milk

Salt and ground black pepper to taste

**PREPARATION TIME
7 MINUTES**

**COOKING TIME
36 MINUTES**

1 In a large saucepan or Dutch oven, bring water to a boil over high heat. Meanwhile, cut kielbasa into 4 pieces; slash each piece on the diagonal about ¼-inch deep. Add the kielbasa to the boiling water, cover the pan, and boil for 5 minutes. Meanwhile, peel and cut potatoes crosswise into ½-inch-thick slices.

2 Using a slotted spoon, transfer the kielbasa to a bowl, cover, and keep it warm. Add the potatoes to the water in the saucepan; return it to a boil. Reduce the heat to moderate, cover, and cook the potatoes until they are almost tender, about 8 minutes.

3 Add frozen green peas to the potatoes; cook the peas until they are thawed, 1 to 2 minutes. Reserving 1 cup of the potato-cooking water, drain the potatoes and peas; transfer them to another bowl and set them aside.

4 In the same saucepan, melt butter over moderate heat. Add onion and sauté until soft, about 5 minutes. Stir in flour until well mixed; gradually stir in the reserved potato-cooking water. Cook, stirring constantly, until thickened and smooth, about 10 seconds.

5 Stir half-and-half into the onion mixture. Gently fold in the cooked potatoes and peas. Season the creamed vegetables with salt and pepper. Transfer to a serving dish, top with the kielbasa, and serve.

Shelf Magic

Pineapple and bratwurst sausage make a sensational combination. Serve the kebabs on a bed of quick-cooking white rice.

BRATWURST KEBABS

Preheat the broiler. Cut **5 fully cooked bratwursts** into 1½-inch chunks; set them aside. Drain **one 8-ounce can pineapple chunks**, reserving **1 tablespoon of the juice**. On three 12-inch skewers, alternate the bratwurst and pineapple chunks. In a cup or small bowl, combine **½ cup pineapple preserves**, **1 tablespoon Dijon mustard**, and the reserved 1 tablespoon pineapple juice.

Meanwhile, place the kebabs on the rack over a broiler pan. Brush them with some of the preserves mixture. Broil the kebabs 4 inches from the heat until they are heated through, about 2 to 4 minutes, stopping frequently to turn them and brush with more of the preserves mixture. Place the kebabs on a platter and serve.
SERVES 3

MIXED SAUSAGES WITH SAUERKRAUT

One Serving: **Calories** 685 **Protein** 23g **Carbohydrates** 26g **Fat** 52g **Cholesterol** 115mg **Sodium** 2118mg

4 **knackwurst (about 1 pound)**

8 **ounces bratwurst**

1 **large yellow onion**

1 **large cooking apple**

1 **package (16 ounces) sauerkraut**

2 **tablespoons (¼ stick) butter or margarine**

1 **teaspoon caraway seeds**

2 **bay leaves**

½ **cup canned reduced-sodium chicken broth**

½ **cup dry white wine**

2 **tablespoons firmly packed light brown sugar**

 PREPARATION TIME
7 MINUTES

COOKING TIME
31 MINUTES

FOOD NOTE *Sauerkraut is a traditional specialty of Bavaria and the Black Forest. German sausage is its perfect accompaniment.*

1 Cut each knackwurst and bratwurst sausage in half crosswise. Slice onion; peel and core apple and cut it into cubes. Rinse and drain sauerkraut thoroughly.

2 In a 5-quart Dutch oven or kettle, melt butter over moderate heat. Add the sausages and cook until they are lightly browned, about 4 minutes, turning them occasionally to cook evenly. Using a slotted spoon, transfer the sausages to a bowl. Add the onion to the Dutch oven and sauté until soft, about 5 minutes.

3 Add the sauerkraut, apple, caraway seeds, bay leaves, broth, wine, and sugar to the onion; bring the mixture to a boil. Reduce the heat to low, cover, and simmer for 15 minutes.

4 Return the sausages to the Dutch oven, cover, and continue cooking just until they are heated through, about 2 more minutes. Drain the liquid from the pan. Arrange the sausages and sauerkraut on a warm serving platter, discard the bay leaves, and serve.

SWEET AND SOUR FRANKS

One Serving: **Calories** 527 **Protein** 15g **Carbohydrates** 39g **Fat** 36g **Cholesterol** 69mg **Sodium** 1255mg

1 **can (20 ounces) pineapple chunks packed in juice**

1 **tablespoon cornstarch**

2 **tablespoons sugar**

2 **tablespoons distilled white vinegar**

2 **tablespoons ketchup**

1 **pound frankfurters**

1 **large green bell pepper**

1 **tablespoon vegetable oil**

Hot cooked rice (optional)

 PREPARATION TIME
5 MINUTES

COOKING TIME
11 MINUTES

1 Into a small bowl, drain the juice from pineapple chunks. Set the pineapple aside. Stir cornstarch, sugar, vinegar, and ketchup into the pineapple juice; set the mixture aside. Slice frankfurters diagonally ½ inch thick; seed and cut bell pepper into strips.

2 In a large skillet, heat vegetable oil over moderately high heat. Add the frankfurter slices and cook until they are lightly browned, 3 to 4 minutes. Stir in the bell pepper and sauté until it is crisp-tender, 3 to 4 minutes.

3 Stir the pineapple juice mixture into the franks and bell pepper; bring the mixture to a boil. Continue cooking, stirring constantly, until thickened, 3 to 4 minutes. Stir in the pineapple chunks and cook until heated through. Transfer the franks to a warm serving platter and serve with cooked rice, if desired.

PASTA AND GRAINS

SPAGHETTINI ALLA PUTTANESCA (PAGE 220)

PASTA

Pasta is one of the shortest routes to a quick and satisfying meal. Whether you're planning a casual supper or an elegant dinner party, pasta will do on any occasion.

PENNE PRIMAVERA

One Serving: **Calories** 725 **Protein** 18g **Carbohydrates** 98g **Fat** 29g **Cholesterol** Trace **Sodium** 71mg

1 **pound penne or other short tubular pasta**

4 **ounces green beans, cut into 2-inch lengths**

1 **small bunch (12 ounces) broccoli, cut into 2-inch lengths**

8 **ounces asparagus, trimmed to use tips only**

4 **ounces snow peas, tips and strings removed**

2 **large carrots, julienned**

2 **tablespoons chopped fresh basil or oregano (or 2 teaspoons, dried)**

For the vinaigrette

½ **cup olive oil**

3 **tablespoons wine vinegar**

2 **teaspoons prepared mustard**

1 **clove garlic, finely chopped**

Salt and ground black pepper to taste

 PREPARATION TIME
20 MINUTES

COOKING TIME
25 MINUTES

SERVING SUGGESTION *This springtime favorite is delicious served hot or cold. Any fresh vegetables can be substituted, depending on availability. Try using fresh green peas, cauliflower, red bell pepper, or zucchini. Finish the meal with fresh orange slices in caramel sauce.*

1 In a stockpot, bring 4 quarts of water to a boil. Cook penne in the boiling water according to package directions or until it is tender but still firm to the bite.

2 Meanwhile, into another stockpot with a steaming rack or steamer insert, pour 1 inch of water and bring it to a boil.

3 On a heatproof plate placed on the rack, or in the steamer insert, steam green beans for 2 minutes; add the remaining vegetables and steam an additional 3 to 4 minutes or until they are crisp-tender. (Alternatively, cook the vegetables directly in boiling water, one at a time.) Drain the vegetables thoroughly and place them in a large bowl with the herbs.

4 To make the vinaigrette, using a fork, beat all of the vinaigrette ingredients together in a cup. Pour the mixture over the vegetables and herbs. Drain the pasta thoroughly. Add the pasta to the vegetables and toss gently. Serve immediately.

TIME SAVERS

PRECOOKED PASTA
With the use of a microwave oven, pasta can easily be cooked ahead and reheated in just minutes:

Cook the pasta according to package or recipe directions. Drain the cooked pasta and immediately rinse it in cold water to stop the cooking. Drain it again and toss it gently with a little olive oil. Place it in an airtight container, and refrigerate it for up to two days.

To reheat the pasta, place it in a microwave-safe covered dish and microwave on high power for about one minute, stopping halfway through the cooking time to stir. If the the pasta is not hot, continue cooking and testing it at 15-second intervals.

ORZO WITH GARDEN VEGETABLES

One Serving: **Calories** 617 **Protein** 21g **Carbohydrates** 93g **Fat** 18g **Cholesterol** 42mg **Sodium** 353mg

- **1 pound orzo (rice-shaped pasta)**
- **¼ cup (½ stick) butter or margarine**
- **1 large white onion, chopped**
- **1 medium-size red bell pepper, cored, seeded, and slivered**
- **4 ounces mushrooms, sliced**
- **1 teaspoon dried oregano, crumbled**
- **½ cup grated Parmesan cheese**
- **Salt and ground white pepper to taste**

 PREPARATION TIME
8 MINUTES

COOKING TIME
27 MINUTES

SERVING SUGGESTION *This light main course also makes an excellent dish to serve as an accompaniment to beef or chicken. As a side dish it will make 6 to 8 servings.*

1 In a stockpot, bring 4 quarts of water to a boil. Cook orzo in the boiling water according to package directions or until it is tender but still firm to the bite.

2 Meanwhile, in a large skillet, melt butter or margarine over moderate heat. Add chopped onion and sauté until soft, about 5 minutes. Add pepper slivers, sliced mushrooms, and oregano; continue sautéing for 5 more minutes.

3 Drain the pasta thoroughly and transfer it to a serving bowl. Toss gently with the onion mixture and Parmesan cheese. Season with salt and pepper and serve immediately.

RIGATONI WITH BEANS AND VEGETABLES

One Serving: **Calories** 442 **Protein** 18g **Carbohydrates** 62g **Fat** 14g **Cholesterol** 6mg **Sodium** 192mg

- **2 medium-size carrots**
- **1 small bunch (12 ounces) broccoli**
- **8 ounces rigatoni (large tube-shaped pasta)**
- **3 tablespoons olive oil**
- **1 small head escarole, coarsely sliced (about 8 cups)**
- **2 cloves garlic, finely chopped**
- **1 can (10 ½ ounces) white kidney beans (cannellini), drained and rinsed**
- **⅓ cup grated Parmesan cheese**
- **Salt and ground white pepper to taste**

 PREPARATION TIME
6 MINUTES

 COOKING TIME
28 MINUTES

DIET NOTE *Carrots, broccoli, escarole, and white kidney beans join with pasta and cheese to create a delicious vegetarian meal that is rich in vitamins and minerals. To reduce the calories, the amount of olive oil can be cut down to 2 tablespoons.*

1 In a stockpot, bring 4 quarts of water to a boil. Thinly slice carrots and cut broccoli into 2-inch lengths. Cook rigatoni and the carrots in the boiling water for 9 minutes. Stir in the broccoli and continue cooking until the rigatoni, carrots, and broccoli are just tender but still firm to the bite, 2 to 3 minutes.

2 Meanwhile, in a large skillet, heat oil over moderate heat. Add escarole and garlic and sauté until the escarole is just wilted, about 2 minutes. Stir in white kidney beans and cook until heated through, about 3 minutes.

3 Drain the pasta, carrots, and broccoli thoroughly and transfer the mixture to a serving bowl. Toss gently with the escarole-bean mixture and Parmesan cheese. Season the rigatoni with salt and pepper and serve immediately.

ANGEL HAIR WITH ZUCCHINI

ANGEL HAIR WITH ZUCCHINI

One Serving: **Calories** 520 **Protein** 16g **Carbohydrates** 69g **Fat** 20g **Cholesterol** 16mg **Sodium** 533 mg

¼ cup olive oil

3 medium-size zucchini, cut into 2- by ½-inch strips

2 green onions, cut into 1-inch lengths

1 clove garlic, finely chopped

2 cups reduced-sodium chicken broth

12 ounces capelli d'angelo (angel-hair pasta)

2 ounces feta cheese, crumbled (½ cup)

1 large tomato, halved, seeded, and diced

Salt and ground black pepper to taste

 PREPARATION TIME **10 MINUTES**

 COOKING TIME **20 MINUTES**

COOK'S TIP *The fine strands of angel-hair pasta cook very quickly—start testing it after only one minute to avoid overcooking.*

1 In a stockpot, bring 4 quarts of water to a boil. Meanwhile, in a large skillet, heat oil over moderately high heat. Add zucchini and sauté until it is lightly browned, about 10 minutes. Stir in green onions and garlic and sauté l more minute.

2 Add chicken broth to the zucchini and bring the mixture to a boil. Remove the skillet from the heat, keeping it warm.

3 Cook pasta in the boiling water according to package directions or until it is tender but still firm to the bite. Drain the pasta thoroughly and transfer it to a serving bowl.

4 Gently toss the zucchini mixture into the pasta. Add crumbled feta cheese and diced tomato; mix well. Season the pasta with salt and pepper; serve immediately.

PASTA VERDE

One Serving: **Calories** 481 **Protein** 10g **Carbohydrates** 37g **Fat** 33g **Cholesterol** 5mg **Sodium** 268mg

- **1 pound rotelle or fusilli (wheel-shaped or cork-screw-shaped) pasta**
- **2 cloves garlic, halved**
- **¼ cup shelled pistachios or pine nuts**
- **1 cup fresh basil (do not use dried)**
- **½ cup parsley**
- **½ cup olive oil**
- **⅓ cup grated Parmesan cheese**
- **Salt and ground black pepper to taste**
- **Additional grated Parmesan (optional)**

PREPARATION TIME **5 MINUTES**

COOKING TIME **23 MINUTES**

SERVING SUGGESTION *This pasta topped with classic pesto sauce goes well with simple bruschetta: Italian bread covered with chopped tomatoes lightly tossed with basil, vinegar, and olive oil.*

1 In a stockpot, bring 4 quarts of water to a boil. Cook pasta in the boiling water according to package directions or until it is tender but still firm to the bite.

2 Meanwhile, using a food processor or electric blender, finely chop garlic and nuts. Add basil, parsley, and oil; process until the herbs are puréed. Add cheese and process just until well mixed. Season the mixture with salt and pepper.

3 Drain the pasta thoroughly and transfer it to a serving bowl. Toss gently with the sauce until well mixed. Sprinkle with additional Parmesan cheese, if desired, and serve immediately.

BAKED SHELLS

One Serving: **Calories** 401 **Protein** 22g **Carbohydrates** 36g **Fat** 18g **Cholesterol** 77mg **Sodium** 983mg

- **1 container (15 ounces) part-skim ricotta cheese**
- **8 ounces mozzarella cheese, coarsely grated (2 cups), divided**
- **1 large egg**
- **2 tablespoons chopped fresh parsley, oregano, or basil (or 2 teaspoons, dried)**
- **¼ teaspoon salt**
- **1 jar (27 ½ or 30 ounces) prepared plain spaghetti sauce**
- **8 ounces medium-size (1-inch) pasta shells**
- **Additional herb sprigs (optional)**

 PREPARATION TIME **5 MINUTES**

 COOKING TIME **40 MINUTES**

COOK'S TIP *To avoid overcooking pasta that is going to be baked, drain the partially cooked pasta and run cold water over it.*

1 Preheat the oven to 375°F. Lightly grease a 13- by 9-inch baking dish. In a stockpot, bring 4 quarts of water to a boil. Meanwhile, in a medium-size bowl, combine ricotta, 1 cup mozzarella, egg, herbs, and salt until well mixed. In a medium-size saucepan, heat spaghetti sauce over moderately high heat.

2 Partially cook pasta shells in the boiling water for half the time given in the package directions. Drain the pasta thoroughly and rinse it with cold water. Return the pasta to the stockpot and toss it gently with the ricotta mixture.

3 Pour about half of the spaghetti sauce into the bottom of the prepared dish. Spoon the pasta and cheese mixture over the sauce. Spoon the remaining spaghetti sauce over the shells. Sprinkle with the remaining mozzarella.

4 Bake the pasta until it is hot and bubbly, 20 to 25 minutes. Garnish with herb sprigs, if desired, and serve.

FETTUCCINE WITH SALMON

FETTUCCINE WITH SALMON

One Serving: **Calories** 578 **Protein** 21g **Carbohydrates** 69g **Fat** 23g **Cholesterol** 70mg **Sodium** 415mg

2 **cups half-and-half**	
2 **tablespoons (¼ stick) butter or margarine**	
1 **teaspoon grated lemon peel**	

PREPARATION TIME
10 MINUTES

COOKING TIME
28 MINUTES

FOOD NOTE *The rich gets richer when you add smoked salmon to this creamy sauce, making it an ideal dish for a special occasion.*

- 2 **cups half-and-half**
- 2 **tablespoons (¼ stick) butter or margarine**
- 1 **teaspoon grated lemon peel**
- 12 **ounces dried or 1 pound fresh spinach fettuccine**
- 4 **ounces sliced smoked salmon, cut into thin strips**
- ¼ **cup grated Parmesan cheese**
- 1 **tablespoon snipped fresh dill**

  Ground black pepper to taste

1 In a large stockpot, bring 4 quarts of water to a boil. Meanwhile, in a large saucepan, heat half-and-half, butter, and lemon peel over moderate heat until just hot, but not boiling. Reduce the heat to low and cook until the mixture is slightly thickened, about 10 minutes.

2 Cook fettuccine in the boiling water according to package directions or until it is tender but still firm to the bite.

3 Meanwhile, remove the half-and-half mixture from the heat. Stir in smoked salmon, Parmesan cheese, and snipped dill. Season the mixture with black pepper.

4 Drain the pasta thoroughly and transfer it to a serving bowl. Add the salmon mixture and toss gently. Serve immediately.

ROTELLE WITH CHEESE AND WALNUTS

One Serving: **Calories** 527 **Protein** 13g **Carbohydrates** 41g **Fat** 35g **Cholesterol** 50mg **Sodium** 222mg

1 **pound rotelle or fusilli (wheel-shaped or cork-screw-shaped pasta)**

1 **tablespoon butter or margarine**

1 **cup walnut pieces**

½ **cup half-and-half**

½ **cup canned reduced-sodium chicken broth**

4 **ounces mascarpone or cream cheese, softened**

Ground black pepper to taste

2 **tablespoons chopped parsley**

 PREPARATION TIME
3 MINUTES

 COOKING TIME
23 MINUTES

DIET NOTE *Walnuts provide a good source of protein, B vitamins, and minerals. Here the crunchy texture of the sautéed nuts contrasts deliciously with the creamy sauce.*

1 In a stockpot, bring 4 quarts of water to a boil. Cook pasta in the boiling water according to package directions or until it is tender but still firm to the bite.

2 Meanwhile, in a small saucepan, melt butter over low heat. Add walnuts and sauté until lightly toasted, about 1 minute. Add half-and-half and chicken broth. Increase the heat to moderately high and gently bring to a boil.

3 Reduce the heat. Add the cheese to the half-and-half mixture and whisk until the liquid is smooth. Season with pepper and stir in chopped parsley.

4 Drain the pasta thoroughly and transfer it to a serving bowl. Pour the sauce over the pasta and toss gently. Serve immediately.

LINGUINE WITH CLAM SAUCE

One Serving: **Calories** 673 **Protein** 35g **Carbohydrates** 90g **Fat** 17g **Cholesterol** 51mg **Sodium** 345mg

1 **pound dried or 1¼ pound fresh linguine**

¼ **cup olive oil**

2 **cloves garlic, finely chopped**

2 **tablespoons all-purpose flour**

¼ **teaspoon ground white pepper**

2 **bottles (8 ounces each) clam juice**

3 **tablespoons dry white wine (optional)**

2 **cups cooked clams (or two 10-ounce cans baby clams, drained)**

3 **tablespoons chopped parsley**

 PREPARATION TIME
6 MINUTES

 COOKING TIME
28 MINUTES

COOK'S TIP *Small, fresh clams, simmered until their shells open, make the best sauce for this dish. However, since fresh may not be available, ready-to-use cooked clams are a good alternative. To prevent precooked clams from becoming tough, cook them briefly.*

1 In a stockpot, bring 4 quarts of water to a boil. Cook the linguine in the boiling water according to package directions or until it is tender but still firm to the bite.

2 Meanwhile, in a large saucepan, heat oil over moderate heat. Add chopped garlic and sauté for 15 seconds. Stir in flour and white pepper. Stir in clam juice and white wine, if desired; bring the mixture to a boil, stirring occasionally. Stir in clams and continue cooking until they are just heated through.

3 Drain the pasta thoroughly and transfer it a serving bowl. Add the clam sauce and parsley, and toss it gently. Serve immediately.

SPAGHETTINI ALLA PUTTANESCA

One Serving: **Calories** 564 **Protein** 18g **Carbohydrates** 95g **Fat** 12g **Cholesterol** 3mg **Sodium** 909mg

1 **pound spaghettini (thin spaghetti) or vermicelli**

2 **tablespoons olive oil**

4 **cloves garlic, finely chopped**

4 **anchovy fillets, coarsely chopped**

1 **can (35 ounces) whole peeled plum tomatoes, chopped, liquid reserved**

½ **cup pitted black olives, cut in half**

¼ **cup drained capers**

1 **teaspoon dried oregano, crumbled**

⅛ **teaspoon dried red pepper flakes, or to taste**

2 **tablespoons chopped parsley**

PREPARATION TIME
8 MINUTES

COOKING TIME
25 MINUTES

FOOD NOTE *This traditional dish has deep peasant roots, as do most quick and economical Italian pastas; it is named for Italy's ladies of the evening. Serve it with a Chianti or other hearty red Italian wine to complement its zesty flavor.*

1 In a stockpot, bring 4 quarts of water to a boil. Cook spaghettini in the boiling water according to package directions or until it is tender but still firm to the bite.

2 Meanwhile, in a large saucepan, heat oil over moderate heat. Add chopped garlic and anchovies; cook gently until the anchovies are very soft, about 3 minutes. Stir in chopped tomatoes with their liquid, olives, capers, oregano, and red pepper flakes. Cook 5 minutes, stirring occasionally.

3 Drain the pasta thoroughly and transfer it to individual serving plates. Pour the sauce over the hot spaghettini and garnish each serving with parsley. Serve immediately.

NEW TUNA NOODLE CASSEROLE

One Serving: **Calories** 318 **Protein** 17g **Carbohydrates** 13g **Fat** 21g **Cholesterol** 86mg **Sodium** 427mg

8 **ounces farfalle (bow-tie-shaped pasta) or medium-width egg noodles**

1 **package (8 ounces) Neufchâtel or cream cheese, softened**

1 **cup sour cream**

½ **cup milk**

1 **can (6⅛ ounces) tuna packed in water, drained and flaked**

¼ **cup chopped green onions**

2 **tablespoons finely chopped red bell pepper**

Salt and ground black pepper to taste

2 **ounces Cheddar cheese, grated (½ cup)**

PREPARATION TIME
5 MINUTES

COOKING TIME
40 MINUTES

FOOD NOTE *This American classic never fails to provide an easy and healthy family meal. Here it is updated with bow-tie pasta, but die-hard traditionalists can stay with egg noodles if they prefer. Grated Monterey Jack works well in place of the Cheddar cheese.*

1 Preheat the oven to 375°F. In a stockpot, bring 4 quarts of water to a boil. Partially cook noodles in the boiling water for half the time given in the package directions.

2 Meanwhile, grease a 1½-quart casserole. In a large bowl, combine cream cheese, sour cream, and milk until smooth and creamy. Stir in flaked tuna, chopped green onions, and chopped bell pepper. Season with salt and pepper.

3 Drain the noodles thoroughly and stir them into the tuna mixture. Place the noodles in the prepared casserole and sprinkle with cheese. Bake until the mixture is bubbly and the top is browned, about 25 minutes, and serve.

SHELLS WITH SHRIMP SAUCE

Shells with Shrimp Sauce

One Serving: **Calories** 387 **Protein** 27g **Carbohydrates** 48g **Fat** 5g **Cholesterol** 166mg **Sodium** 639mg

- **1 pound medium-size (1-inch) pasta shells**
- **1 tablespoon olive oil**
- **2 cloves garlic, finely chopped**
- **¼ teaspoon dried red pepper flakes, or to taste**
- **1 can (28 ounces) whole, peeled plum tomatoes, chopped, liquid reserved**
- **1 cup dry white wine**
- **1 teaspoon dried basil, crumbled**
- **12 ounces cooked shelled and deveined shrimp**
- **1 cup frozen green peas**
- **Salt to taste**

 PREPARATION TIME
5 MINUTES

 COOKING TIME
30 MINUTES

SERVING SUGGESTION *Steamed broccoli florets and a glass of crisp white wine make light accompaniments to this low-calorie main dish. Another medium-size pasta such as fusilli (corkscrew-shaped pasta) can be used in place of the shells, if you prefer.*

1 In a stockpot, bring 4 quarts of water to a boil. Cook pasta in the boiling water according to package directions or until it is tender but still firm to the bite.

2 Meanwhile, in a large saucepan, heat oil over moderate heat. Add garlic and pepper flakes; sauté for 1 minute. Add tomatoes with their liquid, wine, and basil. Bring to a boil over high heat. Reduce the heat to low, partially cover the pan, and simmer for 10 minutes.

3 Add shrimp and peas to the sauce; cook over high heat until both are heated through. Season with salt.

4 Drain the pasta thoroughly and it transfer to a serving dish. Toss the shrimp sauce gently into the pasta and serve immediately.

Start with some Pasta

It's official—pasta has progressed from its humble Italian roots to conquer the world. Pasta is the perfect staple to have on hand for a quick dinner for the family or guests; some of the tastiest sauces can be ready to eat before the water has had time to boil.

Here are six simple sauces that require only a few ingredients and very little time. When you're choosing which shape of pasta to use, a general rule is that thinner sauces suit longer, finer pastas, and thicker sauces go best with short ones. Estimate about one pound of dried pasta to make four main-course servings. Top the pasta with one of these easy sauces.

◄ **MEAT SAUCE** In a large saucepan, heat **1 Tbsp. olive oil**. Add **1 lb. ground beef, 1 large yellow onion**, chopped, and **2 cloves garlic**, chopped. Cook until the beef is well browned. Pour off any excess fat. Add **one 28-oz. can tomato purée, ½ cup red wine or beef broth, 2 Tbsp. chopped parsley**, and **1 tsp. dried basil**. Bring the sauce to a boil. Reduce the heat to low, cover, and simmer for 15 minutes. Season with **salt and pepper**.

► **CHEESE SAUCE** Using a food processor or electric blender, purée **1 cup ricotta cheese, ¼ cup grated Parmesan cheese, 2 cloves garlic**, and **¼ cup half-and-half** until smooth. In a large saucepan, heat **2 Tbsp. olive oil**. Add **1 small red bell pepper**, cored, seeded, and slivered, and **4 green onions** cut into ½-inch slices (white and green parts). Sauté for 3 minutes. Add the cheese mixture to the pepper mixture and heat through (do not boil). Season with **salt and pepper**.

▼ CREAMY CLAM SAUCE In a large saucepan, heat **2 Tbsp. olive oil**. Add **2 green onions**, chopped, and **3 cloves garlic**, chopped. Sauté until the onions are soft, about 3 minutes. Whisk in **one 8-oz. package cream cheese**, softened, **one 6 ½-oz. can chopped clams**, and **½ cup dry white wine or water**. Cook until heated.

▲ OLIVE-MARINARA SAUCE In a large saucepan, heat **2 Tbsp. olive oil**. Add **1 yellow onion**, sliced, and **2 cloves garlic**, chopped. Sauté 3 minutes. Stir in **one 16-oz. can tomatoes** and **one 6-oz. can tomato paste**. Add **1 cup red wine or beef broth**, **½ cup pitted black olives**, halved, and **1 tsp. dried oregano**. Bring to a boil; reduce heat, cover, and simmer 15 minutes. Add a **pinch cayenne pepper** and **sugar**.

▼ BROCCOLI PESTO SAUCE Using a food processor or electric blender, finely chop **¼ cup pecans** and **3 cloves garlic**. Add **1 cup olive oil**, **one 10-oz. package frozen chopped broccoli**, thawed, and **1 cup parsley**. Process until fairly smooth. Transfer to a medium-size bowl. Stir in **½ cup grated Parmesan cheese**. Season the sauce with **salt and pepper**.

▲ MUSHROOM-ZUCCHINI SAUCE Cut **8 oz. mushrooms** into quarters; cut **2 small zucchini** into 3- by ½-inch sticks. In a large skillet, melt **3 Tbsp. butter**. Sauté zucchini for 2 minutes. Add the mushrooms and cook until tender. Stir in **1 Tbsp. all-purpose flour**. Stir in **1 cup chicken broth**, **½ cup half-and-half**, **2 Tbsp. chopped parsley**, and **¼ tsp. pepper**. Bring sauce to a boil over moderately high heat, stirring constantly.

CREAMY PESTO CHICKEN PASTA

One Serving: **Calories** 654 **Protein** 33g **Carbohydrates** 91g **Fat** 15g **Cholesterol** 67mg **Sodium** 457mg

3 tablespoons butter or margarine

8 ounces boneless, skinless chicken breasts, cut into strips

2 cloves garlic, chopped

¼ cup all-purpose flour

⅛ teaspoon ground black pepper

1 pound fusilli (corkscrew-shaped pasta) or spaghetti

1 cup canned reduced-sodium chicken broth

½ cup milk

1 cup lightly packed chopped parsley

1 cup lightly packed fresh basil (do not use dried)

⅓ cup grated Parmesan cheese

Additional fresh basil leaves (optional)

PREPARATION TIME **10 MINUTES**

COOKING TIME **25 MINUTES**

1 In a stockpot, bring 4 quarts of water to a boil. Meanwhile, in a large skillet, melt butter over moderate heat. Add chicken and sauté until lightly browned, about 7 minutes. Using a slotted spoon, transfer the chicken to a bowl, keeping it warm.

2 Add chopped garlic to the skillet and sauté for a few seconds. Stir in flour and ground black pepper, and cook until the mixture becomes bubbly. Remove the skillet from the heat. Cook fusilli or spaghetti in the boiling water according to package directions or until it is tender but still firm to the bite.

3 Meanwhile, using a wire whisk, gradually stir chicken broth into the flour mixture until blended. Gradually stir in milk. Return the skillet to moderate heat. Cook the mixture until it is thickened, stirring constantly, 2 to 3 minutes.

4 Using a food processor or electric blender, purée the sauce; add parsley and basil and continue puréeing the sauce until it turns green, stopping frequently to scrape the sides of the container.

5 Drain the pasta thoroughly and transfer it to a serving bowl. Add the creamy pesto sauce, the chicken strips, and cheese; toss it gently until it is well mixed. Garnish with additional basil leaves, if desired, and serve immediately.

Shelf Magic

These two simple, meatless pasta sauces require no cooking—the heat of the pasta warms the sauce on its own. With one pound of dried, cooked fusilli, penne, or spaghetti, you'll have a substantial side dish or a light main course.

ARTICHOKE-OLIVE SAUCE

Drain **one 6-ounce jar artichoke hearts**, reserving 2 tablespoons oil. Chop the artichokes; place them in a medium-size bowl. Add **1 tablespoon chopped parsley**, **one 2¼-ounce can sliced black olives**, drained, the reserved oil, **salt and pepper**. Drain **cooked pasta** and toss with the sauce. **SERVES 4**

BASIL AND PINE-NUT SAUCE

In a small skillet, heat **1 tablespoon olive oil**. Lightly sauté **2 tablespoons pine nuts**. Drain the **cooked pasta**; gently toss it with **1 tablespoon butter or margarine, 1 tablespoon chopped fresh basil or parsley**, and the sautéed pine nuts. Sprinkle a **pinch of paprika** over the top of each serving. **SERVES 4**

SPICY SESAME NOODLES WITH CHICKEN

SPICY SESAME NOODLES WITH CHICKEN

One Serving: **Calories** 625 **Protein** 30g **Carbohydrates** 72g **Fat** 24g **Cholesterol** 33mg **Sodium** 397mg

12 ounces dried or 1 pound fresh linguine

1 tablespoon sesame seeds

2 tablespoons vegetable oil

8 ounces boneless, skinless chicken breasts, thinly sliced

1/3 cup smooth peanut butter

1/2 cup hot water

1 tablespoon soy sauce

1 tablespoon distilled white vinegar

1 tablespoon honey

1 tablespoon Oriental sesame oil

1/4 teaspoon dried red pepper flakes

1 green onion, sliced diagonally

 PREPARATION TIME
4 MINUTES

COOKING TIME
26 MINUTES

DIET NOTE *It doesn't take a fortune cookie to tell you that good health is in your future with this high-protein noodle dish.*

1 In a stockpot, bring 4 quarts of water to a boil. Cook linguine in the boiling water according to package directions or until it is tender but still firm to the bite.

2 Meanwhile, in a large skillet, toast sesame seeds over moderate heat until golden, shaking the pan constantly. Place the seeds in a small bowl and set aside. In the same skillet, heat vegetable oil. Add chicken slices and stir-fry until cooked through, about 2 to 3 minutes. Remove the skillet from the heat.

3 In a medium-size bowl, blend peanut butter and water. Stir in soy sauce, vinegar, honey, sesame oil, and pepper flakes. Drain the pasta thoroughly and transfer it to a serving bowl.

4 Stir the peanut-butter mixture into the linguine until well mixed. Toss the linguine with the chicken and its juices; sprinkle with the toasted sesame seeds and green onion, and serve immediately.

CHICKEN CACCIATORE OVER PASTA

One Serving: **Calories** 621 **Protein** 41g **Carbohydrates** 60g **Fat** 21g **Cholesterol** 86mg **Sodium** 831mg

3 tablespoons all-purpose flour

¼ teaspoon salt

¼ teaspoon ground black pepper

1 pound boneless, skinless chicken breasts, cut into ½-inch pieces

3 tablespoons olive oil

1 large yellow onion, sliced

1 jar (14 ounces) prepared plain spaghetti sauce

½ cup dry red wine

12 ounces dried or 1 pound fresh fettuccine

1 large green bell pepper, chopped

PREPARATION TIME 5 MINUTES

COOKING TIME 40 MINUTES

1 In a large stockpot, bring 4 quarts of water to a boil. Meanwhile, in a plastic food-storage bag, combine flour, salt, and pepper. Add chicken pieces; shake to coat with the flour mixture.

2 In a large skillet, heat oil over moderate heat. Add the chicken pieces and sauté until browned on all sides, about 5 minutes.

3 Stir onion into the chicken. Cook until the onion is slightly soft, about 3 minutes. Stir spaghetti sauce and wine into the chicken mixture; increase the heat to high and bring the mixture to a boil. Reduce the heat to low, cover the skillet , and simmer the chicken for 15 minutes, stirring occasionally.

4 Meanwhile, cook fettuccine in the boiling water according to package directions or until it is tender but still firm to the bite.

5 Add bell pepper to the chicken and continue cooking until the chicken is fork-tender, about 5 more minutes. Drain the pasta thoroughly and transfer it to a serving bowl. Top it with the chicken pieces and the sauce; serve immediately.

SPAGHETTI WITH BACON AND VEGETABLES

One Serving: **Calories** 710 **Protein** 29g **Carbohydrates** 44g **Fat** 46g **Cholesterol** 73mg **Sodium** 1224mg

8 ounces sliced lean bacon, cut into 2-inch lengths

1 pound spaghetti

3 tablespoons vegetable oil, divided

1 red bell pepper, cored, seeded and cut into strips

1 green bell pepper, cored, seeded and cut into strips

1 small (12 ounces) eggplant, unpeeled, quartered lengthwise then sliced

½ cup grated Romano or Parmesan cheese

½ cup half-and-half

Salt and pepper to taste

PREPARATION TIME 10 MINUTES

COOKING TIME 24 MINUTES

1 In a stockpot, bring 4 quarts of water to a boil. Meanwhile, in a large skillet (preferably with nonstick coating), cook bacon pieces over moderate heat until they are lightly browned and crisp.

2 Remove the bacon and drain it on paper towels. Discard the bacon fat. Using paper towels, wipe the skillet clean.

3 Cook spaghetti in the boiling water according to package directions or until it is tender but still firm to the bite.

4 Meanwhile, in the skillet, heat 2 tablespoons of oil over moderate heat. Add red and green peppers and eggplant; sauté until softened, about 5 minutes. (Add 1 more tablespoon of oil if necessary.)

5 Drain the pasta thoroughly and return it to the stockpot. Stir in cheese and half-and-half. Season with salt and pepper. Transfer the spaghetti to a serving bowl. Top with the vegetables and the bacon; toss gently and serve immediately.

HAM AND SPINACH-FETTUCCINE ALFREDO

Ham and Spinach-Fettuccine Alfredo

One Serving: **Calories** 920 **Protein** 42g **Carbohydrates** 98g **Fat** 42g **Cholesterol** 273mg **Sodium** 1294mg

- **1 pound dried or 1¼ pound fresh spinach fettuccine**
- **2 tablespoons (¼ stick) butter or margarine**
- **8 ounces cooked smoked ham, cut into strips**
- **2 tablespoons all-purpose flour**
- **1¾ cups milk**
- **¾ cup heavy cream**
- **½ cup grated Parmesan cheese**
- **Salt and ground white pepper to taste**
- **Additional grated Parmesan cheese (optional)**

PREPARATION TIME
4 MINUTES

COOKING TIME
26 MINUTES

SERVING SUGGESTION *When you want a pasta splurge, this is it. Serve it alongside radicchio with feta cheese, chives, and vinaigrette.*

1 In a stockpot, bring 4 quarts of water to a boil. Cook fettuccine in the boiling water according to package directions or until it is tender but still firm to the bite. (Cook fresh pasta at the end of Step 3.)

2 Meanwhile, in a large skillet, melt butter over moderate heat. Add ham and sauté until lightly browned, about 2 to 3 minutes. Stir in flour until well mixed. Gradually stir in milk until well blended. Bring the sauce to a boil, stirring constantly.

3 Reduce the heat to low; stir in cream. Heat the sauce until just hot, but not boiling, about 1 minute. Stir cheese into sauce until smooth. Season the sauce with salt and pepper.

4 Drain the pasta thoroughly and transfer it to a serving dish. Top the fettuccine with the ham sauce and additional Parmesan cheese, if desired, and toss gently. Serve immediately.

THAI PORK AND NOODLES

One Serving: **Calories** 537 **Protein** 30g **Carbohydrates** 70g **Fat** 15g **Cholesterol** 140mg **Sodium** 587mg

8 ounces ½-inch-thick boneless pork cutlets

2 tablespoons soy sauce

3 cloves garlic, finely chopped

1 teaspoon minced fresh ginger (or ¼ teaspoon ground ginger)

Pinch cayenne pepper

12 ounces dried or 1 pound fresh linguine

2 medium-size carrots, peeled and sliced

2 tablespoons vegetable oil, divided

2 large eggs, beaten

8 ounces bean sprouts

1 tablespoon chopped cilantro (or chopped parsley)

PREPARATION TIME
10 MINUTES

COOKING TIME
26 MINUTES

SERVING SUGGESTION *A plate of sliced star fruit and oranges makes a beautiful finish for this Asian-inspired dish.*

1 In a stockpot, bring 4 quarts of water to a boil. Meanwhile, trim the fat from pork. Cut the pork into strips about ¼-inch thick. In a medium-size bowl, combine the pork strips, soy sauce, garlic, ginger, and cayenne pepper. Let it stand 20 minutes to marinate.

2 Cook linguine and carrots together in the boiling water until they are tender but still firm to the bite, 9 to 11 minutes. (If you are using fresh linguine, cook the carrots for 4 minutes before adding the pasta.)

3 In a large skillet, heat 1 tablespoon of oil over moderate heat. Pour beaten eggs into the pan and fry until the underside is set; turn the eggs over and cook the other side. Transfer the eggs to a plate and cut them into ½-inch strips; set aside.

4 In the same skillet, heat the remaining oil over high heat. Add the pork and stir-fry until it is lightly browned, 3 to 4 minutes. Add bean sprouts and cook until they are slightly wilted, about 1 more minute.

5 Drain the linguine and carrots; transfer them to a serving bowl. Add the pork mixture, the egg strips, and cilantro. Toss gently and serve.

ZITI AL FORNO

One Serving: **Calories** 545 **Protein** 21g **Carbohydrates** 47g **Fat** 30g **Cholesterol** 46mg **Sodium** 1345mg

12 ounces ziti or other short tubular pasta

4 ounces pepperoni sausage

4 ounces Fontina or mozzarella cheese, sliced

2 cups prepared plain spaghetti sauce

¼ cup grated Parmesan cheese

2 tablespoons sliced black olives

PREPARATION TIME
5 MINUTES

COOKING TIME
38 MINUTES

1 Preheat the oven to 400°F. In a stockpot, bring 4 quarts of water to a boil. Partially cook ziti in the boiling water for half the time given in the package directions.

2 Meanwhile, lightly grease 4 small individual oval baking dishes, or one 12- by 7-inch shallow baking dish. Cut pepperoni into ½-inch cubes and cut Fontina cheese into small strips.

3 Drain the pasta thoroughly and return it to the stockpot. Add spaghetti sauce and the pepperoni to the ziti and toss gently. Divide the ziti among the prepared small baking dishes, or place it in the large baking dish. Top with the Fontina and Parmesan cheeses.

4 Bake until the cheese is melted and golden, 15 to 20 minutes. Garnish with olive slices and serve.

SPAGHETTI TUSCAN STYLE

One Serving: **Calories** 566 **Protein** 24g **Carbohydrates** 57g **Fat** 27g **Cholesterol** 57mg **Sodium** 1508mg

- **8** ounces sweet Italian sausage, casings removed
- **1** small yellow onion, finely chopped
- **2 ½** cups prepared plain spaghetti sauce
- **1** teaspoon dried oregano, crumbled
- **1** tablespoon butter or margarine
- **1** package (10 ounces) frozen chopped spinach, cut into pieces
- **1** tablespoon milk
- **⅓** cup grated Parmesan cheese, divided
- **12** ounces spaghetti

PREPARATION TIME
10 MINUTES

COOKING TIME
25 MINUTES

SERVING SUGGESTION *A basket of bread and some extra Parmesan are the only accompaniments this hearty bowl of pasta needs.*

1 In a stockpot, bring 4 quarts of water to a boil. Meanwhile, in a large skillet (preferably with nonstick coating), cook sausage over moderate heat until well browned, stirring occasionally to break up the meat. Drain excess fat. Stir in onion and cook for 2 minutes.

2 Increase the heat to high; add spaghetti sauce and oregano to the sausage and onion mixture and bring it to a boil. Reduce the heat to low, cover, and simmer the sauce for 15 minutes.

3 Cook pasta in the boiling water according to package directions or until it is tender but still firm to the bite.

4 Meanwhile, in a medium-size saucepan, melt butter over moderate heat. Add frozen spinach, cover, and cook it until it is thawed, stirring occasionally, about 5 minutes. Uncover the pan and continue cooking the spinach until any liquid in the pan evaporates, about 1 minute. Remove the pan from the heat; stir in milk and half of the cheese.

5 Drain the pasta thoroughly and transfer it to a serving bowl. Cover it first with the sausage sauce, then with the spinach mixture. Sprinkle the remaining cheese on top. Serve immediately.

Shelf Magic

With a jar of prepared spaghetti sauce in the cupboard and a few extra ingredients, the possibilities are endless for a delicious pasta sauce. Cook one pound of dried spaghetti or penne while you're making the sauce.

SPICY TOMATO-BACON SAUCE

In a medium-size saucepan, heat **one 30-ounce jar prepared plain spaghetti sauce**. Meanwhile, cut **4 ounces lean bacon** into short strips. In a small skillet, heat **1 teaspoon olive oil**; sauté the bacon. Add the bacon and **½ teaspoon red pepper flakes** to the sauce. Serve over **cooked pasta**.
SERVES 4

ZUCCHINI-TOMATO SAUCE

In a medium-size saucepan, heat **one 30-ounce jar prepared plain spaghetti sauce**. Meanwhile, slice **1 medium-size zucchini** and chop **1 small yellow onion**. In a small skillet, heat **1 tablespoon olive oil**; sauté the zucchini and onion. Add the mixture to the sauce. Serve over **cooked pasta**.
SERVES 4

PENNE WITH SHRIMP AND PEPPERS

One Serving: **Calories** 614 **Protein** 34g **Carbohydrates** 92g **Fat** 11g **Cholesterol** 132mg **Sodium** 188mg

1 pound penne (quill-shaped pasta)

1 large red pepper

1 clove garlic

2 medium-size zucchini

2 tablespoons olive oil

12 ounces large uncooked shelled and deveined shrimp (thawed if frozen)

2 tablespoons chopped fresh basil (or 2 teaspoons dried basil, crumbled)

Salt and ground black pepper to taste

2 tablespoons grated Parmesan cheese

Additional basil sprigs (optional)

 PREPARATION TIME
10 MINUTES

 COOKING TIME
30 MINUTES

COVER RECIPE *This light, pretty main-dish pasta goes well with classic accompaniments—a mixed salad and a loaf of French bread.*

1 In a stockpot, bring 4 quarts of water to a boil. Cook penne in the boiling water according to package directions or until it is tender but still firm to the bite.

2 Meanwhile, coarsely chop red pepper and finely chop garlic. Cut zucchini in half lenthwise, then slice them crosswise.

3 In a large skillet, heat olive oil; cook shrimp until they turn pink, 3 to 5 minutes. Add the garlic and chopped pepper to the skillet. Cook until the pepper is tender, about 3 minutes. Add the zucchini and basil. Cook until the zucchini are tender, about 3 more minutes.

4 Drain the pasta and transfer it to a warm serving platter. Add the shrimp mixture, season with salt and pepper, and toss gently. Sprinkle with Parmesan, garnish with basil, if desired, and serve.

CINCINNATI CHILI SPAGHETTI

One Serving: **Calories** 541 **Protein** 29g **Carbohydrates** 55g **Fat** 23g **Cholesterol** 65mg **Sodium** 794mg

1 tablespoon vegetable oil

1 medium-size yellow onion, chopped

1 small green bell pepper, halved, cored and diced

1 pound ground beef

2 tablespoons chili powder, or to taste

½ teaspoon ground cumin

1 jar (27 ½ or 30 ounces) plain spaghetti sauce

1 can (16 ounces) red kidney beans, drained

Salt to taste

12 ounces spaghetti

Additional chopped yellow onion and bell pepper (optional)

Grated Cheddar cheese (optional)

 PREPARATION TIME
5 MINUTES

COOKING TIME
40 MINUTES

1 In a stockpot, bring 4 quarts of water to a boil. Meanwhile, in a large skillet, heat oil over moderate heat. Add chopped onion and green pepper; sauté for 5 minutes. Stir in ground beef and cook until browned, about 3 minutes. Stir in chili powder and cumin until well mixed; cook 1 more minute.

2 Add spaghetti sauce to the meat mixture and bring to a boil over high heat. Reduce the heat to low, cover, and simmer the sauce for 15 minutes. Add drained kidney beans and simmer 5 more minutes. Season the sauce with salt.

3 Meanwhile, cook spaghetti in the boiling water according to package directions or until it is tender but still firm to the bite.

4 Drain the pasta thoroughly and transfer it to individual serving plates. Pour an equal amount of the chili sauce over each serving, and garnish with the additional onion, green pepper, and cheese, if desired. Serve immediately.

LASAGNE-STYLE BOW-TIE PASTA

LASAGNA-STYLE BOW-TIE PASTA

One Serving: **Calories** 662 **Protein** 38g **Carbohydrates** 68g **Fat** 26g **Cholesterol** 130mg **Sodium** 934mg

- 8 **ounces farfalle (bow-tie–shaped pasta)**
- 1 **tablespoon vegetable oil**
- 1 **small yellow onion, chopped**
- 8 **ounces ground turkey or lean ground beef**
- 1 **jar (14 ounces) prepared plain spaghetti sauce**
- 1 **cup part-skim ricotta or low-fat cottage cheese**
- 1 **large egg**
- 2 **tablespoons grated Parmesan cheese**
- 4 **ounces mozzarella cheese, grated (1 cup)**

 PREPARATION TIME
7 MINUTES

 COOKING TIME
38 MINUTES

FOOD NOTE *Enjoy the robust flavors of lasagna in only a fraction of the time it takes to create the traditional version.*

1 Preheat the oven to 425°F. Grease an 8-inch square baking dish. In a stockpot, bring 4 quarts of water to a boil. Partially cook pasta in the boiling water for half the time given in the package directions.

2 Meanwhile, in a large skillet, heat oil over moderate heat. Add onion and sauté for 1 minute. Stir in ground turkey and cook until it is lightly browned, about 3 minutes. Add spaghetti sauce; bring to a boil. Reduce the heat to low, partially cover the skillet, and simmer the sauce for 5 minutes.

3 In a small bowl, combine ricotta, egg, and Parmesan. Drain the pasta thoroughly. Layer half of the pasta in the prepared baking dish. Spoon the cheese mixture over the pasta. Spoon half of the meat sauce over the cheese mixture, and sprinkle with half of the mozzarella. Layer the remaining pasta, sauce, and mozzarella.

4 Cover the pan with aluminum foil and bake for 15 minutes. Uncover the pan and bake an additional 5 to 8 minutes, or until heated through, and serve.

GRAINS

From everyday white rice to exotic couscous, grains offer a delicious, versatile range of easy accompaniments and filling main-course dishes.

CRUNCHY GRANOLA

One Serving: **Calories** 274 **Protein** 7g **Carbohydrates** 40g **Fat** 13g **Cholesterol** 12mg **Sodium** 111mg

¼ **cup (½ stick) butter or margarine**

¼ **cup honey**

1 **teaspoon ground cinnamon**

2 **cups old-fashioned rolled oats**

2 **cups corn or wheat cereal squares (such as Chex)**

1 **cup shelled sunflower seeds**

⅔ **cup raisins**

 PREPARATION TIME
5 MINUTES

COOKING TIME
27 MINUTES

SERVING SUGGESTION *Served with milk, and a glass of orange juice on the side, this healthy alternative to store-bought cereal makes a quick, light morning meal. It's also good over ice cream or yogurt.*

1 Preheat the oven to 350°F. In a small saucepan, melt butter over moderate heat. Stir in honey and cinnamon; set the mixture aside.

2 Line a large jelly-roll or roasting pan with aluminum foil; coat the foil with nonstick vegetable spray. In a large bowl, carefully toss oats, cereal squares, and sunflower seeds with the honey mixture; spread the mixture into the prepared pan.

3 Bake the granola, stirring it several times during baking, until it is golden and dry, 25 minutes. Remove the granola from the oven, stir in raisins, and let cool before serving or placing in a storage container.

MULTI-GRAIN HOT CEREAL

One Serving: **Calories** 237 **Protein** 9g **Carbohydrates** 46g **Fat** 3g **Cholesterol** 2mg **Sodium** 63mg

2 **cups water**

1 **cup apple juice**

1 **cup quick or old-fashioned rolled oats**

½ **cup yellow cornmeal**

¼ **cup wheat germ**

½ **cup coarsely chopped dried apple**

½ **teaspoon ground cinnamon**

1 **to 1½ cups skim milk**

Brown sugar to taste

 PREPARATION TIME
5 MINUTES

 COOKING TIME
12 MINUTES

DIET NOTE *Among its many benefits, oats contain soluble fiber, which slows down the body's absorption of sugars in the blood. Here oats join apple juice and cornmeal for a heartwarming breakfast.*

1 In a large saucepan, combine water, apple juice, oats, cornmeal, wheat germ, dried apple, and cinnamon. Bring the mixture to a boil, stirring constantly.

2 Reduce the heat, cover, and cook the cereal, stirring occasionally, 5 minutes. (The cereal should be the consistency of stiff mashed potatoes. If it becomes too stiff, stir in more water or juice.)

3 Add 1 cup milk to the cereal and stir until it reaches a creamy consistency, adding more milk if necessary. Spoon the cereal into serving bowls, sprinkle each with a spoonful of brown sugar, and serve.

RICE PILAF

One Serving: **Calories** 362 **Protein** 7g **Carbohydrates** 52g **Fat** 14g **Cholesterol** 15mg **Sodium** 233mg

- 2 **tablespoons (¼ stick) butter or margarine**
- 2 **ounces vermicelli or spaghettini (very thin spaghetti), broken into small pieces (½ cup)**
- 1 **small yellow onion, chopped**
- 1 **cup long-grain white rice**
- 3 **cups reduced-sodium chicken broth**
- 1 **tablespoon vegetable oil**
- 2 **tablespoons pine nuts**
- 1 **small red bell pepper, cored, seeded, and julienned**

PREPARATION TIME **8 MINUTES**

COOKING TIME **30 MINUTES**

1 In a medium-size saucepan, melt butter over moderate heat. Add vermicelli and cook until it is lightly browned, stirring constantly, about 2 minutes. Stir in onion and rice and sauté 1 minute. Add broth and bring the mixture to a boil over moderately high heat.

2 Reduce the heat to low, cover, and simmer the rice mixture until the rice is tender and the liquid has been absorbed, about 20 minutes.

3 Meanwhile, in small skillet, heat oil over moderate heat. Add pine nuts and sauté until golden. Using a slotted spoon, remove the nuts and set aside. Add red pepper to the skillet and sauté until it is crisp-tender, about 3 minutes. Remove the skillet from the heat.

4 Using a fork, toss the rice mixture with the bell pepper. Spoon the pilaf into a serving dish, sprinkle the top with the pine nuts, and serve.

HAM FRIED RICE

One Serving: **Calories** 288 **Protein** 10g **Carbohydrates** 30g **Fat** 14g **Cholesterol** 86mg **Sodium** 456mg

- 1 **tablespoon butter or margarine**
- 1²/₃ **cups water**
- 1 **cup long-grain white rice**
- 3 **tablespoons vegetable oil, divided**
- 2 **large eggs**
- 4 **ounces baked ham, cubed**
- 1 **small yellow onion, chopped**
- 1 **cup frozen green peas, thawed under warm running water**
- 1 **tablespoon soy sauce**
- 1 **tablespoon Oriental sesame oil**

PREPARATION TIME **5 MINUTES**

COOKING TIME **28 MINUTES**

1 In a medium-size saucepan, bring butter and water to a boil over high heat. Stir in rice. Reduce the heat to moderately low, partially cover the pan, and simmer until most of the liquid has been absorbed, about 5 minutes.

2 Stir the rice with a fork. Reduce the heat to low, cover, and continue cooking until the rice is tender and all of the liquid has been absorbed, about 15 minutes.

3 Meanwhile, in a large skillet, heat 1 tablespoon vegetable oil over moderately high heat, swirling the pan to coat evenly. In a small bowl, beat eggs. Add the eggs to the skillet and fry until they are set, turning them once with a spatula. Transfer the cooked eggs to a plate and cut them into 2- by ½-inch strips. Set the eggs aside.

4 In the same skillet, heat 1 tablespoon vegetable oil. Add ham; cook until lightly browned. Transfer the ham to the eggs and set aside.

5 Heat the remaining 1 tablespoon of vegetable oil in the skillet. Add onion and stir-fry for 1 minute. Stir in peas; cover and cook until tender, 2 or 3 minutes. Gently stir in the rice, eggs, ham, soy sauce, and sesame oil. Cook until heated through. Serve immediately.

FESTIVE MEXICAN RICE

FESTIVE MEXICAN RICE

One Serving: **Calories** 287 **Protein** 5g **Carbohydrates** 50g **Fat** 7g **Cholesterol** Trace **Sodium** 172mg

- **2 tablespoons vegetable oil**
- **1 cup long-grain white rice**
- **1 small yellow onion, chopped**
- **2 cloves garlic, chopped**
- **1 can (8¼ ounces) whole, peeled tomatoes, chopped**
- **1¼ cups canned reduced-sodium chicken broth**
- **1 large carrot, cut into short strips**
- **¼ cup canned chopped green chilies**
- **½ cup frozen green peas**

PREPARATION TIME
5 MINUTES

COOKING TIME
22 MINUTES

SERVING SUGGESTION *With flour tortillas on the side, this colorful rice dish rounds out a meal of beef or chicken deliciously.*

1 In a large skillet, heat oil over moderately high heat. Add rice and cook it until it is golden, stirring constantly, about 3 minutes. Add onion and cook for 2 minutes, stirring occasionally. Stir in garlic and tomatoes with their juice until well mixed.

2 Add broth, carrot, and chilies. Increase the heat to high and bring to a boil. Reduce the heat to low, cover, and simmer for 10 minutes.

3 Add peas; cover and cook until the rice is tender and the liquid has been absorbed, about 5 more minutes. Serve immediately.

JAMBALAYA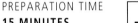

One Serving: **Calories** 352 **Protein** 23g **Carbohydrates** 49g **Fat** 28g **Cholesterol** 123mg **Sodium** 650mg

- 2 **tablespoons vegetable oil**
- 8 **ounces large uncooked shelled and deveined shrimp, thawed if frozen**
- 1 **large yellow onion**
- 1 **small green bell pepper**
- 1 **medium-size stalk celery**
- 1 **clove garlic**
- 8 **ounces andouille (or other smoked pork sausage), thinly sliced**
- 1 **cup long-grain white rice**
- 1½ **cups canned reduced-sodium chicken broth**
- 1 **can (14½ or 16 ounces) whole, peeled tomatoes, drained and chopped**
- 1 **teaspoon dried thyme leaves, crumbled**
- ½ **teaspoon hot red pepper sauce**
- 1 **bay leaf**
  Salt and ground black pepper to taste

 PREPARATION TIME
15 MINUTES

COOKING TIME
24 MINUTES

FOOD NOTE *This traditional New Orleans fish and rice dish is a meal in itself. A culinary cousin of the Spanish paella, jambalaya was adapted by Creole cooks making use of their local ingredients. Inlanders can use thawed frozen shrimp for fine results.*

1 In a large saucepan, heat oil over moderate heat. Add shrimp and sauté until they are firm and pink, about 1 minute. Using a slotted spoon, remove the shrimp from the pan and set them aside.

2 Chop onion, core and chop bell pepper, and chop celery and garlic. Add the onion, bell pepper, celery, garlic, and sausage to the pan. Cook, stirring frequently, for 2 minutes. Add rice and stir to coat.

3 Stir chicken broth, tomatoes, thyme, pepper sauce, and bay leaf into the rice mixture. Increase the heat to high and bring the mixture to a boil. Reduce the heat to low, cover, and simmer until the rice is almost tender and the liquid has been absorbed, about 20 minutes.

4 Using a fork, stir the shrimp into the rice mixture. Cover and cook until the shrimp are reheated, 5 more minutes. Discard the bay leaf, and season the jambalaya with salt and pepper. Place it in a serving bowl and serve immediately.

TIME SAVERS

RICE

- Quickly add a delicious, nutty flavor to plain long-grain white rice: Brown it in a skillet (without oil) over moderate heat. Once it's toasted, cook the rice as the label directs.

- Another quick way of adding extra flavor to plain white rice is to simmer the rice in chicken or beef broth or a combination of broth and water, rather than using water alone.

- Save time on meals by cooking rice dishes a couple of days before you need them. Many grain dishes (excluding risotto) can be cooked in advance and frozen, then thawed and gently reheated.

- For perfect risotto, be sure to use the Italian short-grain rice called Arborio. Do not rinse the rice—the starch that coats each grain is essential for making the rice so creamy.

- You can quickly tell if the saucepan you're using to cook rice is large enough if you remember that rice triples or quadruples in bulk after it's cooked.

- Keep the grains of white rice from sticking by adding a tablespoon of oil or butter to the water before cooking.

- Rice cooks best in a heavy pan—the bottom layer is less likely to scorch, and it makes cleanup much easier.

SKILLET PAELLA

SKILLET PAELLA

One Serving: **Calories** 771 **Protein** 39g **Carbohydrates** 47g **Fat** 46g **Cholesterol** 169mg **Sodium** 878mg

2	tablespoons olive oil
4	chicken thighs (about 1½ pounds)
1	medium-size green bell pepper
1	small yellow onion
2	cloves garlic
1	cup long-grain white rice
1	teaspoon turmeric
⅛	teaspoon saffron threads (optional)
1	can (8 ounces) stewed tomatoes
1½	cups water
8	ounces cooked smoked sausage (kielbasa, garlic sausage or chorizo), sliced
	Salt and ground black pepper to taste
	Parsley sprigs

 PREPARATION TIME
5 MINUTES

COOKING TIME
40 MINUTES

COOK'S TIP *Emphasize the dish's Spanish flavor by adding three or four tablespoons of red wine in the last minutes of cooking.*

1 In a 10-inch skillet (preferably with nonstick coating) or a 5-quart Dutch oven, heat oil over moderately high heat. Add chicken thighs and cook them until browned on each side, about 10 minutes.

2 Meanwhile, cut bell pepper into ½-inch-wide strips. Chop onion and garlic. When browned, remove the thighs from the pan and set aside.

3 Add the pepper strips to the pan; sauté for 1 minute. Using a slotted spoon, remove the peppers and set them aside. Add the onion, garlic, and rice to the pan; sauté for 5 minutes. Stir in turmeric and saffron, if desired. Add tomatoes and water; increase the heat to high and bring to a boil. Continue boiling for 2 minutes, stirring occasionally.

4 Place the chicken over the rice. Reduce the heat to low, cover, and simmer until the chicken and rice are almost tender, 15 minutes.

5 Stir sausage and the pepper strips into the rice. Cook until the rice is tender and the sausage is heated through, 5 more minutes. Season the paella with salt and pepper, garnish with parsley, and serve.

STEWED VEGETABLES WITH COUSCOUS

One Serving: **Calories** 433 **Protein** 11g **Carbohydrates** 80g **Fat** 8g **Cholesterol** 5mg **Sodium** 661mg

2 tablespoons olive oil

1 large yellow onion, chopped

2 cups vegetable broth (made with vegetable stock cubes and water)

2 sweet potatoes (1 pound), peeled, cut into 1-inch chunks

2 medium-size zucchini, thickly sliced

1 cup canned chick-peas (garbanzo beans), drained

⅓ cup raisins

2 cloves garlic, chopped

2½ cups water

1 tablespoon butter or margarine

1 box (10 ounces) quick-cooking couscous (1½ cups)

1 can (8 ounces) tomato sauce

Salt and ground black pepper to taste

 PREPARATION TIME
13 MINUTES

COOKING TIME
27 MINUTES

FOOD NOTE *This North African specialty originated with the Berbers— it was traditionally steamed in a special pot over a stew, where it could best absorb the flavor of the spices. This dish pairs nicely with spicy lamb or chicken. Garnish it with fresh cilantro leaves.*

1 In a large saucepan, heat oil over moderate heat. Add onion and sauté until soft, about 5 minutes. Stir in vegetable broth, sweet potatoes, zucchini, chick-peas, raisins, and garlic. Raise the heat to high and bring the mixture to a boil. Reduce the heat, cover, and simmer just until the potatoes are fork-tender, about 10 minutes.

2 Meanwhile, in a medium-size saucepan, bring water and butter to a boil. Add couscous and boil for 1 minute, stirring frequently. Remove the pan from the heat, cover it tightly, and let it stand until all of the water has been absorbed, 5 to 10 minutes.

3 Stir tomato sauce into the vegetable mixture; simmer for 5 more minutes. Season the vegetables with salt and pepper.

4 Fluff the couscous with a fork and mound it onto the center of a rimmed serving platter or pasta bowl. Gently spoon the stewed vegetables around the couscous to form a border, and serve.

CALIFORNIA KASHA PILAF

One Serving: **Calories** 320 **Protein** 13g **Carbohydrates** 31g **Fat** 16g **Cholesterol** 83mg **Sodium** 117mg

2 tablespoons (¼ stick) butter or margarine

1 large yellow onion, chopped

2 medium-size stalks celery, sliced

1 large egg

1 cup coarse or whole kasha (buckwheat groats)

2 cups water

1 teaspoon ground sage

1 teaspoon ground thyme

1 cup raisins

½ cup coarsely chopped walnuts

Salt to taste

PREPARATION TIME
5 MINUTES

COOKING TIME
25 MINUTES

1 In a large skillet, melt butter or margarine over moderate heat. Add chopped onion and sliced celery; sauté until the vegetables begin to soften, about 3 minutes.

2 In a small bowl, mix egg with kasha; add the mixture to the vegetables in the skillet. Cook the kasha until the grains are dry and separated, stirring constantly, about 1 minute.

3 Add water, sage, and thyme to the kasha mixture. Increase the heat to high and bring the mixture to a boil. Reduce the heat to low, cover, and cook the kasha until it is almost tender, about 10 minutes.

4 Stir raisins and walnuts into the kasha. Continue cooking until the kasha is tender and all the liquid has been absorbed, about 5 more minutes. Season with salt and serve immediately.

POLENTA WITH FONTINA CHEESE SAUCE

One Serving: **Calories** 444 **Protein** 18g **Carbohydrates** 38g **Fat** 26g **Cholesterol** 228mg **Sodium** 435mg

- **6 ounces Fontina cheese, coarsely grated (1½ cups)**
- **½ cup milk**
- **4½ cups water, divided**
- **1½ cups yellow cornmeal**
- **2 tablespoons (¼ stick) butter or margarine**
- **3 large egg yolks**
- **Pinch ground white pepper**
- **Thinly sliced mushrooms (optional)**

PREPARATION TIME
5 MINUTES

COOKING TIME
25 MINUTES

FOOD NOTE *Polenta—a smooth, warming cornmeal mixture—is a northern Italian classic that comes in many guises. Combined as it is here with Fontina cheese, it creates what Italians call* fonduta. *It makes a nourishing vegetarian dish.*

1 In a medium-size bowl, combine cheese and milk. Set the mixture aside. To make the polenta, in a medium-size saucepan, bring 3½ cups of water to a boil. In a small bowl, combine the remaining 1 cup of water and cornmeal. Stir the cornmeal mixture into the boiling water. Cook, stirring constantly, until thickened, about 5 minutes.

2 Reduce the heat to low, cover, and continue cooking the cornmeal 5 more minutes. Remove the pan from the heat and set it aside, keeping the mixture warm.

3 Meanwhile, partially fill the lower part of a double boiler with water and bring it to a boil. Reduce the heat to very low. In the upper part of the double boiler, melt butter over hot, not simmering, water. Add the cheese mixture and stir until the cheese melts. Add egg yolks and continue stirring until the mixture is smooth. Stir in pepper.

4 Spoon the polenta to form individual mounds on warm serving plates. Using the back of a spoon, make an indentation in each mound. Pour an equal amount of the cheese sauce into each indentation. Garnish each serving with mushrooms, if desired, and serve.

Here are two ways to use quick-cooking rice to make a delicious side dish.

ORANGE RICE

In a medium-size saucepan, combine **1½ cups orange juice, 1 tablespoon butter or margarine**, and **1 teaspoon grated orange peel**. Bring to a boil. Stir in **1½ cups quick-cooking rice**. Cover the pan and remove it from the heat. Let stand for 5 minutes. Stir in **½ cup broken pecans**. **SERVES 4**

CURRIED RICE

In a medium-size saucepan, combine **one 14½-ounce can chicken broth, ⅓ cup raisins, 1 tablespoon curry powder**, and **1 tablespoon butter or margarine**. Bring to a boil. Stir in **1½ cups quick-cooking rice**; cover. Remove from heat. Let stand for 5 minutes. Stir in **⅓ cup chopped peanuts**. **SERVES 4**

POLENTA PIZZA

POLENTA PIZZA

One Serving: **Calories** 542 **Protein** 19g **Carbohydrates** 48g **Fat** 31g **Cholesterol** 25mg **Sodium** 1266mg

3 cups water, divided

1½ cups yellow cornmeal

¼ teaspoon salt

2 tablespoons olive oil

1 medium-size yellow onion

4 ounces mushrooms

1 cup plain spaghetti sauce or pizza sauce

4 ounces thinly sliced pepperoni

¼ cup sliced black olives

4 ounces mozzarella cheese, grated (1 cup)

 PREPARATION TIME
10 MINUTES

 COOKING TIME
35 MINUTES

SERVING SUGGESTION *Serve simple mixed greens with this easy twist on pizza—a cornmeal base with traditional pizza toppings.*

1 Preheat the oven to 400°F. Lightly grease a 12-inch pizza pan or large baking sheet. To make the cornmeal crust, in a medium-size saucepan, bring 1½ cups water to a boil. Meanwhile, in a medium-size bowl, combine the remaining 1½ cups water, cornmeal, and salt. Using a wire whisk, stir the cornmeal mixture into the boiling water.

2 Cook the cornmeal until it thickens, stirring occasionally, about 2 minutes. Spread the cornmeal in an even layer over the pizza pan, or form a 12-inch round on the baking sheet, making a slight rim around the edge. Bake for 15 minutes.

3 Meanwhile, slice onion and mushrooms. In a large skillet, heat oil over moderate heat. Add the onion; sauté 3 minutes. Add the mushrooms; sauté until softened, 3 minutes. Remove from the heat.

4 Remove the crust from the oven and spread it with spaghetti sauce. Arrange the onions and mushrooms, pepperoni, and olives over the sauce. Sprinkle the pizza with mozzarella cheese; bake it until the topping is bubbly, about 15 minutes. Cut into wedges and serve.

VEGETABLE RISOTTO

One Serving: **Calories** 453 **Protein** 15g **Carbohydrates** 65g **Fat** 15g **Cholesterol** 26mg **Sodium** 514mg

2 cups canned reduced-sodium chicken broth

2 cups water

2 tablespoons (¼ stick) butter or margarine

1 tablespoon olive oil

1 small yellow onion, finely chopped

1 clove garlic, finely chopped

1½ cups Arborio rice or medium-grain white rice

1 small zucchini, sliced

4 ounces small broccoli florets (1 cup)

½ cup frozen green peas, thawed under warm running water

⅓ cup grated Parmesan cheese

Additional grated Parmesan cheese (optional)

 PREPARATION TIME **8 MINUTES**

COOKING TIME **22 MINUTES**

COOK'S TIP *To produce classic, creamy Italian risotto, add the broth and water mixture to the rice in small doses, stirring frequently. This main course is at its best when served as soon as it is done.*

1 In a medium-size saucepan, bring broth and water to a boil over moderate heat. Meanwhile, in a large saucepan, melt butter with oil over moderate heat. Add onion and garlic to the butter and oil; sauté for 1 minute. Add rice to the onion mixture and cook, stirring constantly with a wooden spoon, for 2 minutes.

2 Add 2 cups of the hot broth and water to the rice mixture, ½ cup at a time, stirring frequently, allowing all of the broth to be absorbed before adding more.

3 Add zucchini, broccoli and 1 more cup of the broth and water. Cook for 5 more minutes, uncovered, stirring occasionally. Continue to add the broth and water until the mixture is creamy and the rice is cooked but still firm to the bite. (Not all of the broth may be needed.)

4 Stir peas and cheese into the rice mixture and continue cooking until the peas are heated through, about 1 minute. Serve the risotto immediately, passing additional Parmesan on the side, if desired.

CHEESE-TOPPED BARLEY WITH MUSHROOMS

One Serving: **Calories** 248 **Protein** 8g **Carbohydrates** 34g **Fat** 9g **Cholesterol** 23mg **Sodium** 237mg

2 tablespoons (¼ stick) butter or margarine

1 medium-size onion, sliced

8 ounces small mushrooms, halved (2¼ cups)

1 clove garlic, chopped

1 bay leaf

2 cups reduced-sodium chicken broth

1 cup quick-cooking pearl barley (not regular barley)

1 ounce Cheddar cheese, coarsely grated (¼ cup)

1 green onion top, chopped

PREPARATION TIME **6 MINUTES**

COOKING TIME **17 MINUTES**

FOOD NOTE *Quick-cooking pearl barley is a refined form of whole-grain barley; it's main benefit is that it can be cooked in a fraction of the time. This cheese-topped version makes a healthy side dish.*

1 In a large saucepan, melt butter over moderate heat. Add onion and sauté until slightly softened, 3 minutes. Stir in mushrooms, garlic, and bay leaf; continue sautéing until the mushrooms are slightly softened, about 2 minutes.

2 Stir in chicken broth and barley. Increase the heat to high and bring the mixture to a boil. Reduce heat to low, cover, and simmer the barley until it is tender and all of the liquid has been absorbed, 10 to 12 minutes. Discard the bay leaf. Spoon the barley into a serving dish, top it with cheese and green onion, and serve immediately.

EGGS AND CHEESE

BAKED EGGS FLORENTINE (PAGE 257)

Eggs and Cheese

For an elegant brunch or a light supper, here is a savory selection of egg and cheese dishes.

Corn Soufflé–Stuffed Peppers

One Serving: **Calories** 277 **Protein** 12g **Carbohydrates** 37g. **Fat** 11g **Cholesterol** 225mg **Sodium** 324mg

4 large flat-bottomed red or green bell peppers (about 8 ounces each)

²/₃ cup milk

²/₃ cup yellow cornmeal

¹/₄ cup water

1 tablespoon butter or margarine

¹/₄ teaspoon salt

  Pinch ground black pepper

4 large eggs, separated, at room temperature

¹/₂ cup canned corn kernels (or frozen corn kernels, thawed)

1 tablespoon chopped green onion top (green part only)

 PREPARATION TIME
15 MINUTES

 COOKING TIME
30 MINUTES

SERVING SUGGESTION *Pair this vegetarian supper with mixed greens and lightly sautéed zucchini ribbons sliced with a potato peeler.*

1 Preheat the oven to 400°F; grease a 9-inch round baking dish. Slice the tops off peppers and reserve. Core and seed the pepper cups. Stand the peppers upright in the prepared dish. (Trim a thin slice off the bottom of any peppers that will not stand up.) Place the reserved tops in the dish next to the cups.

2 In a medium-size saucepan, heat milk over moderate heat until scalded. Meanwhile, in a small bowl or cup, mix cornmeal and water; stir the cornmeal mixture into the scalded milk.

3 Cook the cornmeal until thickened, stirring constantly, about 2 minutes. Stir in butter, salt, and pepper. Remove the pan from the heat; beat in egg yolks, corn, and onion top.

4 In a medium-size bowl, using an electric mixer, beat egg whites until they are stiff but not dry. Stir a heaping spoonful of the whites into the cornmeal mixture to lighten it. Fold the cornmeal mixture into the remaining whites. Spoon an equal amount into each pepper.

5 Bake the soufflés until they are puffed and golden brown, 25 to 30 minutes. Place the pepper tops next to each pepper, and serve.

Time Savers

Egg Whites
• After using egg yolks in a recipe, cooks are often left with extra whites. A quick way to store the whites is to freeze them in an ice cube tray, then transfer them to a freezer bag. They'll keep for a month.

• When beating egg whites, always start with eggs at room temperature for the greatest volume. If you forget to take the eggs out of the refrigerator ahead of time, let them stand in a bowl of warm water for a few minutes before beating.

• Folding in egg whites is easier if you first stir a quarter of the whites into the mixture to lighten it. Add the remaining whites and cut them into the mixture with a rubber spatula, using a circular motion and turning the bowl as you mix.

SPANISH POTATO OMELET

One Serving: **Calories** 364 **Protein** 11g **Carbohydrates** 40g **Fat** 19g **Cholesterol** 212mg **Sodium** 426mg

6 tablespoons olive oil, divided

4 large baking potatoes (about 2 pounds) peeled and cut into ⅛-inch slices

1 large yellow onion, thinly sliced

½ cup water

½ teaspoon salt

1 clove garlic

1 can (14½ or 16 ounces) tomatoes, drained and chopped

½ cup reduced-sodium chicken broth

⅛ teaspoon saffron threads, crumbled

6 large eggs

 PREPARATION TIME **20 MINUTES**

 COOKING TIME **25 MINUTES**

1 In a large skillet or Dutch oven, heat 4 tablespoons of olive oil over low heat. Add potatoes and onion, carefully stirring to coat with oil. Add water and salt; cover and cook, stirring occasionally, until the potatoes are tender but not browned, about 15 minutes.

2 Meanwhile, to prepare the sauce, heat 1 tablespoon of olive oil in a medium-size saucepan over moderately high heat. Add garlic and sauté for 15 seconds. Stir in tomatoes, broth, and saffron. Cover and bring to a boil. Reduce the heat to low and simmer for 15 minutes.

3 In a large bowl, beat eggs. Stir the cooked potato mixture into the eggs. In a 10-inch skillet or omelet pan, preferably with nonstick coating, heat remaining 1 tablespoon of olive oil over moderately low heat. Add the egg mixture and spread to an even layer. Cover and cook the omelet until the underside of the eggs begins to brown and the top begins to set, about 8 minutes.

4 Place a baking sheet upside-down over the skillet and carefully invert the omelet onto the baking sheet. Slide the omelet, topside-down, back into the skillet; continue cooking until it is browned on the other side, about 3 minutes.

5 Transfer the omelet to a platter and cut it into wedges. If desired, press the sauce through a strainer into a bowl to extract as much pulp as possible and remove the seeds. Serve the omelet immediately, passing the sauce separately.

MIXED VEGETABLE EGG SCRAMBLE

One Serving: **Calories** 203 **Protein** 11g **Carbohydrate** 9g **Fat** 14g **Cholesterol** 333mg **Sodium** 319mg

2 tablespoons (¼ stick) butter or margarine

1 small zucchini, quartered lengthwise and sliced

1 medium-size carrot, very thinly sliced

1 small red onion, sliced

½ cup frozen green peas

6 large eggs

⅓ cup water

¼ teaspoon salt

¼ teaspoon dried oregano, crumbled

 PREPARATION TIME **7 MINUTES**

COOKING TIME **17 MINUTES**

1 In a large skillet (preferably with nonstick coating) melt butter or margarine over moderate heat. Add sliced zucchini, carrot, and onion; sauté for 5 to 7 minutes. Reduce the heat to low. Stir in peas, cover the skillet, and continue cooking until the vegetables are tender, about 5 minutes.

2 Meanwhile, in a medium-size bowl, beat eggs, water, salt, and oregano. When the vegetables are done, pour the egg mixture into the skillet. Stir gently from the edge toward the center of the skillet until the eggs begin to set, 2 to 3 minutes. Cover and cook a few more minutes, until the eggs are just set. Serve immediately.

SPINACH SOUFFLÉ

Spinach Soufflé

One Serving: **Calories** 312 **Protein** 14g **Carbohydrates** 16g **Fat** 22g **Cholesterol** 450mg **Sodium** 566mg

4 tablespoons (½ stick) butter or margarine

1 small yellow onion, finely chopped

1 package (10 ounces) frozen chopped spinach, cut into coarse chunks

¼ cup all-purpose flour

1 cup milk

½ teaspoon salt

6 large eggs, separated, at room temperature

PREPARATION TIME
8 MINUTES

COOKING TIME
36 MINUTES

COOK'S TIP *It's best to fold the spinach mixture into the beaten egg whites very gradually for the most dramatic results.*

1 Preheat the oven to 325°F. In a medium-size saucepan, melt butter over moderate heat. Add onion and sauté until soft, about 5 minutes. Add spinach, cover, and cook until thawed, shaking the pan occasionally, about 3 minutes. Remove the lid and continue cooking until all of the liquid has evaporated, about 1 more minute.

2 Stir flour into spinach until well mixed. Gradually stir in milk and salt. Cook until the mixture thickens, stirring constantly, about 1 minute. Remove the pan from the heat and stir in egg yolks.

3 In a large bowl, using an electric mixer, beat egg whites until stiff but not dry. Fold in the spinach. Spoon the mixture into a 2-quart soufflé dish. Bake until the soufflé is puffy and golden, 25 to 30 minutes. (Do not open the oven during baking.) Serve immediately.

BASQUE EGGS

BASQUE EGGS

One Serving: **Calories** 368 **Protein** 21g **Carbohydrates** 9g **Fat** 28g **Cholesterol** 580mg **Sodium** 466mg

2 tablespoons olive oil

1 medium-size yellow onion, thinly sliced

1 small bell pepper, cut into thin strips

6 ounces baked ham, cut into thin strips

1 can (8 ounces) tomatoes, drained and chopped

2 large garlic cloves, crushed

1 teaspoon dried basil, crumbled

8 large eggs

¼ teaspoon salt

⅛ teaspoon ground black pepper

1 tablespoon butter or margarine

 PREPARATION TIME
15 MINUTES

 COOKING TIME
12 MINUTES

SERVING SUGGESTION *Known in Spain as a* piperade, *this colorful main course goes well with sliced, sautéed potatoes. Precook the potatoes slightly in boiling water before sautéeing.*

1 In a large saucepan, heat oil over moderate heat. Add onion and bell pepper; sauté for 2 to 3 minutes. Stir in ham, tomatoes, garlic, and basil. Continue cooking, stirring occasionally, for 3 minutes. Remove the pan from the heat, cover, and set aside.

2 In a medium-size bowl, beat eggs, salt, and black pepper. In a large skillet or omelet pan (preferably with nonstick coating), melt butter over low heat, swirling the pan to coat evenly.

3 Pour the egg mixture into the skillet and cook until the edge begins to set, about 1 minute. Using a wooden spoon or spatula, push the set egg toward the center, allowing the uncooked egg to run to the bottom of the skillet. Repeat until only a thin layer of the uncooked egg remains on top.

4 Spoon the ham and tomato mixture evenly over the eggs. Cook, uncovered, until the eggs are just set. Serve immediately.

Ham and Apple Puffy Omelet

One Serving: **Calories** 340 **Protein** 17g **Carbohydrates** 14g **Fat** 24g **Cholesterol** 458 **Sodium** 359mg

2 **medium-size red cooking apples**

1 **tablespoon lemon juice, divided**

6 **large eggs, separated**

2 **tablespoons water**

½ **teaspoon salt**

3 **tablespoons butter or margarine, divided**

2 **teaspoons light brown sugar**

6 **ounces baked ham, cut into thin strips**

Parsley

 PREPARATION TIME **15 MINUTES**

COOKING TIME **15 MINUTES**

1 Preheat the oven to 400°F. Slice the apples in half and remove the cores. Chop three of the apple halves into ¼-inch pieces. Thinly slice the remaining half lengthwise. In a small bowl, toss the apple pieces with ½ tablespoon lemon juice. In a separate bowl, toss the apple slices with the remaining ½ tablespoon of lemon juice. Set aside.

2 In a large bowl, using an electric mixer, beat egg whites until stiff but not dry. In a small bowl, again using the electric mixer, beat yolks, water, and salt until the mixture has thickened and become pale yellow, 5 minutes. Fold the yolk mixture into the beaten egg whites.

3 In an oven-safe 12-inch skillet, melt 1 tablespoon of butter over moderately low heat, swirling the pan to coat evenly. Add the egg mixture and cook until the bottom is golden, about 5 minutes. Place the skillet in the oven and bake until the top of the omelet is golden and springs back when lightly touched, 5 to 10 minutes.

4 Meanwhile, in a medium-size saucepan, heat brown sugar with the remaining 2 tablespoons of butter. Add the chopped (not sliced) apples and ham. Sauté until the apples are tender, 4 to 5 minutes. Remove the pan from the heat.

5 To serve, loosen the omelet from the skillet. Spoon the apple and ham mixture over half of the omelet. Fold the omelet over the filling and slide it onto a serving platter. Garnish with parsley and the remaining uncooked apple slices, and serve immediately.

Variation: Western puffy omelet

One Serving: **Calories** 259 **Protein** 12g **Carbohydrate**s 8g **Fat** 20g **Cholesterol** 342mg **Sodium** 633mg

Preheat the oven to 400°F. Melt 2 tablespoons of butter in a medium-size skillet over moderate heat. Add **1 small green bell pepper**, *chopped,* **2 small zucchini**, *chopped, and* **1 small onion**, *chopped. Sauté the vegetables until soft, about 5 minutes.*

Add to the vegetables **1 can (14½ or 16 ounces) tomatoes**, *drained and chopped,* **¼ cup sliced black olives**, **1 teaspoon dried basil, crumbled**, *and* **¼ teaspoon ground black pepper**. *Cook until heated through, stirring occasionally, about 2 minutes. Cover the skillet and keep the vegetables warm.*

Prepare the omelet as directed in Steps 2 and 3 above. To serve, loosen the baked omelet from the skillet and transfer it to a large serving platter. Spoon the vegetable mixture on top of the omelet and sprinkle with **½ cup grated Monterey Jack cheese**. *Cut the omelet into wedges and serve immediately.*

CHINESE EGG PANCAKES

One Serving: **Calories** 220 **Protein** 19g **Carbohydrates** 8g **Fat** 13g **Cholesterol** 255mg **Sodium** 614mg

4 large eggs

8 ounces tiny cooked shrimp (about 1½ cups), thawed and drained if frozen

8 ounces bean sprouts (about 3 cups), chopped

¼ cup chopped green onion

2 to 3 tablespoons vegetable oil, divided

For the Oriental sauce

1 cup canned reduced-sodium chicken broth

1 tablespoon cornstarch

1 teaspoon soy sauce

¼ teaspoon sugar

½ teaspoon Oriental sesame oil

PREPARATION TIME
10 MINUTES

COOKING TIME
18 MINUTES

1 To prepare the sauce, in a small saucepan, combine broth, cornstarch, soy sauce, and sugar. Bring to a boil over high heat, stirring constantly. Stir in sesame oil. Remove from the heat; keep warm.

2 In a large bowl, beat eggs, shrimp, bean sprouts, and onion. Heat a large skillet (preferably with nonstick coating) over moderate heat until hot. Add 1 tablespoon vegetable oil, swirling the pan to coat.

3 Spoon about ⅓ cup of the egg mixture into the skillet for each pancake. Fry the pancakes, 2 or 3 at a time, until the underside is golden brown and set, about 1 minute. Using a spatula, turn each pancake and fry the other side. Transfer the pancakes to a serving platter and keep them warm.

4 Repeat to cook the remaining egg mixture, adding more vegetable oil as necessary. Place two pancakes on each plate and pour an equal amount of the sauce over each serving. Serve immediately.

EGGS BENEDICT

One Serving: **Calories** 409 **Protein** 14g **Carbohydrates** 15g **Fat** 33g **Cholesterol** 282mg **Sodium** 241mg

4 large eggs

4 slices Canadian-style bacon

2 English muffins, split

Paprika

For the hollandaise sauce

3 large egg yolks

2 tablespoons lemon juice

⅛ teaspoon salt

Pinch cayenne pepper

⅓ cup butter or margarine, softened

PREPARATION TIME
5 MINUTES

COOKING TIME
12 MINUTES

1 To make the sauce, half fill the lower part of a double boiler with water and bring it to a boil. In the upper part of the double boiler, beat egg yolks lightly. Stir in lemon juice, salt, and cayenne pepper. Place over the boiling water. (The upper pan should not touch the water.)

2 Stirring the sauce constantly, add butter, one teaspoon at a time. Stir until the mixture has thickened and all of the butter is added, 5 minutes. Remove the pan from the heat, cover, and set it aside.

3 In a small skillet, bring 1 inch of water to a boil. Keep the water at a gentle boil. Break the eggs, one at a time, into a small dish, and slide each one into the water. Poach the eggs to desired doneness.

4 Meanwhile, in a large skillet, cook Canadian bacon for 1 minute on each side or until slightly browned. Toast muffins. Top each muffin half with a slice of bacon. Using a slotted spoon, transfer one poached egg to each slice of bacon.

5 If necessary, thin the sauce slightly with a tablespoon of hot water. Spoon sauce over each egg. Garnish with paprika and serve.

CORNED BEEF HASH WITH EGGS

CORNED BEEF HASH WITH EGGS

One Serving: **Calories** 534 **Protein** 23g **Carbohydrates** 36g **Fat** 34g **Cholesterol** 214mg **Sodium** 613mg

3 medium-size all-purpose potatoes (about 1 pound), cooked, peeled, and cut into ½-inch cubes

8 ounces cooked corned beef, cut into ½-inch cubes

2 medium-size yellow onions, chopped

1 green bell pepper, chopped

¼ cup milk

2 tablespoons all-purpose flour

2 tablespoons chopped parsley

3 tablespoons vegetable oil

4 large eggs

Additional chopped parsley (optional)

 PREPARATION TIME
18 MINUTES

 COOKING TIME
27 MINUTES

SERVING SUGGESTION *Serve America's favorite one-skillet break-fast with whole-wheat toast or warm muffins on the side.*

1 In a large bowl, combine potatoes, corned beef, onions, bell pepper, milk, flour, and parsley. In a large skillet, preferably with nonstick coating, heat oil over moderate heat. Add the hash mixture and, using a spatula, pack it down firmly to form a solid cake. Cook the hash until the underside begins to brown, about 10 minutes.

2 Reduce the heat to low. Continue cooking the hash, shaking the skillet occasionally to prevent it from sticking, until the underside is crusty and well browned, about 10 more minutes.

3 Using the back of a spoon, make four indentations in the hash. One at a time, break eggs into a saucer and slip them into the indentations. Increase the heat to moderate, cover the skillet and cook just until the eggs are just set, about 6 minutes. Cut the hash into wedges, garnish with chopped parsley, if desired, and serve immediately.

SAUSAGE AND BROCCOLI CUSTARD

One Serving: **Calories** 475 **Protein** 21g **Carbohydrates** 14g **Fat** 39g **Cholesterol** 209mg **Sodium** 617mg

1 **tablespoon butter or margarine**

1 **pound pork breakfast sausage (bulk or patties)**

1 **small yellow onion, chopped**

1 **package (10 ounces) frozen cut broccoli**

4 **large eggs**

1 **teaspoon prepared mustard**

2 **cups milk**

Pinch ground black pepper

Pinch ground nutmeg

Pimiento slivers (optional)

PREPARATION TIME
4 MINUTES

COOKING TIME
41 MINUTES

1 Preheat the oven to 350°F. In a large skillet, melt butter or margarine over moderately high heat. Add sausage and chopped onion. Cook until the sausage is well browned, stirring occasionally to break it into pieces, about 10 minutes.

2 Meanwhile, prepare frozen cut broccoli according to package directions. Drain thoroughly. Stir the cooked broccoli into the cooked sausage mixture.

3 Grease a 9-inch square baking dish. In a large bowl, beat eggs and mustard until well mixed. Beat in milk, pepper, and nutmeg. Stir the broccoli and sausage mixture into the egg mixture and pour it into the prepared baking dish.

4 Bake until the custard is set and a knife inserted in the center comes out clean, 30 to 35 minutes. Cut the custard into rectangles. Sprinkle each serving with pimientos, if desired, and serve immediately.

HUEVOS RANCHEROS

One Serving: **Calories** 318 **Protein** 17g **Carbohydrates** 20g **Fat** 19g **Cholesterol** 555mg **Sodium** 161mg

4 **6-inch corn tortillas**

1 **tablespoon vegetable oil**

8 **large eggs**

½ **cup prepared mild tomato salsa**

2 **ounces Monterey Jack cheese, coarsely grated (½ cup), divided**

Cilantro leaves (optional)

PREPARATION TIME
5 MINUTES

COOKING TIME
12 MINUTES

1 Preheat the oven to 350°F. Wrap tortillas tightly in aluminum foil and warm them in the oven for 10 to 15 minutes. Maintain the oven temperature. (Alternatively, heat the tortillas in the microwave oven according to package instructions at the end of Step 2.) In a small saucepan, heat salsa over low heat, covered, until hot.

2 Meanwhile, in a 12-inch skillet (preferably with nonstick coating) heat oil over moderate heat. Carefully break eggs, one at a time, into the skillet. When the edges of the egg whites are set, reduce the heat to low. Cover the skillet and cook until the egg yolks are just set, 2 to 3 minutes, or to taste.

3 Place the warm tortillas on individual serving plates. Top each tortilla with two fried eggs and sprinkle with some of the grated cheese. Spoon an equal amount of the warm salsa over each serving and top with the remaining cheese.

4 Place the plates in the preheated oven for 2 minutes (or in the microwave for a few seconds), to melt the cheese. Garnish each serving with cilantro, if desired, and serve immediately.

EGGS WITH CREAM CHEESE AND LOX

EGGS WITH CREAM CHEESE AND LOX

One Serving: **Calories** 281 **Protein** 17g **Carbohydrates** 2g **Fat** 22g **Cholesterol** 462mg **Sodium** 333mg

8 **large eggs**

2 **tablespoons sour cream**

Pinch ground black pepper

1 **tablespoon butter or margarine**

1 **package (3 ounces) cream cheese, cut into ½-inch cubes**

2 **ounces lox or smoked salmon, cut into narrow strips**

Snipped dill

PREPARATION TIME
5 MINUTES

COOKING TIME
7 MINUTES

SERVING SUGGESTION *Warm croissants served with jam or marmalade round out this elegant brunch dish, a combination of eggs with the rich tastes of cream cheese and smoked salmon.*

1 In a large bowl, beat eggs and sour cream. Stir in pepper. In a large skillet (preferably with nonstick coating) melt butter over moderately low heat, swirling the pan to coat evenly. Add the egg mixture and cook, lightly stirring, until the eggs begin to set, about 4 minutes.

2 Distribute cream cheese and lox evenly over the top of the scrambled eggs. Reduce the heat to low, cover, and cook just until the cream cheese begins to soften, 1 to 2 minutes. Garnish with dill and serve.

BAKED EGGS PROVENÇAL

BAKED EGGS PROVENÇAL

One Serving: **Calories** 239 **Protein** 14g **Carbohydrates** 6g **Fat** 19g **Cholesterol** 432mg **Sodium** 359mg

1 tablespoon olive oil

1 tablespoon butter or margarine

6 large eggs

2 ounces Gruyère cheese, coarsely grated (½ cup)

2 green onions, chopped

½ teaspoon dried tarragon or basil, crumbled

¼ teaspoon salt

¼ teaspoon ground black pepper

2 medium-size tomatoes, sliced

 PREPARATION TIME
10 MINUTES

COOKING TIME
15 MINUTES

DIET NOTE *This easy main dish lets you enjoy the sunny flavors of the south of France without overloading on calories.*

1 Preheat the oven to 400°F. In a shallow 8-inch oval baking dish, place oil and butter. Place the dish in the oven to melt the butter.

2 In a large bowl, beat eggs lightly; stir in grated cheese, chopped onions, tarragon, salt, and pepper.

3 Remove the dish from the oven; swirl to coat it evenly with the oil mixture. Pour in the egg mixture and arrange the tomato slices on top. Bake until the eggs are just set, about 15 minutes, and serve.

CREAMED EGGS AND LEEKS

One Serving: **Calories** 409 **Protein** 18g **Carbohydrates** 34g **Fat** 22g **Cholesterol** 262mg **Sodium** 488mg

4 **large eggs**

1 **pound small leeks, trimmed, cleaned and thinly sliced**

2 **medium-size all-purpose potatoes, peeled and cut into ¼-inch pieces**

2 **tablespoons (¼ stick) unsalted butter or margarine**

2 **tablespoons all-purpose flour**

½ **teaspoon dry mustard**

1 **cup milk**

4 **ounces mild Cheddar cheese, coarsely grated (1 cup), divided**

¼ **teaspoon salt**

Pinch ground black pepper

1 **tablespoon chopped fresh chives or parsley**

PREPARATION TIME
15 MINUTES

COOKING TIME
30 MINUTES

1 In a medium-size saucepan, place eggs and cover with cold water. Bring the water to a boil over high heat. Remove the pan from the heat and let it stand, covered, for 15 minutes.

2 Meanwhile, half fill a large saucepan with water and bring it to a boil. Add leeks and potatoes. Reduce the heat to low, partially cover the pan, and cook until the potatoes are fork-tender, about 10 minutes. Drain the vegetables. Drain the eggs and rinse them with cold water. Shell the eggs, cut them in half lengthwise, and set aside.

3 In a medium-size saucepan, melt butter over moderate heat. Add flour and mustard; stir until well mixed. Gradually stir in milk. Cook the mixture, stirring constantly, until it is smooth and thick, about 2 minutes. Stir in half the cheese, salt, and pepper. Continue stirring just until the cheese melts. Remove the pan from the heat.

4 Preheat the broiler. In a shallow 10- by 8-inch baking dish, place potatoes and leeks. Arrange the eggs, round sides up, in the center of the dish on top of the vegetables. Pour the sauce over the eggs and sprinkle with the remaining cheese. Broil just until the cheese is lightly browned, a few seconds. Sprinkle with chives and serve immediately.

BAKED EGGS FLORENTINE

One Serving: **Calories** 292 **Protein** 17g **Carbohydrates** 13g **Fat** 19g **Cholesterol** 249mg **Sodium** 525mg

3 **tablespoons butter or margarine**

4 **ounces mushrooms, sliced (1 cup)**

3 **tablespoons all-purpose flour**

¼ **teaspoon pepper**

⅛ **teaspoon ground nutmeg**

⅛ **teaspoon salt**

1 **cup milk**

1 **package (10 ounces) frozen chopped spinach, thawed, drained, and squeezed dry**

½ **cup grated Parmesan cheese, divided**

4 **large eggs**

PREPARATION TIME
15 MINUTES

COOKING TIME
23 MINUTES

1 Preheat the oven to 350°F. Grease four shallow 8-ounce baking dishes. In a medium-size saucepan, melt butter over moderate heat. Add mushrooms and sauté until they are soft, about 3 minutes. Stir in flour, pepper, nutmeg, and salt until well mixed.

2 Gradually stir milk into the mushroom mixture; cook until the mixture thickens, stirring constantly, about 5 minutes. Add chopped spinach and stir to combine.

3 Spoon the spinach mixture evenly around the edges of the prepared dishes, forming a depression in the center of each dish. Sprinkle each serving with 1 tablespoon of Parmesan cheese.

4 Break 1 egg into each depression; sprinkle each egg with 1 tablespoon of the remaining cheese. Bake until the eggs are just set, 13 to 18 minutes. Serve immediately.

CRUSTLESS GARDEN QUICHE

One Serving: **Calories** 540 **Protein** 22g **Carbohydrates** 34g **Fat** 37g **Cholesterol** 312mg **Sodium** 805mg

4 large eggs

1 cup buttermilk baking mix (Bisquick)

¼ cup olive oil

¼ teaspoon Italian seasoning

3 ounces baked ham, cubed

4 green onions, chopped

2 medium-size tomatoes, seeded and chopped

¼ cup sliced mushrooms

4 ounces Swiss or Jarlsberg cheese, coarsely grated (1 cup), divided

 PREPARATION TIME **10 MINUTES**

COOKING TIME **25 MINUTES**

COOK'S TIP *You'll only have to use one mixing bowl to prepare this simple, filling brunch or supper main dish. While it's baking, make a green salad with toasted pine nuts to go with it.*

1 Preheat the oven to 400°F. Grease a 9-inch pie plate. In a large bowl, whisk eggs, baking mix, oil, and Italian seasoning until well blended. Stir in ham, onions, tomatoes, mushrooms, and ¾ cup cheese.

2 Spoon the egg mixture into the prepared pie plate and sprinkle it with the remaining ¼ cup cheese. Bake until the quiche is golden brown and a knife inserted in the center comes out clean, 25 to 30 minutes. Cut into wedges and serve immediately.

ITALIAN-STYLE FRITTATA

One Serving: **Calories** 292 **Protein** 18g **Carbohydrates** 17g **Fat** 18g **Cholesterol** 327mg **Sodium** 373mg

8 ounces red potatoes

1 package (9 ounces) frozen artichoke hearts

6 large eggs

½ teaspoon dried rosemary, crumbled

¼ teaspoon salt

2 tablespoons olive oil

2 ounces mozzarella cheese, coarsely grated (½ cup)

1 tablespoon grated Parmesan cheese

Chopped parsley (optional)

 PREPARATION TIME **6 MINUTES**

COOKING TIME **34 MINUTES**

FOOD NOTE *A frittata is the Italian version of an omelet. It tastes just as good room-temperature as it does hot from the skillet.*

1 Fill a large saucepan with 2 inches of water, cover, and bring to a boil. Meanwhile, scrub potatoes and cut them into ¼-inch-thick slices.

2 Add the potatoes to the boiling water, cover, and cook until they are almost fork-tender, about 10 minutes. Add frozen artichoke hearts, cover, and continue cooking until the artichokes are thawed, 3 to 4 minutes. Drain the vegetables and pat them dry.

3 Preheat the broiler. In a medium-size bowl, beat eggs, rosemary, and salt until well mixed. In an oven-safe 10-inch skillet or omelet pan, heat oil over moderately high heat, swirling the pan to coat evenly. Add the potatoes and artichokes and cook until lightly browned, about 5 minutes, stirring gently.

4 Reduce the heat to moderately low. Add the egg mixture, cover, and cook until the eggs are almost set, 7 to 8 minutes.

5 Sprinkle the eggs with both cheeses. Place the skillet under the broiler and cook the frittata until the eggs are set and the cheese melts and begins to brown, 1 to 2 minutes. Sprinkle with parsley, if desired. Cut the frittata into wedges and serve immediately.

SMOKED SALMON AND DILL FRITTATA

SMOKED SALMON AND DILL FRITTATA

One Serving: **Calories** 359 **Protein** 24g **Carbohydrates** 4g **Fat** 27g **Cholesterol** 533mg **Sodium** 661mg

7 **large eggs**

¼ **cup sour cream**

1 **tablespoon snipped fresh dill (or ½ teaspoon dill weed)**

¼ **teaspoon salt**

¼ **teaspoon ground white pepper**

4 **ounces thick-sliced smoked salmon, julienned**

2 **tablespoons (¼ stick) butter or margarine**

4 **ounces Gruyère, Swiss or Jarlsberg cheese, grated (1 cup)**

Additional sour cream, salmon caviar, and dill sprigs (optional)

PREPARATION TIME
5 MINUTES

COOKING TIME
12 MINUTES

SERVING SUGGESTION *Serve this light lunch with a glass of white wine. Cut into squares, the frittata makes a terrific appetizer.*

1 Preheat the broiler. In a medium-size bowl, beat eggs, sour cream, dill, salt, and pepper until well mixed. Stir in smoked salmon.

2 In an oven-safe 10-inch skillet or omelet pan, melt butter over moderate heat, swirling the pan to coat evenly. Pour in the egg mixture. Reduce the heat to moderately low, cover, and cook just until almost set, about 10 minutes. Sprinkle the frittata with cheese.

3 Place the skillet under the broiler and broil the frittata until the eggs are set and the cheese melts and begins to brown, about 1 minute. Cut the frittata into wedges and garnish each serving with additional sour cream, caviar, and dill, if desired. Serve immediately.

Ham and Cheese Roulade

One Serving: **Calories** 354 **Protein** 24g **Carbohydrates** 15g **Fat** 23g **Cholesterol** 272mg **Sodium** 1166mg

⅓ **cup butter or margarine**

½ **cup all-purpose flour**

2 **cups milk**

⅛ **teaspoon ground black pepper**

6 **large eggs, separated, at room temperature**

1 **package (8 ounces) thin-sliced American cheese (12 slices)**

¼ **cup watercress leaves**

6 **ounces thin-sliced packaged ham (6 slices)**

Watercress sprigs (optional)

PREPARATION TIME
11 MINUTES

COOKING TIME
29 MINUTES

SERVING SUGGESTION *A spoonful of mixed berries goes well with this roulade, which is much easier to make than it looks.*

1 In a medium-size saucepan, melt butter over moderate heat. Stir in flour and cook until bubbly, about 1 minute. Remove the pan from the heat. Using a wire whisk, gradually stir in milk. Return to moderate heat; cook, stirring constantly, until thickened, about 4 minutes. (Do not boil.) Remove the pan from the heat. Stir in pepper.

2 Preheat the oven to 400°F. In a small bowl, beat egg yolks lightly. Beat in a small amount of the hot milk mixture. Slowly stir the yolk mixture into the remaining hot milk mixture, and set it aside.

3 Grease a 15½- by 10½-inch jelly-roll pan. Line the bottom with wax paper; grease and flour the paper. In a large bowl, using an electric mixer, beat egg whites until stiff but not dry. Fold the yolk mixture gently into the beaten whites. Spread into prepared pan. Bake until the surface is firm, 20 to 25 minutes. Maintain the oven temperature.

4 Cover the omelet with aluminum foil and invert it onto a large baking sheet, top side down. Peel off the wax paper. Arrange cheese slices evenly over the omelet, sprinkle with watercress, and top with ham.

5 Starting from a short edge, roll up the omelet, using the foil to help lift it as it is rolled. Transfer the omelet, seam side down, to an oven-safe serving platter. Place the platter in the oven until the roulade is heated through, 3 to 4 minutes. Garnish the roulade with watercress, if desired, and serve immediately.

This quick lunch takes less than 10 minutes to prepare. Although this recipe is for the microwave, it can easily be done on top of the stove.

Mexican Cheese Melts

Cut half of an **8-ounce package of processed cheese with jalapeño peppers** into cubes. In a 1-quart microwave-safe casserole, mix cheese with **2 tablespoons milk**. Cook on high power, covered, for 1 to 2 minutes or until cheese is melted, stirring once. On **two toasted English muffin halves,** place a slice of **tomato** and two slices of **avocado**. Spoon cheese over each. **SERVES 2**

VARIATIONS ON THE BASIC OMELET

Once you've mastered the basic method for making an omelet, you've gained innumerable options for a quick, light meal. The delicately flavored envelope can hold any combination of meat, cheese, vegetables, or savory sauces.

If you're going to fill the omelet, it's always better to cook the filling first; the omelet cooks very quickly and it requires your undivided attention. These fillings are enough to fill four omelets, but they can easily be cut down for fewer servings.

BASIC OMELET In a large bowl, beat **2 eggs, 2 Tbsp. water**, and **a pinch salt and pepper**. In a medium-size skillet or omelet pan, melt **1 tsp. butter or margarine** over moderately high heat, swirling the pan to coat evenly. Pour the egg mixture into the pan. Cook, without stirring, until the omelet starts to bubble around the edge, about 20 seconds. As the bottom begins to set, slide a spatula underneath to lift the cooked egg and allow the uncooked mixture to flow under it. Cook until the bottom is lightly browned, 2 to 3 minutes. Spoon the **prepared filling** across half of the omelet. Fold the plain half over the filling and serve.

◄ **PRIMAVERA FILLING** In a large skillet, heat
¼ **cup olive oil** over moderate heat. Add **2
medium-size red bell peppers**, cut into thin strips,
and sauté for 2 minutes. Add **2 small zucchini**, cut
into 2-inch sticks, **2 small yellow onions**, sliced, and
1 tsp. dried basil. Sauté until the vegetables are crisp-
tender, 6 to 7 minutes. Season the filling with **salt and pepper.**

◄ **BROCCOLI CHEESE FILLING** In a large saucepan, cook **1 lb.
frozen broccoli florets** according to package directions. Drain and
set aside. In the same saucepan, melt **2 Tbsp. butter or margarine**
over moderate heat. Stir in **2 Tbsp. all-purpose flour** and **2 drops
hot red pepper sauce**. Stir in **1 cup milk**; cook until thickened,
stirring constantly. Stir in **1 cup grated Cheddar cheese** until just
melted. Fold in the cooked broccoli; season with **salt and pepper.**

► **WALNUT AND GOAT CHEESE FILLING** Preheat the oven to 400°F. Spread **4 Tbsp.
chopped walnuts** into a baking dish. Toast the walnuts until lightly browned, about
5 minutes, shaking the dish halfway through cooking. Remove from the oven and
let the walnuts cool slightly. In a small bowl, crumble **1 to 2 oz. goat cheese**;
stir in **1 Tbsp. sour cream**. Stir in toasted walnuts.

► **ASPARAGUS ORIENTAL FILLING** Slice **1½ lbs. fresh
asparagus** diagonally. In a large skillet, heat **2 Tbsp.
vegetable oil** over moderately high heat. Add
1 large onion, sliced; sauté for 5 minutes. Stir
in the asparagus and sauté until crisp-
tender, about 5 minutes. Stir in **1½ tsp.
soy sauce, 1½ tsp. Oriental sesame oil,
and 1½ tsp. sesame seeds.**

► **AVOCADO SOUTHWEST FILLING** In a medium-size
bowl, combine **1 peeled and cubed avocado, 2 chopped
plum tomatoes, ¼ cup prepared tomato salsa, 1 Tbsp.
chopped green onion** and **a pinch salt and pepper**. Prepare
omelet as directed. Just before folding the omelet, sprinkle the
filling with a small handful of **grated Monterey Jack cheese**. Spoon a
dollop of **sour cream** on top of each omelet just before serving.

THREE-CHEESE CHARLOTTE

THREE-CHEESE CHARLOTTE

One Serving: **Calories** 469 **Protein** 27g **Carbohydrates** 35g **Fat** 26g **Cholesterol** 281mg **Sodium** 719mg

1²/₃ **cups milk**

1 **tablespoon butter or margarine**

6 **slices day-old or lightly toasted whole-wheat bread**

4 **large eggs, separated, at room temperature**

1 **can (5 ounces) evaporated milk**

2 **ounces Fontina or Gouda cheese, coarsely grated (½ cup)**

2 **ounces Jarlsberg or Swiss cheese, coarsely grated (½ cup)**

1 **ounce blue cheese, crumbled (¼ cup)**

⅛ **teaspoon ground white pepper**

Pinch ground nutmeg

 PREPARATION TIME
10 MINUTES

COOKING TIME
28 MINUTES

FOOD NOTE *Though charlotte is usually a sweet dish, this version is a savory main course sure to satisfy the most ardent cheese lover.*

1 Preheat the oven to 350°F. In a medium-size saucepan, heat milk over moderate heat until scalded, stirring frequently. Grease a shallow oval 12- by 9-inch baking dish with 1 tablespoon butter.

2 Cut four slices of bread in half diagonally; cut the remaining two slices into small cubes. Using a spatula, briefly dip the bread halves into the scalded milk and line the side of the baking dish with them, overlapping the edges. Add the bread cubes to the remaining milk. Let the bread cubes stand to absorb as much milk as possible.

3 In a large bowl, beat egg yolks, evaporated milk, the bread cubes and any remaining milk, and the cheeses. Stir in pepper and nutmeg.

4 In a medium-size bowl, using an electric mixer, beat the egg whites until stiff but not dry. Fold the whites into the cheese mixture. Pour the mixture over the bread. Bake the charlotte until golden and a knife inserted in the center comes out clean, 25 to 30 minutes; serve.

INDIVIDUAL CHEDDAR SOUFFLÉS

One Serving: **Calories** 333 **Protein** 17g **Carbohydrates** 9g **Fat** 26g **Cholesterol** 275mg **Sodium** 497mg

3 tablespoons butter or margarine

3 tablespoons all-purpose flour

¼ teaspoon salt

⅛ teaspoon cayenne pepper

1¼ cups milk

4 ounces mild Cheddar cheese, coarsely grated (1 cup)

4 large eggs, separated, at room temperature

PREPARATION TIME
10 MINUTES

COOKING TIME
31 MINUTES

COOK'S TIP *Be sure to start with the eggs at room temperature. If they're refrigerator-cold, soak them awhile in warm water.*

1 Preheat the oven to 325°F. In a medium-size saucepan, melt butter over moderate heat. Add flour, salt, and cayenne pepper; stir until well mixed. Gradually stir in milk. Cook until the mixture thickens, stirring constantly, 4 to 5 minutes. Remove the pan from the heat. Stir in cheese until just melted.

2 In a small bowl, beat egg yolks lightly. Beat in a small amount of the hot cheese mixture. Slowly stir the yolk mixture into the remaining cheese mixture; set aside.

3 Place four 10-ounce ramekins or soufflé dishes on a rimmed baking sheet for easier handling. In a medium-size bowl, using an electric mixer, beat egg whites until they are stiff but not dry. Fold in the cheese mixture. Spoon the mixture into the dishes. Using the back of a spoon, make an indentation around each soufflé about an inch from the rim to create a top-hat effect after baking.

4 Bake the soufflés until they are puffy and lightly browned, 25 to 30 minutes. (Do not open the oven during baking.) Serve immediately.

MOZZARELLA RAMEKINS

One Serving: **Calories** 230 **Protein** 16g **Carbohydrates** 11g **Fat** 14g **Cholesterol** 290mg **Sodium** 348mg

1 tablespoon olive oil

4 small zucchini, sliced (4 cups)

1 clove garlic, finely chopped

4 large eggs

4 ounces low-fat mozzarella cheese, coarsely grated (1 cup)

¼ cup packaged dried bread crumbs

1 tablespoon chopped parsley

¼ teaspoon salt

⅛ teaspoon red pepper flakes

PREPARATION TIME
10 MINUTES

COOKING TIME
21 MINUTES

SERVING SUGGESTION *This light meal can be made more substantial by serving it with a loaf of crusty garlic bread and a fresh chopped-tomato and basil salad.*

1 Preheat the oven to 400°F. Grease four individual 3½-inch ramekins or small shallow oval baking dishes. In a large skillet, heat oil over moderate heat. Add zucchini and garlic and sauté until the zucchini is tender, about 5 minutes. Remove the pan from the heat.

2 In a large bowl, combine eggs, cheese, bread crumbs, parsley, salt, and pepper flakes. Stir the zucchini into the egg mixture.

3 Spoon the egg and zucchini mixture into ramekins or dishes and bake until set, 15 to 20 minutes. Serve immediately.

HERBED GOAT-CHEESE TART

One Serving: **Calories** 753 **Protein** 17g **Carbohydrates** 54g **Fat** 51g **Cholesterol** 193mg **Sodium** 820mg

½ **package (15 ounces) refrigerated ready-to-bake pie crust (1 crust)**

2 **tablespoons (¼ stick) butter or margarine**

2 **cloves garlic, finely chopped**

2 **tablespoons all-purpose flour**

1 **teaspoon dried basil or oregano, crumbled**

½ **teaspoon dried thyme leaves, crumbled**

¾ **cup milk**

2 **large eggs, separated, at room temperature**

8 **ounces chèvre or other soft, mild goat cheese, crumbled (2 cups)**

PREPARATION TIME
8 MINUTES

COOKING TIME
35 MINUTES

1 Preheat the oven to 400°F. Press pie crust into a 9- or 10-inch tart pan with a removable bottom, trimming the pastry evenly with the edge of the pan. Using a fork, pierce the bottom and side of the pastry to prevent it from puffing during baking. Set the tart pan containing the pie crust on a pizza pan for easier handling. Bake the crust until it is partially cooked, 10 minutes.

2 Meanwhile, in a medium-size saucepan, melt butter over moderate heat. Add garlic and sauté for 15 seconds. Stir in flour, basil, and thyme leaves; gradually stir in milk. Cook until the mixture thickens, stirring constantly, 1 to 2 minutes. Remove the pan from the heat.

3 In a small bowl, beat egg yolks lightly. Beat in a small amount of the hot milk and flour mixture. Slowly stir the yolk mixture into the remaining milk and flour mixture. Set the mixture aside. In a small bowl, using an electric mixer, beat egg whites until they are stiff but not dry. Fold in the yolk mixture.

4 When the tart shell is done, remove it from the oven and reduce the temperature to 375°F. Distribute the cheese in the crust. Gently spoon the egg mixture over the cheese. Bake until the filling is golden brown and a knife inserted in the center comes out clean, 25 to 30 minutes. Remove the rim of the pan and serve the tart immediately.

Shelf Magic

This spicy dip is ideal for parties—serve it with a plate of crackers and sliced fresh vegetables, or with a basket of chips.

EASY CHEESE DIP

In a 1-quart microwave-safe casserole, combine ⅓ **cup beer or apple juice** and several dashes of **hot red pepper sauce**. Cook, uncovered, on high power until it is very hot, 1 to 2 minutes. Meanwhile, toss together **4 ounces cubed American cheese, 2 tablespoons canned chopped green chilies** (optional), **1 tablespoon all-purpose flour,** and ½ **teaspoon dry mustard.**

Stir the cheese into the beer mixture. Cook, uncovered, on high until the cheese melts and the mixture is heated through, 2 to 4 minutes, stirring once every minute. Stir in **2 to 3 tablespoons milk** to make the mixture of dipping consistency. Serve the dip with a basket or plate of **crackers, chips, or vegetable sticks.**
MAKES ¾ CUP

SPINACH CHEESE PIE

SPINACH CHEESE PIE

One Serving: **Calories** 356 **Protein** 14g **Carbohydrates** 28g **Fat** 22g **Cholesterol** 155mg **Sodium** 329mg

1 **package (10 ounces) frozen chopped spinach**

1 **cup all-purpose flour**

½ **cup whole-wheat flour**

¼ **teaspoon salt**

⅓ **cup plus 1 tablespoon canola or olive oil**

3 **tablespoons cold water**

½ **cup cottage cheese**

½ **cup half-and-half**

4 **large eggs**

¼ **cup grated Parmesan cheese**

1 **teaspoon dried thyme leaves, crumbled**

 PREPARATION TIME
15 MINUTES

COOKING TIME
30 MINUTES

SERVING SUGGESTION *Sautéed onions with strips of red and yellow bell peppers make a colorful accompaniment to this easy supper or brunch dish. Garnish with sprigs of parsley.*

1 Thaw spinach in the microwave or in a colander under warm running water. Drain the spinach and squeeze it dry.

2 Meanwhile, to make the pie crust, in a medium-size bowl, combine all-purpose and wheat flours with salt. Stir in oil; add water, a tablespoon at a time, just until the pastry holds together when pressed into a ball. Between sheets of wax paper, roll out the pastry to form a 10-inch round. Fit it into a 9-inch pie pan.

3 Preheat the oven to 400°F. Using a food processor or electric blender, process cottage cheese and half-and-half until smooth. (Alternatively, press the cheese through a fine strainer into a bowl, then stir in half-and-half.) In a medium-size bowl, beat eggs lightly. Stir in the cottage-cheese mixture, Parmesan, and thyme. Stir in the spinach.

4 Pour the spinach mixture into the pie crust. Bake until a knife inserted in the center comes out clean, 25 to 30 minutes, and serve.

CHEESE FONDUE

One Serving: **Calories** 507 **Protein** 32g **Carbohydrates** 11g **Fat** 32g **Cholesterol** 104mg **Sodium** 800mg

1 pound Gruyère, Swiss, or Jarlsberg cheese, coarsely grated (4 cups)

2 tablespoons all-purpose flour

¼ teaspoon ground black pepper

⅛ teaspoon ground nutmeg

1¼ cups dry white wine

2 tablespoons kirsch or brandy

1 clove garlic, quartered

Any combination of cubed French bread, breadsticks, small mushrooms, broccoli florets, cut carrots, zucchini, or bell peppers for dipping

PREPARATION TIME
5 MINUTES

COOKING TIME
18 MINUTES

FOOD NOTE *Originally a Swiss peasant dish, fondue remains a favorite for entertaining—everyone loves dipping into the pot. Arrange the platter with the freshest, most colorful vegetables.*

1 In a medium-size bowl, mix cheese with flour, pepper, and nutmeg. In a medium-size saucepan or fondue pot that can be used on top of the stove, heat wine, kirsch, and garlic almost to a boil over moderately high heat, about 3 minutes. Remove and discard the garlic.

2 Reduce the heat to low. Add the floured cheese to the wine mixture gradually, by handfuls, stirring constantly until the cheese melts. Arrange bread, breadsticks, and/or vegetables on a serving platter.

3 If using a saucepan, place the cheese fondue over a table-top burner, or place the fondue pot on its stand. (Keep the temperature low to prevent the cheese from becoming hard and sticking to the pan.) To serve, let each person spear the bread and vegetables with long-handled forks and dip the food into the fondue.

CHILES RELLENOS

One Serving: **Calories** 793 **Protein** 24g **Carbohydrates** 16g **Fat** 73g **Cholesterol** 316mg **Sodium** 52mg

8 canned whole mild green chilies

8 ounces Monterey Jack cheese

5 large eggs, separated, at room temperature

¼ teaspoon salt

6 tablespoons all-purpose flour, divided

Vegetable oil for frying

Prepared mild tomato salsa

PREPARATION TIME
19 MINUTES

COOKING TIME
25 MINUTES

1 Rinse and seed chilies; pat dry. Cut cheese into 8 strips to fit inside chilies. Through the open stem end, insert the cheese into the chilies.

2 In a large bowl, beat egg whites until stiff but not dry. In a small bowl, beat the egg yolks until thick and pale yellow, about 5 minutes. Beat in salt and 4 tablespoons of flour. Stir some of the whites into the yolk mixture, then fold the yolk mixture into the remaining whites.

3 In a large skillet, heat ¼ inch of oil to 375°F. On a sheet of wax paper, dust the chilies with the remaining flour. Heat the salsa.

4 Drop about ¼ cup of the egg mixture into the hot oil. Quickly spread the mixture into an oval shape a little larger than the chili; place a stuffed chili in the middle of the egg mixture. Top and enclose the chili with another spoonful of the egg mixture. Turn and fry the stuffed chili until it is golden brown. Fry two or three chilies at a time.

5 Drain the chilies on paper towels, keeping them warm while frying the rest. Serve immediately with the heated salsa on the side.

WELSH RAREBIT

One Serving: **Calories** 512 **Protein** 20g **Carbohydrates** 42g **Fat** 28g **Cholesterol** 82mg **Sodium** 851mg

- 3 **tablespoons butter or margarine**
- 3 **tablespoons all-purpose flour**
- ¼ **teaspoon salt**
- ¼ **teaspoon dry mustard**
- 3 **or 4 drops hot red pepper sauce**
- 1⅓ **cups milk**
- ⅓ **cup beer**
- 1 **teaspoon Worcestershire sauce**
- 6 **ounces sharp Cheddar cheese, coarsely grated (1½ cups)**
- 8 **slices white or rye bread, toasted and kept warm**

PREPARATION TIME
6 MINUTES

COOKING TIME
7 MINUTES

COOK'S TIP *If you prefer, toasted English muffin halves can be used in place of the bread. Garnish each serving with pickled onions or gherkins to make this traditional British dish its most authentic. It's an ideal solution to a quick late supper.*

1 Preheat the broiler. In a medium-size saucepan, melt butter over moderate heat. Add flour, salt, mustard, and pepper sauce; stir until well mixed. Gradually stir in milk, beer, and Worcestershire sauce. Cook until the mixture thickens, stirring constantly, about 5 minutes. Stir in cheese until it is just melted.

2 Arrange the toast on a baking sheet. Pour the hot cheese mixture over the toast. Broil just until the cheese begins to brown, a few seconds. Serve immediately.

BAKED CHEESE AND SAUSAGE

One Serving: **Calories** 498 **Protein** 28g **Carbohydrates** 21g **Fat** 34g **Cholesterol** 100mg **Sodium** 815mg

- 1 **pound red potatoes, halved**
- 8 **ounces Gruyère cheese**
- 8 **ounces kielbasa (or other cooked smoked garlic sausage)**
- **Pinch ground black pepper**
- **Gherkins or cocktail-size pickled onions (optional)**

PREPARATION TIME
4 MINUTES

COOKING TIME
30 MINUTES

COOK'S TIP *It takes only four ingredients to put together this filling winter warmer. The hearty combination of potatoes, garlic sausage, and cheese stands on its own as a complete meal. You may want a glass of cool, light beer to go with it.*

1 In a large saucepan, bring 2 inches of water to a boil over high heat. Reduce the heat to low. Add potatoes, cover, and cook just until fork-tender, about 15 minutes.

2 Meanwhile, cut and discard rind from cheese. Cut the cheese into ¼-inch-thick slices. Remove the casing from kielbasa. Cut the sausage diagonally into ½-inch-thick slices.

3 Preheat the oven to 375°F. In a 9- or 10-inch shallow baking dish, arrange the cooked potatoes, cut sides up, around the edge of the dish. Place the kielbasa in the center of the dish. Arrange the cheese over the potatoes, overlapping the slices if necessary.

4 Bake until the cheese is completely melted and the sausage is heated through, 10 to 15 minutes. Sprinkle the cheese with a pinch of black pepper and garnish the dish with gherkins or pickled onions, if desired. Serve immediately.

VEGETABLES

RATATOUILLE (PAGE 282)

SIDE-DISH VEGETABLES

Flavorful and healthy fresh vegetables provide some of the
simplest first-course and accompaniment dishes.

ASPARAGUS DIJONNAISE

One Serving: **Calories** 167 **Protein** 4g **Carbohydrates** 6g **Fat** 16g **Cholesterol** 3mg **Sodium** 188mg

1½ **pounds asparagus**

¼ **cup olive oil**

1 **tablespoon white-wine vinegar**

1 **tablespoon Dijon mustard**

1 **teaspoon dried tarragon, crumbled**

2 **tablespoons sour cream**

Salt and ground black pepper to taste

2 **tablespoons finely chopped red onion**

 PREPARATION TIME **15 MINUTES**

COOKING TIME **10 MINUTES**

COOK'S TIP *When the asparagus is cooked, remove it from the heat and plunge it quickly into cold water in order to stop the cooking.*

1 In a large skillet, bring ½ inch of water to a boil over high heat. Meanwhile, cut or break off the tough ends of the asparagus. Using a vegetable peeler, peel the lower half of each asparagus.

2 Add the asparagus to the boiling water. Reduce the heat to low, cover, and cook the asparagus until they are crisp-tender, 8 to 10 minutes. Drain and rinse the asparagus with cold water. Pat them dry with paper towels, and place them on a serving platter. Refrigerate while preparing the sauce.

3 In a small bowl, using a wire whisk, beat oil with vinegar, mustard, and tarragon until well mixed. Beat in sour cream until smooth. Season the mixture with salt and pepper.

4 Spoon the mustard mixture across the center of the asparagus, sprinkle it with chopped red onion, and serve immediately.

FRENCH-STYLE PEAS

One Serving: **Calories** 149 **Protein** 6g **Carbohydrates** 18g **Fat** 6g **Cholesterol** 15mg **Sodium** 283mg

1½ **cups shredded iceberg lettuce, divided**

1 **package (16 ounces) frozen green peas, partially thawed in hot water**

2 **green onions, chopped**

1 **teaspoon sugar**

2 **tablespoons (¼ stick) butter or margarine**

Salt and ground white pepper to taste

 PREPARATION TIME **10 MINUTES**

COOKING TIME **5 MINUTES**

FOOD NOTE *This traditional French method of cooking peas uses steam from the moisture in the lettuce. Garnish with fresh mint.*

1 In a medium-size saucepan, place ¾ cup shredded lettuce. Cover the lettuce with partially thawed peas and chopped green onions. Sprinkle with sugar and dot with pieces of butter. Top the peas with the remaining ¾ cup shredded lettuce.

2 Cover the saucepan; cook the lettuce and peas over moderately low heat until the peas are tender, 4 to 5 minutes, shaking the pan occasionally. Season with salt and pepper. Transfer the vegetables to a bowl, and serve immediately.

CREOLE GREEN BEANS

One Serving: **Calories** 81 **Protein** 3g **Carbohydrates** 14g **Fat** 3g **Cholesterol** 3mg **Sodium** 170mg

12 ounces green beans, trimmed and cut into 2-inch lengths

2 slices bacon

1 medium-size white onion, chopped

¼ cup chopped green bell pepper

1 can (14½ or 16 ounces) diced tomatoes, drained

1 teaspoon sugar or to taste

Salt and ground black pepper to taste

	PREPARATION TIME		COOKING TIME
	13 MINUTES		**23 MINUTES**

SERVING SUGGESTION *The tomato sauce and crisp-tender beans make this the perfect accompaniment for broiled chicken or pork.*

1 In a large saucepan, bring 1 inch of water to a boil over high heat. Add cut beans and return the water to a boil. Reduce the heat to low, cover, and cook the beans, stirring once, until they are crisp-tender, about 8 minutes.

2 Meanwhile, in a large skillet, cook bacon over moderate heat until crisp. Leaving the bacon drippings in the skillet, drain the bacon on paper towels. Drain the cooked beans and set them aside.

3 Add onion and bell pepper to the drippings in the skillet; cook until soft but not brown, about 4 minutes. Stir in tomatoes and sugar; cook for 15 minutes, stirring occasionally.

4 Stir the beans into the tomato mixture. Season with salt and pepper, and transfer them to a serving dish. Crumble the bacon over the beans, and serve immediately.

SAUTÉED BROCCOLI ITALIANO

One Serving: **Calories** 134 **Protein** 4g **Carbohydrates** 9g **Fat** 11g **Cholesterol** 0mg **Sodium** 41mg

1 bunch broccoli (about 1½ pounds)

3 tablespoons olive oil

1 clove garlic, finely chopped

½ cup water

1 ripe plum tomato, seeded and chopped

1 tablespoon red-wine vinegar

¼ teaspoon red pepper flakes

Salt to taste

	PREPARATION TIME		COOKING TIME
	9 MINUTES		**13 MINUTES**

DIET NOTE *Broccoli is full of good things, so be sure to take your share. It's high in fiber, calcium, and vitamins A, C, E, and K.*

1 Trim and set aside the woody ends of broccoli stalks; cut tops into florets. Using a vegetable peeler, peel the stalks and cut them diagonally into ¼-inch-thick slices.

2 In a 5-quart Dutch oven or stockpot, heat oil over moderate heat. Add the sliced broccoli stalks and sauté for 5 minutes. Stir in garlic, water, and the florets. Cover and cook the broccoli until it is crisp-tender, about 5 more minutes. Remove the Dutch oven from the heat.

3 Using a slotted spoon, transfer the broccoli to a serving bowl, leaving any liquid in the Dutch oven. Add tomato, vinegar, and pepper flakes to the liquid. Cook over low heat until the mixture is just heated through. Season with salt. Pour the tomato mixture over the broccoli, and serve immediately.

TART-AND-SWEET RED CABBAGE

One Serving: **Calories** 99 **Protein** 2g **Carbohydrates** 11g **Fat** 6g **Cholesterol** 16mg **Sodium** 72mg

1 **small head red cabbage (about 1¼ pounds)**

1 **small yellow onion**

2 **tablespoons (¼ stick) butter or margarine**

1 **tablespoon cider vinegar**

2 **teaspoons light or dark brown sugar**

Salt and ground black pepper to taste

 PREPARATION TIME
5 MINUTES

COOKING TIME
16 MINUTES

COOK'S TIP *If you have a food processor, use it to shred the cabbage to make preparation time even quicker.*

1 Discard any tough outer leaves from cabbage. Cut the cabbage in half through the core; cut out and discard the core. Cut the cabbage crosswise into thin slices or shreds. Chop onion.

2 In a large saucepan, melt butter over moderate heat. Add the onion and sauté until soft, about 5 minutes. Add vinegar, brown sugar, and the cabbage, tossing to coat with the onion mixture.

3 Cover the pan and cook the cabbage until it is crisp-tender, stirring occasionally, 8 to 10 minutes. Season the cabbage mixture with salt and pepper; spoon into a bowl, and serve immediately.

ROASTED RED POTATOES

One Serving: **Calories** 266 **Protein** 5g **Carbohydrates** 47g **Fat** 7g **Cholesterol** 0mg **Sodium** 148mg

1½ **pounds small red potatoes**

1 **medium-size yellow onion, sliced ¼ inch thick**

2 **tablespoons olive oil**

1 **teaspoon dried rosemary, crumbled**

¼ **teaspoon garlic powder**

Salt and ground black pepper to taste

 PREPARATION TIME
10 MINUTES

COOKING TIME
20 MINUTES

1 Preheat the oven to 350°F. Scrub unpeeled potatoes and pat them dry with paper towels. Cut each potato into quarters.

2 In a 13- by 9-inch baking pan, combine the potatoes and onion. Add oil, rosemary, and garlic powder; toss until well mixed. Bake the potatoes until tender and browned, 20 to 25 minutes, stirring occasionally. Season with salt and pepper, and serve immediately.

TIME SAVERS

VEGETABLES

• Many supermarkets now have salad bars, which can save preparation time when you cook fresh vegetables by doing all the cleaning and cutting for you. Look for broccoli florets, bell peppers, and mushrooms.

• Broccoli stalks will cook faster if you peel off the outer fibrous layer first.

• Frozen tiny peas do not need cooking if they are to be used in salads. Place them in a strainer and rinse under hot water until defrosted.

• Quickly ripen tomatoes: Pierce some holes in a brown paper bag and keep the unripened tomatoes in it, out of the refrigerator, until ready to use. The same works for avocados, which will ripen even faster if you put an apple in with them.

LOW-FAT MASHED POTATOES

One Serving: **Calories** 163 **Protein** 6g **Carbohydrates** 30g **Fat** 2g **Cholesterol** 7mg **Sodium** 180mg

1½ **pounds all-purpose potatoes**

⅓ **cup plain low-fat yogurt**

⅓ **cup part-skim ricotta or low-fat cottage cheese**

Salt and ground black pepper to taste

2 **tablespoons chopped fresh herbs (parsley, basil, or chives)**

 PREPARATION TIME
15 MINUTES

 COOKING TIME
15 MINUTES

DIET NOTE *Cream is out, and protein and calcium are in, in this low-fat version of mashed potatoes. Keep in the extra nutrients by leaving the potatoes unpeeled.*

1 Peel potatoes, if desired, and cut them into 1-inch chunks. Place the potatoes in a large saucepan; add enough cold water to cover them. Cover the saucepan and bring the potatoes to a boil over high heat. Reduce the heat to moderate; continue cooking the potatoes until tender, about 15 minutes.

2 Meanwhile, using an electric blender or a food processor fitted with the chopping blade, process yogurt and ricotta until the mixture is completely smooth.

3 Drain the potatoes and return them to the saucepan. Heat the potatoes over moderate heat to evaporate the excess moisture, 30 seconds to 1 minute. Remove the pan from the heat.

4 Using a potato masher or a hand-held electric mixer, beat the yogurt mixture into the boiled potatoes until smooth. Season with salt and pepper. Stir in chopped herbs; transfer the potatoes to a bowl, and serve immediately.

POTATO PANCAKES

One Serving: **Calories** 294 **Protein** 6g **Carbohydrates** 49g **Fat** 8g **Cholesterol** 52mg **Sodium** 562mg

4 **large all-purpose potatoes (about 2 pounds)**

1 **small yellow onion**

1 **large egg**

2 **tablespoons all-purpose flour (or matzo meal)**

1 **teaspoon salt**

¼ **teaspoon ground black pepper**

Vegetable oil

Sour cream (optional)

PREPARATION TIME
10 MINUTES

COOKING TIME
12 MINUTES

1 Preheat the oven to 200°F. Peel and coarsely grate potatoes and onion into a large bowl. Stir in egg, flour, salt, and pepper. Line a baking sheet with a double layer of paper towels.

2 In a large skillet, heat ¼ inch of oil over moderately high heat. One heaping tablespoon at a time, drop the potato mixture into the hot oil; flatten each one slightly with a spatula. Fry three or four pancakes at a time until the edges are brown and crispy, about 4 minutes. Turn them over and continue cooking until they are golden brown, about 1 more minute.

3 Drain the pancakes on the prepared baking sheet. Keep the cooked ones warm in the oven while cooking the remaining pancakes. Place the pancakes on a warm platter; serve with sour cream, if desired.

BAKED POTATO CAKES

BAKED POTATO CAKES

One Serving: **Calories** 204 **Protein** 3g **Carbohydrates** 25g **Fat** 11g **Cholesterol** 1mg **Sodium** 35mg

3 tablespoons olive oil, divided

1 clove garlic, finely chopped

2 large baking potatoes, preferably round in shape (about 1 pound)

1 tablespoon chopped fresh thyme (or 1 teaspoon dried thyme leaves, crumbled)

1 tablespoon grated Parmesan cheese

Ground black pepper

Thyme sprigs (optional)

PREPARATION TIME
13 MINUTES

COOKING TIME
20 MINUTES

SERVING SUGGESTION *These make an excellent side dish, along with a spinach, carrot, and zucchini salad. Serve with chicken or beef.*

1 Preheat the oven to 450°F. Generously brush a large baking sheet with 1½ tablespoons oil. In a small saucepan, heat the remaining 1½ tablespoons oil over moderate heat. Add garlic and sauté until just golden, about 1 minute. Remove the pan from the heat.

2 Peel potatoes and cut them crosswise into very thin (⅛ inch) slices. Divide the slices into 8 equal portions. For each potato cake, arrange the slices overlapping in a circular pattern about 4 inches in diameter on the baking sheet, making a total of 8 cakes.

3 Brush the cakes with the garlic oil. Sprinkle with thyme, Parmesan, and pepper. Bake the cakes until tender and lightly browned, 15 to 20 minutes, pressing them several times during baking with a spatula so the slices stick together. Garnish with thyme, if desired, and serve.

GINGERED SWEET POTATOES

One Serving: **Calories** 311 **Protein** 3g **Carbohydrates** 62g **Fat** 6g **Cholesterol** 16mg **Sodium** 89mg

4 sweet potatoes (about 2 pounds)

2 tablespoons (¼ stick) butter or margarine

1 tablespoon finely chopped fresh ginger (or 1 teaspoon ground ginger)

⅛ teaspoon ground cinnamon

¼ cup firmly packed light brown sugar

Salt and ground black pepper to taste

| | PREPARATION TIME **10 MINUTES** | | COOKING TIME **18 MINUTES** |

SERVING SUGGESTION *This delicious variation on traditional sweet potatoes still goes perfectly with baked ham or roast turkey for a holiday meal. On less special occasions, serve it with chicken.*

1 In a large saucepan, bring 2 inches of water to a boil over high heat. Meanwhile, peel sweet potatoes and cut them into ½-inch-thick slices. Add the sweet-potato slices to the boiling water. Cover the saucepan and return the water to a boil. Reduce the heat to low and cook the potatoes until tender, about 8 minutes.

2 Meanwhile, in a large skillet, melt butter or margarine over moderate heat. If using chopped fresh ginger, add ginger and cinnamon; cook for 1 minute. Stir in brown sugar and heat until the sugar dissolves. (If using ground ginger, add ginger and cinnamon at the same time as the brown sugar.)

3 Drain the sweet potatoes and add them to the sugar mixture in the skillet. Cook until the potatoes are coated with the sugar mixture, stirring gently. Season with salt and pepper; transfer the potatoes to a bowl, and serve.

ORANGE-GLAZED PARSNIPS

One Serving: **Calories** 172 **Protein** 2g **Carbohydrates** 30g **Fat** 6g **Cholesterol** 16mg **Sodium** 74mg

1½ pounds parsnips

1 cup water

1 large or 2 medium-size oranges

2 tablespoons (¼ stick) butter or margarine

2 tablespoons light or dark brown sugar

2 teaspoons lemon juice

Salt and ground white pepper to taste

1 tablespoon chopped parsley

| | PREPARATION TIME **17 MINUTES** | | COOKING TIME **20 MINUTES** |

1 Peel parsnips and cut them into 3- by ½-inch sticks. In a large skillet, bring the parsnips and water to a boil over moderate heat. Reduce the heat to low, cover, and cook the parsnips until they are crisp-tender, about 8 minutes.

2 Meanwhile, finely grate only the orange part of the orange peel to measure 1 tablespoon of grated peel. Cut the orange in half and squeeze out ¼ cup juice.

3 Uncover the skillet and increase the heat to moderately high. Add the orange juice, orange peel, butter, brown sugar, and lemon juice to the parsnips; stir to combine. Continue cooking until the liquid is reduced to a syrupy consistency and the parsnips are glazed, stirring occasionally, about 7 minutes.

4 Season the parsnips with salt and pepper. Transfer to a serving dish, sprinkle with parsley, and serve.

SPINACH-FILLED TOMATOES

SPINACH-FILLED TOMATOES

One Serving: **Calories** 219 **Protein** 10g **Carbohydrates** 27g **Fat** 10g **Cholesterol** 27mg **Sodium** 355mg

4 **large tomatoes**
1¼ **pounds fresh spinach**
2 **tablespoons (¼ stick) butter or margarine**
1 **small yellow onion, sliced**
2 **tablespoons all-purpose flour**
1 **cup milk**
2 **tablespoons half-and-half**
¼ **teaspoon ground nutmeg**
   Salt and ground black pepper to taste

 PREPARATION TIME
10 MINUTES

 COOKING TIME
15 MINUTES

SERVING SUGGESTION *These make an attractive first course with whole-wheat or sourdough rolls.*

1 Preheat the oven to 400°F. Using a sharp knife, cut off and discard a ¼-inch slice from the stem end of tomatoes. Scoop out and discard the seeds and pulp. Place the tomatoes upside-down on paper towels to drain. Meanwhile, rinse and drain spinach; discard any large stems.

2 Place the spinach in a Dutch oven or stockpot. Cover and cook over high heat until the leaves are just wilted, stirring occasionally, about 3 minutes. Drain the spinach in a colander, pressing the leaves to extract the water. Chop the spinach and set it aside.

3 In the same Dutch oven, melt butter over moderate heat. Add onion and sauté until soft, about 5 minutes. Stir in flour until well mixed. Gradually stir in milk and bring the mixture to a boil. Stir in the spinach, half-and-half, and nutmeg; cook until the spinach is heated through. Season the mixture with salt and pepper.

4 Fill each tomato with an equal amount of the spinach mixture. Place the filled tomatoes in an ungreased baking dish. Bake until the tomatoes are heated through, 3 to 5 minutes. Serve immediately.

RATATOUILLE

One Serving: **Calories** 192 **Protein** 3g **Carbohydrates** 16g **Fat** 14g **Cholesterol** 0mg **Sodium** 191mg

1 **medium-size yellow onion**
1 **clove garlic**
1 **medium-size zucchini**
1 **small eggplant (about 8 ounces)**
1 **medium-size green bell pepper**
¼ **cup olive or vegetable oil**
1 **can (14½ or 16 ounces) diced tomatoes**
2 **teaspoons dried basil or oregano, crumbled**
  Salt and ground black pepper to taste

PREPARATION TIME
9 MINUTES

COOKING TIME
36 MINUTES

1 Chop onion and garlic, and slice zucchini. Trim the ends off eggplant and cut it into 1-inch cubes. Core and seed bell pepper and cut it into 1-inch pieces.

2 In a 5-quart Dutch oven, heat oil over moderate heat. Add the onion and sauté until soft, about 5 minutes. Stir in the eggplant, bell pepper, zucchini, and garlic; cook for 5 minutes, stirring occasionally.

3 Add undrained diced tomatoes and dried basil to the Dutch oven; bring the mixture to a boil. Reduce the heat to low and partially cover the pan. Cook the vegetables until they are tender, stirring occasionally, about 25 minutes.

4 Season the ratatouille with salt and black pepper to taste. Spoon it into a serving bowl and serve immediately, or cover and refrigerate it to serve chilled later.

MICROWAVE VERSION

In a large microwave-safe dish or casserole, place oil and onion. Cover the dish and cook on high power until the onion softens, 3 to 4 minutes, stirring halfway through the cooking time. Stir eggplant, pepper, zucchini, garlic, and basil into the onion. Replace the cover and cook on high for 10 minutes, stirring twice during cooking.

Drain tomatoes. Stir the tomatoes into the eggplant mixture. Continue cooking, uncovered, on high power, until the vegetables are tender, about 15 minutes, stirring twice during cooking. Season with salt and pepper, and serve.

Shelf Magic

Corn on the cob and mashed potatoes get special treatment for extra taste.

CURRIED CORN ON THE COB

Cook **4 ears frozen corn on the cob** according to package directions. Melt **3 tablespoons butter**. Stir in **1 teaspoon curry powder**; cook for 1 minute. Drain the corn; brush curry butter over them, and serve.
SERVES 4

DRESSED MASHED POTATOES

Prepare 4 servings **instant mashed potatoes** according to package directions, except reduce the amount of water by ¼ cup. Stir in ¼ **cup creamy Italian salad dressing**. Top with **2 tablespoons crumbled bacon**.
SERVES 4

STUFFED ZUCCHINI

STUFFED ZUCCHINI

One Serving: **Calories** 151 **Protein** 6g **Carbohydrates** 13g **Fat** 9g **Cholesterol** 69mg **Sodium** 337mg

4 **small zucchini (about 1¼ pounds)**

2 **tablespoons (¼ stick) butter or margarine**

1 **small yellow onion, chopped**

1½ **cups fresh bread crumbs**

¼ **cup chopped parsley**

1 **teaspoon Italian herb seasoning**

Salt and ground black pepper to taste

1 **large egg**

2 **tablespoons grated Parmesan cheese**

 PREPARATION TIME
10 MINUTES

COOKING TIME
25 MINUTES

COOK'S TIP *You can easily turn this into a main course dish by doubling the quantities, making a light, low-calorie meal.*

1 Preheat the oven to 400°F. Grease a 13- by 9-inch baking pan. Cut each zucchini in half lengthwise. Scoop out and reserve the centers, leaving a ¼-inch-thick shell. Place the zucchini shells, cut side down, into the baking pan. Bake until crisp-tender, about 10 minutes.

2 Meanwhile, dice the zucchini centers. In a medium-size saucepan, melt butter over moderate heat. Add onion and the diced zucchini; sauté until soft, about 5 minutes. Stir in bread crumbs, chopped parsley, and Italian herb seasoning. Season with salt and pepper. Remove the pan from the heat.

3 In a small bowl, beat egg lightly; stir it into the bread-crumb mixture until well mixed. Remove the zucchini shells from the oven, turn them over and sprinkle them lightly with salt and pepper. Fill the zucchini with the crumb mixture and sprinkle them with cheese. Bake until the crumbs are lightly browned, about 15 minutes, and serve.

VARIATIONS ON THE BASIC BAKED POTATO

With the use of the microwave oven, you can have four piping hot baked potatoes in less than half the time they would take in a conventional oven. Once the potatoes are done, don't stop there—make of meal of them by whipping up one of these easy variations and adding soup or salad on the side. Each recipe makes four servings.

BASIC MICROWAVE BAKED POTATOES Scrub **four 8-oz. baking potatoes** well and, using a fork, pierce the potatoes all over. Evenly space them on a microwave-safe plate. Microwave the potatoes on high power until they are tender, 20 to 25 minutes, turning potatoes over and rearranging them halfway through the cooking time. Fill or top the hot potatoes with the **topping** of your choice.

▶ **CHILI TOPPING** In a medium-size saucepan, heat **one 16-oz. can chili con carne** over moderate heat until hot and bubbly; remove the pan from the heat. Cut an X in the top of each of **4 baked potatoes**. Using a fork, fluff up the potato pulp. Top each potato with ¼ of the chili, a handful each of **coarsely grated Monterey Jack cheese** and **shredded lettuce**, and a spoonful of **prepared tomato salsa.**

◀ **CREAM-CHEESE TOPPING** In a small bowl, combine **½ cup softened cream cheese** with **2 Tbsp. creamy Italian or garlic salad dressing**, **2 Tbsp. chopped red bell pepper**, and **2 Tbsp. finely chopped pine nuts** until well mixed. Cut an X in the top of each of **4 baked potatoes**. Using a fork, fluff up the potato pulp. Top each with some of the cream-cheese mixture.

▶ **VEGETABLE-PEPPERONI TOPPING** In a large skillet, heat **1 Tbsp. olive oil** over moderate heat. Add **1 small yellow onion**, sliced, and **¼ cup julienned green pepper**; sauté until soft, about 5 minutes. Add **1 clove garlic**, chopped, and **½ tsp. dried oregano leaves**; sauté for 10 seconds. Remove the skillet from the heat. Stir in **2 ounces pepperoni**, cut into half slices. Cut an X in the top of each of **4 baked potatoes**. Using a fork, fluff up the potato pulp. Top each with some vegetable-pepperoni mixture. Sprinkle with **grated Parmesan cheese**, if desired.

◀ **CHEESE AND HERB TOPPING** Cut **4 baked potatoes** horizontally in half. Leaving ¼-inch-thick potato shells, scoop out the potato pulp into a bowl. Add **2 oz. coarsely grated sharp Cheddar cheese**, **¼ cup plain low-fat yogurt**, **2 Tbsp. chopped parsley**, and **1 Tbsp. chopped chives** to the potato pulp and mix well. Season with **salt and pepper** to taste. Spoon the mixture back into the potato shells and reheat them in the microwave until hot, about 4 minutes. Sprinkle each potato with **paprika**, if desired.

MAIN-COURSE VEGETABLES

These healthy vegetable dishes—some with meat and some vegetarian—are hearty enough to make a complete meal.

TOFU WITH STIR-FRIED VEGETABLES

One Serving: **Calories** 399 **Protein** 16g **Carbohydrates** 29g **Fat** 27g **Cholesterol** 0mg **Sodium** 736mg

½ cup plus 1½ tablespoons cornstarch, divided

1½ tablespoons soy sauce

1 package (16 ounces) extra-firm tofu

⅓ cup vegetable oil

12 ounces green beans

1 large red bell pepper

10 ounces mushrooms, sliced

3 cloves garlic, finely chopped

1 cup vegetable broth or canned reduced-sodium chicken broth

 PREPARATION TIME
18 MINUTES

 COOKING TIME
27 MINUTES

DIET NOTE *Derived from the soy bean, tofu is rich in vegetable proteins and contains no cholesterol. Add rice on the side.*

1 In a cup, combine 1½ tablespoons cornstarch with soy sauce; set the mixture aside. Drain tofu and cut it crosswise into four slices. Using a paper towel, pat the slices to remove the excess moisture. Cut each slice in half diagonally to form a triangle.

2 On a sheet of wax paper, place the remaining cornstarch. Dip the tofu triangles in the cornstarch to coat them thoroughly on all sides; set them aside. In a wok or large skillet (preferably with nonstick coating), heat oil over moderately high heat.

3 Add the tofu and cook, turning them carefully, until golden brown on all sides, 10 to 12 minutes. Meanwhile, cut green beans diagonally into 1½-inch lengths. Core and seed bell pepper and cut it into strips.

4 Transfer the tofu to a plate. Add mushrooms and garlic to the wok; stir-fry for 2 minutes. Add the green beans and broth; bring the mixture to a boil. Reduce the heat to low, cover, and cook until the beans are crisp-tender, about 7 minutes.

5 Increase the heat to moderately high. Add the bell pepper and the soy-sauce mixture to the vegetables; cook until the mixture is thickened and bubbly, about 2 minutes. Add the tofu and stir gently. Cook until heated through, about 2 more minutes, and serve.

TIME SAVERS

BAKED POTATOES
When you're baking potatoes in the conventional oven, there are two simple ways that you can speed up the cooking time. With either method you'll save about 15 minutes.

The first method: Cut the scrubbed potatoes in half lengthwise. Place the halves, cut sides down, on a greased baking sheet, then bake.

The second method: Stick a metal prong or baking nail through the center of the whole potato, then bake. The metal conducts the heat so the potato bakes both inside and out.

Using either method, bake the potatoes in a 425°F oven until they are tender, about 35 minutes.

HAM-STUFFED ACORN SQUASH

Ham-Stuffed Acorn Squash

One Serving: **Calories** 325 **Protein** 12g **Carbohydrates** 48g **Fat** 11g **Cholesterol** 42mg **Sodium** 632mg

2 large acorn squash (about 1¼ pounds each)

3 tablespoons butter or margarine, divided

1 green onion, chopped

1 cup slivered or finely cubed smoked ham

½ teaspoon dried thyme leaves, crumbled

⅔ cup water

½ cup quick-cooking couscous

¼ cup raisins

2 tablespoons honey or maple syrup

Salt and ground black pepper to taste

 PREPARATION TIME
12 MINUTES

 COOKING TIME
33 MINUTES

SERVING SUGGESTION *This low-calorie, satisfying main dish goes well with a salad of endive, raddichio, and artichoke hearts.*

1 Cut each acorn squash in half lengthwise. Scoop out and discard the seeds. Partially fill a large skillet or stockpot with 1 inch of water. Add the squash and bring to a boil over high heat. Reduce the heat to low, cover, and cook until the squash is fork-tender, 15 to 20 minutes.

2 Meanwhile, in a large saucepan, melt 1 tablespoon butter over moderate heat. Add green onion; sauté until soft, about 1 minute. Stir in ham, thyme, and water; bring to a boil. Stir in couscous and raisins. Remove the pan from the heat, cover, and let it stand until the couscous softens, about 15 minutes.

3 Preheat the broiler. Drain the cooked squash and place the halves, cut side up, on the rack over a broiler pan. Place ½ tablespoon each of butter and honey into each cavity. Sprinkle with salt and pepper.

4 Broil the squash 4 inches from the heat until the butter melts. Brush the cut surfaces of the squash with the butter mixture from the cavity. Continue broiling until lightly browned, 3 to 4 minutes. Spoon the ham mixture into the squash cavities, and serve.

BLACK-EYED PEAS WITH RICE

One Serving: **Calories** 337 **Protein** 10g **Carbohydrates** 57g **Fat** 8g **Cholesterol** 0mg **Sodium** 281mg

1 medium-size yellow onion

1 clove garlic

2 tablespoons vegetable oil

1 cup long-grain white rice

2 cups water

1 package (10 ounces) frozen black-eyed peas

1 package (9 ounces) frozen cut green beans

3 tablespoons snipped dill (or 1 tablespoon dill weed)

Salt and ground black pepper to taste

 PREPARATION TIME
5 MINUTES

COOKING TIME
25 MINUTES

1 Chop onion; finely chop garlic. In a large saucepan, heat oil over moderate heat. Add the onion and sauté until soft, about 5 minutes. Add the garlic and rice; stir until well mixed. Add water; increase the heat to high and bring the mixture to a boil.

2 Add frozen black-eyed peas to the rice mixture; stir to break up the frozen chunks. Continue cooking, uncovered, for 10 minutes. Add frozen green beans, stirring to break up the chunks. Reduce the heat to low, cover, and cook until the beans are heated through and the rice is tender, about 5 minutes.

3 Stir dill into the rice and bean mixture; season with salt and pepper. Place the mixture in a large dish, and serve.

VEGETABLE GRATIN ON TOAST

One Serving: **Calories** 364 **Protein** 13g **Carbohydrates** 28g **Fat** 22g **Cholesterol** 21mg **Sodium** 746mg

2 cloves garlic

1 large yellow onion

1 large zucchini

1 large yellow squash

1 large ripe tomato

1/4 cup olive oil

4 1/2-inch-thick slices Italian bread

1/2 teaspoon dried thyme leaves, crumbled

1/2 teaspoon salt

4 ounces provolone cheese, sliced

2 tablespoons grated Parmesan cheese

 **PREPARATION TIME**
15 MINUTES

 **COOKING TIME**
30 MINUTES

FOOD NOTE *This filling and economical vegetable and cheese supper is made rich with the flavors of Italy. Serve it with risotto.*

1 Preheat the oven to 400°F. Lightly grease a 2-quart shallow baking or gratin dish. Finely chop garlic; slice onion. Cut zucchini and yellow squash diagonally into 1/4-inch-thick slices. Slice tomato.

2 In a large skillet, heat oil over moderate heat. Add the garlic and sauté for 1 minute. Remove the skillet from the heat.

3 Brush bread slices on both sides with half of the garlic oil. Set the skillet with the remaining oil aside. Place the bread in the prepared dish and bake until golden, about 8 minutes, turning once halfway through the baking time.

4 Meanwhile, cook the onion in the skillet with the remaining garlic oil over moderate heat for 3 minutes. Add the zucchini, yellow squash, thyme, and salt; sauté until soft, about 5 minutes.

5 Spoon half of the vegetable mixture over the toasted bread; top each with an equal amount of provolone cheese slices. Spoon the remaining vegetable mixture over the cheese; top it with the tomato slices, and sprinkle with Parmesan cheese. Bake until the vegetable mixture is heated through, about 10 minutes, and serve.

VEGETARIAN CHILI

One Serving: **Calories** 283 **Protein** 13g **Carbohydrates** 43g **Fat** 9g **Cholesterol** 15mg **Sodium** 936mg

1 **medium-size yellow onion**

2 **small zucchini**

1 **medium-size green bell pepper**

1 **can (16 or 19 ounces) red kidney beans**

1 **tablespoon vegetable oil**

2 to 3 **teaspoons chili powder**

1 **teaspoon ground cumin**

½ **teaspoon salt**

1 **can (28 ounces) crushed tomatoes**

1 **package (10 ounces) frozen corn kernels**

2 **ounces Cheddar cheese, coarsely grated (½ cup)**

PREPARATION TIME
8 MINUTES

COOKING TIME
25 MINUTES

COOK'S TIP *If you prefer your chili very mild or fire-alarm hot, adjust the amount of chili powder accordingly.*

1 Chop onion and dice zucchini; core, seed, and chop bell pepper. Drain and rinse kidney beans; set them aside. In a 5-quart Dutch oven or kettle, heat oil over moderate heat. Add the onion and bell pepper; sauté until soft, about 5 minutes. Stir in chili powder, cumin, and salt; cook for 1 minute.

2 Stir the beans, zucchini, undrained tomatoes, and corn into the onion mixture. Increase the heat to moderately high and bring the mixture to a boil. Partially cover the pan, reduce the heat to low, and simmer the mixture for 15 minutes, stirring occasionally.

3 Ladle the chili into serving bowls, top each with an equal amount of grated Cheddar cheese, and serve.

VEGETARIAN STUFFED PEPPERS

One Serving: **Calories** 428 **Protein** 22g **Carbohydrates** 43g **Fat** 22g **Cholesterol** 48mg **Sodium** 1007mg

4 **large green, red, or yellow bell peppers (about 8 ounces each)**

1 **medium-size red onion**

1 **small zucchini**

1 **clove garlic**

1 **tablespoon vegetable oil**

1 **can (16 or 19 ounces) red kidney beans, drained and rinsed**

1 **teaspoon dried oregano or basil, crumbled**

8 **ounces mozzarella cheese, diced**

2 **cups prepared plain spaghetti sauce**

PREPARATION TIME
9 MINUTES

COOKING TIME
35 MINUTES

1 Cut each bell pepper lengthwise in half and remove the seeds. In a 12-inch skillet, bring ½ inch of water to a boil over high heat. Add the pepper halves, cover, and cook until the peppers are crisp-tender, about 5 minutes. Meanwhile, chop red onion, dice zucchini, and finely chop garlic.

2 Drain the bell peppers; remove them from the skillet and set them aside. In a medium-size saucepan, heat oil over moderate heat. Add the chopped onion and zucchini; sauté until soft, about 5 minutes. Stir in the chopped garlic and sauté for 10 seconds. Remove the saucepan from the heat.

3 Stir beans, oregano, and cheese into the onion mixture. Fill each pepper half with an equal amount of the mixture. Pour spaghetti sauce into the skillet.

4 Arrange the peppers, filled sides up, in the skillet. Cover the skillet and bring the sauce to a boil over high heat. Reduce the heat to low and continue cooking until the vegetables are heated through and the cheese is melted, about 15 minutes. Transfer the peppers to a platter, spoon the sauce over them, and serve immediately.

MUSHROOM AND ONION PIE

Mushroom and Onion Pie

One Serving: **Calories** 421 **Protein** 15g **Carbohydrates** 35g **Fat** 24g **Cholesterol** 99mg **Sodium** 741mg

- ¼ cup (½ stick) butter or margarine
- 1½ pounds mushrooms, sliced
- 1 large yellow onion, sliced
- ⅓ cup all-purpose flour
- ½ cup dry white wine
- 1 container (8 ounces) cottage cheese
- ¼ cup chopped parsley
- ½ teaspoon salt
- ¼ teaspoon ground white pepper
- ½ package (15 ounces) refrigerated ready-to-bake pie crust
- 1 egg yolk
- 2 tablespoons water

 PREPARATION TIME
15 MINUTES

 COOKING TIME
30 MINUTES

DIET NOTE *With only a top crust on this pie, the calorie count is kept under control. Serve this tasty supper with a bowl of new potatoes.*

1 Preheat the oven to 425°F. In a large skillet, melt butter over moderately high heat. Add mushrooms and onion; sauté until soft, about 10 minutes. Stir in flour until well mixed. Stir in wine and cook until thickened, about 1 minute. Remove the pan from the heat.

2 Stir cottage cheese, chopped parsley, salt, and white pepper into the mushroom mixture. Pour the mixture into an ungreased 9-inch pie plate. Place the pie crust over the filling and press the edge to seal it onto the plate; flute the edge decoratively, if desired.

3 In a cup, mix egg yolk with water; brush the mixture over the pie crust. Cut slits in a decorative design into the crust to allow the steam to escape during baking. Bake the pie until the crust is golden brown and the filling is bubbly, 15 to 20 minutes, and serve.

Eggplant Parmigiana

One Serving: **Calories** 373 **Protein** 13g **Carbohydrates** 23g **Fat** 25g **Cholesterol** 79mg **Sodium** 561mg

1 medium-size eggplant
(about 1 pound)

1 large egg

2 tablespoons water

¹/₃ cup all-purpose flour

¹/₂ teaspoon dried oregano,
crumbled

4 tablespoons vegetable oil,
divided

¹/₃ cup grated Parmesan
cheese

1 cup prepared plain
spaghetti sauce

4 ounces mozzarella cheese,
coarsely grated (1 cup)

PREPARATION TIME
15 MINUTES

COOKING TIME
22 MINUTES

SERVING SUGGESTION *This Italian favorite can easily serve eight as an accompaniment; it would go well with chicken or veal.*

1 Peel eggplant and cut it crosswise into ¹/₂-inch-thick slices. In a pie plate, beat egg with water. On a sheet of wax paper, combine flour and oregano. Dip the eggplant slices first into the egg mixture, then into the flour mixture, shaking off the excess.

2 In a large skillet, heat 2 tablespoons oil over moderately high heat. Add enough eggplant to cover the bottom of the skillet without crowding; cook until golden brown, turning once, about 3 minutes on each side. Drain the eggplant on paper towels.

3 Add the remaining 2 tablespoons of oil to the skillet; cook the remaining eggplant until golden, and drain.

4 Wipe out the skillet with paper towels. Return the eggplant slices to the skillet, overlapping to fit if necessary. Sprinkle with Parmesan cheese. Top with spaghetti sauce and mozzarella cheese. Cover and cook over moderately low heat until heated through, 5 to 7 minutes. Spoon the eggplant onto plates, and serve immediately.

Mixed Vegetable Stew

One Serving: **Calories** 215 **Protein** 8g **Carbohydrates** 26g **Fat** 10g **Cholesterol** 15mg **Sodium** 364mg

8 ounces Swiss chard

4 ounces mushrooms

12 baby carrots (about
8 ounces)

4 ounces snow peas

4 green onions

2 tablespoons (¹/₄ stick)
butter or margarine

1 tablespoon olive oil

1 clove garlic, chopped

1 cup hot water

1 package (10 ounces)
frozen baby lima beans

Salt and ground black
pepper to taste

1 tablespoon chopped
parsley

PREPARATION TIME
15 MINUTES

COOKING TIME
15 MINUTES

1 Cut the stems of chard into 1-inch lengths; slice the green chard leaves into ¹/₂-inch-wide ribbons. Cut mushrooms in half, cut carrots in half lengthwise, remove the strings from snow peas, and cut onions into ¹/₂-inch lengths.

2 In a 5-quart Dutch oven, heat butter with oil over moderately high heat. Add the green onions and sauté for 30 seconds. Stir in the chard stems, mushrooms, carrots, garlic, water, and frozen lima beans. Bring to a boil, stirring to thaw the beans. Reduce the heat to low, cover, and cook until the carrots are almost tender, 8 to 10 minutes.

3 Add the chard leaves and snow peas to the vegetable mixture. Continue cooking until the vegetables are crisp-tender, about 4 more minutes. Season the mixture with salt and pepper. Spoon the mixture into a bowl, sprinkle it with parsley, and serve immediately.

SALADS

SEAFOOD ROMAINE SALAD (PAGE 314)

SIDE-DISH SALADS

As a light accompaniment to your main dish, this bright range of salads will add a healthy touch in very little time.

SPINACH SALAD WITH ORANGES

One Serving: **Calories** 253 **Protein** 5g **Carbohydrates** 22g **Fat** 19g **Cholesterol** 0mg **Sodium** 314mg

¼ cup slivered almonds

3 navel or Valencia oranges

½ small red onion

4 cups torn fresh spinach leaves

For the red-wine vinegar dressing

¼ **cup vegetable oil**

¼ **cup red-wine vinegar**

1 **tablespoon sugar**

½ **teaspoon salt**

¼ **teaspoon ground black pepper**

 PREPARATION TIME
14 MINUTES

 COOKING TIME
4 MINUTES

SERVING SUGGESTION *This colorful salad mixes the tart and sweet tastes of spinach and fruit—it's excellent with barbecued meat.*

1 In a large skillet, heat oil for the dressing over moderate heat. Add almonds and cook until golden, 2 to 3 minutes. Remove the skillet from the heat. Using a slotted spoon, transfer the almonds to a small bowl, leaving the oil in the skillet.

2 To make the dressing, add vinegar, sugar, salt, and pepper to the vegetable oil in the skillet; stir until the sugar dissolves. Set aside.

3 Peel oranges and slice crosswise. Thinly slice red onion. In a salad bowl, combine the oranges, onion slices, and spinach leaves. Sprinkle with the almonds. Add the dressing, toss gently, and serve.

Shelf Magic

Here are two easy side-dish salads—one a Moroccan salad made with bulgur, and the other a potato salad with blue cheese dressing. Either one makes a terrific side dish for a barbecue or picnic.

WARM TABBOULEH SALAD

In a large saucepan, bring **3 cups water** to a boil. Stir in **1½ cups bulgur**. Remove the pan from the heat, cover, and let it stand until the bulgur is soft, about 13 minutes.

Meanwhile, dice **1 large tomato**. Chop **3 green onions** and ¼ **cup shelled pistachio nuts**. In a large bowl, combine the tomato, onion, nuts, ½ **cup sliced pitted dates**, **1 tablespoon each chopped parsley and chopped mint**. Stir in ½ **cup prepared lemon salad dressing** and the bulgur.
SERVES 6

PARMESAN POTATO SALAD

In a large salad bowl, combine **two 16-ounce cans sliced potatoes**, drained, and **one 8-ounce can cut green beans**, drained. Drain **one 6-ounce jar marinated artichoke hearts** and cut them in half; add to mixture.

In a small bowl, combine ½ **cup prepared blue cheese salad dressing** and ¼ **cup grated Parmesan cheese**. Toss gently into potato mixture. Serve immediately, or cover and refrigerate. Stir in **1 cup cherry tomatoes**, halved, just before serving.
SERVES 6

ORIENTAL SALAD

One Serving: **Calories** 201 **Protein** 3g **Carbohydrates** 10g **Fat** 18g **Cholesterol** 0mg **Sodium** 271mg

8 ounces snow peas

1 cup bean sprouts

1 large carrot, cut into matchstick strips

12 thin slices cucumber, halved

For the Oriental dressing

¼ cup vegetable oil

1 tablespoon Oriental sesame oil

1 tablespoon rice vinegar or distilled white vinegar

1 tablespoon soy sauce

½ teaspoon ground ginger

½ teaspoon sugar

Pinch red pepper flakes

PREPARATION TIME
11 MINUTES

COOKING TIME
11 MINUTES

1 In a medium-size saucepan, bring 2 inches of water to a boil over high heat. Meanwhile, remove the tips and strings from snow peas. Rinse and drain bean sprouts.

2 Drop the snow peas into the saucepan of boiling water; when the water returns to a boil, drain the snow peas into a colander; rinse them with cold water, and drain well. Transfer the peas to a large bowl and add the sprouts, carrot, and cucumber slices.

3 To make the dressing, in a small jar or cruet, combine vegetable oil and sesame oil. Add vinegar, soy sauce, ginger, sugar, and pepper flakes. Cover and shake until well mixed. Pour the dressing over the vegetables. Toss to mix well, and serve immediately.

VARIATION: ORIENTAL CHICKEN SALAD

One Serving: **Calories** 294 **Protein** 23g **Carbohydrates** 10g **Fat** 19g **Cholesterol** 43mg **Sodium** 326mg

Add **2 tablespoons vegetable oil** *and* **two 6-ounce boneless, skinless chicken-breast halves** *to the list of ingredients above. In a medium-size skillet, heat 2 tablespoons oil over moderate heat. Cook chicken until the juices run clear, about 3 minutes on each side. Remove the chicken; slice it into ¼-inch-thick slices. Prepare the salad as in Steps 1, 2, and 3 above, adding the chicken just before the dressing.*

CALICO COLESLAW

One Serving: **Calories** 275 **Protein** 3g **Carbohydrates** 18g **Fat** 23g **Cholesterol** 17mg **Sodium** 196mg

1 small head green cabbage

½ small head red cabbage

1 large carrot

1 medium-size red apple

Salt and ground black pepper to taste

For the yogurt dressing

½ cup mayonnaise

⅓ cup low-fat yogurt

2 tablespoons apple juice

1 tablespoon cider vinegar

1 teaspoon celery seeds

PREPARATION TIME
18 MINUTES

COOKING TIME
0 MINUTES

1 Cut green cabbage in half; remove core, and coarsely shred the cabbage. Repeat with red cabbage. Peel and coarsely grate carrot. Remove core from apple and cut into ¼-inch dice.

2 In a large bowl, lightly toss the green and red cabbage with the carrot and apple until well mixed.

3 To make the dressing, in a small bowl, whisk together mayonnaise, yogurt, apple juice, vinegar, and celery seeds.

4 Add the dressing to the vegetables and apple; toss until coated. Season the salad with salt and pepper. Serve immediately, or cover and refrigerate until ready to serve.

CALIFORNIA SALAD

CALIFORNIA SALAD

One Serving: **Calories** 256 **Protein** 8g **Carbohydrates** 16g **Fat** 20g **Cholesterol** 30mg **Sodium** 321mg

- **2 cups alfalfa sprouts**
- **1 can (14 ounces) artichoke hearts in water, drained**
- **3 ripe plum tomatoes**
- **1 ripe avocado**
- **2 tablespoons grated Parmesan cheese**
- **½ cup prepared Caesar salad dressing**

PREPARATION TIME
15 MINUTES

COOKING TIME
0 MINUTES

SERVING SUGGESTION *If you prefer, substitute shredded lettuce for the alfalfa sprouts. Serve the salad as a starter on individual plates.*

1 On a serving platter, spread alfalfa sprouts to an even layer. Cut artichoke hearts in half, or in quarters if they are large. Slice tomatoes. Arrange the artichokes and tomatoes on the sprouts.

2 Cut avocado in half, remove the pit, peel, and slice. Arrange the avocado slices on the platter with the sprouts. Sprinkle the salad with cheese, drizzle it with dressing, and serve immediately.

MUSHROOM ASPARAGUS SALAD

One Serving: **Calories** 108 **Protein** 6g **Carbohydrates** 10g **Fat** 7g **Cholesterol** 0mg **Sodium** 272mg

3 cups water

1 pound fresh asparagus

½ cup white-wine vinegar

½ teaspoon salt

½ teaspoon dried thyme leaves, crumbled

16 mushroom caps

8 small romaine lettuce leaves

2 tablespoons slivered pimiento or roasted red bell pepper

2 tablespoons extra-virgin olive oil

 PREPARATION TIME **15 MINUTES**

 COOKING TIME **10 MINUTES**

SERVING SUGGESTION *This spring salad is pretty enough to serve as a first course for a special dinner party. It's ideal before lamb or fish.*

1 In a large skillet, bring water to a boil over high heat. Meanwhile, snap the tough ends off asparagus. If desired, peel the lower half of each asparagus spear.

2 Add the asparagus to the boiling water; reduce the heat to moderate and cook the asparagus until just crisp-tender, 8 to 10 minutes.

3 Using a slotted spoon, transfer the asparagus from the boiling water to a plate lined with paper towels; set it aside to cool. Meanwhile, add vinegar, salt, and thyme leaves to the water in the skillet. Bring the mixture to a boil and add mushrooms. Return the mixture to a boil. Remove the mushroom mixture from the heat and let it cool.

4 To serve, line each of four individual salad plates with two romaine leaves, overlapping to form a fan shape. Pat the asparagus dry and arrange it in a fan shape over the romaine.

5 Drain the mushrooms and toss with pimientos. Arrange the mushroom mixture at the base of the asparagus stems. Drizzle oil over the asparagus and mushroom mixture, and serve immediately.

TOMATO AND MOZZARELLA SALAD

One Serving: **Calories** 221 **Protein** 5g **Carbohydrates** 24g **Fat** 16g **Cholesterol** 6mg **Sodium** 181mg

3 large ripe tomatoes, sliced

1 pound mozzarella cheese

1 cup red cherry tomatoes or pear-shaped yellow tomatoes

¼ cup fresh basil leaves

For the olive oil dressing

½ cup olive oil

3 tablespoons red-wine vinegar

¼ teaspoon salt

⅛ teaspoon ground black pepper

PREPARATION TIME **45 MINUTES**

COOKING TIME **0 MINUTES**

1 Cut large tomatoes into ¼-inch-thick slices, and cut mozzarella into ¼-inch-thick slices; cut cherry tomatoes in half.

2 On a serving platter, arrange alternating slices of tomatoes and mozzarella cheese around the edge of the platter. Place the cherry tomatoes in the center. Cover and refrigerate the salad for 30 minutes or until ready to serve.

3 Meanwhile, prepare the dressing. In a small jar or cruet, combine olive oil, red-wine vinegar, salt, and pepper. Cover and shake the dressing until mixed.

4 Just before serving, tear or cut basil leaves into slivers and sprinkle them over the tomato salad. Shake the dressing, drizzle it over the salad, and serve.

CREAMY CUCUMBER SALAD

One Serving: **Calories** 90 **Protein** 2g **Carbohydrates** 8g **Fat** 6g **Cholesterol** 13mg **Sodium** 286mg

2 large cucumbers, chilled
½ small yellow onion

For the sour cream dressing
½ cup sour cream
1 teaspoon dill weed
1 tablespoon cider vinegar
1 teaspoon sugar
½ teaspoon salt
¼ teaspoon white pepper

 PREPARATION TIME
10 MINUTES

COOKING TIME
0 MINUTES

1 To make the dressing, in a large bowl, combine sour cream, dill, vinegar, sugar, salt, and pepper until well mixed. Refrigerate until the salad is ready to serve.

2 Peel cucumbers, cut them in half lengthwise, and remove seeds; cut them crosswise into thin slices. Thinly slice onion. Fold the cucumber and onion into the dressing. Spoon the salad into a serving dish, and serve immediately.

SHREDDED CARROT AND BEET SALAD

One Serving: **Calories** 217 **Protein** 2g **Carbohydrates** 24g **Fat** 14g **Cholesterol** 0mg **Sodium** 207mg

3 large carrots (about 12 ounces), peeled
¼ cup raisins
3 medium-size beets (about 11 ounces), peeled

For the sweet and sour dressing
½ cup vegetable oil
2 tablespoons red-wine vinegar
1 teaspoon sugar
½ teaspoon dry mustard
¼ teaspoon salt

 PREPARATION TIME
30 MINUTES

COOKING TIME
0 MINUTES

1 Using a hand grater or a food processor fitted with the shredding blade, shred carrots and place them in a small bowl. Add raisins. Shred beets and place them in another small bowl.

2 To make the dressing, in a small jar or cruet, combine oil, vinegar, sugar, mustard, and salt. Cover and shake until well mixed. Pour half of the dressing over each bowl of vegetables. Toss each until coated. Cover and refrigerate 15 minutes or until ready to serve.

3 To serve, on a platter, arrange the beets in the center and surround them with the carrots. Serve immediately.

MARINATED CHICK-PEA SALAD

One Serving: **Calories** 330 **Protein** 12g **Carbohydrates** 40g **Fat** 18g **Cholesterol** 0mg **Sodium** 303mg

1 small cucumber
1 small green bell pepper
6 red radishes
1 can (16 or 19 ounces) chick-peas, drained
½ cup pitted black olives (preferably Greek), halved
¼ cup prepared Italian dressing
Lettuce leaves
4 cherry tomatoes, halved

 PREPARATION TIME
40 MINUTES

COOKING TIME
0 MINUTES

1 Peel cucumber and remove the seeds; cut it into chunks. Core and seed bell pepper and cut it into strips. Trim and slice radishes.

2 In a medium-size bowl, combine the cucumber chunks, bell pepper, radishes, chick-peas, and olives. Pour dressing over the salad and toss lightly. Cover and refrigerate for at least 30 minutes.

3 Line a serving platter with lettuce leaves. Mound the marinated salad over the leaves. Garnish with cherry tomatoes, and serve.

BROCCOLI-ORANGE SALAD

BROCCOLI-ORANGE SALAD

One Serving: **Calories** 82 **Protein** 2g **Carbohydrates** 9g **Fat** 5g **Cholesterol** 0mg **Sodium** 16mg

2 **cups broccoli florets**

2 **cups cauliflower florets**

Salt and ground black pepper to taste

2 **cups thinly sliced red cabbage**

Red cabbage leaves (optional)

For the orange dressing

2 **tablespoons canola oil (or other vegetable oil)**

1 **small yellow onion, sliced**

2 **teaspoons cornstarch**

½ **cup orange juice**

 PREPARATION TIME
8 MINUTES

 COOKING TIME
26 MINUTES

COOK'S TIP *To cool the broccoli and cauliflower quickly, plunge the cooked vegetables into a large bowl of ice water.*

1 To make the dressing, in a medium-size saucepan, heat oil over moderate heat. Add onion and sauté until soft, about 5 minutes. Stir in cornstarch; stir in orange juice and bring to a boil. Cook until the mixture thickens slightly. Remove the saucepan from the heat. Pour the mixture into a large bowl and refrigerate to cool quickly.

2 Meanwhile, in a large saucepan, bring 2 inches water to a boil over high heat. Add broccoli and cauliflower; cook until just crisp-tender, about 7 minutes. Drain the vegetables and rinse with cold water. Add the vegetables to the orange dressing and toss until coated. Season with salt and pepper. Cover and refrigerate until ready to serve.

3 To serve, add sliced cabbage to the vegetable mixture and toss until well mixed. Line a serving platter with cabbage leaves, if desired; top with the salad, and serve immediately.

CORN AND BEAN SALAD

One Serving: **Calories** 155 **Protein** 4g **Carbohydrates** 11g **Fat** 12g **Cholesterol** 0mg **Sodium** 551mg

3 cups cooked corn kernels

1 can (16 ounces) red kidney beans, drained and rinsed

1 can (drained weight 3.8 ounces) sliced pitted black olives

1 small red bell pepper

Curly endive leaves

For the cumin dressing

6 tablespoons vegetable oil

3 tablespoons cider vinegar

1½ teaspoons Dijon mustard

¾ teaspoon salt

¾ teaspoon ground cumin

¼ teaspoon sugar

PREPARATION TIME
40 MINUTES

COOKING TIME
0 MINUTES

1 To make the dressing, in a medium-size bowl, whisk together oil, vinegar, mustard, salt, cumin, and sugar until well mixed.

2 Stir corn, kidney beans, and olives into the bowl with the dressing; toss until coated. Cover and refrigerate for at least 30 minutes.

3 Keeping bell pepper whole, remove the core and seeds. Cut the pepper crosswise into ¼-inch-thick rings.

4 To serve, line a platter with endive leaves. Spoon the corn mixture over the endive, top with the bell pepper rings, and serve.

VARIATION: THREE-BEAN SALAD

One Serving: **Calories** 177 **Protein** 5g **Carbohydrates** 15g **Fat** 13g **Cholesterol** 0mg **Sodium** 472mg

Omit corn kernels and red bell pepper from the list of ingredients above. Add **one 14.5-ounce can cut green beans,** *drained,* **one 14.5-ounce can cut wax beans,** *drained, and* **⅓ cup chopped onion** *to the list of ingredients. Prepare dressing as in Step 1, above. Stir in all of the beans and the onion; cover and refrigerate for at least 30 minutes. Line a platter with endive leaves. Spoon the bean mixture over the leaves, and serve.*

WARM RICE SALAD

One Serving: **Calories** 295 **Protein** 5g **Carbohydrates** 44g **Fat** 11g **Cholesterol** 0mg **Sodium** 335mg

3 tablespoons vegetable oil, divided

1 small onion, sliced

1 cup long-grain white rice

2½ cups water

1 cup frozen green peas

1 cup sliced celery

1 tablespoon red-wine vinegar

½ teaspoon salt

½ teaspoon dried tarragon, crumbled

¼ teaspoon ground black pepper

PREPARATION TIME
5 MINUTES

COOKING TIME
35 MINUTES

1 In a large skillet, heat 1 tablespoon oil over moderate heat. Add onion and sauté until soft, about 5 minutes. Stir rice into the onion in the skillet and add water. Bring the rice to a boil. Reduce the heat to low, cover, and cook the rice for 10 minutes.

2 Using a fork, gently stir frozen peas into the rice mixture. Cover and continue to cook the rice and peas until they are tender and all the liquid has been absorbed, about 5 minutes. Remove the skillet from the heat and let the rice stand, covered, for 5 minutes.

3 Meanwhile, in a large bowl, combine celery, 2 tablespoons oil, vinegar, salt, tarragon, and pepper. Stir in the cooked rice and toss until coated. Serve the salad warm or at room temperature.

WARM WINTER SALAD

WARM WINTER SALAD

One Serving: **Calories** 410 **Protein** 6g **Carbohydrates** 26g **Fat** 33g **Cholesterol** 24mg **Sodium** 349mg

8 small red potatoes, unpeeled and halved

1 pint Brussels sprouts, trimmed, or 1 package (10 ounces) frozen Brussels sprouts

½ pound carrots, peeled and sliced diagonally

1 tablespoon chopped parsley or chives

For the creamy mustard dressing

¾ cup mayonnaise

1 tablespoon Dijon mustard

1 tablespoon cider vinegar

2 teaspoons celery seeds

Salt and ground black pepper to taste

PREPARATION TIME
15 MINUTES

COOKING TIME
20 MINUTES

SERVING SUGGESTION *This platter of red potatoes and Brussels sprouts with creamy mustard dressing is a natural with roast beef or chicken; it can also serve two as a hearty vegetarian lunch.*

1 In a saucepan of boiling water, cook potatoes until tender, about 20 minutes. In another saucepan of boiling water, cook sprouts and carrots until crisp-tender, about 10 minutes.

2 Meanwhile, make the dressing. In a small bowl, using a wire whisk, combine mayonnaise, mustard, vinegar, and celery seeds. Season with salt and pepper.

3 Drain the vegetables and arrange them decoratively on a serving platter, allowing them to cool slightly. Spoon some of the mayonnaise dressing over the vegetables; sprinkle with parsley. Serve immediately, passing the remaining dressing on the side.

VARIATIONS ON THE BASIC GREEN SALAD

A fresh green salad is a menu standard that tends not to get the attention it deserves. Torn lettuce leaves with a chopped tomato may be fine sometimes, but why not make the salad worth the trouble? Below is a recipe for a basic salad using a fresh combination of greens. Once you've mixed them together, look to the suggestions on the right for dressing and toppings that will really make the salad exciting. Each dressing makes ½ cup. The basic salad and toppings are all sufficient to serve four.

BASIC GREEN SALAD Wash and dry **1 bunch arugula, 1 small head radicchio, 1 small head Boston lettuce**, and **12 oz. fresh spinach**. (One bunch romaine lettuce may be substituted for the arugula and radicchio.) Into a large salad bowl, tear the greens into bite-size pieces.

Prepare the dressing and additional ingredients from one of the recipes at the right; serve immediately.

◄ TOMATO BASIL DRESSING In a food processor or blender, combine **2 medium-size tomatoes**, skinned and seeded, **3 Tbsp. olive oil, 1 Tbsp. white-wine vinegar, 1 tsp. tomato paste, 1 tsp. sugar, 4 to 6 fresh basil leaves** or **$^1/_2$ tsp. dried basil.** Blend until smooth. Season to taste with **salt** and **ground black pepper.** Prepare the **basic green salad**; top with **chopped hard-cooked egg, chopped cucumber,** and **prepared croutons.** Toss with dressing and serve.

◄ CURRIED YOGURT DRESSING In a food processor or blender, combine **$^1/_2$ cup plain yogurt, 2 Tbsp. mango chutney, 1 tsp. curry powder, 1 tsp. lime juice, 6 to 8 fresh mint leaves** or **$^1/_2$ tsp. dried mint.** Blend until smooth. Season with **salt** and **ground black pepper.** Prepare the **basic green salad**; top with **orange segments** or **sliced apple** and sprinkle with **chopped peanuts.** Toss with dressing and serve.

► TANGY COCKTAIL DRESSING In a bowl, combine **$^1/_4$ cup mayonnaise, 2 Tbsp. tomato ketchup, 1 Tbsp. chopped parsley, 1 green onion,** finely chopped, **1 Tbsp. chopped stuffed olives, 1 Tbsp. lemon juice** and **1 tsp. paprika.** Prepare the **basic green salad**; top with **4 oz. canned or imitation crabmeat.** Toss with dressing and serve.

► HORSERADISH CREAM DRESSING In a bowl, combine **$^2/_3$ cup sour cream, 1 Tbsp. creamed horseradish, 2 Tbsp. lemon juice, salt** and **ground black pepper.** Prepare the **basic green salad**; top with **4 oz. shredded cooked beef, 1 medium-size chopped tomato,** and **$^1/_2$ cup shredded zucchini.** Toss with dressing and serve.

► WALNUT AND GARLIC DRESSING In a small jar or cruet, combine **6 Tbsp. walnut oil, 1 Tbsp. red-wine vinegar, 2 Tbsp. finely chopped walnuts** and **1 clove garlic,** crushed. Shake well to combine. Season to taste with **salt** and **ground black pepper.** Prepare the **basic green salad**; top with **3 to 4 oz. sliced goat's cheese, $^1/_4$ cup chopped walnuts,** and **1 sliced pear.** Toss with dressing and serve with **whole-wheat toast triangles.**

MACARONI VEGETABLE CHEESE SALAD

MACARONI VEGETABLE CHEESE SALAD

One Serving: **Calories** 471 **Protein** 11g **Carbohydrates** 32g **Fat** 34g **Cholesterol** 37mg **Sodium** 363mg

4 ounces Cheddar cheese

1 small zucchini

1 small carrot

8 ounces elbow macaroni

¾ cup mayonnaise

¼ cup plain low-fat yogurt

¼ cup prepared Italian dressing

Salt and ground black pepper to taste

Carrot curls (optional)

 PREPARATION TIME
8 MINUTES

 COOKING TIME
26 MINUTES

SERVING SUGGESTION *This healthy version of macaroni salad makes an ideal accompaniment to cold meats for a buffet supper.*

1 In a large saucepan, bring 3 quarts water to a boil over high heat. Meanwhile, using a hand grater or food processor, coarsely grate cheese, zucchini, and carrot into a large bowl; set aside.

2 Add macaroni to the boiling water and cook according to package directions or until it is tender but still firm to the bite. Stir mayonnaise, yogurt, and Italian dressing into the cheese and vegetables.

3 Drain the macaroni in a colander and rinse with cold water until the macaroni is cold, 1 to 2 minutes. Stir the well-drained macaroni into the cheese mixture. Season with salt and pepper.

4 Transfer the macaroni salad to a serving bowl and garnish with carrot curls, if desired. Serve immediately, or cover and refrigerate until ready to serve.

THREE-POTATO SALAD

One Serving: **Calories** 334 **Protein** 4g **Carbohydrates** 34g **Fat** 21g **Cholesterol** 11mg **Sodium** 273mg

1 **pound all-purpose potatoes**

2 **small sweet potatoes (about 6 ounces each)**

8 **ounces small red potatoes**

¹⁄₃ **cup prepared Italian or oil-and-vinegar dressing**

¹⁄₂ **cup mayonnaise**

¹⁄₄ **cup water**

1¹⁄₂ **tablespoons prepared mustard**

2 **green onions, chopped**

¹⁄₄ **cup chopped fresh basil, tarragon, or parsley**

Salt and ground black pepper to taste

PREPARATION TIME
9 MINUTES

COOKING TIME
29 MINUTES

1 In a Dutch oven or stockpot, bring 2 inches water to a boil over high heat. Meanwhile, peel all-purpose and sweet potatoes and cut them into 1-inch cubes. Cut unpeeled red potatoes into quarters. Drop the all-purpose and red potatoes into the boiling water. Cover and return the water to a boil. Boil the potatoes for 5 minutes.

2 Add the sweet potatoes to the Dutch oven and continue cooking the potatoes until tender, about 7 more minutes. Drain the potatoes in a colander and rinse with cold water to cool. Transfer the potatoes to a large bowl and drizzle with Italian dressing. Gently toss the potatoes until coated. Cover and refrigerate at least 5 minutes.

3 In a small bowl, combine mayonnaise, ¹⁄₄ cup water, and mustard until smooth. Stir in chopped green onions and basil. Fold the mayonnaise mixture into the potatoes. Season with salt and pepper. Serve the potato salad immediately or cover and refrigerate until ready to serve.

CREAMY PASTA SALAD

One Serving: **Calories** 406 **Protein** 9g **Carbohydrates** 42g **Fat** 23g **Cholesterol** 26mg **Sodium** 42mg

1 **small yellow onion**

1 **clove garlic**

1 **large red bell pepper**

6 **ounces penne (quill-shaped pasta)**

3 **tablespoons olive or vegetable oil**

1 **cup broccoli florets**

1 **tablespoon red-wine vinegar**

1 **cup fresh basil (or 1 cup watercress plus 1 table-spoon dried basil)**

1 **cup sour cream**

Salt and ground black pepper to taste

PREPARATION TIME
10 MINUTES

COOKING TIME
25 MINUTES

1 In a large saucepan, bring 3 quarts water to a boil over high heat. Meanwhile, slice onion and chop garlic. Core and seed bell pepper and cut it into thin strips.

2 Add penne to the boiling water and cook according to package directions or until it is tender but still firm to the bite.

3 Meanwhile, in a large skillet, heat oil over moderate heat. Add the onion and sauté until soft, about 5 minutes. Stir in the bell pepper, broccoli florets, and garlic. Cook until crisp-tender, about 4 minutes. Remove the pan from the heat; stir in vinegar.

4 Drain the pasta and rinse it well with cold water to cool quickly. Return the pasta to the large saucepan. Using a blender or food processor, purée basil with sour cream until the mixture is smooth.

5 Add the creamy basil dressing to the cooked pasta and toss gently until coated. Season with salt and pepper to taste. Transfer the pasta salad to a large serving bowl, top it with the sautéed vegetables, and serve immediately.

Melon Fruit Salad

One Serving: **Calories** 192 **Protein** 2g **Carbohydrates** 25g **Fat** 11g **Cholesterol** 0mg **Sodium** 15mg

1 **small cantaloupe**
1 **medium-size peach**
2 **ripe red plums**
1 **cup green seedless grapes**

For the honey-mint dressing
3 **tablespoons vegetable oil**
1 **tablespoon chopped mint**
1 **tablespoon lemon juice**
1 **teaspoon honey**

 PREPARATION TIME
15 MINUTES

COOKING TIME
0 MINUTES

1 Cut cantaloupe in half lengthwise and scoop out the seeds. Cut the cantaloupe into thin slices and cut the peel off each slice. Cut peach and plums in half, discard the pits, and cut into slices. On a serving platter, arrange grapes with the sliced fruits.

2 To make the dressing, in a small jar or cruet, combine oil, chopped mint, lemon juice, and honey. Cover and shake until well mixed. Drizzle the dressing evenly over the fruit, and serve immediately.

Apple Grape Salad

One Serving: **Calories** 301 **Protein** 2g **Carbohydrates** 23g **Fat** 24g **Cholesterol** 16mg **Sodium** 176mg

2 **stalks celery**
1 **large Granny Smith apple**
1 **cup red seedless grapes**
¼ **cup dried apricots**
2 **tablespoons sliced almonds**
½ **cup mayonnaise**
2 **tablespoons apple juice or cider**
Salt and ground white pepper to taste
Lettuce leaves

 PREPARATION TIME
12 MINUTES

COOKING TIME
3 MINUTES

1 Cut celery stalks into ¼-inch slices. Core apple and cut it into ¾-inch cubes. Cut grapes in half; cut apricots into quarters. Place almonds in a small skillet; toast them over moderate heat, stirring frequently, 2 to 3 minutes.

2 In a medium-size bowl, combine the celery slices, apple cubes, grapes, and apricots. Stir in mayonnaise and apple juice until well mixed. Season the salad with salt and pepper. Cover and refrigerate until ready to serve.

3 To serve, line a serving dish with lettuce leaves. Spoon the apple mixture into the center and sprinkle the salad with the toasted almonds. Serve immediately.

Time Savers

Salads
• Use scissors to snip fresh herbs and leaves directly into the salad bowl rather than taking the time to chop them. If exact measurements are required, snip the greens into a measuring cup. Firm fruit such as dried apricots, as well as cooked meats, can also be cut with scissors.

• For quickest salads, use the prewashed and packaged lettuces available at the supermarket.

• When making salads in which precision is not essential, don't waste preparation time by measuring each ingredient to exact specifications. The amounts given are approximate; use your eye to guide you.

WATERCRESS PEAR SALAD

WATERCRESS PEAR SALAD

One Serving: **Calories** 362 **Protein** 6g **Carbohydrates** 26g **Fat** 28g **Cholesterol** 13mg **Sodium** 245mg

1 **bunch watercress**

2 **ripe Bartlett or Comice pears**

½ **cup crumbled blue cheese**

⅓ **cup sliced pitted prunes**

¼ **cup chopped walnuts**

For the raspberry vinegar dressing

⅓ **cup olive oil**

2 **tablespoons raspberry vinegar**

Salt and ground black pepper to taste

PREPARATION TIME
21 MINUTES

COOKING TIME
0 MINUTES

COOK'S TIP *Red-wine vinegar may be used in place of the raspberry vinegar. Either way, this makes an elegant starter.*

1 Remove thick watercress stems and discard. Cut pears in half lengthwise, remove the cores, and cut lengthwise into slices.

2 On four individual serving plates, arrange an equal amount of the watercress, pears, cheese, and prunes; sprinkle with walnuts.

3 To make the dressing, in a small jar or cruet, combine oil, vinegar, salt and pepper. Cover and shake until well mixed. Drizzle the dressing over each salad, and serve immediately.

MAIN-COURSE SALADS

Bursting with fresh flavors and filling enough to make a complete meal, these easy salads can be made in a flash.

MEDITERRANEAN SALAD

One Serving: **Calories** 502 **Protein** 16g **Carbohydrates** 28g **Fat** 37g **Cholesterol** 48mg **Sodium** 1031mg

- 1 **small red onion**
- 4 **ounces mushrooms**
- 2 **cloves garlic**
- 2 **ripe tomatoes**
- 1 **cucumber**
- 4 **ounces sliced salami**
- 6 **tablespoons olive oil, divided**
- 2 **cups 1-inch cubes Italian bread**
- 2 **tablespoons red-wine vinegar**
- **Salt and ground black pepper to taste**
- 4 **cups torn firm salad greens such as curly endive or romaine lettuce**
- 1/2 **cup fresh basil (optional)**
- 4 **ounces feta cheese, crumbled**

PREPARATION TIME
15 MINUTES

COOKING TIME
10 MINUTES

COOK'S TIP *Try another Mediterranean flavor by substituting a small can of tuna, drained and flaked, for the salami, and omitting the feta.*

1 Thinly slice onion and mushrooms. Chop garlic and cut tomatoes into 1-inch chunks. Peel cucumber and cut it into 1/4-inch-thick slices. Cut sliced salami into strips.

2 In a 4-quart saucepan, heat 2 tablespoons oil over moderate heat. Add the onion and sauté until soft, about 5 minutes. Add the mushrooms and garlic; cook until soft, about 3 minutes. Remove the saucepan from the heat. Stir in bread cubes; set aside to cool.

3 Meanwhile, in a small jar or cruet, combine the remaining 4 tablespoons olive oil, vinegar, salt, and pepper. Cover and shake the dressing until well mixed.

4 To serve, in a salad bowl, toss the tomatoes, cucumber, salad greens, and basil if desired. Top with the salami, cheese, and the bread mixture. Drizzle the dressing over the salad. Toss gently, and serve.

Shelf Magic

You'll be packing a wholesome lunch if you take this salad along as the main dish. Add an apple or some sliced melon on the side.

WHITE BEANS WITH TUNA

Drain one **16-ounce can white kidney beans** (cannellini) and rinse with cold water. Drain **two 6 1/8-ounce cans tuna packed in water.** Cut **3 ripe plum tomatoes** into 1/2-inch cubes. Finely chop **1 green onion.**

In a large bowl, combine the beans, tomatoes, green onion, 1/4 **cup olive oil, 2 tablespoons lemon juice, 1 clove garlic,** finely chopped, 1/2 **teaspoon dried oregano,** and **2 tablespoons chopped parsley.**

Gently fold the tuna into the bean mixture. Season with **salt and ground black pepper.** Serve the salad immediately, or cover the bowl and refrigerate until ready to serve. Toss lightly before serving.
SERVES 4

Antipasto Salad Bowl

One Serving: **Calories** 417 **Protein** 16g **Carbohydrates** 28g **Fat** 28g **Cholesterol** 37mg **Sodium** 1268mg

8 ounces salami

8 ounces mushrooms

1 small red bell pepper

1 can (drained weight 6 ounces) large pitted black olives, chilled

1 can (8 to 10½ ounces) chick-peas, chilled

1 jar (6 ounces) marinated artichoke hearts, chilled

2 tablespoons olive oil

1 tablespoon red-wine vinegar

½ teaspoon dried oregano, crumbled

Escarole leaves

PREPARATION TIME
21 MINUTES

COOKING TIME
0 MINUTES

SERVING SUGGESTION *Serve this robust salad with a basket of warm Italian bread and garlic butter. There probably won't be room for a pasta course, but crunchy amaretti cookies with ice cream follow perfectly for dessert.*

1 Using a sharp knife, cut salami into ¾-inch cubes. Slice mushrooms; core and seed bell pepper and cut it into 1-inch pieces. Drain olives; drain and rinse chick-peas.

2 In a large bowl, combine the salami, mushrooms, bell pepper, olives, chick-peas, and artichoke hearts with their marinade. Add oil, vinegar, and oregano.

3 To serve, line a shallow glass salad bowl with escarole. Spoon the salami mixture into the center and serve immediately, or cover and refrigerate until ready to serve.

Broccoli and Lentil Salad

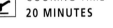

One Serving: **Calories** 340 **Protein** 18g **Carbohydrates** 34g **Fat** 16g **Cholesterol** 12mg **Sodium** 158mg

1 cup dried lentils

2 cups water

2 cups broccoli florets

1 green onion, chopped

½ cup prepared ranch-style dressing

Salt and ground black pepper to taste

8 red radishes

¼ cup toasted sunflower seeds

Additional ranch-style dressing (optional)

PREPARATION TIME
20 MINUTES

COOKING TIME
20 MINUTES

1 Rinse and drain dried lentils. In a medium-size saucepan, bring the lentils and 2 cups water to a boil over high heat. Reduce the heat to low, cover, and simmer the lentils until they are tender but firm, 15 to 20 minutes.

2 Meanwhile, in a small saucepan, bring 1 inch of water to a boil over high heat. Drop broccoli into the boiling water and return the water to a boil, uncovered. Cook the broccoli until crisp-tender, about 2 minutes. Drain the broccoli and rinse with cold water. Place the broccoli around the edges of a shallow serving dish and refrigerate.

3 Drain the cooked lentils and rinse them with cold water. In a medium-size bowl, combine the lentils with chopped green onion and ranch-style dressing. Season with salt and pepper. Refrigerate the lentils until cool, at least 10 minutes. Meanwhile, slice radishes or cut them into rose shapes.

4 To serve, mound the lentils in the center of the broccoli on the serving dish, and sprinkle with toasted sunflower seeds. Garnish the salad with the radishes. Serve immediately, passing additional dressing on the side, if desired.

PINEAPPLE–COTTAGE CHEESE SALAD

PINEAPPLE–COTTAGE CHEESE SALAD

One Serving: **Calories** 214   **Protein** 13g   **Carbohydrates** 33g   **Fat** 4g   **Cholesterol** 7mg   **Sodium** 349mg

1   **container (16 ounces) low-fat cottage cheese**

1   **can (8 ounces) crushed pineapple packed in juice, drained**

2   **tablespoons raisins**

1   **tablespoon chopped fresh mint**

2   **Red Delicious or McIntosh apples, chilled**

   Curly red-leaf lettuce leaves

2   **tablespoons chopped walnuts**

   Mint sprigs (optional)

PREPARATION TIME
10 MINUTES

COOKING TIME
0 MINUTES

DIET NOTE *This ideal low-calorie lunch turns plain cottage cheese into something to look forward to. Serve it with whole-wheat rolls.*

1 In a small bowl, combine cottage cheese, drained pineapple, raisins, and chopped mint. Cover and refrigerate until ready to serve.

2 Just before serving, quarter and core apples but do not peel. Cut the apples into thin wedge-shape slices.

3 Line four individual serving plates with lettuce leaves. Mound an equal amount of the cheese mixture on top of the lettuce; surround with the apple slices, and sprinkle with chopped walnuts. Garnish the plates with mint sprigs, if desired, and serve immediately.

SEAFOOD ROMAINE SALAD

One Serving: **Calories** 309 **Protein** 22g **Carbohydrates** 9g **Fat** 21g **Cholesterol** 48mg **Sodium** 237mg

12 ounces cod, orange roughy, or halibut

1 small head romaine lettuce

1 can (2 ounces) anchovy fillets

1 cup prepared croutons

2 tablespoons grated Parmesan cheese

Ground black pepper to taste

For the lemon-garlic dressing

1/3 cup vegetable oil

2 tablespoons lemon juice

1 clove garlic, finely chopped

1 teaspoon Worcestershire sauce

1/4 teaspoon dry mustard

 PREPARATION TIME **25 MINUTES**   COOKING TIME **5 MINUTES**

COOK'S TIP *You can easily create a simple version of Caesar salad by omitting the white-fish fillets altogether. Be sure to use fresh, crisp lettuce that is rinsed and dried thoroughly.*

1 Preheat the broiler. To prepare the dressing, in a small jar or cruet, combine oil, lemon juice, garlic, Worcestershire sauce, and mustard. Cover and shake the dressing until well mixed.

2 Place fish on a greased rack over the broiler pan. Drizzle 1 tablespoon of the dressing over the fish. Broil the fish 4 inches from the heat until it flakes easily when tested with a fork, about 5 minutes. Transfer the fish to a plate and let it cool for 10 minutes.

3 Meanwhile, rinse and dry romaine. Tear the leaves into bite-size pieces and place them in a salad bowl. Drain anchovies and cut them in half crosswise. Break the cod into small chunks and remove any bones. Add the fish, anchovies, and croutons to the romaine.

4 Shake the remaining dressing, and drizzle it over the salad. Sprinkle with cheese and pepper, toss gently until coated, and serve.

DILLED SALMON AND BEAN SALAD

One Serving: **Calories** 329 **Protein** 25g **Carbohydrates** 13g **Fat** 20g **Cholesterol** 54mg **Sodium** 674mg

1 1/2 pounds green beans

2 cans (7 1/2 ounces) salmon, drained and skinned

2 ounces sliced smoked salmon or lox, cut into strips

1/2 small red onion, thinly sliced

Lettuce leaves

For the dill and lemon dressing

1/4 cup olive oil

2 tablespoons lemon juice

1 tablespoon snipped dill (or 1 teaspoon dill weed)

1/2 teaspoon dry mustard

Salt and ground black pepper to taste

 PREPARATION TIME **15 MINUTES**   COOKING TIME **8 MINUTES**

1 In a 4-quart saucepan, bring 4 inches of water to a boil over high heat. Snap tips off green beans. Drop the beans into the boiling water and return the water to a boil. Cook the beans until crisp-tender, about 4 minutes. Drain the beans and rinse with cold water. Place the beans in a bowl and refrigerate until ready to serve.

2 To make the dressing, in a large bowl, whisk together olive oil, lemon juice, snipped dill, and dry mustard. Season the dressing with salt and pepper to taste.

3 Fold canned salmon, smoked salmon, and onion into the bowl with the dressing; toss gently until coated. Cover and refrigerate the salmon mixture until ready to serve.

4 Just before serving, line a platter with lettuce leaves. Add the beans to the salmon mixture and toss gently. Mound the salmon mixture on the lettuce, and serve immediately.

SHRIMP COUSCOUS SALAD

SHRIMP COUSCOUS SALAD

 4

One Serving: **Calories** 425 **Protein** 25g **Carbohydrates** 52g **Fat** 11g **Cholesterol** 166mg **Sodium** 215mg

- **4** tablespoons olive or vegetable oil, divided
- **1** small zucchini, sliced
- **1** clove garlic, finely chopped
- **1** teaspoon curry powder
- **1½** cups vegetable broth or water
- **1½** cups quick-cooking couscous
- **12** ounces medium-size uncooked, shelled and deveined shrimp, thawed if frozen
- **3** ripe plum tomatoes, diced
- **2** tablespoons chopped parsley
- **1** tablespoon red-wine vinegar

  Salt and ground black pepper to taste

PREPARATION TIME
10 MINUTES

COOKING TIME
15 MINUTES

COOK'S TIP *This healthy grain salad is delicious served warm or cold. Be sure to use quick-cooking couscous.*

1 In a large skillet, heat 2 tablespoons oil over moderate heat. Add zucchini and sauté until it softens, about 4 minutes. Stir in garlic and curry powder; cook for 1 minute.

2 Add vegetable broth to the skillet with zucchini and bring it to a boil. Stir in quick-cooking couscous, cover, and remove the skillet from the heat. Let the couscous stand until it softens and absorbs all the liquid, about 10 minutes.

3 Meanwhile, in a large saucepan, bring 2 inches of water to a boil over high heat. Drop shrimp into the boiling water and cook the shrimp until they are pink and firm, about 1 minute. Drain the shrimp.

4 In a large bowl, combine the shrimp, tomatoes, parsley, vinegar, and the remaining 2 tablespoons oil. Stir in the couscous mixture, breaking up the lumps of couscous with a fork. Season the salad with salt and pepper. Serve the salad warm, or cover and refrigerate until ready to serve.

TEX-MEX SALAD

One Serving: **Calories** 490 **Protein** 33g **Carbohydrates** 13g **Fat** 35g **Cholesterol** 115mg **Sodium** 456mg

1 medium-size yellow onion

1 clove garlic

1 medium-size green bell pepper

3 tablespoons vegetable oil

16 ounces lean ground beef or ground turkey

2 teaspoons chili powder

1 teaspoon ground cumin

1 cup prepared chunky tomato salsa

½ medium-size head iceberg lettuce

4 ounces Cheddar cheese, coarsely grated (1 cup)

½ cup sliced pitted black olives

¼ cup sliced red radishes

 PREPARATION TIME **17 MINUTES**

COOKING TIME **9 MINUTES**

SERVING SUGGESTION *Add a basket of warm flour tortillas on the side—you can even make them into burritos by spooning the salad into the tortillas and adding some sour cream.*

1 Chop onion and garlic. Core and seed bell pepper, and cut it into 1-inch pieces.

2 In a large skillet, heat oil over moderately high heat. Add the onion, garlic, and ground beef; cook until the meat is lightly browned. Stir in chili powder and cumin; continue cooking 1 more minute.

3 Remove the skillet from the heat. Stir the bell pepper and tomato salsa into the meat mixture, and set it aside.

4 Thinly slice iceberg lettuce into shreds; line a serving platter with the lettuce shreds. Spoon the meat mixture over the lettuce. Sprinkle the meat mixture with grated cheese, sliced olives, and sliced radishes; serve immediately.

LAYERED CHICKEN SALAD

One Serving: **Calories** 702 **Protein** 24g **Carbohydrates** 20g **Fat** 61g **Cholesterol** 82mg **Sodium** 549mg

6 slices bacon

2 boneless, skinless, chicken-breast halves (about 12 ounces)

1 small head romaine lettuce

3 large ripe tomatoes

2 small avocados

1 cup prepared chunky blue cheese dressing

 PREPARATION TIME **17 MINUTES**

COOKING TIME **13 MINUTES**

1 In a large skillet, cook bacon over moderate heat until crisp. Leaving the drippings in the skillet, remove the bacon to drain on paper towels. Crumble the bacon and set it aside.

2 Using a sharp knife, cut each chicken-breast half crosswise into ⅛-inch-thick slices. In the bacon drippings in the skillet, cook the chicken over moderately-high heat until tender, about 5 minutes. Set the chicken aside to cool slightly.

3 Cut romaine lettuce crosswise into ½-inch-thick slices. Thinly slice tomatoes. Cut avocados in half, remove the pits, and slice the avocados crosswise.

4 To arrange the salad, place the sliced lettuce in the bottom of a large glass salad bowl. Forming layers, add the chicken, then tomatoes, then avocados, spacing them evenly. Add the crumbled bacon and a spoonful of blue cheese dressing in the center. Transfer the remaining dressing to a small bowl or pitcher. Serve the salad, passing the extra dressing on the side.

Beef Noodle Salad

One Serving: **Calories** 624 **Protein** 33g **Carbohydrates** 39g **Fat** 38g **Cholesterol** 61mg **Sodium** 780mg

2 packages (3 ounces each) ramen noodle soup (any flavor)

2 green onions

2 large carrots

12 ounces roast beef, cut into strips

Lettuce leaves

For the peanut-sesame dressing

2/3 cup hot water

1/3 cup creamy peanut butter

2 tablespoons soy sauce

2 tablespoons Oriental sesame oil

1 tablespoon distilled white vinegar

1 teaspoon sugar

Pinch red pepper flakes

 PREPARATION TIME
20 MINUTES

COOKING TIME
11 MINUTES

1 In a large saucepan, bring 2 inches water to a boil over high heat. Add dried ramen noodles (discard the seasoning packets), cover, and reduce the heat to moderate. Cook the noodles just until they are soft, about 3 minutes.

2 Meanwhile, cut green onions lengthwise into thin strips, then crosswise into 2-inch lengths. Peel carrots and cut them into 1/4-inch-thick strips. Drain the ramen noodles in a colander and rinse with cold water. Set the noodles aside.

3 To make the dressing, in a large bowl, using a wire whisk, combine 2/3 cup hot water, peanut butter, soy sauce, sesame oil, vinegar, sugar, and red pepper flakes.

4 Add the cooked noodles, beef and carrot strips, and the green onions to the peanut-butter mixture and fold gently until well mixed. Line a serving platter with lettuce leaves. Spoon the beef noodle salad over the leaves. Serve immediately or cover and refrigerate the salad until ready to serve.

Ham and Smoked Cheese Salad

One Serving: **Calories** 415 **Protein** 26g **Carbohydrates** 6g **Fat** 33g **Cholesterol** 96mg **Sodium** 1106mg

8 ounces turkey ham or smoked ham

8 ounces smoked Gouda or smoked Cheddar cheese

2 stalks celery

Spinach leaves

2 medium-size ripe tomatoes, cut into wedges

For the mustard dressing

1/4 cup vegetable oil

1 tablespoon red-wine vinegar

1 tablespoon Dijon mustard

1 tablespoon snipped chives or green onion tops

Salt and ground black pepper to taste

 PREPARATION TIME
18 MINUTES

 COOKING TIME
0 MINUTES

COOK'S TIP *For variety, instead combining ham and smoked cheese, try putting together chicken cold cuts with Monterey Jack cheese, or thin slices of salami with Edam. This makes an excellent salad to pack for a brown-bag lunch or a picnic.*

1 To make the dressing, in a medium-size bowl, whisk together oil, vinegar, mustard, and chives until well mixed. Season the dressing with salt and pepper.

2 Using a sharp knife, cut ham, smoked cheese, and celery into 1/4-inch-thick strips. Add the ham, cheese, and celery to the bowl with the dressing; toss gently until evenly coated. Rinse spinach leaves and pat them dry; remove the tough stems.

3 Line a serving platter with the spinach leaves. Spoon the salad mixture over the leaves and arrange tomato wedges around the salad. Serve immediately.

WARM SAUSAUGE-ONION SALAD

WARM SAUSAGE-ONION SALAD

One Serving: **Calories** 379 **Protein** 15g **Carbohydrates** 13g **Fat** 31g **Cholesterol** 56mg **Sodium** 935mg

12 **ounces smoked garlic sausage or kielbasa**

8 **ounces mushrooms**

2 **large red onions**

2 **tablespoons olive oil**

1 **tablespoon red-wine vinegar or balsamic vinegar**

1 **teaspoon dried rosemary, crumbled**

1 **clove garlic, finely chopped**

4 **cups arugula leaves**

 PREPARATION TIME
10 MINUTES

COOKING TIME
15 MINUTES

SERVING SUGGESTION *This cold-weather salad goes perfectly alongside a baked potato sprinkled with shredded cheese.*

1 Preheat the oven to 450°F. Using a sharp knife, cut sausage into ½-inch-thick diagonal slices. Cut mushrooms into quarters. Cut onions into ¼-inch-thick slices.

2 In a large open roasting pan, toss the sausage, mushrooms, onions, oil, vinegar, rosemary, and garlic until well mixed. Roast the sausage and vegetables until lightly browned, 15 to 20 minutes, stirring halfway through the roasting time.

3 Meanwhile, rinse arugula leaves and pat them dry. Line a serving platter or four individual serving plates with the arugula. Spoon the sausage and vegetable mixture with the pan juices over the arugula leaves; serve immediately.

Spinach, Bacon, and Egg Salad

One Serving: **Calories** 271 **Protein** 10g **Carbohydrates** 12g **Fat** 22g **Cholesterol** 121mg **Sodium** 344mg

- 1 tablespoon vegetable oil
- 4 slices turkey bacon (made from white and dark turkey meat)
- 2 large eggs, beaten
- 8 cups torn fresh spinach leaves
- 8 ounces mushrooms, sliced
- 2 green onions, sliced

For the cider vinegar dressing

- ¼ cup olive oil
- 1 tablespoon sugar
- 2 tablespoons cider vinegar
- ¼ teaspoon ground black pepper

 PREPARATION TIME **24 MINUTES**

COOKING TIME **12 MINUTES**

COOK'S TIP *If you prefer, you can use regular pork bacon, but there's no need to fry it in oil. Cook the egg in the bacon drippings.*

1 In a large skillet, heat vegetable oil over moderate heat. Add bacon and cook until crisp, turning occasionally. Remove the bacon to drain on paper towels, leaving the drippings in the skillet. Crumble the bacon and set it aside.

2 Add beaten eggs to the skillet and fry until set on the bottom. Turn the eggs over and continue to cook until set throughout. Transfer the eggs to a plate and cut into strips.

3 To make the dressing, in a small jar or cruet, combine olive oil, sugar, vinegar, and pepper. Cover and shake until well mixed.

4 In a large salad bowl, combine spinach, mushrooms, and green onions. Top with the egg strips and bacon and toss gently to mix. Drizzle the dressing over the salad, toss until coated, and serve.

Turkey Pasta Salad

One Serving: **Calories** 654 **Protein** 42g **Carbohydrates** 64g **Fat** 25g **Cholesterol** 116mg **Sodium** 516mg

- 2 stalks celery
- 1 cup red seedless grapes
- 3 cups cubed roast turkey (about 1 pound)
- 8 ounces fusilli (corkscrew-shaped pasta)
  Salt and ground black pepper to taste
  Boston lettuce leaves
- 4 small clusters red seedless grapes (optional)

For the mayonnaise dressing

- 1 cup reduced-calorie mayonnaise
- ½ cup light sour cream
- 2 tablespoons cider vinegar
- 2 tablespoons milk
- 1 teaspoon dried tarragon, crumbled

 PREPARATION TIME **12 MINUTES**

COOKING TIME **18 MINUTES**

DIET NOTE *The healthy dressing for this salad is made with reduced-calorie mayonnaise and light sour cream.*

1 In a large saucepan, bring 2 quarts of water to a boil over high heat. Meanwhile, slice celery. Cut grapes in half. In a large bowl, combine turkey with the celery and grapes.

2 Cook fusilli according to package directions or until it is tender but still firm to the bite. Meanwhile, prepare the dressing. In a small bowl, combine mayonnaise, sour cream, vinegar, milk, and tarragon.

3 Drain the pasta and rinse with cold water; set aside. Pour the dressing over the turkey mixture and gently toss until coated. Season with salt and pepper. Fold in the cooked pasta until well mixed.

4 Rinse lettuce leaves and pat them dry. Line a serving bowl with the lettuce leaves. Spoon the turkey pasta into the prepared bowl. Garnish with small grape clusters, if desired. Serve immediately or cover and refrigerate until ready to serve.

BREADS, CAKES, AND COOKIES

APPLE BRAN MUFFINS (PAGE 331)

BREADS

This selection of sweet and savory breads offers a warming addition to every meal, breakfast through supper.

JALAPEÑO CORN BREAD

One Serving: **Calories** 214 **Protein** 5g **Carbohydrates** 37g **Fat** 5g **Cholesterol** 29mg **Sodium** 244mg

- 1 **cup canned or frozen white or yellow corn kernels**
- 1 **cup yellow cornmeal**
- 1 **cup all-purpose flour**
- ¼ **cup sugar**
- 2½ **teaspoons baking powder**
- ½ **teaspoon salt**
- ⅔ **cup milk**
- 2 **tablespoons vegetable oil**
- 1 **large egg**
- 1 **tablespoon chopped jalapeño peppers**

 PREPARATION TIME
7 MINUTES

COOKING TIME
25 MINUTES

COOK'S TIP *If you prefer less spicy corn bread, you can substitute 1 tablespoon of chopped mild green chilies for the jalapeños. If you like it really hot, increase the jalapeños to 2 tablespoons.*

1 Preheat the oven to 425°F. Grease an 8-inch round baking pan. Drain canned corn kernels, or thaw frozen kernels under warm water.

2 In a large bowl, combine cornmeal, flour, sugar, baking powder, and salt. In a small bowl, combine milk, oil, and egg until well mixed. Stir the milk mixture into the dry ingredients until just moistened. Fold in the corn kernels and jalapeño peppers. Spoon the cornmeal batter into the prepared pan.

3 Bake the corn bread until a toothpick inserted in the center comes out clean, 25 to 30 minutes. Cut the bread into wedges and serve warm.

FLAKY HERBED BISCUITS

One Serving: **Calories** 195 **Protein** 5g **Carbohydrates** 24g **Fat** 9g **Cholesterol** 24mg **Sodium** 427mg

- 2 **cups all-purpose flour**
- 2 **teaspoons baking soda**
- 1 **teaspoon cream of tartar**
- ½ **teaspoon salt**
- 6 **tablespoons (¾ stick) butter or margarine, cut into pieces**
- ¼ **cup chopped fresh dill, basil, or parsley**
- ¾ **cup plain low-fat yogurt**

 PREPARATION TIME
15 MINUTES

COOKING TIME
18 MINUTES

COOK'S TIP *To make splitting the baked biscuits easier, roll out the dough to a ¼-inch thickness, then fold it in half and cut the dough.*

1 Preheat oven to 425°F. In a large bowl, combine flour, baking soda, cream of tartar, and salt. Using a pastry blender or two knives scissor-fashion, cut in the butter until the mixture resembles coarse crumbs.

2 Stir chopped herb into the flour mixture until well mixed. Add yogurt and stir to form a soft dough. Knead the dough very briefly in the bowl just to combine.

3 On a lightly floured surface, using a rolling pin, roll out the dough to a ½-inch thickness. Using a floured 3-inch round cookie cutter, cut out the biscuits and place them on an ungreased baking sheet. Pat the dough scraps together, reroll, and cut out more biscuits. Bake the biscuits until they are golden brown, about 18 minutes. Serve warm.

GARLIC TOAST ⦿4

One Serving: **Calories** 264 **Protein** 7g **Carbohydrates** 35g **Fat** 11g **Cholesterol** 19mg **Sodium** 467mg

8 **¾-inch-thick slices Italian or French bread**
2 **tablespoons (¼ stick) butter or margarine**
1 **tablespoon olive oil**
2 **cloves garlic, very finely chopped**
1 **teaspoon dried basil, crumbled**
2 **tablespoons grated Parmesan cheese**

PREPARATION TIME
4 MINUTES

COOKING TIME
6 MINUTES

1 Preheat the broiler. Arrange bread slices on the broiler rack over a broiler pan; set aside. In a small saucepan, heat butter and oil over moderate heat. Add garlic and basil; cook for 10 seconds. Remove the pan from the heat.

2 Broil the bread about 4 inches from the heat until it is lightly toasted. Turn the slices over. Brush the bread with the garlic mixture and sprinkle with cheese. Continue broiling until the bread is golden brown. Serve immediately.

POPOVERS ⦿6

One Serving: **Calories** 140 **Protein** 6g **Carbohydrates** 17g **Fat** 6g **Cholesterol** 75mg **Sodium** 220mg

2 **large eggs**
1 **cup milk**
1 **tablespoon vegetable oil**
1 **cup all-purpose flour**
½ **teaspoon salt**

PREPARATION TIME
15 MINUTES

COOKING TIME
30 MINUTES

1 Preheat the oven to 425°F. In a small bowl, using an electric mixer, beat eggs until frothy. Beat in milk and oil. Beat in flour and salt until well mixed. Let the batter rest for 10 minutes.

2 Grease 6 popover or medium-size muffin cups. Set the popover cups in a small jelly-roll pan for easier handling. Pour the batter into the prepared cups.

3 Bake the popovers until puffed and well browned, about 30 minutes. Immediately remove the popovers from the cups and serve hot.

Shelf Magic

Keep a couple packages of canned biscuit dough in the refrigerator, then fill your basket with these quick, savory breads:

SKILLET ONION BISCUITS

Chop **1 green onion**. In a large skillet, melt **2 tablespoons butter**. Add **1 teaspoon sugar** and half the onion. Pat biscuits from **two 7½-ounce packages refrigerated biscuit dough** into skillet; sprinkle with remaining onion. Cover and cook over moderate heat until browned, 5 minutes on each side. **SERVES 8**

SPICY PARMESAN PUFFS

SPICY PARMESAN PUFFS

One Serving: **Calories** 116 **Protein** 5g **Carbohydrates** 6g Fat 8g **Cholesterol** 71mg **Sodium** 198mg

¼ **cup water**

¼ **cup milk**

¼ **cup (½ stick) butter or margarine**

½ **cup all-purpose flour**

1 **green onion**

2 **large eggs**

⅓ **cup grated Parmesan cheese**

¼ **teaspoon salt**

¼ **teaspoon cayenne pepper**

Butter (optional)

PREPARATION TIME
10 MINUTES

COOKING TIME
30 MINUTES

SERVING SUGGESTION *These light, flavorful rolls pair well with a fresh salad or a bowl of hot soup.*

1 Preheat the oven to 400°F. In a medium-size saucepan, combine water, milk, and butter; bring to a boil over moderate heat. Add flour; using a wooden spoon, beat the mixture until it leaves the side of the pan and forms a ball. Remove from the heat and let cool slightly.

2 Meanwhile, lightly grease a baking sheet. Trim and finely chop green onion, including the green top.

3 Beat eggs, one at a time, into the flour mixture until smooth. Stir in cheese, onion, salt, and cayenne pepper. Drop the batter by heaping spoonfuls into 8 mounds, about 2 inches apart, on the prepared sheet. Bake until the puffs are crisp and golden, 25 to 30 minutes. Serve warm with butter, if desired.

PARMESAN ONION BREAD

One Serving: **Calories** 202 **Protein** 4g **Carbohydrates** 18g **Fat** 13g **Cholesterol** 34mg **Sodium** 341mg

- ½ cup (1 stick) butter or margarine, divided
- 1 medium-size yellow onion, finely chopped
- 1 12-inch loaf Italian or sourdough bread
- ¼ cup grated Parmesan cheese

PREPARATION TIME
6 MINUTES

COOKING TIME
26 MINUTES

SERVING SUGGESTION *Next time you serve pasta for dinner, make this crispy cheese and onion bread to go with it.*

1 Preheat the oven to 375°F. In a large skillet, melt 2 tablespoons butter over moderate heat. Add onion and sauté until soft and lightly golden, 5 to 7 minutes. Remove the skillet from the heat and allow the onion to cool slightly.

2 Meanwhile, using a serrated knife, cut bread in half horizontally and place the halves side by side on a long sheet of aluminum foil. Stir the remaining butter into the sautéed onion until melted.

3 Spoon the onion butter over the cut surfaces of the bread; sprinkle with cheese. Keeping the halves open, wrap the bread loosely with the foil and bake for 10 minutes.

4 Open the foil and continue to bake the onion-bread halves until they are crisp and golden, 10 to 15 more minutes. Cut the bread crosswise into slices and serve them warm.

CHEESE-STUFFED FRENCH TOAST

One Serving: **Calories** 382 **Protein** 11g **Carbohydrates** 39g **Fat** 21g **Cholesterol** 143mg **Sodium** 420mg

- 4 1-inch-thick slices white bread
- 1 package (3 ounces) cream cheese, softened
- 1 tablespoon chopped pistachios, almonds, or pecans
- 2 tablespoons apricot or peach preserves
- 2 large eggs
- ½ cup milk
- ½ teaspoon vanilla extract
- ¼ teaspoon ground cinnamon
- 1 tablespoon vegetable oil
- 1 tablespoon butter or margarine
- Confectioners sugar (optional)

PREPARATION TIME
5 MINUTES

COOKING TIME
8 MINUTES

COOK'S TIP *It's better to buy an uncut loaf of bread and slice it yourself so you can be sure the slices are thick enough to hold the cream-cheese filling without falling apart.*

1 Using a serrated knife, cut a pocket in each slice of bread from the top-crust end almost to the bottom-crust end.

2 In a small bowl, combine cream cheese, nuts, and preserves. Spoon about 2 tablespoons of the mixture into the pocket of each slice of bread. In a pie plate, whisk eggs, milk, vanilla, and cinnamon. On a griddle or in a large skillet, heat oil and butter over moderate heat.

3 Dip the stuffed bread slices, one at a time, into the egg mixture, turning to coat both sides and taking care not to squeeze out the cheese filling. Fry the bread on the griddle until golden brown, turning once, about 1½ minutes on each side. Dust with confectioners sugar, if desired, and serve immediately.

OVEN-BAKED FRENCH TOAST

OVEN-BAKED FRENCH TOAST

One Serving: **Calories** 429 **Protein** 14g **Carbohydrates** 65g **Fat** 12g **Cholesterol** 285mg **Sodium** 570mg

1 loaf French bread (about 16 by 3 inches)

4 large eggs

1/2 cup half-and-half

1/4 cup honey

1/2 teaspoon ground nutmeg

1/2 teaspoon vanilla extract

Fresh strawberries (optional)

Warm pancake syrup (optional)

PREPARATION TIME
20 MINUTES

COOKING TIME
16 MINUTES

SERVING SUGGESTION *Brighten your morning with this warming brunch dish and a bowl of fresh strawberries.*

1 Preheat the oven to 500°F. Grease two large baking sheets. Cut French loaf crosswise into 1-inch diagonal slices. In a 13- by 9-inch baking dish, place the bread slices.

2 In a medium-size bowl, whisk together eggs, half-and-half, honey, nutmeg, and vanilla. Pour the egg mixture over the bread and turn the slices to coat evenly. Let the bread soak until the egg mixture is absorbed, about 15 minutes.

3 Place the bread on the prepared baking sheets. Bake until golden, 8 to 10 minutes on each side. Transfer to serving dishes. Top each serving with strawberries and syrup, if desired, and serve.

START WITH A CRÊPE

Crêpes provide the basis for an elegant main course or dessert. They are easy to make and store (see page 27), and ready-prepared ones are widely available. To warm chilled crêpes, wrap them and place them in a preheated 325°F oven for a few minutes. Meanwhile, prepare your filling. Each recipe makes enough to fill eight crêpes, for four servings.

◄ **SPINACH AND CHEESE CRÊPES** In a medium-size saucepan, melt **¼ cup butter** over low heat. Stir in **¼ cup flour** and **⅛ tsp. pepper**. Gradually stir in **1 cup half-and-half**. Cook over moderate heat, stirring, until thickened. Add **two 10-oz. packages frozen chopped spinach**, cooked, and **1 cup grated Swiss cheese**. Cook, stirring, until cheese melts. Spoon mixture onto crêpes, and roll up. Place in greased baking dish; broil 5 minutes.

▼ **CHICKEN-FILLED CRÊPES** Scald **1 cup milk**. Melt **2 Tbsp. butter** in a medium-size saucepan over low heat. Add **2 Tbsp. flour**, stirring constantly. Gradually pour in the hot milk and cook, stirring, until the mixture thickens. Add **1 cup cooked, shredded chicken** and **½ cup sliced mushrooms**. Cook 5 minutes. Fill the crêpes with the mixture; fold and place in greased baking dish. Broil 5 minutes.

▼ **RATATOUILLE-FILLED CRÊPES** In a large skillet, sauté **2 medium-size onions**, sliced, and **2 cloves garlic** in **¼ cup olive oil**. Add **one small eggplant**, cubed, **1 large green pepper**, cut into strips, **2 zucchini**, sliced, **3 tomatoes**, peeled and chopped, **2 Tbsp. chopped parsley**, **2 tsp. salt**, **½ tsp. dried basil**, and **⅛ tsp. pepper**. Cover and simmer 10 to 15 minutes. Uncover and simmer for a few more minutes until the sauce thickens. Divide mixture among crêpes and fold ends under. Place in greased baking dish and broil 5 minutes.

ONE-INGREDIENT COMBINATIONS

SAVORY FILLINGS	SWEET FILLINGS	TOPPINGS
Grated Cheddar cheese	Jam or preserves	Confectioners sugar
Soft cream cheese	Melted chocolate chips	Brandy or liqueur
Scrambled eggs	Chopped fresh fruit	Maple or fruit syrup

▶ **CRÊPES SUZETTE** Make orange butter by creaming **¼ cup butter, 2 tsp. powdered sugar, 2 tsp. strained orange juice, 2 tsp. grated orange peel,** and **1 tsp. orange liqueur**. Spread butter mixture on crêpes. In a large skillet, fry each crêpe, butter side down, until hot, 1 to 2 minutes. Fold in a triangle and pile at the side of pan until all crêpes are cooked. Spread crêpes out and flame with **2 Tbsp. each brandy and Grand Marnier.**

◀ **APPLE CRÊPES** Preheat oven to 375°F. Fry **2 sliced apples** in **2 Tbsp. butter**; sprinkle with **2 Tbsp. sugar**; stir to caramelize. Fill crêpes with apples, fold, and place in a shallow greased baking dish. Bake 8 minutes. Flame with **¼ cup Calvados or brandy**. Spoon **cream** over crêpes.

▶ **PEACH CRÊPES** In a small saucepan, bring **2 cups water** and **¼ cup confectioners sugar** to a boil. Stir until mixture is clear. Add **4 peaches, skinned and sliced**. Cook until soft, about 10 minutes. Meanwhile, prepare **orange butter** as in Crêpes Suzette (above) and spread on crêpes. In large skillet, fry each crêpe, butter side down, 1 to 2 minutes. Fill crêpes with peaches, fold each one into a triangle and return to skillet, spreading them evenly. Flame with **2 Tbsp. Grand Marnier.**

BLUEBERRY PANCAKES

BLUEBERRY PANCAKES

One Serving: **Calories** 313　**Protein** 8g　**Carbohydrates** 41g　**Fat** 12g　**Cholesterol** 85mg　**Sodium** 407mg

1¼ **cups all-purpose flour**

2 **tablespoons sugar**

2 **teaspoons baking powder**

¼ **teaspoon salt**

1¼ **cups milk**

1 **large egg**

3 **tablespoons butter or margarine, melted**

⅔ **cup blueberries**

Warm pancake syrup (optional)

 PREPARATION TIME
5 MINUTES

 COOKING TIME
10 MINUTES

SERVING SUGGESTION *Warm blueberry syrup and a plate of fried bacon will turn this into the perfect Sunday breakfast.*

1 In a large bowl, combine flour, sugar, baking powder, and salt. In a small bowl, combine milk, egg, and butter. Add the milk mixture to the dry ingredients and stir until just moistened. (The batter may be somewhat lumpy.) Fold blueberries into the pancake batter.

2 Lightly grease a griddle or large skillet. Heat the griddle or skillet over moderately high heat.

3 For each pancake, pour about ⅓ cup of the batter onto the hot griddle, cooking a few at a time. Cook the pancakes until several bubbles burst on the top and the bottom is light brown, about 3 minutes. Flip the pancakes and cook the other side until golden brown, about 2 more minutes.

4 Transfer the pancakes to a platter and keep them warm. Repeat to cook the remaining batter, making a total of 8 pancakes. Serve with warm syrup, if desired.

CURRANT SCONES

MAKES

One Piece: **Calories** 164 **Protein** 4g **Carbohydrates** 22g **Fat** 7g **Cholesterol** 51mg **Sodium** 250mg

- **2 cups all-purpose flour**
- **2 tablespoons sugar**
- **1 tablespoon baking powder**
- **½ teaspoon salt**
- **¼ teaspoon baking soda**
- **6 tablespoons (¾ stick) butter or margarine, cut into pieces**
- **½ cup dried currants or raisins**
- **½ cup buttermilk**
- **2 large eggs**

PREPARATION TIME **15 MINUTES**

COOKING TIME **12 MINUTES**

SERVING SUGGESTION *The traditional English tea-time treat goes just as well for breakfast. Spread it with honey or strawberry jam.*

1 Preheat the oven to 425°F. In a large bowl, combine flour, sugar, baking powder, salt, and baking soda. Using a pastry blender or two knives scissor-fashion, cut in the butter until the mixture resembles coarse crumbs.

2 Stir currants into the flour mixture until well mixed. In a small bowl, combine buttermilk and eggs. Add the buttermilk mixture to the dry ingredients and stir to form a soft dough. With floured hands, gently knead the dough very briefly in the bowl just to combine. Divide the dough in half.

3 On a large ungreased baking sheet, carefully pat each piece of dough into a 6-inch round. Using a large knife, cut each round into 6 equal wedges but do not separate the segments. Bake the scones until they are golden brown, 12 to 15 minutes. Separate the wedges and serve them warm.

APPLE BRAN MUFFINS

One Serving: **Calories** 205 **Protein** 5g **Carbohydrates** 32g **Fat** 7g **Cholesterol** 24mg **Sodium** 326mg

- **1 large red baking apple**
- **2½ cups bran flakes, crushed**
- **1¼ cups all-purpose flour**
- **1½ teaspoons baking powder**
- **½ teaspoon baking soda**
- **¼ teaspoon salt**
- **¾ cup buttermilk**
- **¼ cup maple syrup or honey**
- **¼ cup vegetable oil**
- **1 large egg**

PREPARATION TIME **7 MINUTES**

COOKING TIME **20 MINUTES**

SERVING SUGGESTION *These healthy muffins are good with apple butter: Blend a large spoonful of applesauce into some softened butter or margarine, spread it into a small crock, and serve.*

1 Preheat the oven to 375°F. With vegetable shortening or paper liners, grease or line 9 muffin cups. Using a food processor or hand grater, coarsely shred unpeeled apple.

2 In a large bowl, combine crushed bran flakes, flour, baking powder, baking soda, and salt until well mixed. Stir in the shredded apple. In a small bowl, combine buttermilk, maple syrup, oil, and egg. Stir the buttermilk mixture into the dry ingredients until the batter is just moistened. (Do not overmix.)

3 Divide the batter among the prepared muffin cups. Bake until lightly browned, about 20 minutes. Remove the muffins from the cups and serve them warm.

OATMEAL DATE MUFFINS

One Serving: **Calories** 191 **Protein** 4g **Carbohydrates** 30g **Fat** 6g **Cholesterol** 37mg **Sodium** 240mg

3 tablespoons butter or margarine

1 cup all-purpose flour

1 cup quick-cooking oats

¼ cup firmly packed light brown sugar

2 teaspoons baking powder

½ teaspoon salt

½ teaspoon ground cinnamon

½ cup chopped pitted dates

1 cup milk

1 large egg

 PREPARATION TIME
15 MINUTES

COOKING TIME
20 MINUTES

COOK'S TIP *To prevent the dates from sticking to the knife when chopping, place the fruit on the chopping board and sprinkle a little flour over them. If there is time, chill the dates before cutting them for the easiest preparation.*

1 Preheat the oven to 400°F. With vegetable shortening or paper liners, grease or line 9 muffin cups.

2 In a small saucepan, melt butter over moderate heat. In a large bowl, combine flour, oats, brown sugar, baking powder, salt, and cinnamon until well mixed. Stir in dates.

3 In a small bowl, combine milk, egg, and the melted butter. Using a wooden spoon, stir the milk mixture into the dry ingredients until just moistened. (Do not overmix.)

4 Divide the batter among the prepared muffin cups. Bake until lightly browned, 20 to 25 minutes. Remove the muffins from the cups and serve them warm.

ZUCCHINI WHEAT MUFFINS

One Serving: **Calories** 183 **Protein** 4g **Carbohydrates** 25g **Fat** 8g **Cholesterol** 43mg **Sodium** 297mg

1 small zucchini (4 to 5 ounces)

1 cup all-purpose flour

¾ cup whole-wheat flour

¼ cup sugar

1 tablespoon baking powder

1 teaspoon finely grated lemon peel

½ teaspoon salt

¼ teaspoon ground nutmeg

⅓ cup milk

⅓ cup butter or margarine, melted

1 large egg

 **PREPARATION TIME**
9 MINUTES

COOKING TIME
20 MINUTES

COOK'S TIP *To store leftover muffins, wrap the cooled muffins tightly in aluminum foil and refrigerate. To reheat, loosen the foil and place them in a 250°F oven for ten minutes.*

1 Preheat the oven to 400°F. With vegetable shortening or paper liners, grease or line 9 muffin cups. Using a food processor or hand grater, coarsely shred zucchini.

2 In a large bowl, combine all-purpose and whole-wheat flours, sugar, baking powder, lemon peel, salt, and nutmeg until well mixed. Stir in the shredded zucchini. In a small bowl, combine milk, butter, and egg. Stir the milk mixture into the dry ingredients until just moistened. (Do not overmix.)

3 Divide the batter among the prepared muffin cups. Bake until the muffins are lightly browned, 18 to 20 minutes. Remove the zucchini muffins from the cups and serve them warm.

RAISIN GRANOLA MUFFINS

RAISIN GRANOLA MUFFINS

One Serving: **Calories** 180 **Protein** 4g **Carbohydrates** 27g **Fat** 8g **Cholesterol** 27mg **Sodium** 219mg

- 1 **cup buttermilk baking mix (Bisquick)**
- 1 **cup plain granola cereal, divided**
- ¼ **cup raisins**
- 2 **tablespoons brown sugar**
- ⅓ **cup milk**
- 1 **large egg**
- 1 **tablespoon vegetable oil**

PREPARATION TIME
15 MINUTES

COOKING TIME
15 MINUTES

DIET NOTE *Balance these muffins with fresh melon and a small bowl of calcium-rich yogurt, and the meal comes in under 300 calories.*

1 Preheat the oven to 400°F. With vegetable shortening or paper liners, grease or line 8 muffin cups.

2 In a large bowl, combine baking mix, ¾ cup granola, raisins, and brown sugar until well mixed. In a small bowl, combine milk, egg, and oil. Stir the milk mixture into the dry ingredients until just moistened. (Do not overmix.)

3 Divide the batter among the prepared muffin cups. Sprinkle the batter with the remaining ¼ cup granola. Bake until golden brown, 15 to 20 minutes. Remove the muffins from the cups and serve warm.

Cakes

A homemade cake on the table is always something special, and it doesn't have to take hours to make. Bake one of these easy cakes and enjoy a delicious break.

LEMON-GLAZED APRICOT COFFEE CAKE

One Serving: **Calories** 196 **Protein** 2g **Carbohydrates** 26g **Fat** 9g **Cholesterol** 19mg **Sodium** 301mg

- 1 **package (3 ounces) cream cheese**
- ¼ **cup (½ stick) butter or margarine**
- 2 **cups buttermilk baking mix**
- ¼ **cup milk**
- ½ **cup thick apricot preserves**
- 1 **tablespoon sliced almonds**

For the lemon glaze
- ½ **cup sifted confectioners sugar**
- ¼ **teaspoon lemon extract**
- 1 **to 2 teaspoons lemon juice**

 PREPARATION TIME
10 MINUTES

 COOKING TIME
25 MINUTES

COOK'S TIP *The braided effect of this Danish-like cake is much simpler to do than it looks—and well worth the effort.*

1 Preheat the oven to 375°F. Grease a large baking sheet. In a medium-size bowl, using a pastry blender or two knives scissor-fashion, cut cream cheese and butter into baking mix until the mixture resembles coarse crumbs. Add milk and stir until just mixed. On a lightly floured surface, knead the dough 10 to 12 turns.

2 On the prepared baking sheet, roll or pat the dough into a 12- by 8-inch rectangle. Spread preserves lengthwise down the center third of the dough. Make 2½-inch-long cuts in the dough from the long sides toward the center at 1-inch intervals. Fold the strips over the preserves, overlapping alternate strips. Bake 20 to 25 minutes.

3 Meanwhile, to make the lemon glaze, in a small bowl, combine sugar and lemon extract. Add a sufficient amount of the lemon juice to make the glaze the consistency of thin frosting.

4 Place the coffee cake on a serving platter. Drizzle it with the glaze and sprinkle with almonds. Serve warm.

Shelf Magic

This easy chocolate sauce makes a tasty topping for angel food cake. Purchase fresh cake from the bakery section of your supermarket.

CHOCOLATE-COFFEE SAUCE

In a small saucepan, melt **4 tablespoons butter or margarine**. Add **6 ounces chopped semisweet chocolate** and **2 tablespoons water**; stir over low heat until melted. Pour in **5 or 6 tablespoons strong black coffee** and **2 tablespoons brandy**. Sweeten with **1 to 3 tablespoons confectioners sugar**. Place **4 slices angel food cake** on plates, and pour sauce over each. Garnish with **strawberries. SERVES 4**

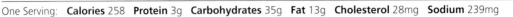

CREAM-FILLED COCOA CUPCAKES

One Serving: **Calories** 258 **Protein** 3g **Carbohydrates** 35g **Fat** 13g **Cholesterol** 28mg **Sodium** 239mg

4 ounces cream cheese, softened

1 large egg, separated

1 cup plus 1 tablespoon sugar, divided

½ cup chocolate chips

1½ cups all-purpose flour

¼ cup unsweetened cocoa powder

1½ teaspoons baking soda

½ teaspoon salt

¾ cup water

⅓ cup vegetable oil

1 tablespoon distilled white vinegar

1 teaspoon vanilla extract

PREPARATION TIME
17 MINUTES

COOKING TIME
25 MINUTES

1 Preheat the oven to 350°F. With vegetable shortening or paper liners, grease or line 12 muffin cups. Using an electric mixer, beat cream cheese with egg yolk and 1 tablespoon of sugar. Stir in chocolate chips; set the mixture aside.

2 In a large bowl, using an electric mixer, combine 1 cup sugar, flour, cocoa, baking soda, and salt. Add the egg white, water, oil, vinegar, and vanilla; beat the mixture until smooth.

3 Divide the cocoa mixture among the prepared muffin cups; drop an equal amount of the cheese mixture on top of each. Bake the cupcakes until a toothpick inserted into the cake comes out clean, about 25 minutes. Cool the cupcakes for 10 minutes in the pan, remove, and serve. Store leftover cupcakes in the refrigerator.

GINGER CAKE WITH LEMON SAUCE

One Serving: **Calories** 420 **Protein** 5g **Carbohydrates** 70g **Fat** 15g **Cholesterol** 82mg **Sodium** 287mg

1¼ cups whole-wheat flour

1 cup all-purpose flour

2 teaspoons ground ginger

1½ teaspoons baking powder

1 teaspoon cinnamon

¼ teaspoon baking soda

¼ teaspoon salt

1 cup firmly packed dark brown sugar

½ cup (1 stick) butter or margarine, softened

2 large eggs

½ cup molasses

¾ cup hot water

For the lemon sauce

1 large lemon

½ cup sugar

2 tablespoons cornstarch

1 cup water

2 tablespoons (¼ stick) butter or margarine

PREPARATION TIME
10 MINUTES

COOKING TIME
35 MINUTES

1 Preheat the oven to 350°F. Generously grease a 9-inch square baking pan. In a medium-size bowl, combine both flours, ginger, baking powder, cinnamon, baking soda, and salt.

2 In a large bowl, using an electric mixer, beat brown sugar and butter until light and fluffy. Gradually beat in eggs and molasses until well mixed. Add the flour mixture a little at a time, alternating with hot water. Pour the batter into the prepared pan. Bake until a toothpick inserted in the center comes out clean, 35 to 40 minutes.

3 Meanwhile, make the lemon sauce. Finely grate only the yellow part of the lemon peel to make 1 teaspoon of lemon zest. Cut the lemon in half and squeeze it to extract ¼ cup lemon juice. In a small saucepan, combine sugar and cornstarch. Stir in water; bring the mixture to a boil over moderately high heat, stirring constantly.

4 Stir butter, the lemon peel, and lemon juice into the sauce mixture. Remove the saucepan from the heat and pour the sauce into a small heatproof pitcher.

5 Let the cake cool in the pan for 5 minutes. Cut the cake into squares and serve it warm, with the lemon sauce on the side.

APPLE-RAÍSIN UPSIDE-DOWN CAKE

APPLE-RAÍSIN UPSIDE-DOWN CAKE

One Serving: **Calories** 305 **Protein** 3g **Carbohydrates** 53g **Fat** 10g **Cholesterol** 51mg **Sodium** 233mg

6 tablespoons (¾ stick) butter or margarine

2 large red baking apples

⅓ cup firmly packed light brown sugar

½ teaspoon ground cinnamon

¼ cup raisins

1⅓ cups cake flour

⅔ cup sugar

2 teaspoons baking powder

¼ teaspoon salt

½ cup milk

1 large egg

1 teaspoon vanilla extract

 PREPARATION TIME
15 MINUTES

 COOKING TIME
30 MINUTES

COOK'S TIP *Place a large, shallow baking pan on the rack under the springform pan to catch any drippings during baking.*

1 Preheat the oven to 375°F. Grease the sides of a 9-inch springform pan. In a small saucepan, melt butter over low heat. Meanwhile, quarter, core, and thinly slice unpeeled apples.

2 Transfer 3 tablespoons of the melted butter to a small bowl and set it aside. Stir brown sugar, cinnamon, and raisins into the remaining butter in the pan. Pour the mixture into the prepared baking pan and spread the apple slices on top. Set the pan aside.

3 In a large bowl, combine flour, white sugar, baking powder, and salt. Add milk, egg, vanilla, and the reserved melted butter. Using an electric mixer at low speed, beat the batter until just combined.

4 Increase the mixer speed to high and continue beating until the batter is smooth, about 1 minute. Spoon the batter over the apples.

5 Bake the cake until a toothpick inserted in the center comes out clean, about 30 minutes. Let cool 5 minutes. Invert it onto a serving plate; wait 1 minute, then remove the pan. Serve warm.

START WITH A POUND CAKE

The simple pound cake is an ideal starting point for a quick and delicious dessert. Start with your own homemade pound cake (see page 28), or pick a ready-made one from the bakery counter or the frozen-foods section at the supermarket.

The loaf-shaped cake works best for these recipes; use a serrated knife to slice through it easily. Then add a scoop of your favorite ice cream, some fresh fruit, or a drizzle of chocolate sauce, and the ordinary becomes something memorable.

▶ **TOFFEE-CHOCOLATE CAKE** In a medium-size saucepan, melt **one 6-oz. package semisweet chocolate chips** over very low heat, stirring often. Remove pan from heat and stir in **2/3 cup sour cream** until smooth. Coarsely crush **two 1 1/8-oz. English toffee candy bars**; set aside. Cut **pound cake** in half horizontally. Place bottom cake layer on serving plate; spread it with one-third frosting. Sprinkle with one-third crushed candy. Top with second layer of cake. Frost cake with the remaining frosting, and sprinkle the remaining candy over the top. Serves 8

◀ **BAKED ALASKA** Preheat the oven to 400°F. Beat **2 large egg whites**, at room temperature, with **a pinch cream of tartar**. Gradually beat in **1/4 cup sugar** until stiff peaks form. Place **four 1-inch-thick slices pound cake** on a small, greased baking sheet or oven-safe tray. Top each slice with one scoop from **1 pint strawberry ice cream**. Spread meringue over the ice-cream-topped cake slices, covering each completely. Bake until meringue is golden brown, 3 to 5 minutes. Serves 4

◀ **RASPBERRY TRIFLES** Thaw **one 10-oz. package frozen raspberries** in quick-thaw pouch according to package directions. Meanwhile, cut **four 1-inch-thick slices pound cake** into cubes and divide among four individual glass serving dishes. Drizzle cake cubes with **4 Tbsp. dry sherry or orange liqueur**. Divide berries and their syrup over the cake cubes. Pour **1 cup prepared instant vanilla pudding mix** over the berries and cake. Garnish each trifle with a dollop of **whipped cream or thawed, frozen cream topping** and **mint sprigs**, if desired. Serves 4

◄ **CAKE AND FRUIT WITH CHOCOLATE FONDUE** In a small saucepan, place **one 6-oz. package semisweet chocolate chips**, **¼ cup sour cream** and **½ cup half-and-half**. Cook over low heat, stirring constantly, until mixture is smooth. Pour chocolate into a small fondue pot and keep warm. On a serving platter, arrange **1½ cups cubed pound cake**, **1 red apple**, cored and cut into cubes, **1 banana**, peeled and cut into chunks, and **1 cup pineapple chunks**. Let each person spear cake and fruit with a fondue fork and dip it into chocolate fondue. If fondue thickens, stir in some **additional half-and-half** and reheat over low heat. Serves 4

▶ **STRAWBERRY SHORTCAKE** In a medium-size bowl, toss **1 pint strawberries**, sliced, with **2 Tbsp. sugar**. Let stand for 15 minutes, stirring occasionally. Beat **½ cup heavy cream** with **1 tsp. sugar** and **¼ tsp. vanilla extract** until soft peaks form. On four individual dessert plates, place half of **eight ½-inch-thick slices pound cake**. Spoon half of the berries with some of their juices and a dollop of whipped cream on each slice. Top with remaining cake, berries, and whipped cream. Serves 4

◄ **PEACH TORTE** Cut **one pound cake** horizontally into three layers. In a small bowl, combine **1 cup chopped peaches** with **¼ tsp. almond extract** and **½ cup vanilla yogurt**. On a serving plate, place bottom cake layer; spread with half of the yogurt mixture. Cover with another cake layer, remaining yogurt mixture, and top cake layer. Spread **¼ cup chocolate fudge topping** over the top layer. Garnish with **additional peach slices**, if desired. Serves 8

BROILED COCONUT CAKE

BROILED COCONUT CAKE

One Serving: **Calories** 314 **Protein** 4g **Carbohydrates** 49g **Fat** 12g **Cholesterol** 70mg **Sodium** 156mg

2 **large eggs**

1 **cup sugar**

1 **cup all-purpose flour**

1 **teaspoon baking powder**

½ **cup milk**

2 **tablespoons (¼ stick) butter or margarine**

For the coconut topping

½ **cup firmly packed light brown sugar**

¼ **cup (½ stick) butter or margarine, softened**

1 **cup sweetened flaked or shredded coconut**

 PREPARATION TIME
11 MINUTES

 COOKING TIME
25 MINUTES

SERVING SUGGESTION *Invite your friends over for a casual dessert, and serve this cake with steaming cappuccino or hot chocolate.*

1 Preheat the oven to 350°F. Grease a 9-inch square baking pan. In a small bowl, using an electric mixer at high speed, beat eggs until foamy. Gradually add white sugar and beat at medium speed until the mixture is light and fluffy, about 5 minutes. Add flour and baking powder; mix at low speed until just combined.

2 In a small saucepan, heat milk and butter until the butter melts. Add the hot milk mixture to the batter and beat until smooth. Pour the batter into the prepared pan. Bake the cake until a toothpick inserted into the center comes out clean, 25 to 30 minutes. Once the cake has been removed from the oven, preheat the broiler.

3 Meanwhile, to make the topping, in a small bowl, combine brown sugar and butter until smooth. Stir in flaked coconut, and set aside.

4 Spread the cake with the topping. Broil it 4 inches from the heat until golden brown, 1 to 2 minutes. Cut into squares and serve warm.

SPICED PECAN CAKE

One Serving: **Calories** 257 **Protein** 4g **Carbohydrates** 34g **Fat** 12g **Cholesterol** 44mg **Sodium** 140mg

1⅓ **cups all-purpose flour**

⅔ **cup sugar**

2 **teaspoons baking powder**

½ **teaspoon ground cinnamon**

¼ **teaspoon ground nutmeg or allspice**

⅔ **cup milk**

¼ **cup (½ stick) butter or margarine, softened**

1 **large egg**

1 **teaspoon vanilla extract**

½ **cup finely chopped pecans**

Confectioners sugar (optional)

Sweetened whipped cream (optional)

PREPARATION TIME	COOKING TIME
10 MINUTES	**25 MINUTES**

1 Preheat the oven to 350°F. Grease and flour an 8-inch round baking pan. In a large bowl, combine flour, sugar, baking powder, cinnamon, and nutmeg.

2 Add milk, butter, egg, and vanilla to the flour mixture. Using an electric mixer at low speed, beat the cake batter until just combined. Increase the speed to medium and continue beating for 1 minute. Stir in pecans; pour the batter into the baking pan.

3 Bake until a toothpick inserted in the center comes out clean, 25 to 30 minutes. Let the cake cool in the pan on a wire rack for 5 minutes. Transfer the cake from the pan to a serving plate. Dust with confectioners sugar, if desired. Serve the cake warm, with whipped cream, if desired.

MICROWAVE VERSION

Increase the amount of butter or margarine to ⅓ cup. Grease a microwave-safe 8-inch round baking dish. Line the bottom of the dish with a round of wax paper. Prepare the batter as above in Steps 1 and 2. Pour the batter into the prepared dish.

Place the dish on a rack or inverted saucer in the microwave oven. Microwave the cake, uncovered, on high power for 10 minutes, rotating the dish a quarter-turn every 3 minutes.

The cake may appear moist on top, but it is done when a toothpick inserted in several places comes out clean. If not, continue cooking on high power until the surface of the cake is nearly dry, 30 seconds to 2 minutes longer. Cool the cake in the dish on a wire rack for 5 minutes. Loosen it, then invert it onto a serving platter; remove the wax paper. Dust with confectioners sugar, if desired, and serve.

TIME SAVERS

FREEZING CAKES
For best results when freezing cakes, first cool the cake completely. Wrap it in plastic wrap, then in heavy foil, and put it in the freezer for up to one month.

THAWING CAKES
For a quick thaw on frozen cakes, use the microwave: Remove all wrapping from the cake; place it on a microwave-safe plate. Heat the cake on low power (10%) till thawed, 5 to 7 minutes, stopping every 3 minutes to give the plate a half-turn. If your microwave's lowest setting is 30%, heat the cake for 3 minutes, stopping once to check.

COOKIES

The cookie jar won't stay full for long if it's filled with a batch of these simple and tasty treats.

SCOTTISH OAT WEDGES

MAKES  8

One Piece: **Calories** 350 **Protein** 5g **Carbohydrates** 41g **Fat** 19g **Cholesterol** 47mg **Sodium** 154mg

¾ **cup (1½ sticks) butter, softened**

⅔ **cup firmly packed light brown sugar**

1 **teaspoon vanilla extract**

¼ **cup all-purpose flour**

3 **cups old-fashioned oats**

 PREPARATION TIME
15 MINUTES

 COOKING TIME
15 MINUTES

FOOD NOTE *In Scotland this snack is known as a flapjack, although its crunchy texture bears no resemblance to a pancake.*

1 Preheat the oven to 350°F. In a large bowl, using an electric mixer, beat butter, brown sugar, and vanilla until fluffy. Beat in flour and half of the oats until well mixed. Using a wooden spoon or by hand, work in the additional oats until the dough just holds together.

2 Press the mixture into an ungreased 9-inch round baking pan. Using a knife, divide the dough into 8 wedges without cutting all the way through to the bottom of the dough.

3 Bake the cookie until it is golden brown, about 15 minutes. Let it cool in the pan, then cut it into wedges and serve.

CINNAMON-SUGAR COOKIES

MAKES  36

One Piece: **Calories** 66 **Protein** Trace **Carbohydrates** 10g **Fat** 3g **Cholesterol** 13mg **Sodium** 31mg

½ **cup (1 stick) butter or margarine, softened**

1 **cup plus 2 tablespoons sugar, divided**

1 **large egg**

½ **teaspoon vanilla extract**

¼ **teaspoon baking powder**

¼ **teaspoon baking soda**

1½ **cups all-purpose flour, divided**

1 **teaspoon ground cinnamon**

 PREPARATION TIME
15 MINUTES

COOKING TIME
30 MINUTES

COOK'S TIP *The dough can be made ahead and frozen in an airtight container. Before baking, thaw it at room temperature.*

1 Preheat the oven to 375°F. In a large bowl, using an electric mixer, beat butter and 1 cup sugar until well mixed. Beat in egg and vanilla until the mixture is smooth.

2 Add baking powder, baking soda, and half of the flour to the butter mixture; beat until smooth and fluffy. Beat in the remaining flour.

3 Drop the dough by rounded teaspoons, about 2 inches apart, on an ungreased baking sheet. In a cup, combine cinnamon with the remaining 2 tablespoons of sugar. Sprinkle some of the cinnamon-sugar over the dropped cookie dough.

4 Bake the cookies until the edges are golden, 10 to 12 minutes. Using a spatula, transfer the cookies to a wire rack to cool. Repeat to bake the remaining cookies, and serve.

LEMON TUILES

MAKES  30

One Piece: Calories 70 **Protein** 1g **Carbohydrates** 4g **Fat** 6g **Cholesterol** 9mg **Sodium** 30mg

²/₃ cup confectioners sugar

¹/₃ cup all-purpose flour

2 large egg whites

1 teaspoon grated lemon peel

¹/₂ teaspoon lemon extract

¹/₂ cup (1 stick) butter or margarine, softened

1 cup sliced blanched almonds

 PREPARATION TIME
15 MINUTES

COOKING TIME
30 MINUTES

SERVING SUGGESTION *These tuiles, or tiles, make a crispy accompaniment to ice cream or fruit for dessert. On their own they are a low-calorie tea-time treat. Be sure to shape the cookies immediately after you take them out of the oven, while they are hot.*

1 Preheat the oven to 400°F. Lightly grease two baking sheets. In a large bowl, combine confectioners sugar and flour. Make a well in the center and add egg whites, lemon peel, and lemon extract. Using a wooden spoon, mix thoroughly; stir in butter. Stir in sliced almonds until well mixed.

2 Drop a portion of the batter by rounded teaspoons, about 2 inches apart, onto the prepared baking sheets (6 cookies on each sheet). Using a fork dipped in cold water, spread the batter out slightly.

3 Bake the cookies, one sheet at time, until the cookies are golden brown, 6 to 8 minutes. Immediately remove the cookies from the baking sheet and drape them over a rolling pin. Allow them to become firm on the rolling pin before transferring them to a wire rack to cool. Repeat to bake the remaining cookies.

BLONDE BROWNIES

MAKES 16

One Piece: Calories 137 **Protein** 2g **Carbohydrates** 16g **Fat** 8g **Cholesterol** 36mg **Sodium** 66mg

5 tablespoons butter or margarine, softened

³/₄ cup firmly packed light brown sugar

2 large eggs

1 teaspoon vanilla extract

³/₄ cup all-purpose flour

1 teaspoon baking powder

³/₄ cup chopped walnuts

 PREPARATION TIME
20 MINUTES

 COOKING TIME
20 MINUTES

COOK'S TIP *A quick way to soften butter that has been stored in the refrigerator is to grate it—it will soften in minutes. This batter can easily be beaten by hand if you'd prefer not to use a mixer.*

1 Preheat the oven to 350°F. Generously grease an 8-inch square baking pan and lightly dust it with flour.

2 In a large bowl, using an electric mixer, beat butter with brown sugar until the mixture is smooth and fluffy. Add eggs and vanilla; beat the mixture until it is well mixed. With the mixer at low speed, beat in flour and baking powder. Using a rubber spatula, fold in walnuts and spread the batter into the prepared pan.

3 Bake the brownies until they are golden brown, 20 to 25 minutes. Cool in the pan for 10 minutes, then cut into 16 pieces and serve, or store them in an airtight container.

LEMON TUILES (RIGHT) AND ALMOND-COCONUT MACAROONS

ALMOND-COCONUT MACAROONS

MAKES  24

One Piece: **Calories** 66 **Protein** 2g **Carbohydrates** 8g **Fat** 4g **Cholesterol** Trace **Sodium** 11mg

- **1 cup blanched slivered almonds**
- **2 large egg whites**
- **²/₃ cup sugar**
- **²/₃ cup sweetened flaked or shredded coconut**
- **½ teaspoon almond extract**

 PREPARATION TIME
10 MINUTES

 COOKING TIME
25 MINUTES

COOK'S TIP *For a smooth finish to the top of the cookies, brush each with a pastry brush dipped in cold water before baking.*

1 Preheat the oven to 325°F. Using an electric blender, chop almonds until finely ground. Spread the ground almonds on a baking sheet. Bake them for 10 minutes to dry.

2 Meanwhile, in a small bowl, using an electric mixer, beat egg whites until soft peaks form. Gradually add sugar, beating constantly, until stiff, glossy peaks form.

3 Grease and flour two baking sheets or line them with parchment paper. Using a rubber spatula, fold coconut, almond extract, and the ground almonds into the beaten egg whites.

4 Drop the batter by rounded tablespoons, about 2 inches apart, onto the prepared baking sheets. Bake the macaroons until the edges are lightly browned, 15 to 20 minutes, switching the baking sheets half way through the cooking time. Cool the cookies on a wire rack.

Favorite Fudge Brownies

MAKES  24

One Piece: **Calories** 201 **Protein** 2g **Carbohydrates** 20g **Fat** 14g **Cholesterol** 55mg **Sodium** 81mg

1 package (12 ounces) semisweet chocolate chips

1 cup (2 sticks) butter or margarine

4 large eggs

1 cup sugar

1 teaspoon vanilla extract

1 cup all-purpose flour

¼ teaspoon baking powder

1 cup chopped walnuts (optional)

 PREPARATION TIME
15 MINUTES

COOKING TIME
25 MINUTES

SERVING SUGGESTION *Kids will love these all-time favorites in a sack lunch or after school with a glass of milk.*

1 Preheat the oven to 350°F. Grease a 13- by 9-inch baking pan. In a medium-size saucepan, melt chocolate chips with butter over low heat, stirring constantly, until smooth. Remove the pan from the heat and let the chocolate mixture cool slightly.

2 Meanwhile, in a medium-size bowl, using an electric mixer, beat eggs until foamy. Gradually add sugar, beating constantly, until the mixture is thick and pale yellow, about 3 minutes. Beat in vanilla.

3 Beat the chocolate mixture into the eggs until well mixed. At low speed, beat in flour and baking powder. Stir in walnuts, if desired. Pour the batter into the prepared pan.

4 Bake the brownies until a toothpick inserted 2 inches from the edge comes out clean, 20 to 25 minutes. (The center will remain soft.) Let the brownies cool slightly and cut them into rectangles.

Variation: Marbled brownies

One Piece: **Calories** 166 **Protein** 2g **Carbohydrates** 16g **Fat** 11g **Cholesterol** 55mg **Sodium** 80mg

Reduce the amount of chocolate chips to ¹/₂ package (1 cup). Melt the chocolate and butter separately. Proceed with Step 2 as above. Beat butter, flour, and baking powder into the egg-sugar mixture. Stir in nuts, if desired.

Pour half of the batter into a second bowl. Stir the chocolate into one of the two bowls of batter. Alternately spoon dollops of the chocolate batter and the white batter into the pan. Run a knife through the batter to give it a marbled effect. Bake as in Step 4 above.

Time Savers

BAKING PREPARATION
• A quick alternative to chopping walnuts is to put the nuts in a plastic bag, seal it tightly, then roll it lightly with a rolling pin.

• To make measuring sticky liquids (such as honey) easier, either rinse the cup in very hot water or spray it with nonstick vegetable spray before measuring.

• You can easily melt chocolate in the microwave: Place it in a small microwave-safe bowl; heat it, uncovered, on high power until shiny, 1 to 2 minutes per ounce.

FAVORITE FUDGE BROWNIES (FAR RIGHT) AND CARAMEL-PECAN SQUARES

CARAMEL-PECAN SQUARES

MAKES 20

One Piece: **Calories** 287 **Protein** 2g **Carbohydrates** 31g **Fat** 18g **Cholesterol** 24mg **Sodium** 86mg

- **2 cups all-purpose flour**
- **1½ cups firmly packed light brown sugar, divided**
- **1 cup (2 sticks) butter or margarine, softened, divided**
- **1½ cups pecan pieces**
- **1 cup semisweet chocolate chips**

 PREPARATION TIME
20 MINUTES

 COOKING TIME
20 MINUTES

COOK'S TIP *Use a heavy pan, uncovered, to melt the chocolate chips. Alternatively, melt them in the microwave or over a double boiler.*

1 Preheat the oven to 350°F. Grease a 13- by 9-inch baking pan. In a large bowl, combine flour, 1 cup brown sugar, and 1 stick butter until well mixed.

2 Press the flour mixture firmly and evenly into the pan to form a crust. Sprinkle the crust with pecans. In a small saucepan, melt the remaining 1 stick of butter with ½ cup brown sugar over moderate heat, stirring constantly, until the mixture begins to boil. Continue boiling for 1 minute, stirring constantly.

3 Spoon the hot sugar mixture evenly over the pecans. Bake until the top is bubbly and the crust is golden brown, about 20 minutes.

4 Meanwhile, in a small saucepan, melt chocolate chips over low heat. Drizzle the melted chocolate over the top of the baked mixture. Let cool, then cut it into 12 pieces and serve.

CHOCOLATE-NUT DROP COOKIES

MAKES

One Piece: **Calories** 135 **Protein** 2g **Carbohydrates** 15g **Fat** 18g **Cholesterol** 19mg **Sodium** 61mg

½ cup (1 stick) butter or margarine, softened

½ cup sugar

¼ cup firmly packed light brown sugar

1 large egg

1 teaspoon vanilla extract

1 cup plus 2 tablespoons all-purpose flour

½ teaspoon baking soda

1 cup semisweet chocolate chips

½ cup chopped walnuts

| PREPARATION TIME **7 MINUTES** | COOKING TIME **20 MINUTES** |

COOK'S TIP *The cookies will bake more evenly if they are done in two batches, rather than all at once.*

1 Preheat the oven to 375°F. Lightly grease two baking sheets. In a large bowl, using an electric mixer, beat butter and both sugars until well mixed. Beat in egg, vanilla, flour, and baking soda until a stiff dough forms. Stir in chocolate chips and chopped walnuts.

2 Drop the dough by rounded teaspoons, about 2 inches apart, onto the prepared baking sheets. Bake until the edges of the cookies are golden, 8 to 10 minutes. Cool the cookies on the baking sheet for 1 minute, then transfer to a wire rack to cool completely. Repeat to bake the remaining dough.

VARIATION: OATMEAL-RAISIN DROP COOKIES

One Serving: **Calories** 107 **Protein** 2g **Carbohydrates** 16g **Fat** 4g **Cholesterol** 19mg **Sodium** 52mg

*Delete chocolate chips and walnuts from the recipe. Reduce the amount of baking soda to ¼ teaspoon. Prepare the dough as in Step 1 above, adding **2 tablespoons milk** with the sugars. Stir **1 cup quick-cooking oats** and **½ cup raisins** into the dough. Drop the cookies by rounded tablespoons; bake for 10 to 12 minutes.*

APPLE-SPICE DROP COOKIES

MAKES

One Piece: **Calories** 98 **Protein** 1g **Carbohydrates** 15g **Fat** 4g **Cholesterol** 19mg **Sodium** 51mg

½ cup (1 stick) butter or margarine, softened

½ cup sugar

¼ cup firmly packed light brown sugar

1 teaspoon ground cinnamon

¼ teaspoon ground nutmeg

1 large egg

1 teaspoon vanilla extract

1 cup plus 2 tablespoons all-purpose flour

¼ teaspoon baking soda

1 cup dried apple, diced

| PREPARATION TIME **8 MINUTES** | COOKING TIME **20 MINUTES** |

1 Preheat the oven to 375°F. In a large bowl, using an electric mixer, beat butter, both sugars, cinnamon, and nutmeg until well mixed. Beat in egg, vanilla, flour, and baking soda until the mixture is thoroughly combined and a stiff dough forms. Using a wooden spoon, stir the dried apples into the dough.

2 Drop the dough by rounded teaspoons, about 2 inches apart, onto an ungreased baking sheet. Bake until the edges of the cookies are golden, 8 to 10 minutes.

3 Cool the cookies on the baking sheet for 1 minute, then transfer to a wire rack to cool completely. Repeat to bake the remaining dough.

DESSERTS

CHOCOLATE PARFAITS (PAGE 367)

FRUIT DESSERTS

The lightest desserts start with fresh fruits of the season.
They make a colorful and healthy finish to any meal.

CHOCOLATE-DIPPED STRAWBERRIES

One Serving: **Calories** 145 **Protein** 1g **Carbohydrates** 19g **Fat** 9g **Cholesterol** 0mg **Sodium** 4mg

3 squares (1 ounce each) semisweet chocolate

1 teaspoon vegetable shortening

1 pint large fresh strawberries, unhulled

 PREPARATION TIME
30 MINUTES

COOKING TIME
5 MINUTES

SERVING SUGGESTION *These sweet bites of fruit and chocolate would make the ideal dessert for a champagne brunch.*

1 Partially fill the bottom part of a double boiler with water; bring to a boil over high heat. Meanwhile, finely chop chocolate. Reduce the heat under the double boiler to moderately low. In the top part of the double boiler, melt the chopped chocolate and shortening over the hot, not boiling, water. (Alternatively, melt the chocolate and shortening in the microwave, stopping frequently to check if they are soft.)

2 Stir the chocolate until smooth. Remove the double boiler from the heat but keep the melted chocolate in the top part over the water.

3 Lightly oil a baking sheet. Rinse strawberries and gently pat them dry. Pour the melted chocolate into a small bowl. Holding each berry by its green top, dip the end halfway into the chocolate. Let the excess chocolate drip off the berry; place it on the prepared baking sheet.

4 Refrigerate the berries until the chocolate is firm, about 15 minutes. Arrange the berries in a single layer on a plate, and serve.

Shelf Magic

Two easy fruit desserts, one cool and one warm, get a dash of spirits to boost the flavor. Serve them with a scoop of vanilla ice cream.

BERRIES WITH LIQUEUR

Gently toss ½ **pint blackberries,** ½ **pint raspberries,** and ½ **pint blueberries** together in a serving bowl. In a cup, combine **1 tablespoon raspberry liqueur or cranberry juice** and **1 tablespoon honey.** Pour over the berries, toss gently, and serve.
SERVES 4

SPICED APRICOTS AND PEARS

Preheat the broiler. Drain **one 16-ounce can apricot halves,** reserving 2 tablespoons syrup, and **one 16-ounce can pear halves.** In a pie plate, mix syrup with **2 tablespoons brandy, 1 tablespoon honey,** and a **pinch cinnamon.** Stir in fruit; broil until browned.
SERVES 4

GRAPE PARFAIT SUPREME

GRAPE PARFAIT SUPREME

One Serving: **Calories** 211 **Protein** 3g **Carbohydrates** 34g **Fat** 8g **Cholesterol** 22mg **Sodium** 29mg

- **1 cup seedless green grapes, halved**
- **1 container (8 ounces) light or fat-free sour cream, divided**
- **3 tablespoons firmly packed light brown sugar, divided**
- **1 cup seedless red grapes, halved**
- **1 cup seedless black grapes, halved**
- **1 tablespoon chopped shelled pistachios**

PREPARATION TIME
20 MINUTES

COOKING TIME
0 MINUTES

COOK'S TIP *This simple dessert is prepared right in the serving bowl, so there are no extra dishes to wash. Use a clear glass bowl to show all the layers.*

1 In a 1-quart stemmed compote or medium-size straight-sided glass bowl, place green grapes. Top with ⅓ cup sour cream and spread to a thin layer to cover the grapes. Sprinkle the sour cream with 1 tablespoon brown sugar.

2 Cover the sugar-cream layer with red grapes; spread with ⅓ cup sour cream and sprinkle with 1 tablespoon brown sugar. Top with black grapes. Spoon dollops of the remaining sour cream in the center of the black grapes. Sprinkle with the remaining brown sugar and chopped pistachios, and serve.

FRESH FRUIT AMBROSIA

One Serving: **Calories** 298 **Protein** 3g **Carbohydrates** 68g **Fat** 3g **Cholesterol** 0mg **Sodium** 8mg

3 large nectarines

2 medium-size ripe bananas

½ cup dark sweet cherries

¼ cup orange juice

2 tablespoons Grand Marnier or orange juice

2 tablespoons flaked coconut

 PREPARATION TIME
20 MINUTES

COOKING TIME
0 MINUTES

1 Cut nectarines in half. Remove the pits and slice the nectarines. Peel and slice bananas. Cut cherries in half and remove the pits.

2 In a medium-size bowl, toss nectarines and bananas with orange juice and Grand Marnier. Pour the fruit mixture into a glass bowl. Sprinkle the fruit with coconut, top it with the cherries, and serve.

CARAMEL BANANAS

One Serving: **Calories** 367 **Protein** 2g **Carbohydrates** 46g **Fat** 22g **Cholesterol** 41mg **Sodium** 163mg

⅓ cup butter or margarine

⅓ cup firmly packed light brown sugar

¼ cup water

4 medium-size bananas (about 1½ pounds)

⅓ cup pecans

Vanilla frozen yogurt or ice cream (optional)

 PREPARATION TIME
2 MINUTES

COOKING TIME
10 MINUTES

1 In a large skillet, melt butter over moderate heat. Stir in brown sugar until it dissolves. Gradually stir in water. Bring the mixture to a simmer; reduce the heat to low and continue simmering the sauce.

2 Peel bananas and cut them crosswise in half. Add the bananas and pecans to the caramel sauce in the skillet; cook until the bananas are just heated through, 5 to 7 minutes, turning them gently in the sauce. Place the bananas and their sauce in small bowls; top them with frozen yogurt or ice cream, if desired, and serve.

STRAWBERRIES IN BLUEBERRY SAUCE

One Serving: **Calories** 350 **Protein** 3g **Carbohydrates** 76g **Fat** 4g **Cholesterol** 11mg **Sodium** 27mg

2 pints ripe strawberries

1 cup sweetened whipped cream or thawed, frozen whipped topping

Mint leaves (optional)

For the blueberry sauce

1 cup fresh or frozen blueberries, thawed

1 cup sugar

1 teaspoon grated orange peel

2 tablespoons blackberry liqueur or brandy

 PREPARATION TIME
12 MINUTES

COOKING TIME
15 MINUTES

1 To make the sauce, in a medium-size saucepan, combine blueberries, sugar, and orange peel. Cook over moderate heat, stirring gently, until the berries burst and the mixture begins to liquify. Simmer 5 minutes, stirring occasionally.

2 Remove the pan from the heat and stir in liqueur. Let the sauce cool for at least 10 minutes or until ready to serve. Meanwhile, rinse and hull strawberries; cut each in half.

3 To serve, divide the blueberry sauce among four dessert bowls and top with strawberries. Spoon whipped cream on top, garnish with mint leaves, if desired, and serve.

GLAZED PINEAPPLE

One Serving: **Calories** 180 **Protein** 1g **Carbohydrates** 35g **Fat** 5g **Cholesterol** 8mg **Sodium** 37mg

1 tablespoon butter or margarine

6 tablespoons orange marmalade

1½ teaspoons lemon juice or lime juice

3 cans (8 ounces each) pineapple slices in unsweetened juice

3 tablespoons sliced almonds

 PREPARATION TIME
13 MINUTES

COOKING TIME
15 MINUTES

COOK'S TIP *If you prefer to use fresh pineapple, buy the prepared slices available at the salad bar section of your supermarket.*

1 Preheat the broiler. In a small saucepan, melt butter over moderate heat. Stir in orange marmalade and cook until it is melted. Stir in lemon juice; remove the saucepan from the heat.

2 Drain pineapple; arrange the pineapple slices on the rack over a broiler pan. Brush the slices with half of the marmalade mixture. Broil the pineapple 4 inches from the heat until lightly browned on one side, 3 to 6 minutes.

3 Turn the pineapple slices over and brush them with the remaining marmalade mixture. Continue broiling until lightly browned, about 3 to 6 more minutes.

4 Sprinkle the pineapple slices with almonds and continue broiling until the nuts are golden brown, 30 seconds to 1 minute. Place the warm pineapple slices on a plate, and serve immediately.

TROPICAL FRUIT SKEWERS

One Serving: **Calories** 140 **Protein** 1g **Carbohydrates** 36g **Fat** 1g **Cholesterol** 0mg **Sodium** 5mg

2 medium-size or 1 large ripe mango

2 tablespoons sugar

1 tablespoon lime juice

1 ripe papaya

1 kiwi fruit

1 large ripe banana

PREPARATION TIME
25 MINUTES

COOKING TIME
0 MINUTES

COOK'S TIP *You could prepare these a short while in advance if you brush the fruit pieces with a little lemon juice. The fruit goes well with yogurt on the side.*

1 Peel mango; cut the pulp from its seed and place it in the container of a food processor or electric blender. Add sugar and lime juice to the mango. Process the mixture until smooth. Pour the mango sauce into a small bowl and refrigerate it while preparing the fruit skewers.

2 Peel papaya and cut it in half. Discard the seeds; cut the papaya into 1-inch chunks. Peel kiwi and cut it in half crosswise; cut each half into four chunks. Peel banana and cut it into ½-inch slices.

3 On four bamboo sewers, alternately thread the fruit pieces, beginning and ending with a kiwi chunk. To serve, pour a little of the mango sauce onto each individual serving plate. Top with a fruit skewer, and serve immediately.

MELON COMPOTE

Melon Compote

One Serving: **Calories** 86 **Protein** 1g **Carbohydrates** 22g **Fat** Trace **Cholesterol** 0mg **Sodium** 10mg

1½ **pounds seeded or seed-less watermelon**

½ **small cantaloupe**

½ **small honeydew melon**

2 **to 3 tablespoons finely chopped fresh mint leaves**

2 **tablespoons honey**

Mint sprigs (optional)

PREPARATION TIME
45 MINUTES

COOKING TIME
0 MINUTES

DIET NOTE *This light dessert will give you your vitamin C for the day, and still satisfy the sweet tooth—all in under 90 calories.*

1 Using a melon-ball cutter, scoop balls of watermelon, cantaloupe, and honeydew. (Alternatively, cut the fruit into ³/₄-inch cubes.) Place the fruit in a large bowl; add chopped mint and honey, and toss the mixture gently. Cover and refrigerate to marinate the melon mixture, at least 30 minutes.

2 Spoon the melon mixture and any accumulated juices into dessert dishes. Garnish each serving with a mint sprig, if desired, and serve.

STUFFED BAKED APPLES

One Serving: **Calories** 311 **Protein** 1g **Carbohydrates** 63g **Fat** 8g **Cholesterol** 16mg **Sodium** 163mg

4 **medium-size red baking apples (about 1⅓ pounds)**

2 **tablespoons (¼ stick) butter or margarine**

½ **cup graham cracker crumbs**

3 **tablespoons raisins**

2 **tablespoons firmly packed light brown sugar**

½ **teaspoon ground cinnamon**

1 **cup apple juice**

¼ **cup maple syrup**

Cream (optional)

PREPARATION TIME
10 MINUTES

COOKING TIME
27 MINUTES

SERVING SUGGESTION *This traditional cold-weather dessert goes well with a pitcher of chilled cream to pour over it.*

1 Preheat the oven to 375°F. Cut apples in half crosswise. Using a melon-ball cutter, core the apple halves, being careful not to cut through to the bottom skin. Place the apple halves, cut side up, in a 13- by 9-inch baking dish.

2 In a small saucepan, melt butter over moderate heat. Remove the pan from the heat and brush the apples lightly with some of the melted butter. Add cracker crumbs, raisins, sugar, and cinnamon to the remaining melted butter in the saucepan. Toss the crumb mixture until well mixed.

3 Fill the cavity of each apple half with some of the crumb mixture, mounding it in the center. In a cup, combine apple juice and maple syrup. Pour a tablespoon of the juice mixture over each apple, and pour the remaining mixture into the dish around the apples.

4 Bake the apples until they are tender, 25 to 35 minutes. Transfer the apples to dessert bowls, add some cream, if desired, and serve.

BRANDY SPICED PEACHES

One Serving: **Calories** 316 **Protein** Trace **Carbohydrates** 74g **Fat** Trace **Cholesterol** 0mg **Sodium** 2g

1 **cup sugar**

1 **cup water**

1 **cinnamon stick (about 3 inches long)**

6 **whole cloves**

¼ **teaspoon ground nutmeg**

4 **large firm ripe freestone peaches (about 2 pounds)**

½ **cup brandy**

Sweetened whipped cream, or frozen whipped topping, thawed (optional)

PREPARATION TIME
5 MINUTES

COOKING TIME
6 MINUTES

1 In a large saucepan, bring 3 inches of water to a boil over high heat. Meanwhile, in a medium-size saucepan, combine sugar, water, cinnamon, cloves, and nutmeg; bring the mixture to a boil over moderately high heat.

2 Place peaches in the boiling water for 1 to 2 minutes to loosen their skins. Drain the peaches and rinse them under cold water. Peel the peaches, cut them in half, and remove the pits.

3 Add the peach halves to the sugar mixture; cook gently until the peaches soften, about 3 minutes. Remove the saucepan from the heat; stir in brandy. Set the peaches aside to cool slightly.

4 Spoon the warm peaches into small dessert bowls with some of their cooking liquid; top with a spoonful of whipped cream, if desired, and serve immediately.

HONEY-BAKED PEARS

One Serving: **Calories** 241 **Protein** 2g **Carbohydrates** 50g **Fat** 6g **Cholesterol** 8mg **Sodium** 31mg

4 firm ripe Bartlett pears (about 1½ pounds)

1 cup orange juice

¼ cup honey

¼ teaspoon ground ginger

1 tablespoon butter or margarine, cut into pieces

2 tablespoons chopped shelled pistachios or toasted almonds

 PREPARATION TIME **10 MINUTES**   COOKING TIME **25 MINUTES**

1 Preheat the oven to 350°F. Peel pears and cut them in half lengthwise. Using a melon-ball cutter, remove the cores with the seeds.

2 Place the pears, cut sides down, in a single layer in a 10- by 6-inch or 12- by 8-inch baking dish. In a small bowl, combine orange juice, honey, and ginger until well mixed. Pour the mixture over the pears. Dot the pears with butter; bake until the pears are just tender, 20 to 30 minutes.

3 Place the pears and their baking liquid in a dish or small bowls, sprinkle them with nuts, and serve immediately.

GINGERED PEACHES WITH YOGURT

One Serving: **Calories** 172 **Protein** 4g **Carbohydrates** 26g **Fat** 6g **Cholesterol** 18mg **Sodium** 98mg

4 medium-size ripe peaches (about 1¼ pounds)

2 tablespoons (¼ stick) butter or margarine

1 container (8 ounces) nonfat vanilla yogurt

2 tablespoons finely chopped crystallized ginger, divided

Mint sprigs (optional)

PREPARATION TIME **7 MINUTES**   COOKING TIME **7 MINUTES**

1 Cut peaches in half. Remove the pits and slice the peaches. In a large skillet, melt butter over moderate heat. Add the peach slices and sauté until softened, about 5 minutes.

2 Stir yogurt and 1 tablespoon crystallized ginger into the peaches until well mixed and just warmed. Remove the skillet from the heat. Place the warm peaches and yogurt in small bowls; sprinkle each serving with an equal amount of the remaining crystallized ginger; garnish with mint sprigs, if desired, and serve.

TIME SAVERS

FRUIT

• For a snack that needs no cooking, make a batch of frozen grapes. Freeze individual seedless grapes on a baking sheet, transfer them to a plastic bag, and seal tightly. They're delicious on their own or mixed into yogurt for dessert.

• Many supermarkets have salad bars these days, which can save a lot of prepration time when making fresh-fruit dishes. The food may cost a bit more, but it can be worth it. Look for cleaned strawberries, cubed cantaloupe and watermelon, and sliced pineapple.

• Some supermarkets sell special plastic bowls to ripen fruit more quickly. The bowls can be very handy, but you can also speed up ripening on your own: Punch some holes in a brown paper bag; place the fruit inside. Leave it out at room temperature for a couple of days.

CINNAMON POACHED PEARS

CINNAMON POACHED PEARS

One Serving: **Calories** 227 **Protein** 1g **Carbohydrates** 56g **Fat** 1g **Cholesterol** 0mg **Sodium** 23mg

1 **can (12 ounces) frozen unsweetened apple juice concentrate**

1 **cup water**

2 **cinnamon sticks (about 3 inches long)**

1/8 **teaspoon ground nutmeg**

4 **firm, ripe Bosc pears with stems (about 1½ pounds)**

Sour cream (optional)

 PREPARATION TIME
2 MINUTES

COOKING TIME
25 MINUTES

COOK'S TIP *These can also be served cold; add a scoop of vanilla ice cream if you want a richer dessert.*

1 In a large saucepan, combine undiluted frozen apple juice, water, cinnamon, and nutmeg; bring to a boil over moderately high heat.

2 Meanwhile, leaving the stems attached, peel pears. Through the bottom end, core the pears. Rinse the pears and place them standing upright in the saucepan with the apple mixture. Cover and bring the mixture to a boil. Immediately reduce the heat to low and simmer the pears until they are just tender, about 25 minutes.

3 Remove the saucepan from the heat. Using a slotted spoon, lift the pears out of the saucepan and place them in a serving bowl. Strain the poaching liquid over the pears and allow them to cool slightly before serving. Serve with sour cream, if desired.

FROZEN DESSERTS

For a sure crowd pleaser, make one of these frozen treats—
they'll provide a cool finale in any season.

MISSISSIPPI MUD PIE

One Serving: **Calories** 837 **Protein** 11g **Carbohydrates** 84g **Fat** 54g **Cholesterol** 167mg **Sodium** 385mg

- 19 **cream-filled chocolate sandwich cookies, finely crushed**
- ¼ **cup (½ stick) butter or margarine, melted**
- ½ **gallon chocolate or coffee ice cream**
- 1 **cup (½ pint) heavy cream, divided**
- 1 **cup (6 ounces) semisweet chocolate chips**
- ¼ **teaspoon ground cinnamon**

PREPARATION TIME
40 MINUTES

COOKING TIME
5 MINUTES

COOK'S TIP *Children and adults love this easy ice cream pie. Make two pies and freeze one for later.*

1 In a medium-size bowl, using a fork, combine crushed cookies and butter. Set aside 1 tablespoon of the crumb mixture. Press the remaining mixture into the bottom and sides of a 9-inch pie plate. Freeze the crust for 10 minutes.

2 Scoop ice cream into balls and place in the crumb crust. Using a rubber spatula, smooth the top of the ice cream. Sprinkle the surface with the remaining crumbs. Return the pie to the freezer.

3 Meanwhile, in a small bowl, using the electric mixer, beat ½ cup heavy cream until stiff peaks form. Using a pastry bag fitted with a star tube, pipe the cream around the edge of the pie. Pipe any remaining cream in the center of the pie. Freeze the pie for at least 15 to 20 minutes or until ready to serve.

4 Meanwhile, in a small saucepan, combine chocolate chips with the remaining ½ cup cream and cinnamon. Cook over moderate heat, stirring constantly, until the chocolate melts and the mixture is smooth and bubbly. Pour the mixture into a small pitcher. Cut the pie into wedges and serve, passing the chocolate sauce on the side.

Shelf Magic

This refreshing ice-cream drink uses gingersnap cookie crumbs for a spicy twist. Serve it in tall glasses with colorful straws.

GINGER-VANILLA SMOOTHIE

In a food processor or blender, crush **6 gingersnap cookies** until coarsely chopped. Using a large spoon, add **1 pint vanilla ice-cream**, slightly softened, and process until smooth. Divide the mixture among four goblets, add a **pinch of nutmeg** to each, and serve immediately.
SERVES 4

QUICK ICE CREAM

One Serving: **Calories** 318 **Protein** 2g **Carbohydrates** 31g **Fat** 22g **Cholesterol** 81mg **Sodium** 25mg

1 cup (½ pint) heavy cream

⅓ cup sugar

1 teaspoon vanilla extract

1 package (20 ounces) frozen unsweetened strawberries, raspberries, sliced peaches, or cherries

PREPARATION TIME
5 MINUTES

COOKING TIME
0 MINUTES

FOOD NOTE *This soft-style ice cream tastes as if it was made in an ice-cream maker, and only takes 5 minutes to prepare. Make sure the fruit is well frozen when you add it to the cream.*

1 Using a food processor with the chopping blade, process cream, sugar, and vanilla until smooth, about 1 minute.

2 Through the feed tube in the food processor, add frozen fruit, a few pieces at a time; process until smooth. Spoon the ice cream into small bowls, and serve immediately.

PINEAPPLE WITH ORANGE SHERBET

One Serving: **Calories** 311 **Protein** 2g **Carbohydrates** 71g **Fat** 3g **Cholesterol** 8mg **Sodium** 54mg

1 medium-size fresh pineapple (about 3 ¼ pounds)

¼ cup sugar

1 tablespoon cornstarch

1 tablespoon rum (optional)

1 large banana

1 pint orange sherbet

Fresh mint sprigs

PREPARATION TIME
27 MINUTES

COOKING TIME
4 MINUTES

COOK'S TIP *Fresh pineapple is worth the extra effort because this dessert looks so special served in bowls made from the rind. If you prefer not to buy a whole pineapple, buy pre-cut fresh pineapple from the supermarket and serve the dessert in small bowls.*

1 Twist the green top off pineapple. Cut the pineapple lengthwise in half. Cut each half crosswise in half. Carefully cut the pineapple flesh away from the rind, leaving a shell about ½-inch thick.

2 Remove the core from the pineapple pieces. Cut the pineapple into ½-inch-thick slices. Using an electric blender or food processor, process enough of the slices to yield 1 cup finely chopped pineapple.

3 Fill the pineapple shells with the remaining pineapple slices. Wrap and refrigerate the pineapple shells until ready to serve.

4 In a medium-size saucepan, combine sugar, cornstarch, and rum if desired. Stir in the chopped pineapple until well mixed. Bring the pineapple mixture to a boil over moderate heat, stirring constantly, until thickened and bubbly. Remove the pineapple mixture from the heat and chill for 10 to 15 minutes.

5 Place a pineapple shell on each of four individual serving plates. Peel and slice banana into approximately 16 slices and divide them among the shells. Scoop orange sherbet onto each shell. Top with the warm pineapple sauce, garnish with mint, and serve immediately.

ICE CREAM TRIFLE

ICE CREAM TRIFLE

One Serving: **Calories** 419 **Protein** 5g **Carbohydrates** 47g **Fat** 24g **Cholesterol** 76mg **Sodium** 194mg

1 **small prepared jelly-roll cake (about 8 inches long), filled with red jelly**

¼ **cup cream sherry or orange juice**

1½ **pints vanilla ice cream**

½ **pint fresh raspberries, rinsed and dried**

½ **cup sweetened whipped cream, or frozen whipped topping, thawed**

2 **tablespoons sliced almonds**

PREPARATION TIME
20 MINUTES

COOKING TIME
0 MINUTES

SERVING SUGGESTION *Use sliced strawberries instead of raspberries if you prefer. Either way, this summery dessert looks spectacular, and takes only minutes to prepare.*

1 Cut jelly-roll cake crosswise into ½-inch-thick slices. In a small shallow glass bowl or footed compote dish, line the bottom and side of the bowl with the cake slices. Sprinkle the cake with sherry.

2 Fill the cake-lined bowl with scoops of ice cream. Top it with raspberries, whipped cream, and almonds. Serve immediately.

Start with a Scoop

You'll never be at a loss for a creative dessert if you keep the freezer stocked with a pint of your favorite ice cream or frozen yogurt. Start with a scoop and add any combination of chocolate sauce, fresh fruit, liqueur, or cookie crumbs, and you've made an irresistibly refreshing treat. For a few ideas for single-ingredient additions, look to the box at the lower right. Each of these recipes serves four, and each may easily be halved or doubled.

◀ PEACH MELBA Thaw **one 10-oz. package frozen raspberries or strawberries in quick-thaw pouch** according to package directions. In a small saucepan, combine **1 Tbsp. sugar** with **2 tsp. corn-starch**; stir in juice from raspberries. Bring syrup to a boil over moderate heat; cook until thickened. Remove from heat and stir in raspberries. Using a blender, purée raspberries and strain them into a bowl; discard seeds. Peel, halve, and pit **4 peaches**. Place 2 peach halves into each of four serving bowls. Scoop **1 pint vanilla ice cream** over peaches; top with sauce.

▶ COCONUT SNOWBALLS Scoop **1 pint vanilla frozen yogurt** into four balls; roll the scoops in **1 cup flaked coconut** until well coated to make snowballs. Place snowballs on a serving plate; refreeze until firm. Just before serving, pour **½ cup pineapple ice-cream topping** over the four snowballs. Garnish plate with **sliced fresh strawberries**.

▶ AMARETTI CHOCOLATE ICE CREAM Place **1 cup crushed amaretti cookies** on a sheet of wax paper. Scoop **1 pint chocolate ice cream** into four balls and roll the balls in the crumbs. Place crumb-coated ice cream balls on a plate and refreeze until firm. To serve, spoon a thin coating of **prepared chocolate topping** onto four small rimmed serving plates. Cut each ice cream ball into four wedges. Arrange wedges on each plate. Garnish each serving with a dollop of **whipped cream** and a **maraschino cherry**.

364

► **ORANGE ICE CREAM WITH BLACK RASPBERRY SAUCE** Using an electric blender or food processor, process **2 cups fresh black raspberries or blackberries** until puréed. Press the berry purée through a fine sieve into a bowl; discard the seeds. Add **1 Tbsp. blackberry liqueur, crème de cassis, or Grand Marnier** and **sugar to taste** to the purée. Serve over scoops from **1 pint orange ice cream or sherbet.**

◄ **WAFFLE À LA MODE** Lightly toast **4 frozen waffles**. In a small saucepan, heat **1 cup canned apple-pie filling** until warm. On each of four small dessert plates, place a toasted waffle. Place scoops from **1 pint vanilla ice cream** on each waffle. Top with warm apple filling; sprinkle with **chopped pecans** and **ground cinnamon.**

► **TUTTI-FRUTTI SUNDAE** In a large bowl, combine **3 Tbsp. sugar, 2 Tbsp. brandy, 1 small diced nectarine, 1 small sliced banana,** and **1 cup fresh or canned dark sweet cherries,** halved and pitted. Place **four ½-inch-thick slices pound cake** into four dessert dishes. Place scoops from **1 pint lemon sherbet** on cake slices. Top with fruit; garnish with **sliced almonds.**

ADD TO YOUR FAVORITE ICE CREAM

Crushed toffee	Crushed sandwich cookies	Crumbled brownies
Warm apricot jam	Butterscotch chips	Chopped peanut-butter cups
Crème de Menthe liqueur	Toasted coconut	Chocolate-covered raisins
Crushed peppermint candy	Granola	Banana chips
Toasted slivered almonds	Candied chestnuts	Chopped candy bars

CAPPUCCINO ICE CREAM CAKES

CAPPUCCINO ICE CREAM CAKES

One Serving: **Calories** 497 **Protein** 7g **Carbohydrates** 63g **Fat** 25g **Cholesterol** 141mg **Sodium** 219mg

4 **prepared individual sponge-cake shells**

½ **cup canned ready-to-spread chocolate fudge frosting**

1 **pint coffee ice cream**

½ **cup sweetened whipped cream or frozen whipped topping, thawed**

Ground cinnamon

4 **cinnamon sticks (optional)**

 PREPARATION TIME
12 MINUTES

 COOKING TIME
0 MINUTES

FOOD NOTE *The flavors of coffee, chocolate and ice cream are combined here in a delicious twist on cappuccino.*

1 Line a small baking sheet with wax paper. Place cake shells on the prepared baking sheet; spread the tops and sides of the cake shells with chocolate fudge frosting.

2 Fill the center of each frosted cake shell with a scoop of ice cream. Freeze the ice cream cakes until ready to serve.

3 Just before serving, place the ice cream cakes on individual dessert plates. Top each with whipped cream and sprinkle with ground cinnamon. Garnish with a cinnamon stick, if desired, and serve.

HOT APPLE PARFAIT

One Serving: **Calories** 388 **Protein** 4g **Carbohydrates** 63g **Fat** 15g **Cholesterol** 35mg **Sodium** 166mg

- **3 large Golden Delicious apples**
- **¼ cup raisins**
- **¼ cup sugar**
- **¼ cup water**
- **½ teaspoon ground cinnamon**
- **1 package (7 ounces) shortbread cookies or vanilla wafers**
- **1 pint vanilla frozen yogurt**
- **¼ cup chopped walnuts**

PREPARATION TIME
20 MINUTES

COOKING TIME
20 MINUTES

1 Peel, core, and coarsely chop apples. In a medium-size saucepan, combine the apples, raisins, sugar, water, and cinnamon; bring the mixture to a boil over moderate heat.

2 Cover the saucepan and cook the apple mixture, stirring occasionally, for 15 minutes. If necessary, uncover the saucepan and continue cooking until all the liquid has evaporated, about 5 more minutes. Meanwhile, place cookies in a plastic food-storage bag. Using a rolling pin, crush the cookies into crumbs, making about 2 cups.

3 Divide half of the cookie crumbs among four parfait glasses or water goblets. Divide the warm apple mixture among the glasses and top with the remaining crumbs. Scoop frozen yogurt onto each parfait glass and sprinkle with walnuts. Serve immediately.

MICROWAVE VERSION

Chop apples as as in Step 1 above. In a microwave-safe, 2-quart casserole, combine apples, raisins, sugar, water, and cinnamon. Microwave on high power for 5 minutes, covered, stirring once during cooking. Uncover and continue cooking on high until the apples are very soft and almost all the liquid has evaporated, 3 to 4 more minutes, stirring once during cooking. Proceed with the recipe as in Steps 2 and 3 above.

CHOCOLATE PARFAITS

One Serving: **Calories** 467 **Protein** 11g **Carbohydrates** 56g **Fat** 24g **Cholesterol** 75mg **Sodium** 189mg

- **½ cup semisweet chocolate chips**
- **2 tablespoons (¼ stick) butter or margarine**
- **1 pint chocolate ice cream**
- **22 vanilla wafers, crushed (about 1 cup)**
- **½ cup sweetened whipped cream, or frozen whipped topping, thawed**
- **2 tablespoons chopped walnuts**
- **4 maraschino cherries with stems (optional)**

PREPARATION TIME
15 MINUTES

COOKING TIME
3 MINUTES

1 In a small saucepan, melt chocolate with butter over low heat, stirring constantly. Remove the saucepan from the heat and set aside. (Alternatively, melt the chocolate and butter in the microwave.)

2 Divide half of the ice cream among four parfait glasses or stemmed water goblets. Sprinkle each portion with half of the cookie crumbs. Repeat with the remaining ice cream and cookie crumbs.

3 Top the chocolate parfaits with whipped cream and chopped walnuts, and maraschino cherries if desired. Pour the melted chocolate into a small pitcher. Serve the parfaits immediately, passing the melted chocolate on the side.

ICE CREAM WITH BUTTERSCOTCH SAUCE

ICE CREAM WITH BUTTERSCOTCH SAUCE

One Serving: **Calories** 683 **Protein** 5g **Carbohydrates** 101g **Fat** 31g **Cholesterol** 109mg **Sodium** 259mg

1 cup firmly packed light brown sugar

⅓ cup dark corn syrup

¼ cup water

4 tablespoons butter or margarine

⅓ cup heavy cream, at room temperature

½ teaspoon rum extract

1 pint vanilla ice cream or frozen yogurt

PREPARATION TIME
14 MINUTES

COOKING TIME
7 MINUTES

COOK'S TIP *Toasted chopped almonds would add a crunchy texture—stir them directly into the sauce, or sprinkle them on top.*

1 In a small saucepan, combine brown sugar, corn syrup, water, and butter. Bring to a boil over moderate heat and continue boiling until the mixture reaches the soft ball stage on a candy thermometer (236°F), about 4 minutes. Remove the pan from the heat and let the mixture cool slightly for about 10 minutes.

2 Add cream and rum extract to the mixture; stir until smooth. Pour the butterscotch sauce into a small pitcher.

3 Scoop ice cream into four dessert dishes and serve immediately, passing the butterscotch sauce on the side.

MINI WHITE ALASKAS

One Serving: **Calories** 615 **Protein** 8g **Carbohydrates** 70g **Fat** 36g **Cholesterol** 202mg **Sodium** 205mg

- **4 prepared individual sponge-cake shells**
- **1 pint strawberry ice cream**
- **1 cup (½ pint) heavy cream**
- **2 tablespoons confectioners sugar**
- **½ teaspoon vanilla extract**
- **½ cup prepared chocolate syrup, divided**

PREPARATION TIME
30 MINUTES

COOKING TIME
0 MINUTES

1 Place cake shells on a small baking sheet or freezer-safe plate. Scoop ice cream into four balls and place one in each cake shell. Freeze the ice cream and shells for 10 minutes.

2 Meanwhile, in a small bowl, using an electric mixer, beat cream with sugar and vanilla until stiff peaks form. Remove the cake shells from the freezer and, using a rubber spatula, quickly frost the ice cream and cake with the whipped cream. Return the frosted cakes to the freezer for 10 minutes or until ready to serve.

3 Just before serving, divide the chocolate syrup among four rimmed individual dessert plates. Using a pancake turner, place the cake shells on top of the sauce, and serve immediately.

TORTONI

One Serving: **Calories** 276 **Protein** 4g **Carbohydrates** 25g **Fat** 17g **Cholesterol** 55mg **Sodium** 102mg

- **1 cup crushed amaretti cookies (or vanilla wafers)**
- **2 tablespoons dark rum (or 1½ tablespoons water with 1 teaspoon rum-flavored extract)**
- **3 tablespoons coarsely chopped maraschino cherries**
- **1 pint vanilla ice cream, slightly softened**
- **3 tablespoons slivered blanched almonds**
- **3 maraschino cherries, halved**

PREPARATION TIME
45 MINUTES

COOKING TIME
0 MINUTES

1 Line 6 muffin-pan cups with fluted aluminum-foil or paper cupcake liners. In a medium-size bowl, combine amaretti crumbs, rum, and chopped cherries until well mixed. Quickly spoon in ice cream and fold gently just to mix. Spoon the ice-cream mixture into foil baking cups and freeze until the ice cream is firm, about 30 minutes.

2 Meanwhile, in a large skillet, heat almonds over moderate heat until toasted or lightly browned, stirring frequently, about 3 minutes. Remove the almonds from the heat and let them cool.

3 Transfer each tortoni cup to a serving plate. Top each with some toasted almonds and a cherry half, and serve immediately.

TIME SAVERS

TOASTED ALMONDS
Make a quick, crunchy garnish for ice-cream desserts by toasting almonds in the microwave: Place ½ cup sliced almonds in a 3-cup microwave-safe glass dish. Cook on high power, uncovered, for 2 to 3 minutes, stopping after each minute to stir. As soon as the almonds begin to brown, remove the dish from the oven and pour the almonds out onto a paper towel to cool. Chop the almonds, if desired, and sprinkle them over the ice cream.

Custards and Soufflés

Turn to one of these easy desserts when the end of the meal calls for something rich and creamy.

Rum Chocolate Mousse

One Serving: **Calories** 485 **Protein** 6g **Carbohydrates** 34g **Fat** 37g **Cholesterol** 221mg **Sodium** 286mg

3 large eggs, at room temperature

¼ cup dark rum

½ cup (1 stick) unsalted butter

4 squares (1 ounce each) semisweet chocolate, finely chopped

¼ cup sugar

Sweetened whipped cream, or frozen whipped topping, thawed (optional)

Chocolate shavings (optional)

PREPARATION TIME
37 MINUTES

COOKING TIME
6 MINUTES

COOK'S TIP *Kahlua makes an excellent substitute for rum if you prefer. This dessert can be made in advance and refrigerated.*

1 Partially fill the bottom part of a double boiler with water; bring to a boil over high heat. Meanwhile, separate eggs. In a small bowl, combine the egg yolks and rum until blended; set aside. Cut butter into tiny pieces; set aside.

2 Reduce the heat under the double boiler to moderately low. In the top part of the double boiler, melt chocolate over the hot, not boiling, water. Add the butter and continue stirring until blended.

3 Remove the top part of the double boiler from the water. Gradually add the egg-yolk mixture and stir until thoroughly blended. Refrigerate the chocolate mixture briefly, while preparing the next step.

4 In a small bowl, using an electric mixer, beat the egg whites until foamy. Gradually add sugar, and continue beating until stiff peaks form. Using a rubber spatula, fold the egg whites into the chocolate.

5 Spoon the mousse into four stemmed wine glasses or dessert bowls. Garnish each serving with whipped cream and chocolate shavings, if desired. Refrigerate until ready to serve, at least 25 minutes.

Shelf Magic

Use a package of pudding mix to whip up this creamy coffee-flavored dessert. Fill tall parfait glasses to show off the layers best.

Mocha Pudding

In a large bowl, using an electric mixer, beat **1 cup heavy cream** with **2 tablespoons sugar** and **1 teaspoon instant-coffee powder** until stiff peaks form. In a separate bowl, prepare **one 3.9-ounce package instant choco-** late pudding and pie filling mix with **2 cups milk** according to package directions. Alternately spoon the mixtures into four glasses. Refrigerate until ready to serve. **SERVES 4**

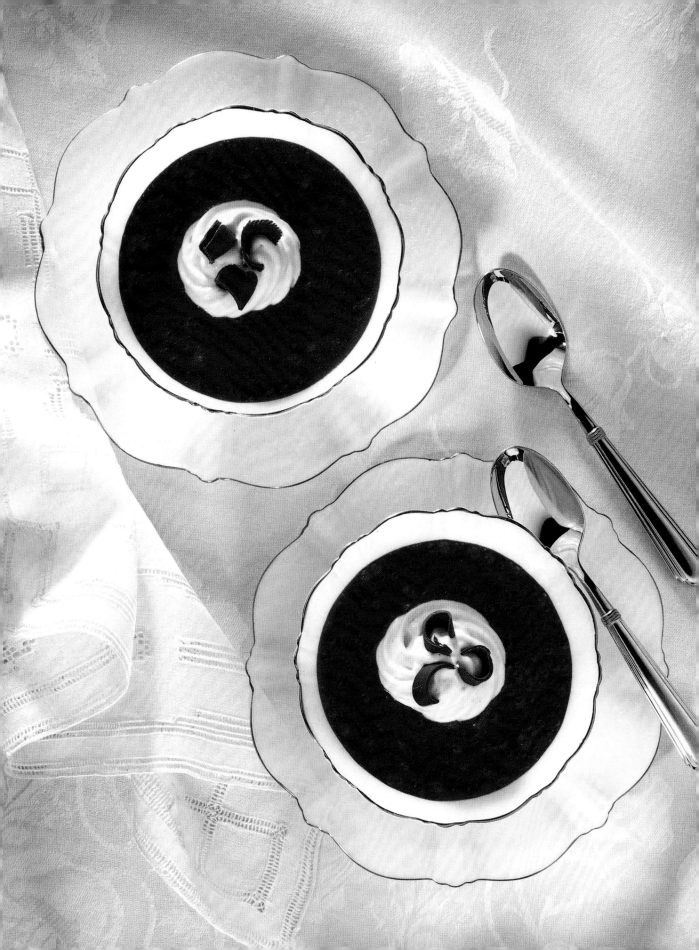

STRAWBERRY MOUSSE

One Serving: **Calories** 299 **Protein** 3g **Carbohydrates** 25g **Fat** 22g **Cholesterol** 81mg **Sodium** 26mg

1 **envelope unflavored gelatin**

¼ **cup orange juice**

1 **package (10 ounces) frozen strawberries in syrup**

1 **teaspoon vanilla extract**

1 **cup (½ pint) heavy cream**

2 **tablespoons confectioners sugar**

PREPARATION TIME
35 MINUTES

COOKING TIME
1 MINUTE

SERVING SUGGESTION *This fruit mousse makes a light, refreshing dessert after a filling meal. Garnish it with sprigs of mint.*

1 In a medium-size saucepan, sprinkle gelatin evenly over orange juice and let it stand 1 minute to soften the gelatin slightly. Cook the mixture over low heat until the gelatin dissolves completely. Remove the saucepan from the heat and stir in frozen strawberries and vanilla until the berries thaw enough to break apart.

2 Using an electric blender or food processor, process the strawberry mixture until smooth. Refrigerate the mixture at least 10 minutes. Meanwhile, in a small bowl, using an electric mixer, beat cream with confectioners sugar until stiff peaks form.

3 Using a rubber spatula, fold the chilled strawberry mixture into the whipped cream until it is well mixed. Spoon the mousse into a large serving bowl, individual glass dessert bowls, or goblets. Refrigerate until the mousse is set, about 15 minutes, and serve.

ZABAGLIONE

One Serving: **Calories** 171 **Protein** 5g **Carbohydrates** 15g **Fat** 8g **Cholesterol** 318mg **Sodium** 13mg

1 **pint fresh strawberries, hulled and sliced**

6 **large egg yolks**

2 **tablespoons sugar**

⅓ **cup Marsala**

PREPARATION TIME
15 MINUTES

COOKING TIME
8 MINUTES

SERVING SUGGESTION *This rich Italian custard can also be served in wine glasses without the fruit; add ladyfingers on the side.*

1 Partially fill the bottom part of a double boiler with water; bring the water to a boil over high heat. Meanwhile, divide strawberries among four stemmed wine glasses and set aside.

2 In the top part of the double boiler (still separate from the bottom part), using an electric mixer, beat egg yolks with sugar until thick and pale yellow, about 4 minutes. Gradually add Marsala, beating until well combined.

3 Reduce the heat under the double boiler to moderately low. Place the top part of the double boiler over the hot, not boiling, water. Continue beating the egg-yolk mixture at medium speed until it begins to hold its shape, about 8 minutes. Spoon the zabaglione over the berries in the glasses and serve immediately. (The zabaglione will separate on standing.)

CHEESECAKE CUPS

CHEESECAKE CUPS

One Serving: **Calories** 207 **Protein** 4g **Carbohydrates** 16g **Fat** 15g · **Cholesterol** 78mg **Sodium** 133mg

6 vanilla wafers

1 package (8 ounces) cream cheese, softened

¼ cup sugar

1 teaspoon vanilla extract

1 large egg

6 ripe strawberries

1 to 2 tablespoons strawberry or apple jelly

PREPARATION TIME
20 MINUTES

COOKING TIME
25 MINUTES

SERVING SUGGESTION *These little cheesecakes make an excellent dessert for a buffet or a tea-time treat.*

1 Preheat the oven to 325°F. Line 6 muffin-pan cups with fluted aluminum-foil cupcake liners. Place one vanilla wafer in each cup. In a small bowl, using an electric mixer, beat cream cheese, sugar, and vanilla until smooth and fluffy. Beat in egg until well mixed.

2 Divide the cream-cheese mixture among the lined cups. Bake the cheesecake cups until they are just set, about 25 minutes. Refrigerate at least 15 minutes or until ready to serve.

3 If desired, just before serving, from the pointed end of each strawberry, make thin parallel cuts to the opposite end, being careful not to cut through the berry. Fan out each berry and place one on top of each cheesecake cup. (Alternatively, slice off the top of each strawberry and place them upside-down in the center of each cheesecake.)

4 In a small saucepan, heat jelly over low heat until it is melted. Brush some of the glaze over each berry. Serve immediately.

BITTERSWEET CHOCOLATE SOUFFLÉS

One Serving: **Calories** 442 **Protein** 15g **Carbohydrates** 47g **Fat** 22g **Cholesterol** 424mg **Sodium** 161mg

1 tablespoon butter or margarine

4 ounces bittersweet chocolate

½ cup sugar, divided

3 tablespoons cherry-flavored liqueur, brandy, or cranberry juice

8 large eggs, separated, at room temperature

1 tablespoon confectioners sugar

PREPARATION TIME
20 MINUTES

COOKING TIME
12 MINUTES

COOK'S TIP *Save time by melting the chocolate in the microwave, checking it frequently until it is soft and able to be stirred.*

1 Preheat the oven to 450°F. Coat the bottom and sides of four 1½-cup individual soufflé dishes with butter. Set the dishes aside on a rimmed baking sheet. Partially fill the bottom part of a double boiler with water; bring to a boil over high heat. Meanwhile, finely chop bittersweet chocolate.

2 Reduce the heat under the double boiler to moderately low. In the top part of the double boiler, melt the chopped chocolate. Stir in ¼ cup sugar and liqueur until blended.

3 Remove the top part of the double boiler from the water. Add egg yolks and stir until thoroughly blended. Refrigerate the chocolate mixture briefly, only while preparing the next step.

4 In a large bowl, using an electric mixer, beat egg whites until foamy. Gradually add the remaining ¼ cup sugar and beat until stiff peaks form. Fold one-fourth of the beaten egg whites into the chocolate mixture until well mixed. Fold the chocolate mixture into the remaining beaten egg whites.

5 Pour the mixture into the soufflé dishes and bake until puffed, 12 to 15 minutes. (Do not open the oven door during baking.) Sift confectioners sugar over the soufflés before serving.

PUMPKIN MOUSSE

One Serving: **Calories** 243 **Protein** 2g **Carbohydrates** 24g **Fat** 17g **Cholesterol** 61mg **Sodium** 28mg

1 cup canned pumpkin

⅓ cup firmly packed light brown sugar

½ teaspoon ground cinnamon

½ teaspoon ground ginger

¾ cup heavy cream

2 tablespoons chopped crystallized ginger, divided

PREPARATION TIME
10 MINUTES

COOKING TIME
0 MINUTES

1 In a medium-size bowl, combine pumpkin, brown sugar, cinnamon, and ginger. In a small bowl, using an electric mixer, beat heavy cream until stiff peaks form.

2 Using a wire whisk or rubber spatula, fold the whipped cream into the pumpkin mixture until well mixed. Fold in 1 tablespoon chopped crystallized ginger.

3 Spoon the pumpkin mousse into four wine glasses or dessert bowls. Sprinkle the top of each serving with the remaining tablespoon of chopped ginger, and serve.

ROCKY ROAD PUDDING

One Serving: **Calories** 312 **Protein** 7g **Carbohydrates** 44g **Fat** 14g **Cholesterol** 138mg **Sodium** 246mg

¹/₃ cup sugar

¹/₃ cup unsweetened cocoa powder

2 tablespoons cornstarch

2 tablespoons all-purpose flour

¹/₈ teaspoon salt

2 cups milk

2 large egg yolks

2 tablespoons (¼ stick) butter or margarine

1 teaspoon vanilla extract

1 cup miniature marshmallows

2 tablespoons chopped peanuts (optional)

 PREPARATION TIME **8 MINUTES**   COOKING TIME **9 MINUTES**

1 In a medium-size saucepan, combine sugar, cocoa powder, cornstarch, flour, and salt. Stir in milk until well mixed. Bring the mixture to a boil over moderate heat, stirring constantly. Continue boiling and stirring for 1 minute. Remove the saucepan from the heat.

2 In a small bowl, beat egg yolks slightly; stir in one-fourth of the cocoa mixture to warm the yolks. Stir the yolk mixture into the remaining cocoa mixture in the saucepan. Return the pan to moderate heat and cook for 1 more minute, stirring constantly. Remove the saucepan from the heat.

3 Stir butter and vanilla into the chocolate pudding until blended. Fold in marshmallows. Spoon the pudding into individual dessert cups or bowls. Top with chopped peanuts, if desired. Serve warm or refrigerate to serve cold.

CHERRY CREAM PUDDING

One Serving: **Calories** 437 **Protein** 6g **Carbohydrates** 23g **Fat** 37g **Cholesterol** 123mg **Sodium** 185mg

1 package (8 ounces) cream cheese, softened

¹/₄ cup confectioners sugar

³/₄ cup heavy cream

1 teaspoon vanilla extract

12 ounces sweet cherries, halved and pitted

4 sweet cherries with stems (optional)

 PREPARATION TIME **20 MINUTES**   COOKING TIME **0 MINUTES**

1 In a small bowl, using an electric mixer, beat cream cheese and sugar until the mixture is smooth and fluffy. Slowly beat in cream and vanilla until soft peaks form.

2 Using a rubber spatula, fold cherries into the cream mixture. Spoon the pudding into four goblets or small glass bowls. Top each serving with a cherry, if desired, and serve.

CHOCOLATE PISTACHIO YOGURT PARFAIT

One Serving: **Calories** 418 **Protein** 16g **Carbohydrates** 58g **Fat** 15g **Cholesterol** 11mg **Sodium** 209mg

1 cup granola cereal

¹/₄ cup mini chocolate chips

¹/₄ cup chopped shelled pistachios

1 container (32 ounces) vanilla yogurt

 PREPARATION TIME **11 MINUTES**   COOKING TIME **0 MINUTES**

1 In a small bowl, combine granola, chocolate chips, and pistachios. In each of four parfait glasses, layer ¹/₃ cup yogurt, followed by 2 tablespoons granola mixture, repeating twice and ending with granola.

2 Serve the yogurt parfaits immediately, or cover with plastic wrap and refrigerate until ready to serve.

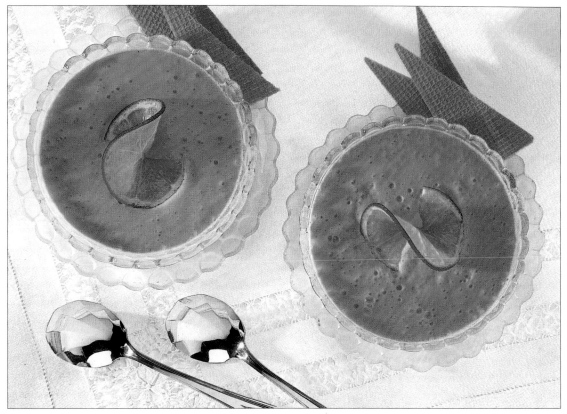

PAPAYA CREAM

PAPAYA CREAM

One Serving: **Calories** 290 **Protein** 6g **Carbohydrates** 41g **Fat** 12g **Cholesterol** 50mg **Sodium** 103mg

1 **envelope unflavored gelatin**

½ **cup water**

2 **tablespoons sugar**

1 **tablespoon lime juice**

1 **large ripe papaya**

1 **pint vanilla ice cream, cut into chunks**

Thin lime slices (optional)

 PREPARATION TIME
30 MINUTES

COOKING TIME
1 MINUTE

SERVING SUGGESTION *The creamy, refreshing texture of this fruit cream contrasts well with sugar cookies or amaretti.*

1 In a small saucepan, sprinkle gelatin evenly over water; let it stand 1 minute to soften the gelatin slightly. Cook over moderately low heat until the gelatin dissolves completely. Remove from the heat and stir in sugar and lime juice. Refrigerate the gelatin mixture while preparing the fruit, about 10 minutes.

2 Cut papaya lengthwise in half. Using a spoon, scoop out seeds and discard. Scoop out the papaya pulp into the container of an electric blender or food processor. Process the pulp with the gelatin mixture until smooth.

3 While the blender or processor is running, add ice cream to the papaya mixture; continue processing until the papaya mixture is just mixed. Spoon the papaya cream into individual glass dessert bowls. Refrigerate until set, about 20 minutes, or until ready to serve. Garnish each with a twisted lime slice, if desired.

PIES AND COBBLERS

These quick pies, tarts, and cobblers make satisfying desserts and coffee-time snacks.

NECTARINE CHEESE TART

One Serving: **Calories** 274 **Protein** 4g **Carbohydrates** 26g **Fat** 18g **Cholesterol** 39mg **Sodium** 220mg

½ **package (15 ounces) refrigerated ready-to-bake pie crusts (1 crust)**

Flour

1 **container (8 ounces) soft-style cream cheese**

2 **tablespoons confectioners sugar**

4 **medium-size ripe nectarines**

3 **tablespoons orange marmalade**

 PREPARATION TIME **28 MINUTES**

COOKING TIME **12 MINUTES**

COOK'S TIP *Overlapping the fruit slices carefully will result in an eye-pleasing dessert, ready to grace the table of a formal dinner.*

1 Preheat the oven to 450°F. Let pie crust stand for 5 minutes. Unfold the crust and peel off one plastic sheet. Lightly dust crust with some flour and smooth out the fold lines. Invert the crust on a baking sheet; remove the second sheet of plastic. Using a fork, pierce crust all over.

2 Fold in the pie-crust edge 1 inch to make a 9-inch-round tart shell. Flute the crust edge to form a ½-inch-high rim. Bake the tart shell until golden brown, 10 to 12 minutes.

3 Meanwhile, combine cream cheese and confectioners sugar. Cut nectarines in half. Remove the pits and cut the nectarines into thin slices. In a small saucepan over low heat, or in a microwave-safe cup in the microwave, melt marmalade.

4 Transfer the baked tart shell to a serving plate and let it cool slightly. Spread the cream-cheese mixture evenly in the shell. Arrange the nectarine slices in concentric circles, overlapping to fit, over the cheese. Brush the nectarines with the melted marmalade, and serve.

Shelf Magic

Refrigerated biscuit dough is easily transformed into these single-serving upside-down cobblers.

PINEAPPLE COBBLERS

Preheat the oven to 450°F. Into each of four 1½-cup ramekins, spread one of **4 teaspoons butter**; sprinkle one of **4 tablespoons brown sugar** over each. Drain **one 8-oz. can pineapple slices**. Place one slice in each ramekin. From **one 4½-ounce package** **refrigerated buttermilk biscuit dough,** shape 1½ biscuits into a circle to fit ramekin. Repeat with remaining biscuits. Bake for 10 minutes. To serve, run a knife around each biscuit; invert each onto a dessert plate. **SERVES 4**

ALMOND SPONGE TART

Almond Sponge Tart

One Serving: **Calories** 398 **Protein** 8g **Carbohydrates** 41g **Fat** 24g **Cholesterol** 166mg **Sodium** 423mg

1 **cup milk**

¼ **cup (½ stick) butter or margarine**

1 **package (12 ounces) frozen pound cake, thawed and crumbled**

1 **tablespoon grated lemon peel**

1 **teaspoon almond extract**

½ **package (15 ounces) refrigerated ready-to-bake pie crust (1 crust)**

¼ **cup black cherry conserve**

2 **large eggs**

¼ **cup sliced almonds**

Sweetened whipped cream, or frozen whipped topping, thawed (optional)

 PREPARATION TIME
15 MINUTES

COOKING TIME
25 MINUTES

COOK'S TIP *This tart uses pound-cake crumbs as a base for its soft texture. Use fresh or thawed, frozen pound cake. Strawberry jam may be used in place of the cherry conserve.*

1 Preheat the oven to 450°F. In a medium-size saucepan, heat milk and butter until melted. Add cake crumbs, lemon peel, and almond extract. Stir well; remove from the heat and set aside.

2 Line a 9-inch pie plate with pie crust and flute the edge decoratively. Spread conserve over the pastry.

3 Using an electric mixer, beat eggs into the cake-crumb mixture. Spoon the mixture over the layer of conserve, flattening it with a spoon. Sprinkle with sliced almonds. Bake until the filling is firm and the crust is golden, about 25 minutes. Serve the tart warm, with whipped cream if desired.

FRESH STRAWBERRY PIE

One Serving: **Calories** 362 **Protein** 4g **Carbohydrates** 57g **Fat** 13g **Cholesterol** 28mg **Sodium** 205mg

²/₃ **cup plus 1 tablespoon sugar, divided**

¼ **cup cornstarch**

1¹/₃ **cups water**

1 **package (6 ounces) strawberry-flavored gelatin**

Ice cubes

2 **pints fresh strawberries, well chilled**

1 **prepared 9-inch pie crust, baked, or graham cracker-crumb crust**

½ **cup heavy cream**

 PREPARATION TIME
30 MINUTES

COOKING TIME
4 MINUTES

FOOD NOTE *Strawberries and cream make a fresh pie filling in this summertime dessert. Make extra whipped cream to serve on the side.*

1 In a small saucepan, combine ²/₃ cup sugar and cornstarch. Stir in water until smooth; bring to a boil over moderate heat, stirring constantly. Continue boiling and stirring for 1 minute; remove the saucepan from the heat. Stir gelatin into the mixture until it dissolves.

2 Fill a large bowl with ice cubes and place the saucepan of gelatin in the ice cubes. Stir the gelatin mixture until it cools and thickens slightly, 2 to 3 minutes. (Do not allow the gelatin to set.) Remove the saucepan from the bowl of ice.

3 Rinse and hull strawberries. Pat the berries dry on a paper towel. Arrange the berries in the pie crust and pour the gelatin mixture over them. Refrigerate the pie at least 20 minutes.

4 Just before serving, prepare the whipped cream. In a small bowl, using an electric mixer, beat cream with 1 tablespoon sugar until stiff peaks form. Spoon the cream around the edge of the pie, and serve.

EASY CRUSTLESS COCONUT PIE

One Serving: **Calories** 271 **Protein** 6g **Carbohydrates** 31g **Fat** 14g **Cholesterol** 130mg **Sodium** 231mg

¼ **cup (½ stick) butter or margarine**

2 **cups milk**

1½ **teaspoons vanilla extract**

4 **large eggs, at room temperature**

1 **cup flaked coconut**

¾ **cup sugar**

½ **cup buttermilk baking mix (Bisquick)**

 PREPARATION TIME
7 MINUTES

COOKING TIME
38 MINUTES

COOK'S TIP *Although this can be served straight from the oven, it's even better chilled, allowing you to make this dessert in advance.*

1 Preheat the oven to 400°F. Grease a 9-inch pie plate. In a small saucepan, melt butter over moderate heat. Add milk and heat just until bubbles appear around the side of the saucepan.

2 Remove the milk mixture from the heat and stir in vanilla. Using an electric blender or food processor, process eggs, coconut, sugar, and baking mix until combined. Add the milk mixture to the egg mixture and process until well blended.

3 Pour the mixture into the prepared pie plate and bake until a knife inserted halfway between the center and edge comes out clean, 30 to 35 minutes. Let the pie stand 5 minutes before cutting. Serve warm or refrigerate to serve chilled later.

BLUEBERRY SHORTCAKES

One Serving: **Calories** 343 **Protein** 5g **Carbohydrates** 49g **Fat** 15g **Cholesterol** 45mg **Sodium** 491mg

³/₄ cup all-purpose flour

¹/₄ cup yellow cornmeal

1 tablespoon sugar

1 teaspoon baking soda

¹/₂ teaspoon baking powder

¹/₄ teaspoon salt

3 tablespoons butter or margarine, cut into tiny pieces

6 tablespoons plain low-fat yogurt

1 pint fresh blueberries

2 tablespoons honey

¹/₂ cup sweetened whipped cream, or frozen whipped topping, thawed

PREPARATION TIME 8 MINUTES

COOKING TIME 20 MINUTES

SERVING SUGGESTION *This fresh alternative to strawberry shortcake works just as well for a party as for a family dessert.*

1 Preheat the oven to 425°F. In a medium-size bowl, combine flour, cornmeal, sugar, baking soda, baking powder, and salt. Using a pastry blender or two knives scissor-fashion, cut in butter until the mixture resembles coarse crumbs. Using a fork, stir in yogurt until a soft dough forms. Lightly knead the dough for a few seconds.

2 On a lightly floured surface, pat or roll the dough to a ¹/₂-inch thickness. Using a floured 3-inch cookie cutter, cut out four dough rounds. Place the dough rounds, or shortcakes, on an ungreased baking sheet. Bake until golden brown, 18 to 20 minutes.

3 Meanwhile, rinse and pick over blueberries. In a medium-size bowl, combine the blueberries with honey, crushing about one-quarter of the berries. Refrigerate the berry mixture until the shortcakes are ready to serve.

4 To serve, split the warm shortcakes in half horizontally. Place the bottom halves on serving plates. Top with half the berries, the top halves of the shortcakes, a dollop of whipped cream, and the remaining berries. Serve immediately.

APPLE CRISP

One Serving: **Calories** 463 **Protein** 4g **Carbohydrates** 86g **Fat** 12g **Cholesterol** 31mg **Sodium** 111mg

4 large Granny Smith apples

¹/₃ cup sugar

2 tablespoons lemon juice

1 teaspoon ground cinnamon

¹/₂ cup firmly packed light brown sugar

¹/₂ cup all-purpose flour

¹/₂ cup quick-cooking oats

¹/₄ cup (¹/₂ stick) butter or margarine, cut into tiny pieces

PREPARATION TIME 15 MINUTES

COOKING TIME 30 MINUTES

1 Preheat the oven to 350°F. Peel, core and slice apples. Place the apples in a large bowl; sprinkle them with sugar, lemon juice, and cinnamon. Toss the apples to coat evenly. Transfer the apples to a 9-inch-square baking dish.

2 In a small bowl, combine brown sugar, flour, and oats. Using a pastry blender or two knives scissor-fashion, cut butter into the flour mixture until it resembles coarse crumbs. Sprinkle the crumb topping over the apple mixture.

3 Bake the apples until the crumb topping is crisp, about 30 minutes. Spoon the warm apple crisp into small bowls and serve immediately, or let the apple crisp cool and serve it at room temperature.

START WITH A CRUMB CRUST

A graham cracker, chocolate, or vanilla crumb crust makes a sweet and simple base for a variety of easy pies. All of these tempting desserts can be whipped up in minutes, then placed in the refrigerator to finish setting up while you enjoy dinner.

Start with your own crumb crust (see page 28 for recipes), or purchase a ready-made one, then choose a filling from this eye-catching group. Each pie serves eight.

◀ **CREAMY STRAWBERRY PIE** Rinse, dry, hull, and slice **1 pint strawberries.** In a small bowl, combine berries and **2 Tbsp. sugar.** Refrigerate. Meanwhile, in a small bowl, beat **1 cup heavy cream** with **1 tsp. vanilla extract** until stiff peaks form. In another bowl, prepare **one 3¼-oz. package vanilla-flavor instant pudding and pie filling mix** with **1 cup milk.** Spoon half of the strawberries into **one 9-inch vanilla- or butter-flavored crumb crust.** Fold whipped cream into pudding. Spoon over strawberries. Top with remaining strawberries. Refrigerate for at least 15 minutes.

▶ **BLACK BOTTOM PUDDING PIE** Melt **2 squares semisweet chocolate;** set aside. Using an electric mixer, beat **1 cup heavy cream** with **1 tsp. vanilla extract** until stiff peaks form. In another bowl, prepare **one 3¼-oz. package vanilla-flavor instant pudding and pie filling mix** with **1 cup milk.** Fold whipped cream into pudding mixture; spoon ½ cup mixture into cooled melted chocolate. Spread chocolate mixture into bottom of **one 9-inch vanilla- or butter-flavored crumb crust.** Pour remaining pudding over it. Refrigerate the pie for at least 20 minutes. Garnish with **chocolate curls.**

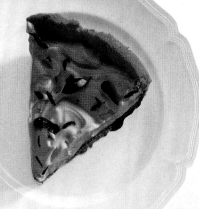

► **COCONUT CREAM PIE** In a large skillet, heat **1⅓ cups flaked coconut** over moderate heat until lightly browned. Let cool. Beat **1 cup heavy cream** with **2 Tbsp. confectioners sugar** and **1 tsp. vanilla extract** until stiff peaks form. Reserve ½ cup toasted coconut. Fold remaining coconut into whipped cream; spread into **one 9-inch graham cracker-crumb crust**. Sprinkle with coconut. Refrigerate for at least 15 minutes.

◄ **BANANA SPLIT PIE** Peel and slice **2 medium-size bananas** into one 9-inch chocolate-flavored crumb crust. Top with scoops from **2 pints vanilla ice cream**. Drizzle ½ **cup prepared chocolate topping** over pie; sprinkle with ½ **cup chopped, toasted almonds**. Freeze for at least 15 minutes.

► **PEANUT BUTTER–CHOCOLATE PIE** Using an electric mixer, beat **1 package (8 oz.) cream cheese** until smooth. Beat in ½ **cup creamy peanut butter, 3 Tbsp. confectioners sugar**, and **2 Tbsp. milk**. In a small bowl, beat **1 cup heavy cream** with **1 tsp. vanilla extract** until stiff peaks form. Fold whipped cream into cream-cheese mixture; spread into **one 9-inch chocolate-flavored crumb crust**. Sprinkle with **grated semisweet chocolate**. Refrigerate for at least 15 minutes.

► **LIME PIE** Whisk **one 14-oz. can sweetened condensed milk** with ½ **cup fresh lime juice** and **2 large egg yolks** until thickened. Pour into **one 9-inch graham cracker-crumb crust**. Freeze for 15 minutes. Spoon **2 cups frozen whipped topping,** thawed, over pie; add **grated lime peel**.

KIWI AND GRAPE PASTRIES

One Serving: **Calories** 317 **Protein** 6g **Carbohydrates** 34g **Fat** 18g **Cholesterol** 11mg **Sodium** 281mg

1 **package (10 ounces) frozen puff-pastry shells (6 shells)**

3 **kiwi fruits**

1 **cup seedless red grapes**

1 **package (3¼ or 3.4 ounces) vanilla-flavor instant pudding and pie filling mix**

2 **cups milk**

Additional kiwi fruit and grapes (optional)

 PREPARATION TIME **25 MINUTES**

COOKING TIME **20 MINUTES**

FOOD NOTE *The kiwi fruits and grapes in a puff-pastry shell make a cool and elegant finale to a dinner party.*

1 Preheat the oven to 400°F. Place frozen pastry shells on an ungreased baking sheet according to package directions. Bake the pastry shells until golden and puffed, 20 to 25 minutes.

2 Meanwhile, peel kiwis and trim off the ends. Slice the kiwis thinly and cut the slices into small pieces. Transfer the kiwis to a medium-size bowl. Cut grapes into quarters and add them to the kiwis.

3 In another medium-size bowl, whisk pudding mix with milk according to package directions. Combine half of the pudding mix with the chopped fruit.

4 Transfer the baked pastry shells to a wire rack. Using a fork, remove the pastry lids and place them on the wire rack. Scoop out and discard any soft pastry inside the pastry shells. Allow the pastry shells to cool slightly, about 5 minutes.

5 Meanwhile, divide the remaining plain pudding among six dessert plates, spreading it over the center of each plate. Place a pastry shell in the center of the pudding. Divide the pudding-fruit mixture among the pastry shells, and top each one with a pastry lid. Decorate with additional kiwi fruit and grapes, if desired. Serve immediately, or refrigerate until ready to serve.

CHOCOLATE BREAD PUDDING

One Serving: **Calories** 375 **Protein** 8g **Carbohydrates** 39g **Fat** 22g **Cholesterol** 101mg **Sodium** 334mg

2 **cups milk**

1 **cup semisweet chocolate chips**

¼ **cup firmly packed light brown sugar**

¼ **cup (½ stick) butter or margarine, melted**

4 **or 5 1-inch slices braided egg bread (or other fresh bread)**

2 **large eggs**

 PREPARATION TIME **15 MINUTES**

 COOKING TIME **30 MINUTES**

1 Preheat the oven to 350°F. Grease a 1-quart casserole. In a small saucepan, heat milk, chocolate, sugar, and butter over moderate heat until melted. Remove the saucepan from the heat and set aside.

2 Cut bread into 1-inch cubes and place in the prepared casserole. In a medium-size bowl, beat eggs. Pour the chocolate mixture onto the eggs and mix well. Pour the egg mixture over the bread cubes.

3 Bake the pudding for 30 minutes or until a knife inserted 1 inch from the side of the casserole comes out clean. (The center may still be slightly soft.) Serve the pudding warm.

PECAN TARTLETS

PECAN TARTLETS

One Serving: **Calories** 361 **Protein** 2g **Carbohydrates** 51g **Fat** 18g **Cholesterol** 12mg **Sodium** 195mg

2 **tablespoons (¼ stick) butter or margarine**

⅔ **cup dark corn syrup**

¼ **cup sugar**

1 **teaspoon vanilla extract**

2 **large eggs**

6 **prepared individual graham cracker-crumb tart shells**

¾ **cup pecans, coarsely chopped**

PREPARATION TIME
7 MINUTES

COOKING TIME
30 MINUTES

COOK'S TIP *These will be so popular you might like to prepare a double batch, storing the extra for a special coffee break.*

1 Preheat the oven to 350°F. In a small saucepan, melt butter. Remove the pan from heat. Stir in corn syrup, sugar, and vanilla; beat in eggs.

2 Place tart shells on a small baking sheet. Pour an equal amount of the syrup mixture into each tart shell. Sprinkle pecans on top.

3 Bake the tartlets until the filling is set, 25 to 30 minutes. Remove the tartlets from the oven and let them cool slightly. Serve warm.

CREAMY BANANA TARTLETS

One Serving: **Calories** 368 **Protein** 4g **Carbohydrates** 40g **Fat** 22g **Cholesterol** 61mg **Sodium** 403mg

1¼ **cups milk**

1 **package (3¼ or 3.4 ounces) vanilla-flavor instant pudding and pie filling mix**

1 **cup (½ pint) heavy cream**

2 **medium-size ripe bananas**

6 **prepared individual graham cracker-crumb tart shells**

 PREPARATION TIME
15 MINUTES

COOKING TIME
0 MINUTES

COOK'S TIP *If you keep some prepared tart shells in your pantry, you will never be at a loss for an easy dessert like this one.*

1 In a medium-size bowl, combine milk with pudding mix and stir to combine, about 45 seconds. Cover the bowl and refrigerate until ready to use.

2 Meanwhile, in a small bowl, using the electric mixer, beat cream until stiff peaks form. Measure ½ cup of the whipped cream and set it aside. Using a rubber spatula, gently fold the remaining whipped cream into the pudding until well mixed.

3 Peel and slice bananas. If desired, reserve six slices for garnish. Place four slices of banana on the bottom of each tart. Spoon half of the pudding mixture into the tart shells. Add a layer of bananas to each tart. Cover the bananas with the remaining pudding. Top each with a dollop of whipped cream and a banana slice, and serve.

CHOCOLATE ALMOND CREAM PIE

One Serving: **Calories** 327 **Protein** 3g **Carbohydrates** 27g **Fat** 24g **Cholesterol** 54mg **Sodium** 332mg

2 **tablespoons (¼ stick) butter or margarine, softened**

1 **bag (7 ounces) flaked coconut**

1 **package (3.9 ounces) chocolate-flavor instant pudding and pie filling mix**

1¼ **cups milk**

1 **cup (½ pint) heavy cream**

½ **teaspoon almond extract**

2 **tablespoons sliced almonds**

 PREPARATION TIME
25 MINUTES

COOKING TIME
20 MINUTES

COOK'S TIP *The easy coconut pie crust used in this dessert makes a versatile base for many fruit-flavored pie fillings.*

1 Preheat the oven to 325°F. On the bottom and side of a 9-inch pie plate, evenly spread butter, covering the pie plate to the outer rim. Pat coconut into the butter. Bake the coconut crust until golden, about 20 minutes. Let the crust cool on a wire rack.

2 Meanwhile, in a medium-size bowl, combine pudding mix with 1¼ cups milk and mix according to package directions. Refrigerate the pudding mix.

3 In a small bowl, using an electric mixer, beat heavy cream until stiff peaks form. Using a rubber spatula, gently fold half of the whipped cream and all of the almond extract into the chocolate pudding until it is well mixed.

4 Spoon the pudding mixture into the cooled coconut crust. Top the pie with the remaining whipped cream and sprinkle with almonds. Refrigerate the pie until ready to serve.

PEACH RASPBERRY CRUMBLE

PEACH RASPBERRY CRUMBLE

One Serving: **Calories** 388 **Protein** 4g **Carbohydrates** 60g **Fat** 15g **Cholesterol** 41mg **Sodium** 129mg

- **4 medium-size firm ripe freestone peaches (about 1⅓ pounds)**
- **½ pint fresh raspberries (or 1 cup frozen unsweetened raspberries)**
- **1 cup flour**
- **½ cup sugar**
- **¼ teaspoon ground nutmeg**
- **⅓ cup unsalted butter, cut into tiny pieces**
- **Light sour cream or vanilla yogurt (optional)**

 PREPARATION TIME
15 MINUTES

 COOKING TIME
25 MINUTES

SERVING SUGGESTION *If you prefer a more substantial dessert, this is also delicious served with a scoop of vanilla ice cream.*

1 Preheat the oven to 375°F. Cut peaches in half. Remove the pits and slice the peaches. In a 10- by 6-inch baking dish, place the peach slices. Sprinkle raspberries over the peaches.

2 In a medium-size bowl, combine flour, sugar, and nutmeg. With fingertips, work butter into the flour mixture until crumbly. Cover the fruit with the crumbly mixture.

3 Bake until the crumb topping is golden brown and the peaches are soft, about 25 minutes. Serve warm, with light sour cream if desired.

INDEX

Page numbers in *italic* type refer to illustrations.

Page numbers in *italic* type refer to illustrations.

Page numbers in *italic* type refer to illustrations.

Page numbers in *italic* type refer to illustrations.

Page numbers in *italic* type refer to illustrations.